Discernment in the Desert Fathers

Διάκρισις in the Life and Thought
of Early Egyptian Monasticism

STUDIES IN CHRISTIAN HISTORY AND THOUGHT

A full listing of all titles in this series
appears at the close of this book

Discernment in the Desert Fathers

Διάκρισις in the Life and Thought
of Early Egyptian Monasticism

Antony D. Rich

Foreword by Benedicta Ward, SLG

Wipf & Stock
PUBLISHERS
Eugene, Oregon

Wipf and Stock Publishers
199 W 8th Ave, Suite 3
Eugene, OR 97401

Discernment in the Desert Fathers
Diakrisis in the Life and Thought of Early Egyptian Monasticism
By Rich, Antony D.
Copyright©2007 Paternoster
ISBN 13: 978-1-55635-339-0
ISBN 10: 1-55635-339-1
Publication date 3/19/2007

Paternoster
9 Holdom Avenue
Bletchley
Milton Keyes, MK1 1QR
PATERNOSTER   Great Britain

STUDIES IN CHRISTIAN HISTORY AND THOUGHT

Series Preface

This series complements the specialist series of *Studies in Evangelical History and Thought* and *Studies in Baptist History and Thought* for which Paternoster is becoming increasingly well known by offering works that cover the wider field of Christian history and thought. It encompasses accounts of Christian witness at various periods, studies of individual Christians and movements, and works which concern the relations of church and society through history, and the history of Christian thought.

The series includes monographs, revised dissertations and theses, and collections of papers by individuals and groups. As well as 'free standing' volumes, works on particular running themes are being commissioned; authors will be engaged for these from around the world and from a variety of Christian traditions.

A high academic standard combined with lively writing will commend the volumes in this series both to scholars and to a wider readership.

Series Editors

Alan P.F. Sell, Visiting Professor at Acadia University Divinity College, Nova Scotia, Canada

David Bebbington, Professor of History, University of Stirling, Stirling, Scotland, UK

Clyde Binfield, Professor Associate in History, University of Sheffield, UK

Gerald Bray, Anglican Professor of Divinity, Beeson Divinity School, Samford University, Birmingham, Alabama, USA

Grayson Carter, Associate Professor of Church History, Fuller Theological Seminary SW, Phoenix, Arizona, USA

This book is dedicated to Benedicta Ward, SLG

Contents

FOREWORD

To be 'discreet' nowadays usually means to be humble and secretive, discreet in demeanour, not obtrusive, a rather dull method of conduct. The word has however a more dynamic history, since it comes from diakresis (διάκρισις), meaning to divide, to weigh rightly. In the Christian tradition it has always been highly esteemed and understood as discretion, discernment, having a right judgment of all things. It has been seen not as merely part of the natural virtue of prudence but as the chief of the direct gifts of the Holy Spirit, both the way into and the fruit of life in Christ. In the first thousand or more years of Christian living, discernment was discussed with complete unanimity, not because each writer repeated what his predecessors said without further thought but because the practice of Christian life continued to make abundantly clear the nature and purpose of discernment.

In the Christian world of fourth century Egypt, with which this book is concerned, 'discernment' could be described as a solid understanding of the will of God, and the mother of virtues, as well as their guide and regulator. Discretion was seen not as good outward behaviour but as a quality that orders and regulates interiorly the more vivid and dramatic virtues. Above all in this tradition, discernment was concerned with the examination of motives for each individual in following Christ. They would say that when the light of discernment was turned towards oneself, it must be ruthless in its refusal of illusion, but when turned towards others it must be truly the light of God which is always positive and loving. It was not seen as a technique or something high-class in a special spiritual world but as part of the way of the cross, where each followed in company with 'a great cloud of witnesses'. It was in walking with God in daily life that discernment had to be sought and applied.

The early writers are unanimous in saying that 'spiritual' matters need as much discernment as 'material' matters. Man is fallen and his sight is wrong in both spheres equally. To be intent on a spiritual way was not necessarily any better than to be absorbed in earthly affairs. Discernment was in fact more necessary in spiritual matters than in material ones, because the danger was greater and more hidden. The Christian was not looking for wisdom from a master but was seeking to become open to the only teacher of the Christian who is Christ. The paradox was that in order to learn from Him and Him only, the blinding pride of self-confidence had to be eliminated and this could only be done by placing oneself in the hands of others. This could apply to long-term issues, such as of the way of life by which to follow Christ or to details of that way. Discernment was sought through others, not for their skill or intelligence but in order to be free to hear the will of God truly.

This way towards discernment in the Christian tradition was always very practical; no-one simply claimed to have discernment, though others might see it in someone else. It was not something valued for its own sake, it was always known in its exercise in practical situations, whether used for oneself or for others. Nor was it an absolute, something that was always the same; on the contrary, it changed both with the person learning it and with those receiving it.

It must always be remembered that discernment was not equated with judgment. The itch to condemn by negative judgment can be transfigured into discernment by seeing only the mercy and goodness of God in others. The way to allow this right judgment to be formed is through humility of heart which in practice involves a consistent refusal to exercise that self-assertion which forms hostile and negative judgments against the neighbour. The true 'judgment' about others which is discernment is the God's eye view, which is always positive. To know the difference between killing judgment and life-giving discernment needs an inner sensitivity. Because humankind is fallen, it is impossible to become discerning easily and naturally by love and concern. Certainly the early writers connect discernment with love, admitting that great love can give someone a particularly sensitive insight into another, but as everyone knows, love is not enough. There is a distorting lens in the eye of the soul which sends the most loving gesture awry without discernment.

Discernment is above all about inner motive and begins with oneself and here the early writers say that the first step towards learning true self-knowledge is to be aware that it is lacking, and so the first virtue needed both in order and in priority is humility. This is not a cringing and rather abstract idea in the desert literature but part of the way out from the illusions of a self-centred world towards an understanding of the reality of humankind before the Creator, of sinners before the Saviour. It is learned with consistency and great practical application, and the most important sign of the reality of this humility in all the desert literature is never for one moment to condemn others.

Discernment is needed within the whole body of the Church, but is not a possession or a skill attained by individuals. Its corporate nature is a reminder that Christianity is not the property of an exclusive and sensitive elite but open to everyone, some of whom will be discerning by nature, others not, but all of whom can become discerning. It is not the equivalent of the enlightened state of the philosopher but a gift of God within the economy of salvation for all. The basic and essential question for each is 'how can I be saved?' and discernment is only to this end.

Discernment is not to be confused either with judging others or with a crippling insistence on getting it right in every way before acting. The results in one filled with this right spirit of discernment always issue in a positive but non-sentimental gentleness which is a God's eye view of all things.

In this book, Dr Rich has explored with exemplary thoroughness the place of discretion in the early Christian monastic world, showing how it was understood and applied, by detailed reference to early monastic texts. These monks were known as the experts, not because they were theologians or writers, but as being the ones who taught by word and by example. He has given an illuminating picture of the content and the outworking of discretion, which can be as useful today as it was in the fourth century.

Benedicta Ward, SLG
Oxford, 2006

PREFACE

This work was originally undertaken as a PhD thesis, but my interest in the significance of διάκρισις in the lives and teaching of the Egyptian Desert Fathers began during sabbatical studies with the Northumbria Community. From general reading came a growing awareness that the acquisition and use of διάκρισις by the Desert Fathers was an important element of their search for God. While there have been a number of articles exploring διάκρισις and διάκρισις πνευμάτων in the early church and Patristic periods, and some academic studies have considered διάκρισις in relation to other aspects of early monastic thought and life, there has been no detailed analysis of the nature and place of διάκρισις in the spirituality of the Egyptian Desert Fathers.

I would like to thank the many scholars who have provided their generous assistance in preparing this book and particularly the following. To Luke Dysinger OSB, particularly for sending me his work in progress on Evagrius' *scholia* on the Psalms. To William Harmless SJ, for his then unpublished Evagrian material and translations. To Francesca Moscatelli OSB for graciously supplying a copy of her out of print work on Evagrius' *de octo spiritibus malitiae*. To Dr Sebastian Brock, Dr Augustine Casiday, Prof. Andrew Louth, Robert Penkett, the late Dom Lucien Regnault, Dr Norman Russell, Rev. Dr Columba Stewart OSB, Rev. Dr Tim Vivian and Roy Adkins for their advice. To the late Dr Martin Selman and Dr Pieter Lalleman for proof reading my Hebrew and Coptic respectively (any mistakes that remain are my own), and Ray Steptoe for his help with material in German. To the library staff of the Bodleian Library, Sackler Library, British Library, Dr Williams's Library and Spurgeon's College Library. Finally, to Sr Benedicta Ward SLG for her constant support and advice, and to whom this book is dedicated.

ABBREVIATIONS

Apophthegmata

Alph.	Alphabetical Collection.
Am	Bohairic Coptic Collection (Amélineau).
App	Latin appendix of Palladius.
Bars	Epistles of Barsanuph and John.
Budge	Syriac Collection (E. A. Wallis Budge).
Ch	Sahidic Coptic Collection (Chaîne).
GSC	Greek Systematic Collection.
J	French trans. of MS *Sinaï* 448 by L. Regnault, *Les Sentences des Pères du Désert série des anonymes* (Spiritualité Orientale 43; Solesmes-Bellefontaine: Abbayes, 1985).
MD	Latin appendix of Martin of Dumio.
Nau	Greek Anonymous Collection.
PE	Greek Anthology of Paul Evergetinos.
SP	Latin supplement (Wilmart).
VP	*Vitae Patrum* (*PL* 73-74).
VP 3	Latin Collection attributed to Rufinus.
VP 5	Latin Systematic Collection of Pelagius and John.
VP 7	Latin Collection of Collection of Paschasius of Dumio.

Reference Works, Journals and Other Works

ANF	*The Ante-Nicene Fathers*, Roberts, A. and J. Donaldson (eds), (digital version in 'The Master Christian Library, Version 5' containing 'The Ages Digital Library Collections' version 2, © 1997, provided by Ages Software, PO Box 1926, Albany, OR 97321-0509, USA. Originally published Buffalo: The Christian Literature Publishing Company, 1885-1896).
BAG	Bauer, W. (ed.), *A Greek-English Lexicon of the New Testament and other Early Christian Literature* (trans.

	W.F. Arndt and F.W. Gingrich; Chicago: University of Chicago Press, 2nd rev. edn, 1979).
BDB	Brown, F., S.R. Driver and C.A.Briggs, (eds), *A Hebrew and English Lexicon of the Old Testament* (Oxford: Clarendon Press, 1951).
BHS	*Biblica Hebraica Stuttgartensia.*
CCL	*Corpus Christianorum Latinorum.*
CSEL	*Corpus Scriptorum Ecclesiasticorum Latinorum.*
CSCO	*Corpus Scriptorum Christianorum Orientalium.*
GCS	*Griechischen Christlichen Schriftsteller.*
HE	*Historia ecclesiastica* (identified by author).
HL	Palladius, *Historia Lausiaca.*
HM	*Historia monachorum in Aegypto.*
JEH	*Journal of Ecclesiastical History.*
JTS	*Journal of Theological Studies.*
Lampe	Lampe, G.W.H. (ed.), *A Patristic Greek Lexicon* (Oxford: Clarendon Press, 1995 [1961]).
LCL	Loeb Classical Library.
Lewis	Lewis, C.T. and C. Short (eds), *A Latin Dictionary* (Oxford: Clarendon Press, 1996 [1879]).
L&S	Liddell, H.G. and R. Scott (eds), *A Greek-English Lexicon*, (Oxford: Clarendon Press, 9th rev. edn with supplement, 1996).
LXX	Septuagint.
NPNF	*The Nicene and Post-Nicene Fathers*, Series 1 Schaff, P. (ed.) and Series 2 Schaff, P. and H. Wace (eds), (Digital version in 'The Master Christian Library, Version 5' containing 'The Ages Digital Library Collections' version 2, © 1997, provided by Ages Software, PO Box 1926, Albany, OR 97321-0509, USA. Originally published New York: The Christian Literature Publishing Company, Series 1 1886-1890, Series 2 1890-1900)
OC	*Orientalia Christiana.*
OCA	*Orientalia Christiana Analecta.*
OCP	*Orientalia Christiana Periodica.*
PG	Ed. J.-P. Migne, *Patrologia Cursus Completus, Series Graeca* (161 vols; Paris, 1857-1866).
Pitra	Evagrius, *scholia in Psalmos* / Origen, *Fragmenta in Psalmos 1-150* (J.B. Pitra).
PL	Ed. J.-P. Migne, *Patrologia Cursus Completus, Series Latina* (221 vols; Paris, 1844-1846).
PO	*Patrologia Orientalis.*
PTS	*Patristische Texte und Studien.*
RAM	*Revue d'Ascétique et de Mystique.*

RB	*Revue Bénédictine.*
ROC	*Revue de l'Orient Chrétien.*
SC	*Sources Chrétiennes.*
Souter	Souter, A. (ed.), *A Glossary of Later Latin to 600 AD* (Oxford: Clarendon Press, 1996 [1949]).
TLG	*Thesaurus Linguae Graecae* (CD ROM E, 1999; University of California, Irvine 3450 Berkley Place Irvine CA 92697-5550, USA). Canon of approximately 11,000 works from over 3,000 Greek authors.
TU	*Texte und Untersuchungen zur Geschichte der altchristlichen Literatur.*
UBS	Greek New Testament (United Bible Societies).
Vg	Vulgate.

General Abbreviations.

attrib.	attributed to
B	Bohairic
ed.	editor
edn	edition
Eng.	English
ep(p).	Epistle(s)
esp.	especially
n(n).	footnote(s)
imp.	impression
lit.	literal(ly)
(l)ln	line(s)
MS(S)	manuscript(s)
repr.	reprint(ed)
S	Sahidic
sp.	spurious
trans.	translation; translated

INTRODUCTION

Διάκρισις and *discretio* are often translated as 'discretion', but in modern usage this English word tends to obscure the meaning of the Greek and Latin. While 'discretion' (from Latin: *discretio*) originally encompassed the Greek and Latin senses of separation, discrimination, judgment and discernment, it has increasingly been used to refer to good behaviour, secrecy and confidentiality. For clarity, then, the Greek and Latin terms are used throughout. By examining the technical use of διάκρισις and *discretio* in a well documented Christian context so different to the modern day Church, it is possible to gain interesting new insights into the nature and application of discernment.

The ability to distinguish between right and wrong and to make right and equitable judgments is fundamental to the morality of all societies. In the Christian tradition this ability is fundamental to righteous living, since it is necessary to make choices between good and evil in order to avoid sin and to live righteously within the will of God. While sin is understood to cause a moral obtuseness, desensitising all consciousness of God and his will, the regenerate soul, indwelt by the Holy Spirit, is capable of knowing both. The role of the Holy Spirit is central to understanding truth, Scripture and doctrine as well as to knowing God.[1] In part the Holy Spirit achieves this by the dissemination of spiritual gifts which include διάκρισις πνευμάτων,[2] but Christians are also expected to develop experience in the use of διάκρισις to discriminate between good and evil.[3] The biblical understanding of διάκρισις in the life of the believer is thus the natural starting point for appreciating what the Desert Fathers understood it to involve.

In the first chapter of this book it will be seen that Scripture develops the meaning of διάκρισις beyond the Classical usage of the term. The theology

---

[1]   Jn 16:5-15.
[2]   1 Cor. 12:10.
[3]   Heb. 5:14.

developed from Scripture in the early church frequently arose as a response to new ideas or heresies and in this process the meaning and use of the word διάκρισις developed as well. The role of the predominantly Origenist Catechetical School of Alexandria is significant to this process, not only because the major theologians associated with it were also closely associated with the nascent monastic movement in the Egyptian desert, but also because Alexandria was a centre of secular philosophical thought. Christianity neither emerged nor developed in a vacuum; the prevailing thought systems and philosophical worldview of the day would inevitably influence early Christian thinking and interpretations of the new faith. Since Neo-Platonic philosophy was highly influential from the third century on and is understood to have made an impact on the emergent theology of the period, this book turns next to consider Plotinus and his work. The first chapter ends by considering Origen, whose speculative theology drew on established philosophical approaches to understanding the nature of existence but also occasioned heated debate and eventual condemnation. The Egyptian desert was to prove a centre for Origenism and thus an appreciation of how Origen viewed διάκρισις is a valuable step towards gaining an understanding of διάκρισις in the thought of the Desert Fathers.

In the last century the shadowy figure of Evagrius Ponticus has come more fully to light with the recovery of many of his works. While his influence on the development of Christian thought has been debated, Evagrius combines Origenism (for which he was condemned in 553AD) with a strongly philosophical approach to faith and finding God. He lived as a monk in the Egyptian desert and also wrote extensively on how the monk should seek God. He thus represents a systematic theologian of the desert who unites the different strands of thought already identified: biblical, philosophical, Origenistic and monastic.

Evagrius is primarily concerned with the interior life of the monk and the union with God of the νοῦς, understood to be the highest level of a person's interior nature. Although Evagrius was renowned for his διάκρισις, he rarely uses the word or its cognates. Nevertheless, there is evidence throughout his works of how διάκρισις was used and understood by monks. By contrast John Cassian, who draws on Evagrius, provides a theology of the desert that is more anecdotal and practical in nature. His extensive writing on *discretio* was particularly valued in the East and his teaching is wholly in keeping with that found in the apophthegms of the Desert Fathers, whom he had visited in Egypt. Thus together, Evagrius and Cassian provide valuable evidence of how διάκρισις / *discretio* was understood, gained and used among the Desert Fathers in Egypt in the fourth and fifth centuries.

The sayings of the Desert Fathers or *Apophthegmata Patrum* are considerable in number, often repeated with major or minor variations in the different collections. Primarily anecdotal, occasionally gnomic but frequently presented as responses to actual questions, they began as an oral tradition that was later committed to writing. Although there is obvious evidence of redaction, in that the sayings are collected under subject headings or grouped according to the name of the main character, the sayings do not represent a systematic theology (as in Evagrius and Cassian) so much as a compendium of *dicta*. These *dicta* nevertheless present a broadly consistent system of thought. It is noted in chapter four that the sayings lay considerable emphasis on διάκρισις and all the sayings understood specifically to relate to διάκρισις have been analysed in chapters four and five.[4] However, it is also noted that unlike other key themes in desert thought, every saying can be interpreted using the key of διάκρισις.

The conclusion is drawn that διάκρισις gradually gained a more specific and technical meaning in monastic thought and mystical theology. However, διάκρισις also emerges not merely as a key element in the spirituality and theology of Egyptian anchoritic monasticism, but also as an essential part of the Christian approach to seeking and knowing God.

---

[4] To facilitate further study two appendices have been provided. The first lists all Scripture texts using διάκρισις, *discretio* and their cognates. The second appendix is a full cross reference list of every saying containing one of this group of words or categorised by the subject heading as relating to them.

CHAPTER 1

Διάκρισις in Late Antiquity

Διάκρισις in Scripture

The meaning of διάκρισις and its cognates[1] in Scripture broadly reflects that found in Classical literature and in the philosophical and theological texts of Late Antiquity. In Classical usage διάκρισις / διακρίνω has the basic sense of judging or making a distinction[2] or, negatively, being indiscriminate.[3] This basic meaning develops to describe separation and division,[4] as opposed to aggregation or combination (σύγκρισις).[5] Διακρίνω in particular can be used as a legal technical term, thus Pindar uses it for making right judgments in the heart (φρήν) rather than as a response to difficult circumstances,[6] Xenophon for judging disputes[7] and Homer of settling an affair.[8] Διάκρισις is sometimes used of difference expressed in quarrel and struggle.[9] The concept expressed by διάκρισις (and its cognates) in Scripture and theological works thus comes to focus on the action of choice between alternatives: discerning, judging, weighing and even wavering between people, things, situations, ideas, doctrines, moral values and so on. Thus, for example, it is used of distinguishing between the Persons of the Godhead,[10] of discerning good and evil,[11] of examination or scrutiny of words,[12] of someone with superior judgment[13]

---

[1] Ἀδιακρισία, ἀδιάκριτος, ἀδιακρίτως, διακρητικός, διακρίνω, διακριτέον, διακριτήριον, διακριτής, διακριτικός, διακριτικότης and διάκριτος.

[2] E.g. the blind distinguishing by feel (Homer, *odyssey* 8.195).

[3] E.g. in plundering raids (Herodotus, *hist.* 3.39).

[4] E.g. sorting flocks of small cattle (Homer, *iliad* 2.475) or combatants breaking off battle (Thucydides, *hist.* 1.105.5).

[5] Plato, *sophista* 243b.

[6] Pindar, *olympia* 8.24. Cf. Plato, *leg.* 11.937b.

[7] Xenophon, *hellenica* 5.2.10.

[8] Homer, *iliad* 20.212.

[9] E.g. decision by battle (Polybius, *hist.* 18.28.3).

[10] Basil the Great, *ep.* 38.4.

[11] Origen, *comm. in Joh.* 6.51.267. Cf. Musonius, *dissert.* discourse 6, lln. 47-48.

[12] Eusebius, *vit. Const.* 4.33.1; *1 Clem.* 48.5.

and of wavering doubt or dispute (i.e. being torn between alternatives).[14] The nearest Latin equivalent for διάκρισις, used frequently to translate it, is *discretio* (from *discerno*), which carries the sense of separation, distinction, discernment and the ability to distinguish.[15,16]

Διάκρισις in the Old Testament

Διάκρισις is only used once in the Septuagint (in Job 37:16) where it translates the *hapax legomenon* מִפְלָשֵׂי (layer [of clouds]).[17] This verse is a continuation of the rhetorical question asked by Elihu in v.15 about whether Job knows how God controls the clouds and lightning; clearly not, only God who is perfect in knowledge can know this. It has been suggested that in v.16 יָדַע governs עַל meaning 'know about' and that the verb for balancing or weighing refers to balancing clouds laden with moisture.[18] The Septuagint use of διάκρισις brings out the sense of weighing, balancing, judging and discerning (cf. *B* ογωτ; *S* ⲘⲒⲚⲈ) the clouds, similar to the use of διακρίνω in Matthew 16:3 when Jesus speaks of discerning or reading the weather.[19] Thus, διάκρισις in the Septuagint (and the Hebrew it translates) refers to Job's ability to discern and understand the nature of the clouds.

Διακρίνω occurs 23 times[20] in the Septuagint. It is most frequently used to translate שָׁפַט (judge, govern, discriminate) and generally denotes the judgment of a case involving two parties, i.e. deciding between two claims and discerning which is right. Thus, Moses explains to Jethro how he sits in

---

[13] Macarius, *de elevatione mentis* 13: 'Those who have διάκρισις and νοῦς, not denying them, inhabit the grace of God, and are not shaken by foul and shameful λογισμοί.'

[14] Clement of Alexandria, *quis dives salvatur* 31.8.

[15] Lewis, p. 589.

[16] The Sahidic and Bohairic Coptic versions of Scripture are generally agreed to date from the period covered by this book or earlier and so provide an indication of how διάκρισις was understood in early Egyptian thought. These use either the Greek word or translate it with words covering the same range of meanings outlined; some examples have been cited to demonstrate this. See also Appendix 1.

[17] הֲתֵדַע עַל־מִפְלְשֵׂי־עָב מִפְלְאוֹת תְּמִים דֵּעִים: (Job 37:16 BHS); BDB (p. 814) defines מִפְלָשֵׂי as 'swaying', 'poising'.

[18] R. Gordis, *The Book of Job: commentary and translation and special studies* (Moreshet Series 2; New York: Jewish Theological Seminary of America, 1978), p. 430. See also N.C. Habel, *The Book of Job: A Commentary* (Old Testament Library; London: SCM Press, 1985), p. 501.

[19] It is debateable whether the translator had Mt. 16:3 in mind. See C. Brown (ed.), *The New International Dictionary of New Testament theology* (4 vols; Grand Rapids: Zondervan, 1986), I, p. 503. (On Mt. 16:3, see below, p. 7).

[20] See Appendix 1 for full list.

judgment and decides (*B* ⲚⲞⲨⲦϤ) cases between the disputants (Exodus 18:16); Solomon asks God (1 Kings 3:9) for the charism of an understanding mind or hearing heart to distinguish between right and wrong in the government of his people when hearing judicial cases (v.11);[21] officials are appointed to judge Israel (1 Chronicles 26:29); and as judges Israel's priests are to decide (*B* ⲦϨⲀⲠ) judicial cases in accordance with God's Law (Ezekiel 44:24). God himself is also presented as Judge: he will judge (*B* ϬⲒ ϨⲀⲠ; *S* ⲪⲒ ϨⲀⲠ) between the idolatrous and faithful in Israel (Ezekiel 20:35-36); as Shepherd of the flock of Israel he will judge or separate out (*B* ⲦϨⲀⲠ) the good and bad sheep, particularly their leaders, (Ezekiel 34:17, 20);[22] and judge (*B* ϬⲒ ϨⲀⲠ...ⲦϨⲀⲠ) the nations for their treatment of his people (i.e. judge between the two; Joel 4:2, 12 LXX). In the heavenly realm God is presented as judging (*B* ⲦϨⲀⲠ) angels (Job 21:22)[23] and also the אֱלֹהִים[24] as he presides over the heavenly court (Psalm 81:1 LXX). The use of διακρίνω to translate שָׁפַט illustrates its sense as a legal technical term for judgment, the discernment between two opposing choices in a judicial case; this is supported by the Coptic evidence.

Διακρίνω is also used in some verses to translate רִיב (judge, plead the cause, execute judgment, contend). These provide two contexts for the use of διακρίνω: a) contention and censure; b) just and righteous rule. In the first instance, Jeremiah laments his birth and rues ever becoming involved in legal accusations against God's people for their breaches of his Law, he feels that he is constantly striving and contending[25] against the entire nation (Jeremiah 15:10) and in Psalm 49:4 (LXX) God is described as coming to judge (*B* ⲦϨⲀⲠ) his people, i.e. to censure them (v.21).[26] In the second instance, Proverbs 31:9 is an injunction to safeguard the rights of the poor by judging and defending them fairly[27] and in Zechariah 3:7 Joshua is sanctified in the heavenly court and given the charge to remain righteous in order to rule (*B* ⲦϨⲀⲠ) over God's people. Both uses reveal dual circumstances that are distinguished and weighed in some way, in the first case a tension between uprightness and disobedience, and in the latter the

---

21   See below (p. 5) on 1 Kgs 3:11 (Vg).

22   Cf. Homer, *odyssey* 8.195.

23   The context and meaning of this verse is debated.

24   Variously interpreted; most probably angels, but possibly the gods of the nations.

25   Διακρίνω.

26   The Hebrew infinitive (reflected in LXX and Vg) makes the subject of the verb uncertain: possibly the heavens and earth are called as judges, but v.6 indicates that the Judge is God.

27   Κρίνω translates שָׁפַט here suggesting some equivalence between διακρίνω and κρίνω, particularly if they are seen as poetic parallels.

route of righteous as opposed to unrighteous rule; selecting righteousness and purity is thus closely associated in Scripture with διάκρισις.

In Job διακρίνω is used to translate two other Hebrew words of broadly similar meaning: בָּחַר (choose, test) in Job 9:14; 15:5 and בָּחַן (examine, scrutinise, test) in Job 12:11; 23:10. This usage is not found elsewhere in the Septuagint. In Job 9:14, Job questions how he could possibly discern the words necessary to argue with God who is infinitely righteous and powerful. This use of διακρίνω to attempt to determine what words to use finds a negative example in Job 15:5, although the Septuagint translation of the Hebrew changes the sense of Eliphaz's words from an accusation of having chosen deceitful words[28] to a failure to discern the words of rulers. Διακρίνω / בָּחַר is thus used of weighing and choosing which words to say, whereas in Job 12:11 διακρίνω / בָּחַן is used of Job testing (*B* ϩⲟⲧϩⲉⲧ; *S* ⲙⲟⲩϫⲧ) the words he hears using his critical faculty in the same way as he might use taste to discriminate between foods. The second use of διακρίνω to translate בָּחַן (Job 23:10) also focuses on testing, but this time it is of God testing Job's way of life as gold might be tested for its purity. Διακρίνω is thus used of examining, weighing and testing the value both of words to be spoken and heard and of a person's manner of life.

The remaining uses of διακρίνω in the Septuagint are single instances of translation. In Leviticus 24:12 it is used for פָּרַשׁ (make distinct, declare) which expresses the will of the Lord being made known to the Israelites regarding a blasphemer. The Septuagint brings out the root meaning of the Hebrew verb, 'separate', i.e. to discern that will or command. In Deuteronomy 33:7 διακρίνω translates רִיב (strive, contend). Although the meaning of the Hebrew of this line is uncertain, it relates to Judah defending itself but also seeking God's help to do so and the Septuagint appears to understand it in this way; thus διακρίνω is used in the sense of a struggle between two causes (cf. *S* ϫⲓ ϩⲁⲡ). Finally, although the Hebrew of Ecclesiastes 3:18 is unclear, בָּרַר (purify, select, choose, test) appears to relate to God making clear to people that they are but animals without him and the Septuagint use of διακρίνω to translate בָּרַר brings out this sense of God judging and weighing between human and beast. Thus, διακρίνω is used of discerning the Divine will and commands, just causes and the nature of existence.

The διάκρισις cognate ἀδιάκριτος is used only in Proverbs 25:1. There is a fluidity of meaning in this word ranging from something mixed or undecided through to something in which there is no discord or uncertainty. In this verse it is used to describe Solomon's proverbs (although it has no direct equivalent in Hebrew or Latin[29]) and may indicate either the unassailable nature of the instructions (παιδεῖαι) that follow or that they

---

[28]   As Vg.

[29]   Nor are גַּם and *quoque* represented in LXX.

are a miscellany. Given the use of ἀδιάκριτος in James 3:17[30] the former is more likely indicating no choice or hesitation between two things and therefore affirming their certainty and veracity.

The five occasions on which the Vulgate uses *discerno* where the Septuagint does not have διάκρισις / διακρίνω provide further insight into the meaning of the word-group. In Leviticus 10:10 *discerno* is used for בָּדַל (divide, separate, make a distinction; LXX διαστέλλω; *B* ογωτ εβολ; *S* πωρ͞x 2ν) and describes the duty of priests to discern what is holy and clean from what is unholy and unclean. In 2 Samuel 19:35 it translates יָדַע (know, discriminate, distinguish; LXX γινώσκω; *S* ειμε) and is used of discerning sweet and bitter tastes (BHS, LXX and *S*: 'good and evil') in a context of judicious bargaining for an alliance between David and Barzillai. 1 Kings 3:11 relates to Solomon's request for wisdom and discernment to govern and judge his people fairly. Whereas διακρίνω and *discerno* are used to translate שָׁפַט in 1 Kings 3:9,[31] here the expression הָבִין לִשְׁמֹעַ מִשְׁפָּט (LXX σύνεσιν τοῦ εἰσακούειν κρίμα) is rendered *sapientiam ad discernendum iudicium* so that *discerno* stands for שָׁמַע / εἰσακούω rather than שָׁפַט / κρίμα. *Discerno* is thus used of the act of judging between two claims rather than the understanding or discernment required to do so, although the context may be said to embrace this as well. In Psalm 42:1 (Vg) *discerno* is used for רִיב (strive, contend; LXX δικάζω) in the Psalmist's prayer for God to plead or distinguish his cause in the face of an unholy nation and rescue him from deceitful[32] men. This sets *discerno* in contrast and opposition to deceit, a juxtaposition found repeatedly in the monastic literature. Finally, in Psalm 67:15 (Vg) *discerno* translates פָּרַשׂ (spread out, scatter; LXX διαστέλλω; *S* πωρ͞x ε2ραι εx͞ν). Although the context and historical background of this verse are uncertain, the sense in the Hebrew and Septuagint versions is a separation of God's people from their enemies, whereas the Vulgate shifts this to God settling or determining (cf. *B* ϵωω εx͞ν) kings over them. The sense nevertheless remains of *discerno* expressing a (Divine) decision. Thus, when *discerno* is used in the Vulgate on occasions where the Septuagint does not use διακρίνω, it is still used of discerning good and evil, deciding justly between two causes or claims (not least in the face of evil and deceit) and of separating out two conflicting parties representing right and wrong.

Διάκρισις in the Old Testament Apocrypha

The only cognate of διάκρισις to appear in the Old Testament apocrypha is διακρίνω; there are four instances. In the longer Greek version of Esther

---

[30] See below, p. 10.
[31] See above, p. 3.
[32] *Dolosus*, δόλιος, מִרְמָה

(probably a later, pre-Christian inflation of the Hebrew text) the additional section following Esther 8:12[33] represents the edict issued by Artaxerxes at Mordecai's behest and E.9 outlines how the authorities are to judge[34] cases fairly; there is also a contrasting context of deceit (E.6). The correct judicial discernment of conflicting causes is also found in Solomon's prayer in Wisdom 9:12 for God's help in governing his people in order to judge them fairly. By contrast elsewhere, idols are said to be incapable of discerning or determining (*B ϩⲁⲡ*) such judgments be it in relation to themselves (LXX Epistle of Jeremiah 1:53, κρίσιν οὐ μὴ διακρίνωσιν αὐτῶν) or more generally (Vg Baruch 6:53, *iudicium non discernent*). Lastly, διακρίνω is used in 4 Maccabees, a late Greek philosophical treatise addressed to Jews on the sovereignty of devout reason over the emotions (4 Maccabees 1:1, 13). In 4 Maccabees 1:14 the writer sets out his intention to distinguish between reason (λογισμός) and emotion (πάθος), the range and nature of the emotions and whether the former rules over the latter. Thus, in the later apocryphal Old Testament, διακρίνω continues to be used of choosing between two conflicting causes and discerning which is right and wrong, of discernment of the inner nature (Epistle of Jeremiah 1:53) and of distinguishing both between and the nature of two psychological concepts.

Διάκρισις in the New Testament

The noun διάκρισις is used only three times in the New Testament,[35] firstly of the ability to distinguish or differentiate between good and evil[36] and also between spirits[37] and secondly of passing judgment.[38] The phrase μὴ εἰς διακρίσεις διαλογισμῶν in Romans 14:1 is not without its problems, since both nouns used in the phrase are capable of different interpretations,[39] but the sense is clear from the context. Those with weaker

---

[33]   LXX Est. E; Vg Est. 16.

[34]   Διακρίνω. Although Vg (16:9) renders the verse differently, it also refers to passing sentence *(ferre sententiam)*.

[35]   The Codex Bezae (folio 429b) version of Acts 4:32 provides a fourth by inserting: καὶ οὐκ ἦν διάκρισις ἐν αὐτοῖς οὐδεμία *(there was not one division among them.* Διάκρισις is translated as *accusatio* in folio 430). Comparing MS cop[G67] with Codex Bezae, Epp concludes that the variants in the latter may be as early as 2nd century (E.J. Epp, 'Coptic Manuscript G67 and the Rôle of Codex Bezae as a Western Witness in Acts', *Journal of Biblical Literature* 85.2 (June, 1966), pp. 197-212).

[36]   Heb. 5:14.

[37]   1 Cor. 12:10.

[38]   Rom. 14:1.

[39]   See e.g. L. Morris, *The Epistle to the Romans* (Leicester: IVP, 1988), p. 478; J. Murray, *The Epistle to the Romans* (The New London Commentary on the New Testament; London: Marshall, Morgan & Scott, 1967), part 2, p. 175.

faith should not be rejected by the strong, nor should the latter enter into debates,[40] disputes or the censorious scrutiny of others' thoughts. Here διάκρισις is being used negatively to express the weighing of thoughts with condemnatory intent.

By contrast Hebrews 5:14 describes the way in which the more mature and advanced in faith have an experience and skill born of practice (ἕξις) that provides them with the sensitivity and ability to distinguish (*B* ϭⲱⲃϯ) what is morally good and evil.[41] The phrase τῶν διὰ τὴν ἕξιν τὰ αἰθητήρια γεγυμασμένα ἐχόντων is significant for arriving at an understanding of how διάκρισις was acquired and used according to the author of Hebrews. The faculties (αἰθητήρια), which represent both the organs of sense and, by extension ethical and spiritual senses, are trained and so διάκρισις is clearly as skill exercised in the mind as well as a spiritual gift as indicated in Scripture elsewhere. Γυμνάζω suggests considerable personal effort, its meaning embracing as it does gymnastic exercise, individual practice and wearing oneself out; furthermore, the perfect tense indicates a continual process. Διάκρισις can thus be acquired through constant human effort and means; it is not exclusively a spiritual gift. Finally, the use of ἕξις is particularly instructive because of the range of meaning associated with this word. While δία τὴν ἕξιν can convey the idea of constant or habitual exercise of the faculties, ἕξις can also refer to a skill, acquired habit or state of mind. Διάκρισις is thus a skill gained through training and effort; while it can be said that it is developed through constant practice, it can also be said that διάκρισις is a state of mind, a disposition as well as an ability to be used, a spiritual faculty of moral discernment and judgment.

Lastly, listed among the gifts of the Holy Spirit in 1 Corinthians 12:10, there is the διάκρισις πνευμάτων (*B* ⲃⲱⲗ ⲙⲡⲛⲁ). This gift follows directly after that of prophecy and it is likely that it particularly refers to the ability to determine the origin of prophetic and ecstatic utterances, i.e. whether actuated by the Holy Spirit or by some demonic source.[42] Thus, διάκρισις is used to express the discernment and distinguishing of thoughts, moral issues and spiritual phenomena and possibly a division between people.[43]

The use of διακρίνω in the New Testament is much more widespread than that of διάκρισις, but it is used for the same range of meanings already discussed. In a saying reminiscent of Job 37:16, Matthew 16:3[44] records Jesus telling the Pharisees and Sadducees that they know how to

---

[40]   As Vg *disceptatio*; *S* ϩⲟⲧϩⲧ; *B* ϩⲓⲟⲓ.

[41]   Cf. Basil the Great, *hom. in Ps* 61.10.

[42]   Cf. 1 Cor. 12:3.

[43]   Acts 4:32 (Codex Bezae).

[44]   Vg 16:3-4a. On Job 37:16 see above, p. 2.

discern (*B* ⲤⲰⲘⲤ) what the weather will be like from the sky,[45] but they are unable to interpret the signs of the times.[46] This, then, refers to the ability to interpret natural phenomena and extends it to include (albeit negatively here) the ability to discern more abstract information which has a spiritual and personal bearing. Thus, in 1 Corinthians 11:29-31 Paul enjoins his readers to self-examination (v.31; *S* ⲘⲞⲨⲰϢⲦ)[47] and to discernment of the body (v.29) when approaching the Eucharist.[48] On both occasions διακρίνω is used, but whereas the process of self-judgment is clear in v.31, the meaning of 'the body' in v.29 is less so. Some early manuscripts have 'the Lord's body' which suggests an early attempt at interpretation. The body may refer to the Host (distinguishing it from common food or discerning the Lord's body in it) or discerning the respective needs of members of the church as the body of Christ at the agape meal.[49] While the former is most likely in the context of v.27, there may be a deliberate dual meaning to the use of 'body' here. In any case, the use of διακρίνω here indicates certainly self and inner discernment (v.31) and also discernment of spiritual issues, most probably in the nature of the Eucharist itself and probably also the corporate nature of its celebration and therefore the discernment of others (v.29). In a similar vein to διάκρισις πνευμάτων in 1 Corinthians 12:10, which most probably relates to prophecy, 1 Corinthians 14:29 refers to the weighing, testing or discerning by the whole church of prophets' words in public worship.[50] In Hebrews 4:12 the word of God is described as *discretor*,[51] capable of discerning the deepest motives and notions of human personality, so that Scripture may be said to be a discerner of all inner dimensions of human existence. Finally, 1 Corinthians 6:5 relates to judging or deciding disputes in the church.[52] Whereas κρίνω might serve equally well here, the compound has probably been used partly because it relates to judging *between* believers and more particularly because the

---

[45] Cf. use of διάκρισις in Gregory of Nyssa, *de vit. Mos.* 1.28 for the distinction between day and night.

[46] MS evidence for vv.2b-3 is weak (*S* omits); possibly a later addition imitating Lk. 12:54-56.

[47] Cf. self-judgment, Ignatius, *ep. to the Ephesians* 5:3; inner deliberation, Hermas, *Visions* 1.2.2.

[48] See above (p. 4) on Job 12:11, 23:10 re testing words and way of life as one would gold.

[49] Cf. differentiating people, *Diognetus* 5.1.

[50] Cf. *Didache* 11.7.

[51] From *discerno*; κριτικός; *S* ⲣⲉϥⲔⲣⲓⲛⲉ; *B* ⲃⲟⲧⲏⲉⲧ.

[52] See above (p. 3) on Ezek. 34:17-20 re God separating out sheep. Cf. Demosthenes, *Phil. ep.* 17.

context is of resolving disputes amicably by arbitration[53] rather than by litigation. Thus, διακρίνω is used of the discernment of meaning, nature and origins in the natural, spiritual and personal interior realms.

The use of διακρίνω to express 'doubt' or 'waver' appears first in the New Testament and probably derives from the sense of disputing and thus being at odds with oneself, i.e. the subject is torn between two options;[54] this is particularly so when διακρίνω is in the passive (i.e. being divided *by* something).[55] In Matthew 21:21 and Mark 11:23 doubt or hesitation[56] are set in contrast to confident faith when Jesus tells his disciples that with undoubting and unwavering faith they will be able to perform miracles. This concept is developed in James 1:6 where διακρίνω (Vg *haesito*; B ⲢϨⲎⲧ B) is used twice to describe someone with faith so unstable that his doubt is expressive of distrust of God. Such people are upbraided for their divided attitude[57] towards God as they waver between trust and distrust. There is a similar use of διακρίνω in Romans 14:23 (S ⲢϨⲎⲧ ⲤⲚⲀⲨ; B ⲢϨⲎⲧ B) where Paul contrasts weak and strong faith. The strong are said to understand that all food is clean, whereas the weak are plagued by doubts about what they should eat. If the latter eats food that his conscience tells him he should not, he does not do so from faith and so, by Paul's definition, he sins. Thus, the doubter fails to discern both his conscience and the dictates of his faith. Διάκρισις is thus a sense of knowing what is right and acting upon this calmly and confidently. In Romans 4:20 the strength of Abraham's faith is seen in its unwavering nature. Thus, wholesome faith is expressed as being unwavering and without doubts, free from the negative aspects of being torn between courses of action or choices. This is not to say that true faith is devoid of διάκρισις, but rather that it chooses to trust in God making possible the proper use of the positive aspects of διάκρισις.

Two further senses in which διακρίνω is used relate to making distinctions between people and contending with them. These meanings are closer than they at first appear since both allude to the ability to weigh matters up; in the first instance people and in the second a situation or cause. Thus, in Acts 10:20 Peter is told in his vision to go with Cornelius' emissaries: possibly without doubt or hesitation (B ⲢϨⲎⲧ B) or, more

---

[53] It is interesting to note, given the excesses and abuses of faith Paul was addressing in the Corinthian church and the need to discern what was right, that διακρίνω is used 5 times and διάκρισις once in 1 Cor.

[54] See L. Morris, *The Epistle to the Romans* (Leicester: IVP, 1988), p. 212, n. 93 and BAG, p. 185. Cf. below (pp. 10-11) on Lk. 11:38.

[55] E.g. Origen, *comm. in Joh.* 13.10.63; John Moschus, *Pratum spirituale* 96 (*PG* 87.2953C).

[56] Vg (both) *haesito*; S (both) ⲢϨⲎⲧ ⲤⲚⲀⲨ; B Mt.: ⲢϨⲎⲧ B; Mk: ⲞⲓⲤⲀⲚⲓⲤ.

[57] Jas. 1:8 δίψυχος.

probably, making no distinctions,[58] i.e. not refusing to go on the grounds that they are Gentiles. The latter sense is more likely, since the same word is used (in the active) in Peter's report of this event in Acts 11:12 (*B* ϩⲏⲧ ⲃ; however Vg *haesito*) when the circumcised believers contend (Acts 11:2 διακρίνω[59]) with him for having met and eaten with Gentiles and again (in the active) in his report to the Jerusalem Council (Acts 15:9) where he says that God made no distinction (*S* ⲡⲱⲣϫ; *B* ⳙⲓⲃϯ) between the Gentiles and themselves (Jews).[60] In Jude 1:9 διακρίνω is used as in Acts 11:2 to describe how the archangel Michael contended with the Devil over the fate of the body of Moses.[61] However, in Jude 1:22 it is used of wavering when the readers are encouraged to show mercy (ἐλεᾶτε) to those who waver (*S* v.23 ϫⲓ ϩⲁⲡ) when faced with false teachers. The earlier use of διακρίνω in Jude 1:9 to describe contention probably gave rise to the emendation of ἐλεᾶτε in some manuscripts to ἐλέγξετε to give 'refute those who are contentious.' In James 2:4 διακρίνω is used in the context of partiality, favouritism and snobbery; the rhetorical question here suggests that in doing so the readers have become evil judges who discriminate (*S* ⳙⲓⲃⲉ; *B* ⳙⲓⲃϯ) wrongly between or against people. Whether the use of ἐν ἑαυτοῖς here is intended to mean an internalised act of discrimination expressed in duplicitous judgment that nominally looks to God while actually being preoccupied with worldly snobbery or whether it refers to the making of unjustified divisions within the church, does not affect the force of διακρίνω being used to describe distinguishing (albeit negatively here) between people. Having said this, the common themes in James of both wavering and of discrimination may indicate an intentional double force to διακρίνω here: wavering between righteous judgment and snobbery *and* making unrighteous distinctions. This is more positively expressed in James 3:17 which describes the nature of heavenly wisdom (which in early Christian literature is interchangeable with 'Spirit') as ἀδιάκριτος, i.e. unwavering or impartial (*B* ⲁⲧϯϩⲁⲡ).[62] Luke 11:38 describes a Pharisee dining with Jesus and observing with surprise that (ἰδὼν ἐθαύμασεν ὅτι) he does not first wash his hands. The Codex Bezae version of this verse

---

[58] Διάκρινω is in the passive. Cf. Hermas, *Mandates* 2.6.

[59] Vg *discepto*; *S* ϫⲓ ϩⲁⲡ; *B* ϭⲓ ϩⲁⲡ. Cf. Ezek. 20:35-36 and Joel 4:12 (LXX) above (p. 3).

[60] The Vulgate's use of *dubito* and *haesito* in Acts 10:20 and 11:12 respectively and of *discerno* in 15:9 may however suggest an early understanding that Peter went both without hesitation *and* without making distinctions; nevertheless, the interpretation given of the Greek provides a more consistent approach.

[61] For a reconstruction of the legend to which this refers, see J.N.D. Kelly, *A Commentary on the Epistles of Peter and of Jude* (Black's New Testament Commentaries; London: Adam & Charles Black, 1969, repr. 1982), pp. 264-65. The sense of dispute is brought out in Vg (*disputo*), *S* (ϫⲓ ϩⲁⲡ) and *B* (ϫⲱ ⲟⲩⲃⲉ).

[62] Cf. Ignatius, *ep. to the Trallians* 1.1.

replaces ἰδὼν ἐθαύμασεν ὅτι with ἤρξατο διακρεινομενος (*sic.*) ἐν ἑαυτῷ λέγειν διὰ τί indicating that the Pharisee weighed the matter up in his mind and passed comment on it.[63] Διακρίνω is thus used here to express interior debate and assessment,[64] possibly of a judgmental nature. In 1 Corinthians 4:7 Paul asks the rhetorical question, 'For who makes you different from anyone else?' which would appear to have a dual answer in the context: a) there is no difference, all believers are forgiven sinners; and b) any difference by virtue of possessing special gifts is granted by God rather than through some superiority on the part of the individual. In either case διακρίνω is used to express a (lack of) distinction between people; it is also used in a context of judgment (v.3), non-judgment and exposure of the heart and inner motives (v.5), the understanding and application of Scripture (v.6) and of self-knowledge (v.7). These verses serve to demonstrate the fluidity with which διακρίνω is used to express wavering and hesitation, the making of distinctions between people and contending with them. The common root, however, lies in making a choice between alternatives.

The διάκρισις / *discretio* word-group, therefore, is used in Scripture to express choice between alternatives. Διάκρισις is used to separate out and weigh up moral, spiritual, natural and psychological aspects of life and arrive at a value judgment concerning them. It is used to evaluate a person's inner or outer life, judicial decisions (hence the sense of contending with people or making evaluations about them), natural and spiritual phenomena (e.g. the weather and prophecy), and words spoken or heard. Διάκρισις is the ability to distinguish and discern matters and so come to a greater understanding of them; an ability which has the potential for both positive and negative use. It is used to distinguish the difference between what is righteous and unrighteous, between good and evil and to determine the spiritual origin of events (e.g. prophecy), the will of God or just causes (e.g. separating out two conflicting parties or causes representing right and wrong). While Scripture continues to use διάκρισις and its cognates within the Classical range of meaning, the New Testament develops the word-group to embrace a new sense, that of wavering and doubting. It can thus express being torn between two options and, negatively, discrimination against people, while the opposite, ἀδιάκριτος, can express certainty and veracity. Furthermore, the word-group begins to be applied in more specifically theological and spiritual senses, and not merely simple acts of judgment. Διάκρισις thus begins, in Scripture, to express a spiritual critical faculty that enables believers to develop their spiritual life.

---

[63]   Codex Bezae, folio 233b (διακρίνω translated as *cogito* in folio 234).

[64]   Cf. Hermas, *Similitudes* 2.1.

The Catechetical School of Alexandria

Having established the use of διάκρισις in Scripture, the main text of Christian spirituality, it is now useful to consider the philosophical and theological background of the period. To gain a clearer appreciation of how διάκρισις was understood in the early church, reference will now be made particularly to Alexandria, which was a centre of theological and secular thought in Late Antiquity. The theology formulated in Alexandria was distinctive from that of other centres such as Antioch and arguably the most influential speculative theologian working there was Origen. The philosophy and theology emanating from Alexandria was closely associated with and supported by the desert monks.[65] Many of the theologians who worked in Alexandria spent time as anchorites and either formulated 'desert theology' (e.g. Evagrius Ponticus and John Cassian) or helped inform its development. A brief overview of the schools of theology and secular philosophy in Alexandria and the interplay between them is thus a valuable starting point for appreciating 'desert theology' and the place of διάκρισις within it.

Christian theology and thought in Egypt in the period under consideration centred on Alexandria and the Catechetical School. Alexandria, founded in 331BC by Alexander the Great, had long been a great centre of learning and it was here that Jewish-Hellenistic literature first found expression in the Septuagint and the works of Philo (c.20BC-c.50AD). The various philosophical systems each had their schools of instruction in Alexandria and so it was perhaps natural that, when Christianity first arrived in the late first century, Christian teachers adopted the same approach. The Catechetical School was probably the first theological school of its kind, but the date of its foundation is unknown.[66] Pantaenus (d.190), a Stoic philosopher, became the first known head of the School following a missionary journey to India.[67] After his death his pupil Clement of Alexandria (c.150-c.215), who sought to reconcile Christian theology with Greek philosophy, became head of the School[68] and trained Origen[69] (c.185-c.254) who in turn succeeded him.[70] Porphyry (c.232-303),

---

[65] The earliest attested use of μοναχός in its institutional sense dates from 324AD in a secular petition for damages, suggesting that the term was well established by that date. (G.H.R. Horsley, *New Documents Illustrating Early Christianity: A review of the Greek inscriptions and papyri published in 1976* (North Ryde, N.S.W: Ancient History Documentary Research Centre, Macquarie University, 1981), pp. 124-26).

[66] Jerome suggests a very early date, possibly as early as Mark the Evangelist (*de vir. inl.* 36; cf. Eusebius, *HE* 2.16.1 where Mark is said to have introduced the Gospel to Egypt and Alexandria) and Eusebius points to its ancient origins (*HE* 5.10.1).

[67] Jerome, *de vir. inl.* 36; Eusebius, *HE* 5.10.1-2.

[68] Clement of Alexandria, *strom.* 1.1.11; Eusebius, *HE* 5.11.2; 6.6.1; 6.13.2.

[69] Jerome, *de vir. inl.* 38.

an ardent defender of Neo-Platonism, claimed that Origen had attended lectures given by the reputed founder of Neo-Platonism, Ammonius Saccas (c.175-242).[71] Ammonius also had a profound influence on Plotinus (c.204-270) who, through his Enneads, handed on what he had learnt from his teacher.[72] The Catechetical School remained strongly Origenist[73] in its theology in the succeeding years: Origen's pupils Heraclas[74] and Dionysius the Great (d. c.264)[75] were successive heads of the School, followed by the Origenist Theognostus (d. c.282) and Pierius, whom Jerome called 'Origen Junior.'[76] Other graduates of the School included Athanasius (c.296-373), Gregory of Nazianzus (329-389), Jerome (c.342-420), Rufinus (c.345-410) and Cyril of Alexandria (d. 444), the last three of whom were taught by Didymus the Blind (c.313-398), a later head of the School who wrote a commentary on Origen's *de principiis*[77] and was later condemned as an Origenist (along with Origen himself and Evagrius) at the Council of Constantinople in 553AD. Many of these scholars (e.g. Pantaenus and Origen) had extensive training in Greek philosophy and were well equipped to conduct the mainly written debate with the Neo-Platonists of Alexandria. However, tension reached a peak in 415AD when Christians brutally murdered Hypatia, the head of the Neo-Platonic School in Alexandria; Cyril, a noted opponent of Neo-Platonism, was suspected of complicity in the crime.[78] The high regard in which Hypatia was held is indicated by the correspondence of Synesius of Cyrene (c.370-413), Bishop of Ptolemais.[79] Thus the Catechetical School and the theology developed there were both strongly Origenist and closely associated with Neo-Platonism, although not

---

[70] Eusebius, *HE* 6.6.1; Jerome, *de vir. inl.* 54.
[71] Porphyry, quoted in Eusebius, *HE* 6.19. While this seems possible, given Origen's interest in Greek philosophy, it should be noted that Porphyry also mentions another Origen (*vit. Plot.* 3, 14 and 20), a common name in Alexandria at the time, and it remains possible that the two have become confused.
[72] *Vit. Plot.* 3; Plotinus' 11 year study under Ammonius would have begun (on Porphyry's dating) around 231AD and whether he was likely ever to have met Origen rests on whether Origen returned to Alexandria between leaving Palestine in 230AD and residing in Caesarea from 231AD; such a visit is probably highly unlikely (see McGiffert's note on Eusebius, *HE* 6.23.4 in NPNF Series 2, Vol. 1, pp. 527-30).
[73] With the possible exception of the School head Peter of Alexandria (d. c.311) whom Quasten says was an anti-Origenist (J. Quasten, *Patrology* (Antwerp: Spectrum, 1964), II, pp. 113-18).
[74] Head 231-c.233; Eusebius, *HE* 6.26.1.
[75] Eusebius, *HE* 6.29.4; Jerome, *de vir. inl.* 69.
[76] Jerome, *de vir. inl.* 76.
[77] Socrates Scholasticus, *HE* 4.25.
[78] *Ibid.* 7.15.
[79] Synesius, *epp.* 10, 15, 16, 33, 81, 124, 136 and 154.

necessarily a wholesale reworking or adoption of the latter. It is therefore appropriate to consider both Neo-Platonism and Origen, to gain some understanding of the thought system in which the Desert Fathers used the term διάκρισις.

The toleration of Christianity decreed by Constantine in the Edict of Milan in 313AD[80] was followed by a more public expression and debate of heresies such as Donatism and Arianism. The Arian controversy centred on Alexandria around Arius and Athanasius and resulted in the Council of Nicaea (325AD) called by Constantine to resolve the dispute over the nature of God. Athanasius implies in his *Vita Antonii*[81] that he met the anchorite Antony the Great in Alexandria when he was called upon to defend his orthodox faith against the Arians (c.338AD).[82] Antony's involvement in the debate and association with Athanasius is evident from Athanasius' record of an earlier visit to Alexandria by Antony during the persecution of Maximin,[83] a letter written by Antony in support of the Alexandrians when they were suffering under a pro-Arian general, Balacius,[84] and his inheritance of Antony's sheepskin, which Athanasius had given him years before.[85] While Antony's concern for the Alexandrians and his support in theological debates and persecutions indicate a close association between the Desert Fathers (not exclusively limited to Antony[86]) and Alexandria, it should be noted that Athanasius was repeatedly out of favour and exiled, which suggests that he had a vested interest not only in personifying his own version of orthodoxy in *Vita Antonii* but also in suggesting a strong friendship with a widely respected figure (even to the point of a deathbed bequest). Antony may not have been an educated man, speaking, and possibly writing, only Coptic, but this did not preclude him or others from engaging occasionally in the theological debates of the day.[87] Senior ecclesiastics are also recorded as sending letters

---

[80] Lactantius, *de mortibus persecutorum* 48; Eusebius, *HE* 10.5.

[81] *Vit. Ant.* 69-71; chapter 71 is in the first person plural, implying that Athanasius was present. Antony also debated Arianism with Didymus the Blind (Socrates Scholasticus, *HE* 4.25). See also Theodoret, *HE* 4.27.

[82] See R.C. Gregg, *Athanasius: The Life of Antony and the Letter to Marcellinus* (New York: Paulist Press, 1980), p. 142, n. 132.

[83] *Vit. Ant.* 46.

[84] *Ibid.* 86.

[85] *Ibid.* 91.

[86] E.g. *VP* 5.4.63.

[87] See e.g. Jerome, *de vir. inl.* 88 (Coptic letters); Palladius, *HL* 21.15 (knew no Greek); *vit. Ant.* 16 (taught in Coptic), 72 (uneducated); Cassian, *conf.* 18.1 (unlettered). By contrast Arsenius is said to have been learned in Latin and Greek (*VP* 5.15.7; Arsenius 6). However, the sophistication of Antony's letters suggests a keen theological mind; see S. Rubenson, *The Letters of St Antony: Monasticism and*

to the monks, bringing the debates to them, such as the Anthropomorphite controversy.[88] Thus the theology of Alexandria and the theology of the desert are closely linked, further warranting an examination of Origen and Neo-Platonism.

Neo-Platonism

Plotinus was among the foremost of Plato's interpreters in Late Antiquity and at the forefront of the Neo-Platonic revival;[89] Porphyry, Iamblichus and Proclus are numbered among his successors and his influence on pagan piety extended throughout Late Antiquity. What little is known of Plotinus' life comes from his biographer and devoted pupil, Porphyry, who records that he would say nothing of his parentage, birthplace or date of birth.[90] Superficially his lifestyle evinces some similarities with that of the Desert Fathers. Porphyry says 'Plotinus ... seemed ashamed of being in the body,'[91] suggesting Plotinus concerned himself little with his physical comfort, but this is probably a reference to his longing for union with the One.[92] His vegetarianism and rejection of bathing[93] find parallels in the monastic lifestyle[94] as do his willingness to teach only earnest enquirers,[95] taking little sleep and only eating every other day,[96] and his apparent humility in the face of those whom he believed had nothing to learn from him.[97] Although Plotinus was unlike the Desert Fathers, who fled renown, in that he had a large following that included many of high rank such as

---

     the Making of a Saint (Studies in Antiquity and Christianity; Minneapolis: Fortress Press, 1995).

[88]   Cassian, *conf.* 10.2.2. On the Anthropomorphite controversy, see below, pp. 35-36, 77.

[89]   Neo-Platonism is a modern term for the Late Antique development of Platonism, particularly under Plotinus, who nevertheless saw his system as essentially Platonist (*Enneads* 5.1.8, cf. *vit. Plot.* 20).

[90]   *Vit. Plot.* 1-2. Eunapius (*vit. soph.* 3.1.1) and later authors claim Plotinus was born in Lyco, or Lycopolis, in Egypt, but there is no real evidence of a particular affinity with Egypt in *vit. Plot.* or *Enneads*, only that Plotinus trained in Alexandria.

[91]   *Vit. Plot.* 1; where, as here, English translations of *vit. Plot.* and *Enneads* are taken from S. MacKenna, *Plotinus: The Enneads* (ed. B.S. Page; London: Faber and Faber, rev. edn, 1961), they are followed by 'MacKenna' in brackets.

[92]   Discussed below, pp. 17-21.

[93]   *Vit. Plot.* 2.

[94]   E.g. Theophilus 3 and *HL* 38.12 respectively.

[95]   *Vit. Plot.* 4, 13, cf. *HL* 21.8-9. Plotinus taught with brevity of language and depth of ideas (*vit. Plot.* 14), which might be said to be similar to the gnomic style of some apophthegms and of Evagrius Ponticus.

[96]   *Vit. Plot.* 8, cf. e.g. Arsenius 14 and Nau 242 respectively.

[97]   *Vit. Plot.* 14. His style was also free of pomp (*vit. Plot.* 18), cf. Poemen 8.

Senators and Emperor Gallienus,[98] nevertheless the response of Senator Rogatianus to his teaching was to renounce his home, possessions and political status and enter an ascetic regime eating only every other day, something which Plotinus called a model of the philosophical life and which is similar to the renunciation of the desert monks.[99] Finally, Porphyry states that Plotinus had the ability to go to the heart of matters very quickly[100] and was guided by the gods,[101] which might be said to be similar to the discernment and Divine guidance valued in the more advanced Desert Fathers. Pagan philosophers and monks alike used asceticism to aid the search for self-knowledge through interior exploration, but such similarities reflect the contemporary understanding of how an individual attempted to understand himself and seek out a higher order of truth, rather than a straightforward adoption of Plotinus' own method.[102]

During Late Antiquity, Greek philosophy increasingly moved away from pure intellectual pursuit to a religious approach to philosophical questions. Plotinus' late coming to philosophy (at 27) is described by Porphyry almost as a religious conversion and the next eleven years were spent training under Ammonius Saccas in Alexandria.[103] Wishing then to understand more of Persian and Indian philosophy he joined the army of Emperor Gordian III and went on the campaign to Persia, but when the Emperor was murdered by his troops in Mesopotamia he returned with some difficulty to Antioch and then removed to Rome (c.244).[104] Porphyry gives Plotinus' age as 38, i.e. c.242 or 243AD, and since Gordian was killed in 243 it is unlikely that Plotinus ever made direct contact with these systems, despite the similarity of ideas. For many years Plotinus showed a marked reluctance to record his philosophical system in writing, following the example of his teacher Ammonius.[105] When Plotinus finally broke his

---

[98]   *Vit. Plot.* 12; Gallienus (c.218-268) was the impetus behind an intellectual renaissance in Rome between 262-267AD. This also indicates, along with his work as an arbiter (*vit. Plot.* 9), the position of influence Plotinus held. It should be noted that the Neo-Platonic quest was generally restricted (in contrast to monasticism) to a cultural, economic and intellectual urban *élite* capable of understanding the philosophical issues involved (see e.g. *vit. Plot.* 7, 9, 12).

[99]   *Vit. Plot.* 7.

[100]   *Ibid.* 13. Porphyry says Plotinus was capable of remarkable penetration into character, e.g. discerning Porphyry's suicidal depression (*ibid.* 11).

[101]   *Ibid.* 23.

[102]   The extent of Plotinus' knowledge of Christianity cannot be fully known; however, he wrote against Gnosticism (*Enneads* 2.9), frequently attacked Christian thinking and encouraged his followers to do the same (*vit. Plot.* 16). Sections of Porphyry's *contra christianos* are preserved in Eusebius, *HE* 6.19.

[103]   *Vit. Plot.* 3.

[104]   *Ibid.*

[105]   *Ibid.*

literary silence, he entrusted the revision and collation of his work to Porphyry, who describes himself as his 'greatest friend,'[106] having spent six years with him.[107] Plotinus' aim (and that of the Neo-Platonic system) was to be united with the One, the Ultimate Being, yet although he longed for this, he only achieved it briefly four times during his acquaintance with Porphyry.[108]

The *Enneads*, Porphyry's revision of Plotinus' writings, present the standard Platonic themes. Plotinus believed that there is an ultimate and immaterial form of reality beyond what can be known through the senses, that intellectual intuition is of greater value than empirical forms of knowing, that there is a sense in which immortality exists and that the universe is essentially good.[109] But his metaphysics go further, asserting that there is one ultimate good, which unites both the natural and the spiritual. He proposes three hypostases: the One or the Good; Νοῦς; and Ψυχή, the realm of sense-perception.[110] The One is the absolute good, containing nothing and void of all but itself,[111] it is in no sense a thing,[112] rather it is the ultimate reality, complete in itself,[113] outside of time and place[114] and 'beyond being'.[115] The One emanates its goodness into all lower beings without any loss from itself and the first result of this emanation is Νοῦς. For Plato, Νοῦς was the realm of Forms and ultimate reality,[116] but for Plotinus there is still here the duality of observer and observed, whereas in the One there is no multiplicity. From Νοῦς, and ultimately therefore from the One, emanates the third and lowest hypostasis, Ψυχή.[117] All living creatures possess Ψυχή, however Ψυχή is

---

[106] *Vit. Plot.* 7. Porphyry notes the appalling state of these works before revision (*ibid.* 8) and describes his redactional work at length (*ibid.* 4-6, 18 and 24-26).

[107] *Ibid.* 4-5.

[108] *Ibid.* 23. Porphyry himself only achieved this once, near the end of his life. See also *Enneads* 4.8.1.

[109] There is also a positive appraisal of traditional culture, classical literature and philosophy.

[110] The three hypostases are discussed in *Enneads* 5.1.

[111] *Enneads* 5.5.13.

[112] *Ibid.* 6.7.38 (nothing can be predicated of the One).

[113] *Ibid* .5.8.7.

[114] *Ibid.* 6.5.11; 6.9.3.

[115] *Ibid.* 4.4.16.

[116] Plato, *rep.* 7.6-7.7, 509d-521b. Plato postulates an hierarchy of mental operation from εἰκασία (conjecture; the realm of impressions), rising to πίστις (belief; the realm of the senses), then διάνοια (deductive reason) and ultimately νόησις (intellection; the realm of vision and ultimate truth); this last is the function of the νοῦς which knows rather than knows about truth.

[117] *Enneads* 5.1.3.

not located in body but body in Ψυχή.[118] The forms of embodied life that emanate from Ψυχή are too weak to emanate.[119] Thus the One becomes many, from the simple comes multiplicity. However, One, Νοῦς and Ψυχή have a common centre,[120] so that Plotinus' system may be represented as both an hierarchical ladder (figure 1 below) and as a series of concentric circles (figure 2 below), the latter being the more representative of his thought. The many (all things, not just human beings) seek to return to the One because their kinship with the One drives them to seek out their true home or Fatherland.[121] They strive towards contemplation, which enables return to the One,[122] longing for the Good and to be united with 'beauty above beauty.'[123] While Plotinus is not concerned with describing how the universe came into existence but with its nature and describing how it is, this emanation from the One and kinship with it could be described as similar to the Christian view of creation in the image of God. Thus there is a process of Emanation (πρόοδος) and Return (ἐπιστροφή),[124] the aim of Neo-Platonism being return to and union with the One, φυγὴ μόνου πρὸς μόνον ('the flight of the alone to the alone'),[125] passing back through the hypostases: embodied life to Ψυχή to Νοῦς to the One.

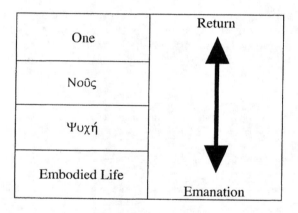

Figure 1

---

[118]   *Ibid.* 3.9.3.
[119]   For this process of 'downward' emanation see *ibid.*4.3.15-17.
[120]   *Ibid.* 4.4.16.
[121]   *Ibid.* 1.6.8.
[122]   *Ibid.* 3.8.1.
[123]   *Ibid.* 6.7.32.
[124]   E.g. *ibid.* 4.8.4-7.
[125]   *Ibid.* 6.9.11.

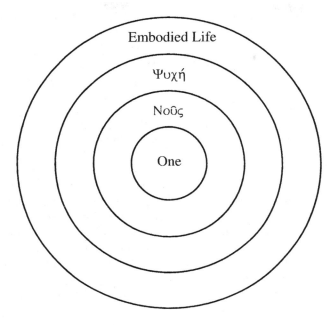

Figure 2

The ascent and return to the One is seen by Plotinus not so much as an upward journey as a personal[126] inward journey:[127]

> ... lifted out of the body into myself; becoming external to all other things and self-encentred; beholding a marvellous beauty; then, more than ever, assured of community with the loftiest order; enacting the noblest life, acquiring identity with the divine...[128]

Union with the One is a withdrawal inwards,[129] looking inwards beyond Noῦς[130] to the point where Noῦς and One become as one, a return to the

---

[126] The personal nature of the ascent to the One is emphasised by Plotinus' view that religious rites are useless for seeking union with the One (*Enneads* 6.6.12; *vit. Plot.* 10).

[127] A. Louth, *The Origins of the Christian Mystical Tradition from Plato to Denys* (Oxford: Clarendon Press, 1981), pp. 36-51 has a helpful summary of this view of Plotinus' system. See also D. Burton-Christie, *The Word in the Desert: Scripture and the Quest for Holiness in Early Christian Monasticism* (New York: Oxford University Press, 1993), pp. 48-54.

[128] *Enneads* 4.8.1 (MacKenna).

[129] 'The Soul withdraws into its own place' (*ibid.* 1.2.5; MacKenna).

[130] *Ibid.* 5.9.2.

centre where there is no longer observer and observed, knower and known,
but rather a state in which there is no longer any differentiation between the
One and individual nature;[131] Νοῦς passes out of itself into the One to
'become the Unity'[132] as their centres coincide.[133] Plotinus describes this
state of union thus:

> There, indeed, it was scarcely vision, unless of a mode unknown; it was a
> going forth from the self, a simplifying, a renunciation, a reach towards
> contact and at the same time a repose, a meditation towards adjustment.
> This is the only seeing of what lies within the holies: to look otherwise is
> to fail.[134]

Plotinus explains that people have forgotten their kinship with the One
through becoming preoccupied with the world around them and so a two
stage process of purification (κάθαρσις) is required to return to the One:
detachment from all that sullies the ψυχή and education (παιδεία) of the
ψυχή so that it becomes reoriented to its true life and can be restored to the
beauty derived from the One.[135] Ascetic practices purify and free the
individual from preoccupation with the world of sense-perception and the
body[136] enabling him to develop personal and civic ἀρετή which, with a
good conduct of life[137] and personal goodness,[138] prepare him for
contemplation.[139] Wisdom and understanding are said to be the
contemplation of all that exists in Νοῦς[140] and it is contemplation of the
Good and aiming for unity of purpose[141] that takes an individual into the
higher realm;[142] thus the individual's inner focus should remain entirely on
the One through contemplation.[143] Asceticism and contemplation are said to

---

[131] *Ibid.* 5.1.1; 6.9.10.
[132] *Ibid.* 6.9.11 (MacKenna).
[133] *Ibid.* 6.9.8.
[134] *Ibid.* 6.9.11 (MacKenna).
[135] *Ibid.* 1.2.4; 5.1.1; cf. Plato, *Phaedo* 10-12, 65a-68b and *rep.* 7.7, 518 respectively.
[136] The body weighs a person down (*Enneads* 6.9.8).
[137] *Enneads* 2.9.15.
   Virtus (plural: *virtutes*) and ἀρετή (plural: ἀρεταί) are used throughout this book as
   they carry not only the sense of moral perfection implied by 'virtue' in English, but
   also strength, power, courage and worth. Thus when the monastic literature is
   considered below, the Latin and Greek terms better convey the disciplines and
   abilities used consciously and tactically to achieve purity.
[138] *Ibid.* 3.1.8-10.
[139] *Ibid.* 1.2.1-3, 7; 4.8.4.
[140] *Ibid.* 1.2.6.
[141] *Ibid.* 4.4.35.
[142] *Ibid.* 1.1.12.
[143] *Ibid.* 6.9.7.

produce an inward simplicity that enables the individual to ascend to the One. Plotinus claims that it is for people to reach out for the ever-present One, which does not itself reach out to people seeking communion with them;[144] a person is to 'call on God ... and pray Him to enter.'[145] However, a person cannot make union with the One happen, he can only prepare himself by concentrating on the One and waiting. When union comes it is sudden and unexpected;[146] he is swept away suddenly on a vision of light;[147] it is probably this concept that lies behind the remark Porphyry found so enigmatic: 'It is for those Beings to come to me, not for me to go to them.'[148]

While this personal quest for union with the highest reality, described in the closing words of the *Enneads* as φυγὴ μόνου πρὸς μόνον, bears no little similarity to mystical theology and the monastic search for God, the aloof, impersonal and indifferent nature of the One is in clear contrast with the nature of the Christian God. This assessment of the One and the solipsistic isolationism of the individual's search for union are challenged by Corrigan.[149] He claims that the phrase φυγὴ μόνου πρὸς μόνον[150] signifies a meeting with another for greater intimacy[151] and a search for identity and self-discovery.[152] For Corrigan, Plotinus' separation and isolation is a stripping away of all that keeps the individual from the One, the final union is a separation from all that is unworthy and the ascent of the soul in Platonism is ultimately a divine gift; this relates closely to monastic mystical theology. While Corrigan's view finds extensive support in the *Enneads*, Louth's opinion that the One is relatively distant and unconcerned with the individual seeking union also carries considerable weight.[153] Plotinus' understanding of the One as the ultimate Good, the Absolute, could be equated with the Christian God, but, notwithstanding its description as 'kind and gentle and more graceful',[154] it is generally presented as far less personal and relatively uninterested.[155] The One has little or no similarity with the Christian God, the process of union stands

---

[144] *Ibid.* 6.9.8.

[145] *Ibid.* 5.8.9 (MacKenna).

[146] *Ibid.* 5.5.8; cf. Plato, *ep.* 7.341.

[147] *Enneads* 6.7.36.

[148] *Vit. Plot.* 10 (MacKenna).

[149] K. Corrigan, '"Solitary" Mysticism in Plotinus, Proclus, Gregory of Nyssa, and Pseudo-Dionysius', *Journal of Religion* 76.1 (January, 1996), pp28-42.

[150] *Enneads* 6.9.11.

[151] E.g. as human sexual union (*ibid.* 3.5.1).

[152] E.g. the fullness and completeness of union described in *ibid.* 6.9.9.

[153] Louth, *The Origins of the Christian Mystical Tradition*, p. 51.

[154] *Enneads* 5.5.12.

[155] E.g. the One 'need seek nothing beyond himself' (*ibid.* 6.7.37; MacKenna) and does not '(reach) out to us or (seek) our communion' (*ibid.* 6.9.8; MacKenna).

opposed to the doctrine of grace since union with the One is portrayed as a chance occurrence and not the result of promise as is found in New Testament and Christian theology.

Plotinus' use of διάκρισις and its cognates is wholly in keeping with that found in Scripture, but particularly focussed on distinguishing between unity (especially in the One) and multiplicity. His most concentrated use of the terms, however, occurs in a discussion of the difference between σύγκρισις (combination) and διάκρισις (separation). He begins by considering the way in which sense-perception (e.g. of colour or taste) may experience either combination or separation in what it experiences[156] and later develops his understanding of their contrasting natures in relation to motion.[157] All motion, he argues,[158] is of one single nature, but any difference perceived in that motion (e.g. up, down or in circles) results from external influences. Σύγκρισις is a motion towards unity, διάκρισις a motion away from it, but the point at which an external force causes either to take place can vary; it can be before, during or after the fact. While this section represents the highest concentration of διάκρισις / διακρίνω in the *Enneads*,[159] it is a philosophical discussion of physical phenomena that illustrates the use of διάκρισις to mean a separation and division, but it is of limited help in clarifying how the term might be understood by early Christian theologians such as Origen in relation to faith and spirituality. Elsewhere διάκρισις / διακρίνω is used of the discernment of Platonic Forms (εἰδοί),[160] of distinguishing phenomena in the natural world,[161] of the νοῦς distinguishing Forms,[162] discerning evil,[163] the ability of the ψυχή to discern what it sees and hears,[164] and self-discernment.[165] Διάκρισις / διακρίνω is used most extensively in relation to the One. It describes the multiplicity of creation that emanates from the One,[166] distinguishing aspects of that created order,[167] distinguishing aspects of being[168] and the human inability to distinguish between the outworking of the Divine Mind (Providence) and what it does.[169] Plotinus describes a second principle next

---

156 *Ibid.* 6.3.17. Cf. Plato, *Sophista* 243b.
157 *Enneads*, 6.3.25.
158 *Ibid.*6.3.24.
159 11 times in *ibid.* 6.3.25.
160 *Ibid.* 1.3.4.
161 *Ibid.* 2.3.13.
162 *Ibid.* 2.4.7.
163 *Ibid.* 2.9.16.
164 *Ibid.* 4.6.2.
165 *Ibid.* 5.4.2; 6.7.39.
166 *Ibid.* 3.3.1.
167 *Ibid.* 3.8.9.
168 *Ibid.* 6.2.8.
169 *Ibid.* 3.4.6.

after the One, which contains both unity and multiplicity, the latter indistinct in the One but becoming distinct in this second principle.[170] Similarly, he speaks of diverse elements within the oneness of the νοῦς as potential diversity.[171] The One is said to contain every ψυχή and νοῦς as distinctly individual but not at the point of separation[172] and διάκρισις / διακρίνω are used to describe the separation of the ψυχή from the One[173] and the discrete individuality of Forms separated from the One.[174] The One is said to be without distinction or division,[175] which quality belongs to the physical world.[176] Finally, when the νοῦς and ψυχή are in the One, they lack division[177] and all distinction disappears when union with the One takes place.[178] Thus, Plotinus uses διάκρισις and its cognates to speak of division, distinction, discernment and separation, but (as is to be expected given the nature of the work) his use of the term is generally to describe the nature of existence rather than in any 'religious' sense. While he does use διάκρισις for the discernment of good and evil, of what is seen and heard and the nature of things in the created order, even in speaking of the One his usage is descriptive of the One rather than of any means of approach or ascent. It will be seen, therefore, that while the use of the word διάκρισις and the practice of it in the religious life described in Late Antique theological and monastic works has similarities with Plotinus, that word-group and what it describes becomes more a technical term in Christian mystical, theological and monastic thought.

Origen

Eusebius of Caesarea (c.260-c.340) claims that Origen was well versed in Scripture from early childhood and trained in the liberal sciences and Greek literature by his father, continuing the latter studies after his father's martyrdom in the Severan persecution.[179] His subsequent assiduous study of Scripture led him to learn Hebrew[180] and gather avidly an extensive

---

[170]   *Ibid.* 5.3.15.
[171]   *Ibid.* 5.9.6, 8.
[172]   *Ibid.* 6.4.14.
[173]   *Ibid.* 4.8.4; 6.4.16.
[174]   *Ibid.* 6.6.17.
[175]   *Ibid.* 6.7.41; 6.9.5.
[176]   *Ibid.* 6.7.14.
[177]   *Ibid.* 4.1.1.
[178]   *Ibid.* 6.7.34; 6.9.10.
[179]   Eusebius, *HE* 6.1-2; since Eusebius was an Origenist (Jerome, *de vir inl.* 81) his opinion of Origen needs to be read with some caution. See also Jerome, *de vir. inl.* 54; Sulpicius Severus, *HS* 2.32. Origen was surnamed Adamantius (man of steel) for his zeal in studying Scripture (Jerome, *ep.* 33.3).
[180]   Contrary to contemporary practice (Jerome, *de vir. inl.* 54).

collection of Jewish works and Scripture translations.[181] His proficiency in
Greek philosophy, particularly Plato, is widely attested in his works and
reported by the early church historians,[182] who say he taught Greek
philosophers and heretics as well as Christians.[183] His pupil Gregory
Thaumaturgus (c.213-c.270)[184] speaks of how Origen taught his pupils to
use philosophy as an essential tool in their theological studies[185] and
alongside this he taught a foundation course in the Liberal Arts.[186] For
Origen, philosophy was essential for piety and the means of gaining
self-knowledge and of discerning good and evil, much as διάκρισις is
understood elsewhere:

> He applauded philosophy and lovers of philosophy ... saying that only
> those live a life truly befitting rational beings, taking care to live rightly
> and seeking to know themselves first ... and then the truly good things,
> which man must pursue, and the really evil things, which he must flee. ...
> Moreover he used to assert that it is not possible for someone to live
> completely piously ... who did not practise philosophy.[187]

However, Origen also urged his students not to assume one philosophy
alone as true:

---

[181]   Eusebius, *HE* 6.16. Origen's Hexapla (fragments extant) was a monumental work
with parallel columns of Old Testament Hebrew, Greek transliteration and the
Greek translations by Aquila, Symmachus, LXX (with supplements where the text
was defective and obeli against words not found in the Hebrew) and Theodotian.
Jerome clearly made extensive use of the work (*ep.* 106).

[182]   E.g. Eusebius, *HE* 6.19 which lists some of the Greek philosophers Origen studied
and reports that Porphyry admired his proficiency. Jerome comments that Origen
sought to harmonise Christian doctrine and Platonism (*ep.* 84.3; *apol. cont.
Ruf.* 1.18).

[183]   E.g. Eusebius, *HE* 6.18.

[184]   Socrates Scholasticus, *HE* 4.27.

[185]   Gregory Thaumaturgus, *Orig. orat. pan.* 9, 11, 13. Gregory also stresses that
Origen taught the practice of ἀρετή by personal example, indicating a perceived
integrity of life and doctrine. Cf. Eusebius (*HE* 6.3.7) who reports that Origen's
doctrine and life were as one and so it is not surprising that when his teaching was
condemned, so was the man (see e.g. Gennadius, *de vir. inl.* 31, 34).

[186]   Gregory Thaumaturgus, *Orig. orat. pan.* 8. He taught the Liberal Arts learnt from
his father (Eusebius, *HE* 6.2.7) as did other teachers of the time. These were first
classified in the fifth century, but the grouping was not fully accepted until the
Middle Ages at which time they were regarded (as by Origen) as essential for
competent study of theology. They consisted: elementary Trivium (grammar,
rhetoric and dialectic) and more advanced Quadrivium (music, arithmetic,
geometry and astronomy).

[187]   Gregory Thaumaturgus, *Orig. orat. pan.* 6.

He neither taught any one of the philosophical theories, nor did he think it fit for us to go with them, but he taught them all, not wishing us to be untested by any Greek doctrine.[188]

Rather, as 'a marvellous and most intelligent hearer of God,'[189] he helped them to discern and select what was useful and true in the various philosophers and encouraged them to devote themselves to God alone;[190] this is an example of διάκρισις being used in study. Thus, Origen was not regarded by his pupil as committed to any one philosophical system, but aimed to seek out truth wherever he could find it and use whatever tools he could find in the philosophical systems of his day to help uncover the deeper meaning of Scripture. Thus in, say, his Commentary on the Song of Songs, it follows that his theology of the ascent to God would be informed by knowledge of Neo-Platonism rather than an adoption of it. Writing of his genius and extensive learning, Jerome describes how Origen taught philosophy widely in the hope of introducing his pupils to faith in Christ.[191] Even in later years when Jerome sought to dissociate himself from Origen, he still praised Origen's commentary work and ability[192] but denied ever

---

[188] *Ibid.* 14.

[189] *Ibid.* 15.

[190] *Ibid.* 15. Origen's teaching style, according to Gregory, was very open and his students had great freedom to explore ideas. (Cf. Plotinus, who would discuss students' questions thoroughly and freely until a solution presented itself; Porphyry, *vit. Plot.* 13). For διάκρισις used to cut through deceitful speech see Gregory Thaumaturgus, *Orig. orat. pan.* 13.

[191] Jerome, *de vir inl.* 54, 65; see also Eusebius, *HE* 6.30. Eusebius (*HE* 6.19.12-14) records that Origen defended his study of Greek philosophy and heresies (as others in the Catechetical School had done) in order to debate effectively with those who held such views. In the latter (also in Jerome, *de vir. inl.* 54), Origen is also reported as saying that Heraclas adopted the Greek philosopher's distinctive *pallium* (probably equivalent to the φαινόλη / φελόνιον, or the φαιλόνης that Paul left at Troas; 2 Tim 4:13) which many Christians who had been professed philosophers retained after conversion; e.g. Justin Martyr (Eusebius, *HE* 4.11.8). Tertullian also praises the quadrangular *pallium* as a silent witness to learning befitting Christians and preferable to the Roman *toga* for its simplicity (*de pall.* 5-6). It became the distinctive dress (ἀνάλαβος) for monks and being cruciform reminded them of faith in Christ (Evagrius, *prak.* prol. 4; Cassian, *inst.* 1.5), but its misuse by those pretending asceticism and piety was anathematised (c.345AD) at the Council of Gangra (Canon 12; cf. Socrates Scholasticus, *HE* 4.23). Further on monastic dress, see below, p. 171.

[192] Jerome, *ep.* 84.2 (c.400AD); yet in *ep.* 84.3 he calls Origen's doctrines poisonous. In his prologue to Origen's homilies on the Song of Songs, Jerome says that he had surpassed himself (*hom. in Cant*, prol.; cf. Rufinus, *de prin. praef. Ruf.*). Cf. Jerome, *ep.* 33.3-4 where there is mixed admiration and concern regarding Origen's orthodoxy.

being an Origenist.[193] Jerome thus had a mixed admiration for Origen, defending his work while refusing to condone his theology, and in doing so he was attempting to exercise διάκρισις. This same need of διάκρισις when considering Origen's work is seen in the advice of the Bishops at the Synod of Alexandria (400AD). They state that Origen should be read cautiously by the wise, acknowledging there to be some good in his work, but rejected by the less able because of the evil in it.[194] The influence of Greek philosophy, particularly Neo-Platonism, evident throughout Origen's works, did not distract his opponents from valuing his work as a commentator, if not as a theologian.

Origen's use of Platonism can be seen in his early (c.230AD) Alexandrian work, *de principiis*.[195] In it he seeks to unite the Greek philosophical world view with Christian doctrine, but in his later (c.249AD) work, *contra Celsum* he is more keenly aware of the distinctions. His grasp of these philosophical issues is evident in his discussion of incorporeality and matter.[196] The Trinity, he claims, is the first principle and cause of everything,[197] being both one and incorporeal,[198] whereas matter is the substance underlying bodies, being created and mutable.[199] Matter, he says, receives qualities[200] and 'is discerned (*discerno*) by the mind alone'[201] and this statement is followed by a discussion of the examination of unfinished matter (i.e. without qualities added) in Psalm 138.16 (LXX) and Enoch 21.1. The mind of the Psalmist is said to examine and separate out its nature using only reason and understanding, and the mind of Enoch to examine and discuss it to discern the same.[202] Διάκρισις is thus being used to understand the nature of existence, but created beings cannot comprehend the uncreated Trinity.[203] Such beings are immortal[204] and have

---

[193]   Jerome, *ep.* 84.3. Jerome was, however, a translator of Origen (see e.g. *de vir. inl.* 135).

[194]   Gennadius, *de vir. inl.* 19.

[195]   *De principiis* was regarded as particularly controversial. Since most of Origen's Greek original is lost and Rufinus states that he corrected the heretical passages while remaining faithful to Origen's thought when he translated it into Latin (*de prin. praef. Ruf.*) the extent to which the original expressed Platonism is a matter of conjecture. Furthermore, Rufinus claims he was not a defender or champion of Origen (*apol. Anas.* 7).

[196]   *De prin.* 4.3.15; 4.4.5-7.

[197]   *Ibid.* 4.3.15.

[198]   *Ibid.* 4.4.5.

[199]   *Ibid.* 4.4.6.

[200]   Cf. *Enneads* 6.1.10.

[201]   *De prin.* 4.4.7; cf. *Enneads* 3.6.15.

[202]   *De prin.* 4.4.8.

[203]   *Ibid.* 4.4.8. Cf. Gregory Thaumaturgus, *Orig. orat. pan.* 8.

[204]   *De prin.* 4.4.9.

an intellectual and rational nature, which requires a corporeal garment.[205]
Even in his practical work, *de oratione*, the 'daily Bread' (ἄρτος
ἐπιούσιος) in the Our Father leads into a discussion of the Platonic and
Stoic views of substance (ὑπόστασις) and being (οὐσία),[206] an argument he
bases on the derivation of ἐπιούσιος from οὐσία.[207] He concludes that
οὐσία can be distinguished (διακρίνω) in different ways, that the bread is
spiritual (νοητός) and therefore 'imparted to the νοῦς and the ψυχή gives a
part of its own strength to the one who provides himself with food from
it.'[208] Origen is thus applying Platonic philosophy to the practical exercise
of prayer and using διάκρισις to determine the nature of what is happening
within it as well as the nature of οὐσία itself.

While Origen develops his theology by using Platonic philosophy with
διάκρισις he adamantly remains a Christian philosopher. He begins *de
principiis* with a standard *regula fidei*, affirming his belief that God had
spoken in Scripture and summarising the doctrine of the Trinity as it was
understood at the time.[209] Elsewhere he asserts his desire for orthodoxy
over heresy[210] and against offending the canon and *regula fidei*.[211]
Furthermore, in his *exhortatio ad martyrium* he advises calm before a
tribunal in order to present Christianity in the most favourable and
persuasive light.[212] Finally, he contrasts the wholehearted commitment and
loyalty engendered by Christ and the rapid rise of Christianity with the
failure of philosophers and philosophy to achieve the same.[213] However,
since Origen also held the widely accepted view that Scriptural wisdom
antedated and informed Greek philosophy[214] (a position Plotinus
challenged[215]), it would be logical to use it discerningly to help interpret
Scripture and gain greater understanding of Christian truth. Greer argues,
rightly, that Origen's condemnation by the Fifth Ecumenical Council
(553AD) arose from seeing his Platonism at the expense of his Christianity,

---

[205] *Ibid.* 4.4.8.
[206] *De orat.* 27.8.
[207] *Ibid.* 27.7.
[208] *Ibid.* 27.9.
[209] *De prin.* pref. 4.
[210] *Hom in Luc.* 16.5.
[211] *Hom in Jos.* 7.6.
[212] *Exhort. ad mart.* 4, 35. This is no theoretical work since Origen had seen persecution at first hand, beginning with his father.
[213] *De prin.* 4.1.1-2.
[214] E.g. *cont. Cels.* 4.21; *comm. in Cant.* 2.5. The claim that Old Testament Law and wisdom antedated the Greek and that Plato was acquainted with Scripture was generally accepted among Jewish and Christian apologists and later writers (See e.g. Josephus, *cont. Ap.* 2.281; Justin Martyr, *apol.* 44.8; 60.1; Eusebius, *praep. Ev.* 11.9.4; Augustine, *de civ. Dei* 8.11).
[215] *Enneads* 2.9.6.

whereas he should be seen as a Christian Platonist who saw himself using the truth he discerned in Plato and the philosophers to understand the truth revealed in Scripture;[216] the maxim 'the truth is true wherever you find it' might well be used to summarise Origen's position.

In Origen's time the doctrines of the Trinity and nature of Christ were being debated and formulated, and his understanding of these shows evidence of the influence of Neo-Platonism. Like the One of Neo-Platonism, God the Father is incorporeal,[217] alone unbegotten[218] and transcendent; truly one (*ex omni parte* μονάς, *et ut ita dicam* ἑνάς; 'in every way unity and, so to speak, oneness'), he is 'the mind and source, from whom is the origin of all intellectual nature or mind.'[219] He alone is ingenerate,[220] truly God (αὐτόθεος[221]) and the 'primal goodness.'[222] Since the Father is omnipotent, Origen advances that he must therefore always have had something over which to exercise his power and so Christ (through whom he exercises that power) and souls were brought into being.[223] Christ is the perfect image of the Father[224] and Origen discerns (διακρίνω) different aspects (ἐπίνοιαι) of his redemptive activity[225] in both his eternal and incarnate natures[226] as he mediates between the Father and the world.[227] The Father begets the Son as a continual and eternal act.[228] He too is God,[229] incorporeal and eternal like the Father,[230] but his deity is

---

[216] R.A. Greer, *Origen: An Exhortation to Martyrdom, Prayer, First Principles, Book IV, Prologue to the Commentary on The Song of Songs, Homily XXVII on Numbers* (The Classics of Western Spirituality; London: SPCK, 1979), p. 6.

[217] *De prin.* 1.1.5; as is the Trinity (*ibid.* 4.3.15).

[218] *Ibid.* 1.2.6

[219] *Ibid.* 1.1.6; cf. *cont. Cels.* 7.38.

[220] *De prin.* 4.2.1; τοῦ δημιουργοῦ, ὅς ἐστιν ἀγέννητος μόνος θεός ('the creator, who is the only uncreated God'). Cf. *Enneads* 6.5.11 where the One is said also to stand outside time.

[221] *Comm. in Joh.* 2.2-3.

[222] *De prin.* 1.2.13.

[223] *Ibid.* 1.2.10; 2.9.1-3. Cf. *Enneads* 6.5.11 where the same is said of the One.

[224] *De prin.* 1.2.6, 13; *comm. in Joh.* 13.25.151.

[225] E.g. *comm. in Joh.* 1.28.200, 1.31.223; Origen also discerns (διακρίνω) the ἐπίνοιαι of νοητός and πνευματικός in Scripture (*ibid.* 1.8.44).

[226] *De prin.* 1.2.1.

[227] *Ibid.* 2.6.1.

[228] *Ibid.* 1.2.4; *hom. in Jer.* 9.4. Cf. *de prin.* 1.2.6: *filii ab eo subsistentia generatur* ('the substance of the Son is generated by him [i.e. the Father]'); but (unlike Neo-Platonism) the Son should not be seen as an emanation as this would divide God.

[229] *Comm. in Joh.* 2.1.10.

[230] *De prin.* 4.4.1. Socrates Scholasticus quotes Athanasius as saying that for Origen 'the Son is co-eternal (συναίδιος) with the Father' (*HE* 6.13). When Beryllus, Bishop of Bostra, claimed that Christ had no personal existence before the

secondary, a δεύτερος θεός ('a second god') united to the Father to a degree beyond every other ψυχή, the pinnacle of all ἀρετή and reason (λόγος),[231] of which he is the fountain.[232] The Son is both fully God and fully Man,[233] but he is θεός, not ὁ θεός, exalted above the other gods[234] and the servant of the Father.[235] The Holy Spirit was, according to Origen, made by the Father through Christ and is 'more honoured than all things and first in order of all that was made by (him).'[236] However, while he is associated in honour and dignity with the Father[237] and is the inspirer of Scripture,[238] Origen says that his origin (created or uncreated) is not clearly discerned (*discerno*).[239] For Origen the Father, Son and Holy Spirit are three Persons or ὑποστάσεις[240] (a term denoting their essential reality) but the Father and Son are numerically distinguishable:[241]

> they are two entities in hypostasis, but one in mind [ὁμόνοια], harmony and identity of will; so he who has seen the Son, 'who is the radiance of glory and the exact representation of the hypostasis' [Hebrews 1:3] of God has seen God himself in him who is the image of God.[242]

Thus they are both distinct and one: 'we are not hesitant at one time to declare two Gods and at another time to declare one God.'[243] Origen variously describes the unity of the Father and Son as a unity of will,[244] the marital unity of one flesh[245] and the unity of spirit between Christ and a

---

incarnation, Origen is said to have convinced him otherwise (Eusebius, *HE* 6.33; Jerome, *de vir. inl.* 60), claiming also that the incarnate God took a human soul (ἔμψυχος) (Socrates Scholasticus, *HE* 3.7).

[231] *Cont. Cels.* 5.39; cf. *comm. in Joh.* 6.39.202 and *de prin.* 2.9; 4.3.7 (Christ is God after the Father). Cf. *Enneads* 5.3.15 (second principle after the One embraces multiplicity and unity).

[232] *Comm. in Joh.* 2.3.20.

[233] *De prin.* pref. 4.

[234] *Comm. in Joh.* 2.2.13-18.

[235] *De prin.* pref. 4; *cont. Cels.* 2.9; 6.60.

[236] *Comm. in Joh.* 2.10.75.

[237] *De prin.* pref. 4.

[238] *Ibid.* 1.3.1.

[239] *Ibid.* pref. 4. Rufinus translates Origen's comment as *natus an innatus* ('born or unborn'; reading γεννητὸς ἤ ἀγέννητος) whereas Jerome (*ep.* 124.2) renders the original Greek as *factus an infectus* ('created or uncreated'; reading γενητὸς ἤ ἀγένητος).

[240] *Comm. in Joh.* 2.10.75.

[241] *Ibid.* 10.37.246; *de orat.* 15.1.

[242] *Cont. Cels.* 8.12.

[243] *Dial. Herac.* 2; cf. *comm. in Joh.* 2.2.15.

[244] *Comm. in Joh.* 13.36.228.

[245] *De prin.* 2.6.3; cf. *dial. Herac.* 3.

righteous man.[246] While for Origen the Three are eternal and distinct, the unity of the Godhead is centred on the Father who is the 'source of divinity;'[247] thus while the Son and Holy Spirit are divine, their divinity derives from the Father, in whom resides the primal goodness which Son and Spirit retain within them from their source.[248] This subordinationism is central to Origen's understanding of the Trinity.[249] Thus, for example, prayer should be not offered to the Son (or anything begotten) but to the Father himself.[250] Origen's hierarchy within the Trinity has a marked similarity with the emanations from the One found in Neo-Platonism;[251] the Father is the source of all existence, the Son of rational nature and the Holy Spirit of holiness.[252] Origen says that through sanctification by the Holy Spirit, a person is capable of receiving Christ, of gaining wisdom, knowledge and purity, and gradually advancing towards the perfection God created the individual to have.[253] Ascent to the Father is by progressive stages[254] through successively higher (as Origen understands it) members of the Trinity; it is a moving deeper into the Godhead and a progressively closer communion or union with him, but with the possibility of lapsing and returning.[255] The believer thus moves from the purity granted by the Holy Spirit through reason in Christ to the Father who is the centre of existence.

Origen's concept of ascent to the Father through successive members of the Trinity is expressed in different ways elsewhere. The three books of Solomon are said to instruct the believer successively bringing him closer to God as each discipline is mastered. Firstly, Proverbs teaches Ethics enabling moral behaviour to be modified, Ecclesiastes teaches Physics and an understanding of the nature of things so that the transient may be cast off in favour of the spiritual, and finally the Song of Songs teaches Enoptics, enabling the seeker after God to see realities hidden behind the visible.[256] Origen sees a similar three-tier progression in the lives of Abraham, Isaac and Jacob, who represent practical obedience, natural philosophy and

---

[246] *Dial. Herac.* 3.
[247] *Comm. in Joh.* 2.3.20.
[248] *De prin.* 1.2.13.
[249] Subordinationism is particularly evident in Arianism and accounts for this heretical view being attributed to Origen (see e.g. Jerome, *ep.* 84.10; *apol. cont. Ruf.* 1.8). For a discussion of Arianism and how Origen relates to it, see R. Williams, *Arius: Heresy and Tradition* (London: SCM Press, 2nd edn, 2001).
[250] *De orat.* 15.1; 16.1; but cf. *cont. Cels.* 5.4-5; 8.13 where prayer is to be offered to the Father through the Son.
[251] Although Origen did not see Christ in this way (*de prin.* 1.2.6).
[252] *De prin.* 1.3.8.
[253] *Ibid.* 1.3.8.
[254] *Hom. in Num.* 27.2.
[255] *De prin.* 1.3.8; cf. 2.9.6.
[256] *Comm. in Cant.* prol. 3; cf. Clement of Alexandria, *strom.* 1.28.176.

inspective science or contemplation of spiritual things respectively.[257] Origen finds a more elaborate sevenfold process in the seven Old Testament songs, which he says reflect the spiritual journey.[258] This suggests that Origen is more concerned with the process of ascent than with any strict number of levels and that he has used the Neo-Platonic concept of ascent as a tool to understand what he found in Scripture. He thus uses διάκρισις to understand the process of ascent to God he sees described in Scripture.

For Origen, the 'inner man' or rational nature yearns to return from its fallen state to the image and likeness of God,[259] but union with God is brief if repeated;[260] this bears a marked similarity to Plotinus and Neo-Platonism.[261] Origen describes union with Christ as ascending above the clouds of the Law, Gospels, prophets and apostles, being lifted up by their doctrine to meet Christ in the spiritual understanding of Scripture.[262] Thus union with God necessarily involves a penetration into the deeper meaning of Scripture,[263] which is the vehicle of Divine inspiration.[264] Indeed, both Scripture and Christ are Λόγος and Christ is incarnate in Scripture.[265] To enter into the mysteries of Scripture, Origen says that complete commitment to studying them watchfully is necessary.[266] He teaches that the Word of God approaches the soul through the window of the senses calling it to forsake the corporeal and visible for the incorporeal and spiritual, since while the soul remains attached to the corporeal it cannot receive the wisdom of God, only observe it with sense-perception;[267] this has a distinctly Neo-Platonic tone. A person continually searches for

---

[257]   *Comm. in Cant.* prol. 3. Origen also finds significance in that they lived in tents and were thus mobile and detached from material possession in their pursuit of God.

[258]   *Ibid.* prol. 4; *hom. in Cant.* 1.1. Songs of Moses, Ex. 15:1-21; of the well, Nm. 21:17-18; of Moses, Dt. 32:1-43; of Deborah, Jdg. 5; of David, 2Kgs 22; the sixth song is taken from Pss 95, 104 in *comm. in Cant.* and Is. 5:1-7 in *hom. in Cant.*; the seventh and highest is the Song of Songs itself.

[259]   *De prin.* 4.4.9. Cf. Neo-Platonic yearning to return to the 'Fatherland' (*Enneads* 1.6.8; see above, p. 18).

[260]   *Hom. in Cant.* 1.7.

[261]   E.g. *vit. Plot.* 23; Enneads 4.8.1; 6.9.11.

[262]   *Frag. in I Thess.* (*PG* 14.1302B-D).

[263]   Macleod argues that 'Origen's mysticism is intimately connected with his central activity as an exegete' and that the knowledge and understanding he sought was the meaning of Scripture (C.W. Macleod, 'Allegory and Mysticism in Origen and Gregory of Nyssa', *JTS* 22.2 (October, 1971), p. 369).

[264]   *De prin.* 4.1.1-7.

[265]   *Philocalia* 15.19.

[266]   *De prin.* 4.2.7.

[267]   *Comm. in Cant.* 3.13. The ascent to God is of the νοῦς rather than the body (*de orat.* 23.2); cf. Evagrius, *de orat.* 35.

God through successive recognitions of truth.[268] Thus, διάκρισις is used both to discern the meaning of Scripture and through it approach union with God. All that stands spiritually opposed to this union is weakened by prayer, which is made by the νοῦς and proceeds from the ψυχή with γνῶσις, reason (λόγος) and faith.[269] For Origen, constant prayer includes acts of ἀρετή and is expressed in an entire life of obedience to God that is 'one great integrated prayer.'[270] It may be said then, that there is a need for διάκρισις in every aspect of daily life to achieve an integrated and wholehearted approach to God as the individual chooses a manner of life that will achieve the goal of union.

Origen's work on the Song of Songs reveals his understanding of the mystical union between God and the soul; the deep personal relationship between Christ (Bridegroom; Word of God) and the individual soul (bride, but also the Church). The soul is said to yearn for union and the wisdom and knowledge it brings.[271] The need of διάκρισις for gaining self-knowledge of the soul and progressing towards God is apparent in his warning to avoid false doctrine and philosophical sects.[272] Furthermore, he equates the 'little foxes' (Song of Songs 2:15) with demonic opposing forces and thoughts that deceive the soul and therefore need to be caught while still small before they take hold of the believer's heart. These he equates with heretical teachers that destroy 'the vineyard of the Lord' and lead people away from 'orthodox belief' and so he warns Christian teachers to be on their guard against them.[273] Thus, in the ascent to God, Origen

---

[268] *Hom. in Num.* 17.4.

[269] *De orat.* 12.1. Since γνῶσις (knowledge) was used of the Christian search for God and of contemplative or mystical knowledge, the Greek word is used throughout this book in preference to the English.

[270] *Ibid.* 12.2. Origen's commitment to study and prayer are aspects of his ascetic discipline (Eusebius, *HE* 6.3.9).

[271] *Comm. in Cant.* 1.1.

[272] *Ibid.* 2.5. Lawson notes that *secta* in early Christian usage denoted Christian sects whereas the synonymous term αἱρήσεις / *haeresis* took the narrower sense of heresy; R.P. Lawson, *Origen: The Song of Songs – Commentary and Homilies* (Ancient Christian Writers 26; New York: Newman Press, 1957) p. 336.

[273] *Comm. in Cant.* 3.15. For fox associations see e.g.: Origen, *cont. Cels.* 4.93 (demons); Chrysostom, *hom.* 32 *in Rom* 16.23 (demons and philosophers); *constitutiones apostolorum* 6.13, 18 (heretics, false teachers and deceivers); Irenaeus, *adversus haereses* 1.31.4 (Gnostic heretic, Valentinus); Ignatius, *ep. to the Philadelphians* 3.4 (the ungodly); Ambrose, *de spiritu sancto* 2.10.109 (deceit of false teachers; removed by the Holy Spirit); Bernard, *serm. in Cant.* 63 (detractors and flatterers); *ibid.* 64 (vainglory and excessive asceticism in more advanced monks); *ibid.* 65 (heresies); Basil the Great, *hom. in hex.* 9.3 (deceit); Gregory of Nazianzus, *orat.* 28.2 (treacherous and faithless soul incapable of heights of contemplation); Ambrose, *de officiis ministrorum* 3.11.75 (deceitful

encourages the use of διάκρισις to decide which teachings to follow and to discern evil thoughts with a view to cutting them off before they become established.

Like Plotinus, Origen holds that the soul has the freewill to choose either to progress towards God by imitating him or fail through neglect,[274] that there are two parts to the soul, the higher in the image of God and the lower preoccupied with the material world,[275] and that human beings have a share in the Spirit of God and kinship with the Divine.[276] Origen understands that souls are immortal by virtue of their participation in the Godhead[277] and pre-exist the body, contracting guilt before God, which determines the physical form they will take;[278] that for him creation is cast down[279] implies their higher origin. Διάκρισις is thus needed to discern good and evil, choosing to move towards God in search of union.

The highly personal relationship and union with God, in which he is actively and willingly involved, is in sharp contrast with the union with the One in Neo-Platonism; for Origen although Man may seek out God, he too comes to Man. The seeker prays for enlightenment from the God and 'the Father knows each single soul's capacity and understands the right time for a soul to receive kisses of the Word in lights and insights of this sort.'[280] God is aware of the individual and concerned about his progress and so Origen explains that the Word of God is variously called Light, Word, Bread, spikenard and so on, adapting himself to address the different senses of the soul, which gains the sense of *discretio* of good and evil (Hebrews 5:14).[281] He says that God also provides angels as guardians,

---

heart); Chrysostom, *ad pop. Antioch.* 12.6 (vice; emulate instead the discernment of bees). Bernard (*serm. in Cant.* 49.4-5) stresses the need of διάκρισις within, as this regulates charity and puts each *virtus* in its place and moderates them, guiding the monk's way of life. Thus there is a continuity of understanding of both the 'little foxes' and more significantly of the central need of διάκρισις in mystical theology and practice.

[274] *Comm. in Cant.* 2.2; *de prin.* 2.9.6; 4.4.9. Cf. *Enneads* 5.1.1, 5.3.3.

[275] *De prin.* 2.10.7. Cf. *Enneads* 2.1.5; 4.4.20-21. Spiritual beings are divided into an immortal thinking part (νοερός) akin to God himself and a rational (λογική) ψυχή (*de prin.* 3.1.13; cf. *comm. in Joh.* 13.33.212: 'If someone is more rational (λογικώτερος) and therefore also a spiritual (νοητός) man, he eats the spiritual (νοητός) bread.').

[276] *De prin.* 1.3.6-7. Cf. *Enneads* 1.6.2, 8.

[277] *De prin.* 4.4.9.

[278] *Ibid.* 3.4.5; cf. 2.9.6 and *Enneads* 4.3.8, 15. See also Jerome, *Letter to Pammachius Against John of Jerusalem* 7.

[279] Καταβολή – *comm. in Joh.* 19.22.149; *de prin.* 3.5.4. Cf. *Enneads* 4.8.5.

[280] *Comm. in Cant.* 1.1 (Lawson, *Origen: The Song of Songs*, p. 62). Cf. the closeness of relationship described by Philo (*de congressu eruditionis gratia* 177).

[281] *Comm. in Cant.* 2.9; cf. 1.4 (see also pp. 7, 50 and n. 90, pp. 87-88 and n. 95).

tutors and governors to support believers in their struggle against demons[282] and so διάκρισις is needed to choose between their conflicting instructions.[283] For Origen the ability to seek union with God varies, but he is accessible through the incarnation and if a believer draws the Word of God to himself in faith, God comes to him readily,[284] turning away none who come in repentance.[285]

This variable ability of individuals to grasp the deeper meaning of Scripture generally and the Song of Songs in particular is demonstrated by Origen's contrasting emphasis on union with God; in his commentary on the Song of Songs it is personal, but in the homilies he concentrates on the Church and those he regards as less advanced in faith. However, he says that the Church and the individual soul are inseparable[286] and so, unlike Neo-Platonism, the search for union is not solitary[287] but made in the context of the Church community. Some, he says, are more perfect and capable of understanding the unseen and mystical, others less so[288] and therefore less able to discern the deeper meaning of Scripture.[289] In keeping with the prevailing Alexandrian approach,[290] Origen is more interested in the allegorical and mystical meaning of Scripture than in the literal. For Origen, the literal meaning of Scripture hides a deeper and unseen meaning[291] and Christ lifts the veil hiding it.[292] Thus, when he interprets allegorically the difference between the maidens and bride in the Song of Songs, he sees the former as yet to achieve the perfection of the bride, who has attained a higher degree of charity in conduct, works, blessedness, wisdom and knowledge.[293] This example brings together the elements of allegory, degrees of ability and the process of ascent. The ascent to God

---

[282]   *Ibid.* 2.3; *cont. Cels.* 8.27; *de orat.* 11.5. Origen says that angels are ministering spirits (*cont. Cels.* 5.4) close to the first principles and provided to help believers (*de prin.* 4.3.14; *cont. Cels.* 8.64).

[283]   Cf. Nau 169. See below, p. 94, n. 144 (for parallels) and p. 112 and n. 255.

[284]   *Comm. in Cant.* 1.4.

[285]   *Ibid.* 2.1.

[286]   *Hom. in Cant.* 2.3, 'which Church is we ourselves.'

[287]   Cf. Aristotle, *eth. Nic* 10.7, 1177a where contemplation is solitary.

[288]   *Comm. in Joh.* 1.30.

[289]   *Comm. in Cant.* prol. 2.

[290]   E.g. Philo Judaeus (c.20BC–c.50AD) describes an ascetic and contemplative community, the Therapeutae, which interpreted Scripture allegorically and sought to discern its hidden and mystical meaning (*de vita contemplativa* 78; Philo used the same method, e.g. in *de migratione Abrahami* 165). Their manner of life has great similarities with early Christian monasticism and Eusebius (*HE* 2.17), questionably, associates the two very closely.

[291]   E.g. *comm. in Cant.* 3.12.

[292]   *De prin.* 4.1.6.

[293]   *Comm. in Cant.* 1.5.

thus requires the development of διάκρισις in order to discern and understand the spiritual, deeper and unseen meaning and mysteries in Scripture.[294]

Origen's views were strongly held among many of the more academic monks. Though less educated, Antony the Great wrote letters of considerable theological depth referring to God as the one ultimate source from which all derive their spiritual essence and to diversity arising through flight from him,[295] which clearly demonstrates Origen's influence as well as being reminiscent of Neo-Platonism. Furthermore, desert theologians Evagrius Ponticus (c.345-399)[296] and John Cassian (c.360-435) emerge in the fourth century with strong Origenist opinions and Jerome claims that the monasteries of Nitria were rife with Origenism.[297] The division between the more and less learned monks in relation to Origenism is amply demonstrated by the late fourth century Anthropomorphite controversy, which centred on whether God is corporeal or incorporeal.

In a record of his visit to Alexandria, Postumianus noted the argument raging between the monks and bishops over Origen's books. The priests declared that the books should not be read or possessed and the bishops maintained that his books had unsound elements. While Origen's supporters claimed that they simply needed to be read with discernment, since heretics had clearly tampered with them, the bishops declared it better to condemn Origen and all his works. When Postumianus read Origen's works for himself, he decided that some elements were good and others blameworthy;[298] he thus uses διάκρισις as Origen's monastic supporters espoused. The civil authorities were next called upon to quell the dispute, but far from suppressing Origenism it was made more widespread as the monks fled.[299]

Origen strongly opposed Anthropomorphism[300] and asserted the incorporeal nature of God throughout his works.[301] However, it is evident that Anthropomorphism and a belief in God's corporeal nature was part of everyday life in the desert from the way Apollo[302] taught monks to prostrate

---

[294] Origen prefers the Christian spiritual understanding of Scripture to Jewish literal interpretations (*hom. in Gen.* 6.1).

[295] Antony, *ep.* 6.56.

[296] E.g. Jerome calls Evagrius an Origenist (*ep.* 133.3).

[297] Jerome, *ep.* 92.

[298] Sulpicius Severus, *dial.* 1.6. Rufinus (*apol. Jer.* 1.15) also claims that heretics had tampered with Origen's works.

[299] Sulpicius Severus, *dial.* 1.7. See below, p. 77.

[300] Rufinus, *apol. Jer.* 1.17.

[301] E.g. *cont. Cels.* 6.70; 7.35; *de orat.* 23.3.

[302] Abba and Amma (Father and Mother, respectively), titles of respect accorded to monks and nuns in the literature under consideration, have been omitted in this work except in quotations.

themselves before visitors as a means of venerating God: 'you have seen your brother, (Scripture) says, you have seen the Lord your God.'[303] Thus when Theophilus,[304] Bishop of Alexandria, circulated a Paschal Letter in 399AD strongly denouncing Anthropomorphism, it was variously received; the intellectuals embraced it, but in Scetis the elderly and advanced ascetic Sarapion cried that they had taken his God away.[305] Sarapion's failure to embrace the doctrine of the incorporeality of God is seen as both ignorance and succumbing to demonic deceit,[306] i.e. as a failure to exercise διάκρισις. There was, then, a division in the understanding of Scripture and doctrine between the intellectual and the less erudite monks. The latter took literally Scripture references to God having eyes, hands and so on, and concluded that God must have a corporeal nature, whereas the more intellectual element (such as Origen and Cassian[307]) understood this metaphorically and held to the incorporeal nature of God. So strong was the feeling of many monks that they entered Alexandria to challenge Theophilus, who calmed them diplomatically by saying: 'When I look upon you, it is as if I beheld the face of God,' which elicited demands to condemn Origen's books to which he acceded.[308] Theophilus thus polarised the situation, but worsened it by pursuing Dioscorus, Ammonius, Eusebius and Euthymius,[309] whom he had previously esteemed but now resented for their condemnation of his avaricious nature. Since they were respected among the monks, he sought to discredit them by exposing their belief in the incorporeality of God to the monks, saying that it was contrary to Scripture. Although he shared this view and the more academic monks were not deceived, the greater number of less erudite monks reacted against the Origenists.[310] This successful if divisive strategy illustrates the strength of feeling both for and against Origen in the desert, where it was the more intellectual element that averred Origenism. Thus in relation to Origen and to doctrine, it is necessary to exercise διάκρισις.

Origen uses the διάκρισις word-group extensively and in keeping with the senses found in Scripture. The discernment of good and evil is a recurrent theme, particularly in association with Hebrews 5:14. Διάκρισις is an organ of sense, which, with purity of heart, dedicated piety and *virtutes* enables the believer to approach God and know him with greater

---

[303] *HM* 8.55. Cf. *vit. Pach.* G¹ 48 re seeing the invisible God in visible man.
[304] Theophilus wrote against both Origen and the Anthropomorphites (Gennadius, *de vir. inl.* 34).
[305] Cassian, *conf.* 10.3.4-5.
[306] *Ibid.* 10.4.
[307] E.g. Cassian, *inst.* 8.3. Cf. Gregory of Nazianzus, *orat.* 42.16.
[308] Socrates Scholasticus, *HE* 6.7; Sozomen, *HE* 8.11.3.
[309] Known as the 'Tall Brothers'.
[310] Socrates Scholasticus, *HE* 6.7.

intimacy.[311] For Origen, there is no greater work than to train oneself in διάκρισις and use it[312] and this need of διάκρισις in order to live the Christian life is also found explicitly stated in the later Pseudo-Macarian homilies.[313] Διάκρισις brings the believer to perfection and maturity by providing him with the ability to distinguish between truth and lies and between allegorical and intelligible meanings, leading him into the wisdom of God and an understanding of truth.[314] Thus for Origen διάκρισις is essential not only to discerning good and evil, but also to interpreting Scripture, living rightly and knowing God more fully.[315] Indeed, to grasp a deeper understanding of God, perceive him inwardly and distinguish the senses of the νοῦς require, for Origen, the ability to use διάκρισις.[316] The veil over the figurative meaning of Scripture is lifted by the gift of God when the enquirer has done all he can to understand it, exercised διάκρισις of good and evil, and prayed for revelation.[317] Διάκρισις is presented as an integral part of the spiritual food needed by the believer,[318] the words of God that nourish the ψυχή.[319] It is used to understand the nature of Christ[320] and to distinguish the image (Christ) from what is made in the image (humanity).[321] Similarly the discernment of true and false prophets requires the gift of διάκρισις πνευμάτων and the ability to distinguish between the genuine and fraudulent, as in coinage.[322] It is significant that Origen makes great use of the word-group in *contra Celsum* drawing attention to Celsus' lack of discernment. In the preface to this work Origen explains his intention to refute Celsus' charges against Christianity, citing the first half of Romans 14:1. While he does not quote the rest of the verse and so use the word διάκρισις here, the context is one of Christian apologetics and the intention is to guide the reader into the truth, a pursuit wholly in keeping with the nature of διάκρισις.[323] Thus, while Origen's use of the διάκρισις word-group reflects its use in Scripture, there is a shift of emphasis to the discernment of right and wrong, good and evil, truth and lies, to

---

[311]   *Cont. Cels.* 3.60.

[312]   *Comm. in Joh.* 6.51.267.

[313]   Pseudo-Macarius, *hom. H* 4.1, *hom. B* 49.1.1.

[314]   *Comm. in Joh.* 13.24.144; 13.37.241; *cont. Cels.* 6.13. Cf. *ibid.* 3.53 re Celsus' failure to discern falsehoods. Celsus' lack of διάκρισις is also seen *ibid.* 1.58; 3.62.

[315]   Thus the word-group is used to praise the Samaritan woman's unwavering faith (*comm. in Joh.* 13.10.63).

[316]   *Comm. in Cant.* 1.4; *cont. Cels.* 7.37.

[317]   *Cont. Cels.* 6.32; *comm. in Joh.* 1.8.44.

[318]   *Comm. in Joh.* 13.33.210.

[319]   *De orat.* 27.5.

[320]   *Comm. in Joh.* 1.28.200.

[321]   *Ibid.* 6.49.252.

[322]   *Frag. in Jer.* 19; *hom in Luc.* 1.3. Cf. *hom in Luc.* 17.107 (see p. 108, n. 234).

[323]   *Cont. Cels.* pref. 6.

understanding deeper spiritual and mystical meaning in Scripture and to the nature of God and the inner life with a view to ascending towards God, entering into a more intimate relationship with him and attaining a higher level of spiritual perfection. As such there is a detectable shift to διάκρισις being a technical term for a charism used in the mystical search for God.

CHAPTER 2

Διάκρισις in Evagrius Ponticus

Having established the Scriptural, philosophical and Origenist background to the developing understanding of διάκρισις and the search for God it is now necessary to consider the work of the first theologian of the desert, Evagrius Ponticus, since his approach to mystical theology and spirituality is strongly philosophical and Origenist.

Evagrius Ponticus (c.345-399AD) was probably born at Ibora in Pontus, but little is known of his early life. However, his ability in διάκρισις and the influence of Origenist thinking on his formation are clearly evident.[1] The principle source of information regarding his life is Palladius,[2] his disciple,[3] who says that he was so pure of νοῦς that he was granted the gifts of 'γνῶσις, wisdom and διάκρισις πνευμάτων.'[4] In *Historia monachorum in Aegypto* he is described as 'a wise and learned man, who was competent in διάκρισις λογισμῶν [discernment of thoughts]'; Rufinus' longer Latin version has 'the grace of *discretio spirituum* [discernment of spirits] and the purging of thoughts.'[5] That Evagrius was valued for his διάκρισις is further

---

[1] A.M. Casiday, *Evagrius Ponticus* (The Early Church Fathers; Routledge: Abingdon, 2006) p. 30, comments that 'the claim that Evagrius himself drew inspiration from Origen ... is beyond dispute.' H.G.E. White, *The Monasteries of the Wâdi 'n Natrûn: Part II – The History of the Monasteries of Nitria and of Scetis* (New York: Metropolitan Museum of Art Egyptian Expedition, 1932), p. 86 says that 'there is no doubt that (Evagrius) was the intellectual center of the Origenist party' and Louth that Origen's 'tradition of intellectualist mysticism ... was developed and bequeathed to the Eastern Church by Evagrius' (Louth, *The Origins of the Christian Mystical Tradition*, p. 74; see also, pp. 100-13).

[2] *HL* 38; the Coptic version is more detailed.

[3] *Ibid.* 23.1. Palladius and Rufinus (*HM* 20.15) knew Evagrius and so provide first hand evidence concerning him.

[4] *HL* 38.10. Evagrius is also described as πνευματοφόρος καὶ διακριτικός ('inspired and discerning'; *ibid.* 11.5).

[5] *HM* 20.15 (Latin: *HM* 27.1). Rufinus, whom Jerome describes him as Evagrius' disciple (*ep.* 133.3), clearly admired Evagrius greatly and praises Evagrius' discernment at length in his Latin translation of *HM*. Sozomen similarly praises

attested by the inclusion of five apophthegms attributed to him in the Greek Systematic Collection's διάκρισις section.[6] While Gennadius[7] and Socrates[8] approve of Evagrius and his works, Jerome, writing some sixteen years after Evagrius' death, describes him as a heretic and hints at his Origenism.[9] The same controversy over Evagrius is reflected in the contrasting opinions of him in modern scholarship.[10] Evagrius was ordained lector by Basil of Caesarea following whose death in 379AD Gregory of Nazianzus ordained him deacon,[11] but after the Second Ecumenical Council (381AD) and as a result of a nascent adulterous affair, he moved to Jerusalem.[12] Here he formed a friendship with Melania the Elder (and Rufinus who later translated some of Evagrius' work[13]) and, after he had been ill, she persuaded him to devote himself to the monastic life.[14] Thus he moved on to Egypt (383AD), first Nitria for two years and thence to Kellia for the final fourteen years of his life;[15] during his time in Egypt he was a disciple of the two Macarii.[16] It was probably through the influence of Basil, Gregory, Melania and Rufinus that Evagrius became familiar with Origen's teaching. Yet it is not until the Fifth Ecumenical Council (553AD) that Evagrius' name begins to be included in anathemata alongside that of

---

Evagrius' skill in 'discerning (διακρίνω) λογισμοί relating to ἀρετή and vice' (*HE* 6.30.6).

[6]   GSC 10.7, 24, 25, 193, 194. See Appendix 2 for parallels.

[7]   *De vir. inl.* 11.

[8]   Socrates Scholasticus, *HE* 4.23.

[9]   Jerome, *ep.* 133.3. Cf. *dial. adv. Pel.* prol. 2.

[10]   A. Casiday, 'Gabriel Bunge and the Study of Evagrius Ponticus: Review Article', *St Vladimir's Theological Quarterly* 48.2 (2004), pp. 249-89 provides an excellent overview of the current state of the modern debate and L. Dysinger, 'The Relationship between Psalmody and Prayer in the Writings of Evagrius Ponticus' (DPhil thesis, St Benet's Hall, Oxford, 1999), pp. 5-10 also summarises some aspects of this controversy.

[11]   *HL* 38.2. Evagrius mentions Gregory and Basil in *gnos.* 44, 45 respectively. Bundy notes that the traditional assertion that he studied under Gregory has been called into question (D. Bundy, 'Evagrius Ponticus: The Kephalaia Gnostica', in V.L. Wimbush (ed.), *Ascetic Behavior in Greco-Roman Antiquity: A Sourcebook* (Studies in Antiquity & Christianity; Minneapolis: Fortress Press, 1990), p. 176, n. 7).

[12]   *HL* 38.2-7.

[13]   Jerome, *de vir. inl.* 17.

[14]   *HL* 38.9; the use of μετημφίασθη suggests that Evagrius reverted to his former mode of dress, i.e. he renewed his monastic way of life; it is widely accepted that Evagrius probably first entered the monastic life under Basil's direction (see Casiday, *Evagrius Ponticus*, pp. 7, 9, 204-205).

[15]   *HL* 38.8-10.

[16]   Socrates Scholasticus, *HE* 4.23.

Origen.[17] The early concern over the Origenist content of his work is demonstrated by the two extant Syriac versions of the *Kephalaia Gnostica*: S[1] has been edited to remove the Origenist content, whereas the more original and unexpurgated version, S[2], retains these.

Evagrius was highly influential in both Eastern and Western asceticism and mysticism.[18] In the West this was primarily through the work of John Cassian (c.360-435AD), but also through Rufinus' Latin translations of his work.[19] Although Cassian never mentions Evagrius by name, it is highly probable 'that Evagrius was the single most important influence on Cassian's monastic theology'.[20] His influence is also seen in such writers as John Climacus, Dionysius the Areopagite, Maximus the Confessor and Simeon the New Theologian as well as extensively in Syriac theologians. His influence continued after the condemnation of his writings, not least because some of them were preserved under the names of more acceptable writers such as Basil and Nilus.[21] The Evagrian corpus is currently an area of active research, but critical texts and translations are widely scattered and often hard to locate; some have yet to be edited. His extant writings are sometimes only available in translations (e.g. into Syriac, Coptic, Armenian or Latin) and what still exists in Greek is often only partial.

The Need of Διάκρισις in Reading Evagrius' Work

Evagrius rarely uses the διάκρισις word-group, but the discernment of spirits, λογισμοί[22] and of spiritual and practical matters is at the centre of

---

[17]   It should be noted, however, that the anathemata appended to the acts of the council were probably added later and so whether Evagrius was condemned of Origenism at the council can be questioned (see Casiday, 'Gabriel Bunge', pp. 293-94).

[18]   See e.g. O. Chadwick, *John Cassian* (Cambridge: Cambridge University Press, 2nd edn, 1968), p. 86 and I. Hausherr, 'Les grands courants de la spiritualité orientale', *OCP* 1 (1935), p. 123.

[19]   See e.g. Jerome, *ep.* 133.3.

[20]   C. Stewart, *Cassian the Monk* (Oxford: Oxford University Press, 1998), p. 11. The connection between Evagrius and Cassian and their ideas is discussed in the next chapter.

[21]   On the re-assignation of such works to Evagrius see e.g. I. Hausherr, 'Le traité de l'oraison d'Évagre le Pontique (Pseudo Nil)', *RAM* 15 (1934), pp. 34-93, 113-70 (esp. 169-70) and 'Nouveaux fragments grecs d'Evagre le Pontique', *OCP* 5 (1939), pp. 229-33.

[22]   Λογισμός is used both positively and negatively, but is frequently used of a temptation, negative preoccupation or passion and has been used in this negative sense throughout this work unless otherwise stated. There is a sense in which the λογισμοί are motivational in nature lying deeper within a person, i.e. beneath sin committed (deed) and sin considered (intent) (cf. *prak.* 48). A monk only sins when he consents to a λογισμός (*prak.* 75. Cf. Nau 169; Cassian, *conf.* 2.16.2 on *discretio*

his teaching, particularly in such works as the *Praktikos*. That Evagrius intended his works to be read with διάκρισις, is evident from the opening and closing words of his trilogy (*Praktikos, Gnostikos, Kephalaia Gnostica*):

> Some things we have concealed and others we have made obscure, lest we give holy things to dogs and throw our pearls to the pigs. [Matthew 7:6] But these things will be manifest to those who have entered upon the same course.[23]

> Scrutinise our words, O our brothers, and explain with zeal the symbols of the centuries, according to the six days of Creation.[24]

Evagrius intends that only experienced ascetics should be able to discern his meaning[25] and monks are expected to advance in understanding of his doctrines as they progress through the trilogy. This is evident from the significance he places on the sequential order of the books and the order and division of the chapters; higher degrees of knowledge and understanding are gained by following the sequence or 'route'.[26] Furthermore, Evagrius appears to use διάκρισις to describe the varied content of his *Epistula ad Melaniam* and διακρίνω to discern its meaning, and later writing of an unwillingness (reminiscent of his intention elsewhere to veil his meaning) to record distinctions (διάκρισις) in the νοῦς, again suggesting the need to use διάκρισις to understand his

---

guiding the monk to avoid giving his consent and *conf.* 7.8.3 on the devil only being able to deceive if the monk consents to his will). See below, p. 150.

[23] *Prak.* prol. 9. He also suggests a veiled and deeper spiritual meaning in *de orat.* prol.

[24] *KG* S[2]; all translations of *KG* 2-6 are from French in A. Guillaumont, *Les six Centuries des 'Kephalaia Gnostica' d'Évagre le Pontique: Édition critique de la version Syriaque commune et édition d'une nouvelle version Syriaque, intégrale, avec une double traduction française* (PO 28.1; Paris: Firmin-Didot, 1958).

[25] Gennadius, *de vir. inl.* 11 also says this is the case.

[26] The sequence is suggested in *prak.* prol. 9 and made more explicit in a request by Evagrius attached to some MSS that future copyists preserve the order and chapter divisions; see J. Muyldermans, *À travers la tradition manuscrite d'Évagre le Pontique: Essai sur les manuscrits grecs conservés à la Bibliothèque Nationale de Paris* (Bibliothèque du Muséon 3; Louvain: Bureaux du Muséon, 1932), pp. 33-34 reproduced in A. and C. Guillaumont, *Évagre le Pontique: Le Traité practique ou le moine* (SC 170, Paris: Cerf, 1971), p. 147 and translated in J. Driscoll, *The 'Ad Monachos' of Evagrius Ponticus: Its Structure and a Select Commentary* (Studia Anselmiana 104; Rome: Abbazia S. Paolo, 1991), p. 3, n. 12; Driscoll also notes the significance of the number and order of the chapters in *ad mon.* (*passim.*). Evagrius also says that the number of chapters is significant in *de orat.* (prol.).

writings.[27] Thus, not only do Evagrius' works address the monk's need and use of διάκρισις, the works themselves need to be read exercising διάκρισις.

Aims and Goals

Evagrius regards διάκρισις as essential to the monastic life and achieving its goals:

> It is absolutely necessary for someone who serves as a soldier in this warfare to seek διάκρισις from the Lord, neglecting nothing that contributes towards the reception of such a gift.[28]

In this progression towards purity and the goals the νοῦς, Evagrius says, uses διάκρισις to examine the inner life:

> διάκρισις is believed [to judge rightly] the fantasies concerning the mind [διάνοια], distinguishing between [διακρίνω] holy and profane, pure and impure λογισμοί.[29]

Furthermore, commenting on Job 12:11 (LXX) on discerning (διακρίνω) words and food, Evagrius speaks of the νοῦς using διάκρισις to discern both γνῶσις of God (the monk's ultimate goal) and intellectual and perceptible things.[30] Evagrius' understanding of the monk's need of

---

27 *Epistula ad Melaniam* 2-3, 17; assuming the accuracy of Frankenberg's translation (W. Frankenberg, *Euagrius Ponticus*, (Abhandlungen der königlichen Gesellschaft der Wissenschaften zu Göttingen, Philologisch-Historische Klasse, Neue Folge, 13.2; Berlin: Weidmannsche Buchhandlung, 1912), p. 613.).

28 *Ep.* 4.5 (cf. Pseudo-Macarius, *hom. H* 4.1, *hom. B* 49.1.1). Translations of *ep.* 4.4-5 are from the Greek in the 13th century *codex Sinaiticus graecus 462* published by C. Guillaumont, 'Fragments grecs inédits d'Évagre le Pontique', in J. Dummer (ed.), *Texte und Textkritik: Eine Aufsatzsammlung* (*TU* 133; Berlin: Akademie-Verlag, 1987), pp. 209-21; this MS contains extracts from several of Evagrius' letters (4, 25, 27, 31, 52, 56, 58).

29 *Ep.* 4.4. G. Bunge, *Evagrios Pontikos: Briefe aus der Wüste* (Sophia Quellen Östlicher Theologie 24; Trier: Paulinus-Verlag, 1986), p. 334, n. 8 suggests that Evagrius is here drawing on his master, Macarius the Egyptian, who was renowned for his διάκρισις (*HL* 17.2).

30 *Schol.* 16-17 in Job 12:11. In his recent compilation of Evagrius' *Scholia in Iob* Casiday defends the attribution of these (and other) *scholia* to Evagrius. While the Hagedorns attributed *schol.* 17 to Evagrius they attributed *schol.* 16, with some uncertainty, to Olympiodoros. Casiday, however, presents good manuscript evidence to suggest that *schol.* 16 is Evagrian and I agree with him that the thought in this *scholion* is consistent with Evagrius' thought elsewhere. See: A.M. Casiday,

διάκρισις may also be illustrated from the *Kephalaia Gnostica*. The νοῦς is said to require 'a sharpened spiritual sense to distinguish spiritual things'[31] so that the monk is able to gain deeper spiritual insight through spiritual θεωρία.[32] The νοῦς is a spiritual organ of sense, which Evagrius equates with ἀπάθεια,[33] that uses διάκρισις both noetically and spiritually. When the monk is immersed in God he can have a true and experiential understanding of God and of spiritual things, whereas outside of God his knowledge is only descriptive.[34] The monk reaches his ultimate goal of γνῶσις of God, via his proximate goal of ἀπάθεια, by exercising διάκρισις in the νοῦς. Immersed in God his νοῦς is free from seeing form and matter,[35] whereas his receptivity to God and γνῶσις of him is lost if he is negligent and turns away from him.[36] Thus, διάκρισις operates within the νοῦς when the monk is living wholly within God and facilitates spiritual understanding and γνῶσις of God, whereas failure to use διάκρισις results in ignorance. For Evagrius, then, διάκρισις is integral to the pursuit of the monk's goals and develops as he progresses towards them.

The high value Evagrius places on γνῶσις of God is repeatedly stressed: it adorns the καρδία like a crown,[37] it is the highest object of love,[38] superior to everything[39] and more important than γνῶσις of any other spiritual entity.[40] Γνῶσις is the essential nature of God[41] and the supreme object of contemplation,[42] acquired by submitting the will to God.[43] The

---

Evagrius Ponticus, pp. 123-24, 224 n. 24; U. Hagedorn and D. Hagedorn (eds), *Die älteren griechischen Katenen zum buch Hiob* (4 vols; *PTS* 40, 48, 53, 59; Berlin: De Gruyter, 1994-2004), II, pp. 104-105.

31 *KG* 1.33 (all translations of *KG* 1 (S²) are by Bundy, 'Evagrius Ponticus').
32 *Ibid.* 1.34; θεωρία (contemplation) is the perception of the νοῦς (intellect) by which it gains spiritual knowledge.
33 *Ibid.* 1.37; ἀπάθεια is a passionless and imperturbable state of purity.
34 *Ibid.* 1.38. This is reminiscent of Plato's hierarchy of mental operation (*rep.* 7.6-7.7, 509d-521b; see above, p. 17, n. 116).
35 *KG* 1.46; cf. *ibid.* 5.15. Cf. Plotinus, *Enneads* 6.7.34 where in union with the One the ψυχή moves beyond all distinctions. Evagrius may refer to such distinctions (διάκρισις) in the context of the unity of God and union with him in *epistula ad Melaniam* 25.
36 *KG* 1.49.
37 *Ad mon.* 27.
38 *KG* 1.86.
39 *Ibid.* 1.87; cf. *ad mon.* 28, 43, 72.
40 *Ad mon.* 110.
41 *KG* 1.89; 2.47.
42 *Ad mon.* 110.
43 *KG* 6.68; *schol.* 4 in Ps. 36:7 (LXX) [*PG* 12.1316]. Evagrius' *schol. in Ps.* are cited according to a text graciously provided by Luke Dysinger OSB and now published on the internet (http://www.ldysinger.com/Evagrius/08_Psalms/00a_start.htm accessed 23 August 2006). It has been reconstructed according to the collation of

monk is thus dependent upon God and his close relationship with him for γνῶσις,[44] which is both the means of ascent to God and his spiritual nourishment;[45] without such γνῶσις the ψυχή is sterile and fruitless.[46]

The acquisition of γνῶσις of God through διάκρισις in an undistracted state of ἀπάθεια is demonstrated by a rare use of διάκρισις / διακρίνω in which Evagrius, citing James 1:5-6,[47] closely associates διάκρισις with γνῶσις of God, as indeed he does in *Scholion* 16 *in* Job 12:11.[48]

If one of the anchorites wishes to receive γνῶσις διακρίσεως from the Lord, let him first eagerly work hard practically at the commandments neglecting nothing and so at the appointed time of prayer, "let him ask for" γνῶσις "from God who gives generously to all and without finding fault, let him ask without hesitating [μηδὲν διακρινόμενος]" and without being thrown about by waves of disbelief, "and it will be given to him." [James 1:5-6] For it is not possible to receive γνῶσις of more practical matters if one is negligent of that which is known, lest someone committing many transgressions becomes responsible for more sins. It is blessed to serve the γνῶσις of God; for it is really dangerous not to do what has been commanded by it, but it is blessed to accomplish everything that has been taught by it.[49] For the νοῦς subject to passion

---

M.-J. Rondeau, based on the 10th century MS *Vaticanus Graecus 754*. Rondeau provides a key to published sources in M.-J. Rondeau, 'Le commentaire sur les Psaumes d'Évagre le Pontique', *OCP* 26 (1960), pp. 307-48, but the Greek is from Rondeau's unpublished collation. Where possible, published sources provided in Rondeau's article are cited after the reference; these are from: Athanasius, *Expositiones in Psalmos*; Origen, *Fragmenta in Psalmos 1-150*; and Origen, *Selecta in Psalmos*.

[44]   *Ad mon.* 120: 'The breast of the Lord is the γνῶσις of God and he who leans back on it will be a theologian.' (cf. Jn 13:25). That the monk should lean back on God (i.e. facing away from him) is reminiscent of Gregory of Nyssa who describes true knowledge of God as moving beyond light into darkness and not seeing, since God transcends all knowledge (*de vit. Mos.* 2.162-163); to follow God is to follow his back, i.e. not to see God's face (*ibid.* 2.253-254). This reveals a high theology of the γνῶσις of God and the importance of submitting to him, while at the same time expressing a deeper realm of γνῶσις, which moves beyond a more basic relationship of following God in what can be seen and perceived to a more advanced state that is prepared to follow in darkness without seeing.

[45]   *Ad mon.* 117: 'Without γνῶσις the καρδία will not be raised up and a tree will not bloom without drinking.'

[46]   *KG* 6.62.

[47]   He replaces σοφία (wisdom) with γνῶσις, suggesting that he regards them as somewhat interchangeable.

[48]   See above, p. 43.

[49]   Cf. Plotinus, *Enneads* 6.7.37: a failure of the νοῦς to perceive (νοεῖν) is unintelligent (ἀνόητος).

wanders about and becomes hard to restrain when it is concerned about matters producing pleasures. But it stops wandering when it has become impassive [ἀπαθής] and encounters incorporeal things which fulfil spiritual desires in it. But it is not possible to acquire γνῶσις, without having made the first, second and third renunciation. The first renunciation is the voluntary abandonment of worldly matters for the sake of the γνῶσις of God; the second is the rejection of evil which comes after by the grace of Christ our Saviour and by the zeal of man; the third renunciation is the separation from ignorance of the things which is made manifest naturally to men in proportion to their κατάστασις.[50]

In these three renunciations can be seen a progression in the acquisition of διάκρισις; first proficiency in works of πρακτική, then overcoming passions and achieving a state of ἀπάθεια and finally γνῶσις of God.[51] This gives διάκρισις a somewhat elevated status[52] as integral to the acquisition of the monk's proximate and ultimate goals. Γνῶσις, and therefore διάκρισις, are received as God's gift when the monk petitions for it, but only if he is maintaining a pure and undistracted life focussed on God and in personal relationship with him. Similarly, on Proverbs 31:9 (LXX),[53] Evagrius says the Psalmist 'calls "poor" someone who has been deprived of γνῶσις and "weak" someone who is impure.'[54] This presents διάκρισις as the strategic instrument for distinguishing between the presence and absence of γνῶσις and purity. Elsewhere monks are warned to pay close attention (implying use of διάκρισις) to the 'demon wanderer' that

---

[50]   Περὶ Λογ. 26 ('For the νοῦς ... spiritual desires in it.' = *KG* S² 1.85). Κατάστασις is an important Evagrian technical term indicating an advanced and settled condition of peace resident in the unconscious. It is disrupted in or after prayer by anger, disturbing the mind's eye (*de orat.* 27, 47). Cassian (*conf.* 3.6; see below, p. 81) also describes these three renunciations, relating them respectively to Proverbs, Ecclesiastes and the Song of Songs (see below, p. 87, n. 89). Cf. John Climacus, *scala parad.* 2.

[51]   Πρακτική refers to ascetic practices used in the pursuit of virtues and purity; hence ascetics are referred to as πρακτικοί.

[52]   There is a close association in James of wisdom and the Holy Spirit (for a discussion see: P.H. Davids, *The Epistle of James: A Commentary on the Greek Text* (The New International Greek Testament Commentary; Exeter: Paternoster Press, 1982), pp. 51-56). Evagrius probably has this in mind, since he states it clearly elsewhere (*epistula ad Melaniam* 7) and so γνῶσις διακρίσεως is associated with the Holy Spirit, giving διάκρισις an elevated status in his doctrine.

[53]   Διάκρινε δὲ πένητα καὶ ἀσθενῆ ('distinguish the poor and weak').

[54]   *Schol.* 298 in Prov. 31:9; *Expositio in Proverbia Salomonis* (C. Tischendorf, *Notitia editionis codicis bibliorum Sinaitici* (Leipzig: F.A. Brockhaus, 1860), p. 112, ln. 13). Διάκρισις is also placed in the context of purity in *schol.* 20 in Eccles. 3:18 (see below, pp. 57-58).

attempts to distract and ruin the νοῦς so that it gradually falls away from γνῶσις of God,[55] since ἀπάθεια is essential in the νοῦς if it is not to wander and the monk is to enter the incorporeal and spiritual realm.[56] Thus διάκρισις is both necessary to acquiring the monk's goals and a product of them, and so it is woven into the whole process of union with God.

The process by which the monk achieves his goals is evident from Evagrius' three tier approach to Christian teaching: practical (πρακτική), natural (φυσική) and theological (θεολογική).[57] Πρακτική relates to ascetic practice used to develop ἀρεταί and overcome vices, φυσική to the contemplation of Scripture and creation, and θεολογική to γνῶσις of God. He then identifies the goals of the monk, to which he frequently refers, as ἀπάθεια ψυχῆς and true γνῶσις of things,[58] particularly of the Trinity.[59] Ἀπάθεια can be equated with Cassian's proximate goal, *puritas cordis* (purity of heart), and since Evagrius relates γνῶσις to knowledge of and union with God and to the Kingdom of God, this too can be equated with Cassian's ultimate goal of ascent to God.[60] This three stage ascent to God is very similar to Origen's use of the three books of Solomon for teaching Ethics, Physics and Enoptics.[61] For union with God, then, the monk must first be cleansed of passions and then delivered from ignorance.[62]

This progression towards union with God is also apparent from Evagrius' distinction between πρακτικοί (ascetics) who understand practical matters and γνωστικοί (knowers) who gain a deeper knowledge of

---

[55] Περὶ Λογ. 9.

[56] *KG* 1.85; cf. Περὶ Λογ. 26.

[57] *Prak.* 1. Cf. *gnos.* 12; *KG* 1.10 (the demons attack each of these aspects); *schol.* 247 in Prov. 22:40.

[58] *Prak.* 2. Jerome is critical of the doctrine of ἀπάθεια (*ep.* 133.3; cf. *comm. in Hierem.* 4.1; *dial. adv. Pel.* prol. 1).

[59] *Prak.* 3.

[60] *Conf.* 1.4-5. Evagrius equates the Kingdom of God with γνῶσις of the Trinity in *prak.* 3. On the equivalence of the proximate and ultimate goals described by Evagrius and Cassian, see below, p. 80, n. 42.

[61] Evagrius relates πρακτική, φυσική and θεολογική to the three books of Solomon in *schol.* 247 in Prov. 22:40 (see below, p. 64). For Origen (*comm. in Cant.* prol. 3) see above, pp. 30-31 (cf. Clement of Alexandria, *strom.* 1.28, quoted by Evagrius in *schol.* 15 in Ps. 76:21 (LXX) [Pitra 76.21]). Cassian adopts the same schema (*conf.* 3.6.4; see above, p. 46, n. 50 and below, p. 87, n. 89).

[62] *De orat.* 37. The process from ἀπάθεια to γνῶσις of God is said to lie by way of ἀγάπη (love), (*ad mon.* 67; cf. 3.), which Evagrius says purifies the heart (*ad mon.* 8.). The fundamental importance of ἀπάθεια and γνῶσις, is evident in the way Evagrius calls them respectively the health and food of the ψυχή, the latter representing the only means of union with the 'holy powers.' (*prak.* 56. Ἀρετή is also said to feed the ψυχή and spiritual prayer the νοῦς; *de orat.* 101).

things.[63] Πρακτικοί develop ἀπάθεια in the ψυχή and γνωστικοί, through an understanding granted by God, are able to discern the deeper meaning of the natural (including themselves) and spiritual order and concentrate on purity.[64] This progression from πρακτικός through ἀπάθεια to γνωστικός[65] is also found in the *Praktikos*: πρακτική purifies the ψυχή,[66] then θεωρία is added,[67] since it is only once the νοῦς has gained ἀπάθεια that it is able to discern the activity of the monk's spiritual enemy.[68] The νοῦς is also empowered for θεωρία of the Divine γνῶσις when γνῶσις works with prayer.[69] The monk does not, then, so much graduate from πρακτικός to γνωστικός as continue as a πρακτικός who increasingly develops the gifts of a γνωστικός, a state in which he is particularly able to exercise διάκρισις as he works towards his goals through careful observation of his spiritual condition. This dual approach to spiritual life (outward and inward) is also evident in Evagrius' two aspects of prayer: πρακτικός and θεωρητικός, the former concentrating on the external and active, the latter being contemplative and discerning inner significance.[70] Διάκρισις is thus necessary to distinguish the different levels of γνῶσις, to weigh and discern what the monk encounters at each level and to apply πρακτική properly in order to achieve his goals.

The three stage progression towards γνῶσις of God is reflected in Evagrius' three aspects of γνῶσις in the νοῦς: of the Trinity; of the incorporeal nature created by it; and contemplation of beings.[71] Like Antony, he understands that the created order needs to be read like a book

---

[63] *Gnos.* 1.

[64] *Ibid.* 2-4; cf. *schol.* 17 in Job 12:11 (see above, p. 43).

[65] Cf. *KG* 1.70 where Evagrius describes five levels of knowledge ranging from γνῶσις of the Trinity (highest) to ἀπάθεια (lowest); the monk must progress through these to achieve γνῶσις of God.

[66] *Prak.* 78. Γνῶσις of God is acquired through πρακτική, which 'becomes a chariot for the rational soul who strives that it might obtain the knowledge of God.' (*KG* S² 1.67).

[67] *Prak.* 79.

[68] *Ibid.* 83.

[69] *De orat.* 86. Γνῶσις and θεωρία are used somewhat interchangeably: γνῶσις δὲ ἐστιν ἡ θεωρία τῆς ἁγίος τριάδος ('knowledge is the contemplation of the holy Trinity', *Schol.* 29 in Ps. 118:66 (LXX) [Pitra 118.65-66]; cf. *KG* 3.42). Dysinger, 'The Relationship between Psalmody and Prayer', pp. 41-42, notes the similarity with Clement of Alexandria (*strom.* 6.7.61.1-3) and Evagrius' tendency to use γνῶσις for higher levels of contemplation.

[70] *De orat.* prol.; the monk is assisted in attaining πρακτική and θεωρητική by the providence of God (*schol.* 8 in Ps. 138:16 (LXX) [Pitra, 138.14-16; *PG* 12.1661]). The terms were already well established (see e.g. Aristotle, *eth. Nic.* 1139a) and Cassian adopts them (*conf.* 14 on spiritual knowledge; see below, p. 87).

[71] *KG* 1.74.

in order to reveal the nature of God[72] and so διάκρισις is used to discern God in his Creation. For Evagrius, γνῶσις of God is the purpose of human existence[73] and it is opposed to ignorance and evil.[74] Through perceptive contemplation (which would require διάκρισις) of the created order, γνῶσις of the Trinity becomes attainable.[75] Ignorance is equated with evil and they are contrasted with γνῶσις in the καρδίαι (hearts) of the more advanced.[76] By placing γνῶσις in the καρδία Evagrius puts it at the centre of human existence where God can be experienced and known and where conscious decisions to eradicate evil and ignorance are made.[77] Evagrius prefers using νοῦς to καρδία but explains that Scripture tends to use the latter as the seat of belief,[78] thus γνῶσις and contemplation, and therefore διάκρισις, operate within the νοῦς / καρδία, the highest spiritual faculty and centre of existence. Διάκρισις can therefore be understood as functioning at the centre of the monk's being enabling him to attain the highest purpose of existence.

Γνῶσις and θεωρία are the key work of the νοῦς,[79] which is accountable to Christ at the Last Judgment,[80] 'the temple of the Holy Trinity'[81] and of the same substance as God:

---

[72]   *Prak.* 92 (quoting *VP* 6.4.16; cf. Antony's debate with the Greek philosophers in *vit. Ant.* 72-80, esp. 78); cf. *gnos.* 48; *KG* 1.14; *schol.* 8 in Ps. 138:16 (LXX) [Pitra, 138.14-16; *PG* 12.1661]. It is through ἀπάθεια and θεωρία that monks are able to recognise the grace of the Creator (*prak.* 53).

[73]   *KG* 1.50, 71, 87.

[74]   *Ibid.* 1.89.

[75]   *Ibid.* 2.16.

[76]   *Ad mon.* 24.

[77]   The καρδία in Scripture and patristic thought represents the totality of human existence, the integration of the physical, spiritual and intellectual. It is the meeting place between the body and the νοῦς (the highest spiritual faculty) where God is encountered and the struggle against demons occurs. It also represents the place where a person thinks, makes moral decisions and obtains wisdom. The concept of the καρδία representing the whole person is common throughout antiquity. In Middle Egyptian the *yb* (heart) represents the seat of the intellect, will and desire, the source of moral awareness and the centre of thought and in Coptic ϩⲏⲧ means both 'heart' and 'mind'. Similarly, in Hebrew, לֵב / לֵבָב represents both heart and human inner nature, mind and will and is the seat of human spiritual and intellectual life. See e.g.: K.T. Ware, 'Prayer in Evagrius of Pontus and the Macarian Homilies', in R. Waller and B. Ward (eds), *An Introduction to Christian Spirituality* (London: SPCK, 1999), pp. 20-23; K.T. Ware, '"Pray Without Ceasing": The Ideal of Continual Prayer in Eastern Monasticism', *Eastern Churches Review* 2 (1968-9), p. 258; T. Špidlík, *The Spirituality of the Christian East: A Systematic Handbook*, (trans. A.P. Gythiel; Cistercian Studies Series 79; Kalamazoo: Cistercian Publications, 1986), pp. 103-107.

[78]   *Schol.* 4 in Ps. 15:9 (LXX) [PG 12.1216] (discussed further below, p. 62).

[79]   *KG* 1.74; cf. *de orat.* 86.

The Kingdom of God is γνῶσις of the Holy Trinity coextensive with the substance [σύστασις] of the νοῦς, and surpassing its incorruption.[82]

The νοῦς purified from sin and λογισμοί (it is healed by γνῶσις[83]) has a natural affinity with the γνῶσις of God[84] and is capable of seeing 'the light of the Holy Trinity at the time of prayer.'[85] Indeed, 'the νοῦς is the light of the Holy Trinity'[86] with which it strives to be mingled.[87] It is, then, the νοῦς that seeks γνῶσις of God, whose nature it shares. Since διάκρισις plays a central role in gaining γνῶσις, exercising θεωρία and overcoming the λογισμοί,[88] and since the νοῦς is its *locus operandi*, διάκρισις may said to be at the centre of Evagrius' spiritual economy and integral to the monk's nature and spiritual endeavours.

The νοῦς is the *locus* of spiritual understanding and of διάκρισις, as is demonstrated by the repeated phrase: 'the νοῦς discerns'.[89] It has spiritual senses equivalent to the natural senses, which it uses to distinguish and discern natural and spiritual matters,[90] and it is in the nature of saints to do this.[91] The νοῦς educates the ψυχή and thereby trains the body so that the monk can enter into γνῶσις of God.[92] To advance towards his spiritual

---

[80]   *Antirr.* prol.; all translations from *Antirrheticus* are by M. O'Laughlin, 'Evagrius Ponticus: Antirrheticus (Selections)', in V.L. Wimbush (ed.), *Ascetic Behavior in Greco-Roman Antiquity: A Sourcebook* (Studies in Antiquity & Christianity; Minneapolis: Fortress Press, 1990), pp. 243-62.
[81]   *Skem.* 34.
[82]   *Prak.* 3. The νοῦς is also equated with Christ (and thereby with γνῶσις of God) in *KG* S² 1.77 where body, ψυχή and νοῦς are ranked in a manner reminiscent of Neo-Platonism, a comparison encouraged by *KG* 1.81 which has γνῶσις resident in the νοῦς and ἀπάθεια in the ψυχή (cf. also *KG* 2.56). The affinity of the νοῦς with God is similar to Origen's theology (see above, pp. 31-32).
[83]   *KG* 3.35.
[84]   *Ibid.* 2.34. Just as γνῶσις is closely associated with the καρδία and volition (*ad mon.* 24) so also the νοῦς is said to be joint with it (*KG* 6.87), further indicating their close relation.
[85]   *Antirr.* prol.
[86]   *KG* S² 3.30.
[87]   *Ibid.* S² 2.29. Cf. the Neo-Platonic return to the Fatherland (see above, p. 18).
[88]   Διάκρισις and λογισμοί in Evagrius is discussed below (pp. 55-62).
[89]   *Schol.* 17 *in* Job 12:11; *KG* 5.58, 59; 6.54.
[90]   *KG* 2.35; *schol.* 16 *in* Job 12:11. Cf. e.g. Origen, *comm. in Cant.* 1.4; 2.9 (see above, p. 33); *de prin.* 1.1.9; Pseudo-Macarius, *hom.* B 49.2.3 (διάκρισις is one of the five senses; cf. *hom. H* 4.7). However, Cassian does not describe the 'spiritual senses' so precisely (see below, pp. 87-88 and n. 95).
[91]   *KG* 6.3.
[92]   *Ibid.* S² 2.56: 'The νοῦς teaches the soul, and the soul the body; and only "the man of God" knows the man of knowledge.'

goals, the monk needs to hold orthodox doctrine within his νοῦς and be responsive to the prompting of the Holy Spirit:

> Sterile is the νοῦς which is deprived of spiritual doctrine, or in which fail the seeds sown by the Holy Spirit.[93]

> In this battle we are in need of spiritual weapons, which are orthodox faith and teaching. These are [revealed in] a perfect fast, brave victories, humility and stillness [ἡσυχία] – being hardly moved or completely unmoved and praying without ceasing.[94]

The monk, in a state of ἀπάθεια, thus strives towards his goals by uniting works of πρακτική (fasting and prayer) and orthodox doctrine. Διάκρισις, operating within the νοῦς, enables the monk to determine right teaching, the correct use of πρακτική and the nature of all that is within and around him.

Evagrius' stress on the νοῦς as the ground of spiritual endeavour and the realm of γνῶσις and θεωρία, is indicative of his more philosophical and noetic approach to mystical theology and spiritual understanding. It is the νοῦς that directs the monk's life:

> Have undistracted sight in your prayer and denying your flesh, and your ψυχή, live according to the νοῦς.[95]

The νοῦς is thus in overall control of ἀπάθεια and πρακτική, and given that the νοῦς uses διάκρισις to govern and direct its activity, διάκρισις can be seen as the guiding force in the pursuit of the monk's goals and as much a mental exercise and discipline as a spiritual gift. For Evagrius the body is weak and struggles to perform works of πρακτική that heal the ψυχή of passions, but constant prayer strengthens the νοῦς for its struggle against the demons;[96] while Evagrius' focus is frequently more on the νοῦς than on the body his emphasis on works of πρακτική is never diminished. Prayer 'is the ascent of the νοῦς to God,'[97] the proper and highest activity of the νοῦς[98] and when offered in a settled state (κατάστασις) of ἀπάθεια, the

---

93   *Ibid.* 6.60.
94   *Antirr.* prol.; ἡσυχία is a state of inner stillness and tranquillity in which the monk can listen attentively to God.
95   *De orat.* 110.
96   *Prak.* 49.
97   *De orat.* 35; cf. Origen, *de orat.* 23.2.
98   *De orat.* 84. Cf. Cassian, *conf.* 9.4 where the metaphor of an unsullied feather rising readily is used of pure prayer unburdened by vice (see below p. 81).

νοῦς is able to ascend to God.[99] Throughout his work it is the νοῦς which works to achieve ἀπάθεια and union with God.[100] Evagrius says that freedom from passion or emotion (πάθος) is only possible when sense-perception (αἴθησις), from which arise desire (ἐπιθυμία) and pleasure (ἡδονή), has been eliminated.[101] Ἀρεταί and vices each blind the νοῦς to the other[102] and so it follows that for the monk to progress, the process of purifying the νοῦς requires a mechanism of spiritual insight into its own state that can distinguish between these; the instrument of this insight would be διάκρισις. Thus, διάκρισις in Evagrius may be seen as an intellectual exercise as well as a spiritual one geared towards the eradication of distracting sense-perception so that God can be known experientially rather than descriptively.

While the νοῦς is the *locus* of γνῶσις of God, ἀπάθεια is resident in the ψυχή.[103] Ἀπάθεια is developed by self-control of the body[104] through the disciplines of πρακτική[105] (which Evagrius equates with the flesh of Christ[106]) and nourishes the monk, thus facilitating his ascent to God.[107] This structure resembles the Neo-Platonic hierarchy of body, ψυχή, νοῦς and One as the body is controlled by the ψυχή which prepares the way for the νοῦς to achieve γνῶσις of God.[108] Ἀπάθεια is developed using πρακτική, is characterised by gentleness and self-control and is associated with wisdom in the καρδία.[109] Evagrius contrasts gentleness with anger[110] which scatters the γνῶσις[111] produced by gentleness.[112] Anger is one of the

---

99   *De orat.* 52. The νοῦς that is 'completely insensitive' (τέλεια ἀναισθησία) in prayer is called blessed (*ibid.* 120). Cf. Cassian, *Conf.* 9.31 where Antony is reported to say that in perfect prayer a monk is unaware of both himself and what he is praying.

100   Evagrius' description of the descent (through negligence) of the νοῦς from and its ascent to union with, God is strongly reminiscent of Neo-Platonism (*KG* 3.28, 42). However, there is also dependence on Christ who leads the reasoning nature to union with God (*ibid.* 4.89).

101   *Prak.* 4.

102   *Ibid.* 62.

103   *KG* 1.81; *gnos.* 2.

104   *Ad mon.* 6. In a state of ἀπάθεια the monk advances beyond the need of self-control and endurance, since he is no longer troubled or affected by outside influences (*prak.* 68).

105   Πρακτική is the spiritual method by which the ψυχή is purified (*prak.* 78) and demonstrates to God a desire for γνῶσις of him (*ibid.* 32).

106   *Ad mon.* 118.

107   *Ibid.* 66.

108   See diagrams above, pp. 18-19.

109   *Ad mon.* 31; *skem.* 3.

110   *Ad virg.* 19.

111   *Ad mon.* 35.

112   *Ibid.* 99.

λογισμοί that need to be eradicated through πρακτική if the monk is to achieve his goals.[113] By locating the struggle to overcome anger and strive towards wisdom in the νοῦς / καρδία where moral decisions are made, by repeatedly emphasising the need to be undistracted and impassive and saying that ἀπάθεια is characterised by self-control, Evagrius implies that overcoming λογισμοί and achieving γνῶσις of God involves conscious decision and choice. Thus the virgin, for example, must choose not to pay attention to or be distracted by, her outward appearance:

> She who has pity upon her bloodshot eyes and the wasting of her flesh, will not delight in her ἀπάθεια ψυχῆς.[114]

Furthermore, the monk is warned that when his νοῦς has begun to develop ἀπάθεια he is driven by vainglory to debauched behaviour, which in the providence of God reminds him that he is not yet perfect. He should, therefore, pay close attention to himself and learn to progress in ἀρετή, resist vice more strongly and so advance, restoring his γνῶσις, θεωρία and prayer and so gain a clearer vision of Christ.[115] This is a decisive and constant act of the will by the monk to rise above his physical nature and to maintain and advance his spiritual state towards ἀπάθεια and eventually γνῶσις. Such watchfulness and choice would need to be conducted using διάκρισις.

Evagrius describes a number of indications that ἀπάθεια has been achieved, for example when all the demons opposing πρακτική have been defeated.[116] Another indication, one that is a key but complex theme in Evagrian mystical theology, is the vision of formless light experienced when the νοῦς is at its intellectual peak.[117] This experience of light is explained sometimes as the νοῦς seeing its own light[118] and sometimes as seeing the light of the Trinity.[119] This formless light is experienced in pure imageless and undistracted prayer.[120] At such a time, the one praying is more fully aware of God and of his own inner nature and state, to the point

---

[113] See below, p. 59.

[114] *Ad virg.* 51.

[115] Περὶ Λογ. 15. The πρακτικός is able to gain an understanding of providence (*ad mon.* 132). Through ἀρεταί and prayer the monk gains insight into the inner meaning of things and thereby of the Creator, who manifests himself in the state of prayer (*de orat.* 51).

[116] *Prak.* 60.

[117] The nature of this sapphire light (*skem.* 2, 4; Περὶ Λογ. 39) is discussed by W. Harmless, 'The Sapphire Light of the Mind: The Skemmata of Evagrius Ponticus', *Theological Studies* 62 (2001), pp. 498-529.

[118] *Prak.* 64; *gnos.* 45; *de orat* 73-74.

[119] *Antirr.* prol.; *skem.* 4, 25, 27; cf. Περὶ Λογ. 40; Cassian, *conf.* 9.25.

[120] *De orat.* 66, 117-120.

that in contemplating God there ceases to be a distinction between the two and there is no longer knower and known.[121] Developing the theme of undistracted prayer, light and the opposition of demons,[122] Evagrius continues:

> The angel God comes and puts an end to every action opposing us with only a word, and stirs the light of the νοῦς to operate without going astray.[123]

'Απάθεια is evidenced, then, by the monk's deeper awareness of the nature of God and of himself and also by his remaining unaffected by demonic attack or deception; being absorbed in God and assisted by him, he is able to discern anything that might lead him astray.[124] In the monastic literature under consideration διάκρισις is frequently set in opposition to deceit and monks are said to use it to see through demonic temptations. Here the νοῦς functions without being deceived (notably with Divine assistance) further suggesting that, for Evagrius, the νοῦς is the *locus operandi* of διάκρισις. Given also the association of διάκρισις with ἀπάθεια it is not surprising that Evagrius says: 'when (the νοῦς) has acquired ἀπάθεια, it will easily perceive the wiles of its enemies'.[125] Thus, when the monk is free from passions (ἀπάθεια) he is able to understand demonic activity and λογισμοί clearly, to remain undisturbed by them[126] and to maintain a constant, detached and critical observation[127] of his inner life and thought over which

---

[121] *KG* S² 4.77, 87. Evagrius says that, 'knowledge of God requires not a debater's soul, but seeing soul' (*KG* S² 4.90; cf. *Enneads* 6.9.10-11), it is an experiential state of mind that is experienced as formless light. Wordless and imageless prayer requires a deaf and dumb νοῦς (*de orat.* 11), is beyond θεωρία of things (*ibid.* 56) and rejects representations (νοήματα, *ibid.* 61), images (*ibid.* 66, 114) and forms (*ibid.* 117) (cf. Cassian, *conf.* 10.11.6), nevertheless prayer is also a conversation of the νοῦς with God (*de orat.* 3, 34, 54; cf. Clement, *strom.* 7.7.39.5, 7.7.41.8, 7.7.42.1, 7.12.73.1), who helps the monk to pray (*de orat.* 62-63). This personal communication and Divine assistance sets Evagrian and Neo-Platonic thought apart. O'Laughlin has helpfully described Evagrius' understanding of the νοῦς as 'a relational element, what we would today call "an interface".' (M. O'Laughlin, 'Evagrius Ponticus in Spiritual Perspective', in E.A. Livingstone (ed.), *Biblica et Apocrypha, Acsetica, Liturgica* (*Studia Patristica* 30; Leuven: Peeters, 1997), p. 229).

[122] *De orat.* 72-73.

[123] *Ibid.* 74.

[124] 'Απάθεια is also recognised in the λογισμοί attacking the monk (*prak.* 56).

[125] *Prak.* 83.

[126] *Ibid.* 67; though unaffected, the monk still experiences attacks (*prak.* 77).

[127] E.g. being self-critical of his motives in prayer (*de orat.* 40).

he is to gain control. This is the function of διάκρισις and reveals it to be a calm and unperturbed observation and awareness of all evil distractions.

This dependence upon God in avoiding deceit as the νοῦς approaches its goals is evident elsewhere. Evagrius explains that the monk crosses over, almost in terms of conversion, from ἐμπαθής (subject to passion) to ἀπάθεια by the mercy of Christ and that he should remember it is Christ who guards him, since this will encourage humility and combat the demon of pride.[128] Similarly, it is with God's help that the νοῦς accomplishes πρακτική and γνῶσις, which lifts the monk up to God and away from the realm of sense-perception.[129] This use of remembrance and the recollection of dependence upon Divine aid is seen elsewhere in the monastic literature as a work of διάκρισις as the monk recalls the true nature of his present state and his reliance upon God's mercy and help in the pursuit of his goals.

Διάκρισις and Λογισμοί

A key theme in Evagrius' writing is the eight principal vices or λογισμοί from which all other vices derive and which distract the monk from his goals:[130] gluttony (γαστριμαργία); fornication (πορνεία); love of money or avarice (φιλαργυρία); grief or depression (λύπη); anger (ὀργή); listlessness or accidie (ἀκηδία); vainglory (κενοδοξία); pride (ὑπερηφανία).[131] Pride is said to be the greatest danger to the monk, the source of the other λογισμοί[132] and 'the first born of the devil'.[133] For Evagrius the order is

---

[128] *Prak.* 33.

[129] *Ibid.* 66.

[130] E.g. the νοῦς troubled by anger is unable to engage in θεωρία (*KG* 6.63).

[131] *Prak.* 6. Gennadius (*de vir. inl.* 11) says that Evagrius was the first to mention or teach on the eight principal vices. On the similarity, however, of Evagrius' eight λογισμοί with Origen see I. Hausherr, 'L'origine de la théorie orientale des huits péchés capitaux', *OC* 30.3 (1933), pp. 164-75 reprinted in 'Études de Spiritualité Orientale', *OCA* 183 (1969), pp. 11-22. Cassian adopts Evagrius' list, discusses λογισμοί at length (*conf.* 5; *inst.*5-12. See below, pp. 93-99) and thereby introduced them to the Latin West. He reverses the order of ὀργή and λύπη and retains the Greek terms (in transliteration) for γαστριμαργία, φιλαργυρία, ἀκηδία and κενοδοξία. Later Gregory the Great (c.540-604) redefined the eight as the Seven Deadly Sins, substituting *invidia* for ἀκηδία, altering the order and removing pride to a special position as the most serious vice and the root of all the others (*mor. in Iob* 31.45.87-88). For a discussion see: R. Gillet, *Grégoire le Grand: Morales Sur Job,* (SC 32; Paris: Cerf, 3rd edn, 1989), pp. 89-93; A. and C. Guillaumont, *Évagre le Pontique: Le Traité practique ou le moine* (SC 170; Paris: Cerf, 1971), pp. 63-84; A. Louth, 'Envy as the Chief Sin in Athanasius and Gregory of Nyssa' (*Studia Patristica* 15, *TU* 128; Berlin: Akademie Verlag, 1984), pp. 458-60.

[132] *Prak.* 14.

significant as they must be tackled sequentially beginning with gluttony,[134] although he does not hold rigidly to this. For example, the demons[135] inspiring gluttony, avarice and vainglory (ἡ τῶν ἀνθρώπων δόξα) are said to attack the monk first, followed by the rest once he is wounded. He equates these three λογισμοί with Christ's temptation in the wilderness and says it is not possible to drive the devil away unless they are despised.[136] The eight λογισμοί broadly affect in turn each of the three parts of the ψυχή identified by Evagrius:[137] the fleshly λογισμοί of gluttony, fornication and avarice attack the ἐπιθυμητικόν (desiring) part; the more inward or psychological λογισμοί of grief, anger and ἀκηδία the θυμικόν (irascible) part; and the more spiritual λογισμοί of vainglory and pride the λογικόν (reasoning) part.[138] The νοῦς is the *locus* of the monk's struggle with the demons[139] and it must be freed from sin so that their attacks can be countered effectively with the appropriate pieces of Scripture (the basic premise of the *Antirrheticus*).[140] Evagrius says that monks cannot prevent λογισμοί from disturbing the ψυχή, but it is within their power to control whether they linger or arouse passions.[141] The monk's battle against the λογισμοί and demons therefore requires that he exercise διάκρισις, discerning the nature of the attack and choosing whether to succumb or not.

---

[133]   Περὶ Λογ. 1. Cf. Gregory the Great, *moralia in Iob* 31.45.87: *vitiorum regina superbia* ('the queen of all the vices is pride').

[134]   Περὶ Λογ. 1; *antirr.* prol. E.g. a monk will succumb to the λογισμός of fornication if he is subject to gluttony (*de octo* 4; cf. *antirr.* 5.30). See also e.g. *prak.* 10 (cf. *Schol.* 313 in Prov. 25:20) and *prak.* 19. The eight λογισμοί form the structure of *antirr.* and *de orat.* (where ὀργή and λύπη are reversed as in Cassian, *inst.* 7 and 8). Pityrion also taught that λογισμοί needed to be conquered in order (*HM* 15.3).

[135]   Evagrius tends to use λογισμοί and demons somewhat interchangeably. When he introduces the eight λογισμοί he speaks of demonic attack indicating the close relation between λογισμοί and the demons that inspire them. He also says that the demons attack anchorites more severely than cœnobites and clearly understands the anchoritic life to be more advanced (*prak.* 5; cf. Περὶ Λογ. 11). Λογισμοί and demons are also closely associated in *ep.* 4.4 where διάκρισις is used to oppose demons inciting λογισμοί.

[136]   Περὶ Λογ. 1. John Climacus (c.579-649) also comments on the eight vices and on this three producing the rest in his step on discernment (*scala parad.* 26. Avarice is not explicitly mentioned here but is identified as one of the three in *ibid.* 17).

[137]   *Prak.* 86; cf. *prak.* 54, *schol.* 127 in Prov. 11:17, *schol.* 72 in Eccles. 11:10.

[138]   Cf. Cassian, *conf.* 24.15.3-4.

[139]   *Antirr.* prol. Λογισμοί darken the νοῦς (especially anger, *prak.* 23-24) and keep it from trusting God (*antirr.* 4.61). On the νοῦς as the *locus* of this struggle, see above p. 49, n. 77.

[140]   'But whenever there is no sin actually in the *nous*, one is able to make answer to the evil one and sin is easily and quickly conquered.' (*antirr.* prol.).

[141]   *Prak.* 6. On the inevitability of attack by λογισμοί and the power to resist them see below, pp. 155-56.

Evagrius stresses the need to discern λογισμοί in the inner person:

Discern [δίκαζε] the λογισμοί in the sanctuary of the καρδία ... for he who is a precise examiner of the λογισμοί is also a true lover of the commandments.[142]

He goes on to warn the monk against being deceived by the demons into thinking that he is prudent, advising him to inspect his καρδία closely and to fight against the λογισμοί he finds there, guarding his senses. Similarly, when the monk advances from being πρακτικός to γνωστικός he is warned to guard against pride in his achievement using 'wise counsel and διάκρισις.'[143] Elsewhere Evagrius says that 'watchfulness and διάκρισις' are needed for purity.[144] The self-examination and watchfulness necessary to overcome λογισμοί and deceit are frequently said to be achieved using διάκρισις in the apophthegms as well.[145] A similar watchfulness using διάκρισις is found in Evagrius' teaching on how it is necessary to consider words carefully before speaking: 'listening to reasons, ask your νοῦς and then having discerned [διακρίνω] you will be ready to give the decree.'[146] Διάκρισις should, then, be used to weigh words heard and spoken. These deliberations take place in the νοῦς where a considered and increasingly intuitive response is formulated. Similarly, commenting on Ecclesiastes 3:18 (LXX) where God is said to judge (διακρίνω) human speech, Evagrius says:

Now he called man's speech his life, since we will give account for every idle word on the day of judgment [cf. Matthew 12.36], on which both the pure and the impure are made manifest.[147]

The monk should, then, use διάκρισις to discern what he says and choose to speak only what is pure.[148] Διάκρισις is thus central to overcoming λογισμοί and advancing towards purity. It is also used as an instrument of debate within the νοῦς to weigh situations and choose how to respond.

---

[142] *Tract. ad Eulog.* 12.
[143] *Ibid.* 24.
[144] *De orat.* 147 (φυλακή καὶ διάκρισις).
[145] See below on watchfulness, pp. 166-71.
[146] *Tract. ad Eulog.* 21; Evagrius teaches about the danger of careless talk, how to suffer abuse and not holding grudges in this passage.
[147] *Schol.* 20 in Eccles. 3:18.
[148] Cf. *schol.* 298 in Prov. 31:9 where διάκρισις is also used of identifying what is pure.

To achieve inner purity the monk must 'utterly destroy evil λογισμοί from his καρδία'.[149] To do this it is necessary to discern the origin of λογισμοί using careful observation to determine whether they derive from angelic, demonic or human origins.[150] Such observation enables the monk to understand the cunning of demons and how the λογισμοί operate, interact and produce different results.[151] Dysinger argues convincingly that Evagrius uses medical language and theory, not least in relation to this keen empirical interior observation.[152] Since the term διάκρισις is extensively used in Classical medical texts for the diagnosis of illness[153] and for the crisis or turning point in an illness,[154] it follows that this interior observation leads to the diagnosis of the monk's inner state and provides the turning point from spiritual illness to spiritual health. By determining which demons lie behind the λογισμοί attacking him, the monk is capable of advancing more easily towards God and defeating his spiritual enemies.[155] However, Evagrius explains that some right λογισμοί are not opposed by demons but by the monk's personal vices[156] and so it is necessary to determine when wrong λογισμοί have a human source. For example, if anger is not resolved before retiring it disturbs the νοῦς at

---

[149] *Ad mon.* 45; cf. *de orat.* 4.

[150] Περὶ Λογ. 8: angelic thoughts concern the true nature of things and the spiritual reasons for them, demonic thoughts know nothing of these and human thoughts only call the image of a thing to mind without passion or greed. Λογισμοί threaten the νοῦς with total destruction and so determining their source is vital for the monk (*antirr.* 5.30), those suggested by demons produce turmoil but can always be rejected, those by angels produce peace but can only sometimes be rejected (*prak.* 80). The angels are said to rejoice in the increase of ἀρεταί and come to fill the monk with spiritual θεωρία, whereas the demons rejoice in the opposite and cast lewd fantasies into the ψυχή (*prak.* 76, cf. *de orat.* 81).

[151] *Prak.* 50. E.g. all the demons teach the ψυχή to love pleasure except λύπη, which cuts off pleasure from it making the monk more resolute if attacked moderately, but encouraging him to give up his way of life if it attacks more severely (Περὶ Λογ. 12). It therefore follows that a monk would need to use διάκρισις to analyse any spiritual attack, to identify which pleasures are wrong for him and to respond to the attack in such a way that he advances towards his goals and not away from them.

[152] Dysinger, 'The Relationship between Psalmody and Prayer', pp. 107-15.

[153] E.g. Hippocrates, *de semine* 3 (αἱ ἐκ νούσων διακρίσιες, 'the crises of sicknesses'); Soranus, *Gynaeciorum libri iv* 3.23.1 (ἡ διάκρισις τῆς σημειώσεως, 'diagnosis of symptoms'). Διάκρισις is also used extensively by Galen. Pachomius uses διάκρισις to distinguish between different types of illness (*vit. Pach.* G[1] 52) and how best to treat the sick (*ibid.* 53).

[154] Hippocrates, *coa praesagia* 133.

[155] *Prak.* 43.

[156] *Ibid.* 30.

night.[157] He then explains that the demons encourage the irascible part (θυμικόν) of the ψυχή to avoid resolving the problem and the desiring part (ἐπιθυμικὸν) to seek out company, but the monk should accede to neither.[158] The demons are thus regarded as seizing the opportunity presented by the monk's anger. To counter anger and the evil and deceptive behaviour it encourages, Evagrius recommends the antirrhetic use of 1 Corinthians 6:7b-8 to remind the monk of his own sinfulness.[159] Thus through discerning self-examination and the antirrhetic use of Scripture the monk gains a more accurate self-awareness of his own spiritual condition and can determine how to behave. Confronted, then, with a λογισμός the monk should analyse it, determine how it is affecting him and, once it is overcome, endeavour to determine how this was achieved so that he can assess his strength and advancement.[160] This process of tactical observation and analysis of λογισμοί as the monk weighs, identifies, diagnoses and determines their effects is expressive of the exercise of διάκρισις.

Reading Evagrius' summary of the eight λογισμοί[161] with διάκρισις in mind suggests that succumbing to them is a failure to exercise διάκρισις. For example: gluttony deceives the monk into thinking that his ascetic practice has given rise to his troubles;[162] fornication incites him to abandon self-control because it appears to be achieving nothing;[163] avarice and λύπη deceive him by undermining his confidence in God's provision[164] (i.e. he fails to discern the true nature of his troubles and the true value of self-control and renunciation). Διάκρισις enables the monk to see through distractions and, since it is the antithesis of deceit, deceptions and distracting cares that would divert him from his pursuit of his goals. Thus in prayer monks are encouraged to be acutely attentive to prevent distraction by cares[165] and even once λογισμοί have been overcome they should

---

[157] *Ibid.* 21.

[158] *Ibid.* 22. Cf. *KG* 1.68 where angels are said to be predominantly νοῦς, human beings ἐπιθυμία and demons θυμός.

[159] *Antirr.* 5.43.

[160] Περὶ Λογ. 19-20. Cf. *ep.* 4.5: this letter discusses the *Antirrheticus* and draws attention to how διάκρισις is essential for the monastic life and is developed using 'self-control, gentleness, watching, withdrawal and frequent prayers lifted up by readings from sacred Scriptures' so that πρακτική may be used to overcome λογισμοί and enter into γνῶσις of God.

[161] *Prak.* 6-14.

[162] *Ibid.* 7.

[163] *Ibid.* 8.

[164] *Ibid.* 9, 10.

[165] *De orat.* 9, cf. 70. Prayer should be perceptive (αἴσθησις) and not merely offered through habit (*ibid.* 41-42). Undistracted prayer is a persistent theme in Evagrius and the hallmark of a true monk (*ibid.* 43). E.g. he should be undistracted by

remain watchful, considering how this was achieved and continuing to reflect on whether they are being deceived by an easy victory:

> When you pray earnestly about λογισμοί examine, if they abate easily, how this happened, lest you suffer an ambush and you are deceived into delivering yourself.[166]

This alert watchfulness, self-examination and guarding against deceit when tackling λογισμοί is frequently associated with the exercise of διάκρισις elsewhere in the monastic literature and Evagrius evidently has this in mind too.[167]

Evagrius also warns against demonic deceit[168] in relation to πρακτική. He says demons try to encourage excessive ascetic acts, such as fasting while weakened by illness,[169] and so the monk needs to discern the degree of πρακτική appropriate for him. To achieve this, the monk needs to know his own ability and degree of advancement. For example, he needs to recognise his continuing need to weep over his sins rather than being deceived into thinking that this is no longer necessary[170] and to see the purifying value of his struggles.[171] Sometimes maintaining his discipline may be a struggle, such as when prayer is difficult or unanswered and he begins to entertain doubts, but he should understand that God uses this to teach him persistence in seeking true prayer.[172] The monk needs διάκρισις to discern his capabilities and status before God as well as the right level of πρακτική and the value of persevering.

As the monk advances in πρακτική he overcomes the passions.[173] For the results to be lasting, however, works of πρακτική need to be applied at the appropriate time and measure,[174] and to time and moderate their use would require discernment.[175] Vices are also said to be overcome by their

---

physical needs (*ibid.* 105-109) since trusting God for these is indicative of trusting him for spiritual needs (*ibid.* 129).

[166] *Ibid.* 133.

[167] See below, pp. 93-99 and pp. 150-66.

[168] Since the Devil is the 'father of lies' (Jn 8:44), demonic activity and deceit are natural partners.

[169] *Prak.* 40.

[170] *De orat.* 78-79.

[171] *Ibid.* 140.

[172] *Ibid.* 29, 34.

[173] *Prak.* 87. Cf. the antirrhetic use of Scripture to overcome λογισμοί in *Antirrheticus*.

[174] *Ibid.* 15. (= GSC 10.25 and parallels; see below, p. 148; see also p. 88).

[175] Διάκρισις would also be needed to ensure that works of πρακτική, intended for overcoming passions, do not become passions or ends in themselves (e.g. tears in prayer, *de orat.* 5-8).

opposing ἀρεταί[176] and so διάκρισις would similarly be needed to apply these. Evagrius says that the development of ἀρεταί is assisted by developing a hatred of demons, which God encourages through his providential abandonment of the monk to indulgences and suffering so that the ψυχή is compelled to return to its original hatred of demons; such perfect hatred is a sign of ἀπάθεια.[177] The combined use of anger and πρακτική against λογισμοί is also found.[178] Evagrius teaches also that one λογισμός can be used to defeat another.[179] He posits two καταστάσεις in the ψυχή deriving respectively from humility, compunction, tears and zeal for both God and the monastic discipline and from the withdrawal of the demons. As the monk approaches the first κατάστασις he becomes more acutely aware of the second,[180] which exposes him to the λογισμοί of vainglory and pride. He says, however, that the λογισμοί of vainglory and fornication cannot attack simultaneously since they promise opposing concepts of honour and disgrace and so he recommends using the one to oppose the other, something he regards as deriving from a highly advanced state of ἀπάθεια.[181] As the monk advances towards ἀπάθεια demonic opposition is said to increase and become more varied, but monks who scrutinise their temptations understand more clearly the attacks upon their ἀπάθεια,[182] which suggests that as the monk becomes more advanced he becomes more skilful in διάκρισις and better able to use his temptations to educate him in self-awareness. The opposition of λογισμοί using antirrhetic Scriptures, opposing ἀρεταί, perfect hatred, πρακτική and other λογισμοί would each require an understanding of how λογισμοί operate and the discernment of which measures to use to overcome them. Discernment would also be needed to appreciate the spiritual value and purpose of both providential abandonment and to learn from temptations suffered. Διάκρισις provides this insight.

---

[176] E.g. *prak.* 20 (anger and hatred overcome by mercy and meekness); *ibid.* 26 (charity and hospitality defeat resentment); *ibid.* 35, 38 (bodily passions overcome by self-control and passions of the ψυχή by ἀγάπη).

[177] Περὶ Λογ. 10. On the natural anger of the ψυχή against demons and λογισμοί see *prak.* 39. On the use of anger against λογισμοί see e.g. Περὶ Λογ. 16-17; *prak.* 24, 42. Evagrius lists five causes of abandonment in *gnos.* 28. His doctrine of providential abandonment (i.e. to lead the monk to repentance) ultimately derives from Origen (*de prin* 3.1.8ff; *de orat* 29.17) whose personal experience of abandonment by God drove him to seek God again (*hom. in Cant.* 1.7).

[178] Περὶ Λογ. 16.

[179] For the use of one sin to oppose another cf. Climacus, *scala parad.* 26 ('On Discernment') where an experienced monk breaks up what is understood to be a sinful homosexual relationship by telling each party that the other slanders him.

[180] *Prak.* 57; cf. *de orat.* 2.

[181] *Prak.* 58.

[182] *Ibid.* 59.

Διάκρισις is thus an essential weapon in the monk's armoury against the demons and the λογισμοί they incite, enabling him to understand what is happening within his νοῦς and ψυχή[183] and to weigh which suggestions and incitements are to be resisted or embraced. For example, demons arouse memories in the monk at prayer to disturb his νοῦς, distract him and make him dispirited[184] and so he is encouraged to guard his memory in prayer[185] and defend what he has gained through it.[186] For Evagrius, spiritual prayer is the arena of battle with the demons, who find it offensive because of the spiritual benefits it affords,[187] and who attack with λογισμοί expressly to weaken the νοῦς and keep the monk from both praying and seeking the Word of God.[188] Such careful weighing of memories and watchful guarding against demons and λογισμοί in prayer, which Evagrius regards as a central activity in the life of the monk, would require διάκρισις.

Διάκρισις and Scripture

Διάκρισις provides the monk with the ability to discern the deeper meaning of Scripture. Commenting on Psalm 15:9 (LXX) Evagrius says: 'He who believes is νοῦς, even anyone who discerns [διακρίνω] words concerning Job.'[189] This would appear to refer back an earlier comment concerning the noble use of good things (Job 2:10), which Evagrius identifies as ἀρεταί and γνῶσις,[190] and more particularly to his subsequent comments on Psalm 15:9 concerning the Holy Spirit who provides the gift of a tongue and also a body (Job 10:11).[191] This draws together a number of themes into association with διάκρισις and its use to understand the deeper meaning of Scripture and its salvific value. Διάκρισις is integral to faith and salvation. The probable back reference suggests διάκρισις is necessary for discerning the correct way to use ἀρεταί and γνῶσις. Finally, the forward reference associates διάκρισις with the activity of the Holy Spirit in the monk's life and quite probably spiritual gifts.

---

[183]   Evagrius says the monk should divide the ψυχή into two, each half encouraging the other (*prak.* 27) suggesting a discrimination and discernment characteristic of διάκρισις.
[184]   *De orat.* 10 and 46.
[185]   *Ibid.* 44.
[186]   *Ibid.* 48.
[187]   *Ibid.* 49.
[188]   *Ibid.* 50.
[189]   *Schol.* 4 in Ps. 15:9 (LXX) [*PG* 12.1216].
[190]   *Schol.* 1 in Ps. 15:1-2 (LXX) [*PG* 12.1209].
[191]   *Schol.* 5-6 in Ps. 15:9 (LXX) [*PG* 12.1216].

Monks need διάκρισις not only to discern the deeper meaning of Scripture, but also to teach it. Commenting on Psalm 111:5 (LXX)[192] he says:

> One must use the passage to those who thoughtlessly disclose the mysteries of sacred Scripture indiscriminately [ἀδιακρίτως]; for Paul says, "So then, let a man consider us as servants of Christ and as stewards of the mysteries of God." [1 Corinthians 4:1][193]

The exegesis of Scripture requires that the monk exercise διάκρισις and only disclose the meaning of Scripture for upright reasons and to those whom it is appropriate. Thus, for example, the more advanced monk or γνωστικός should not reveal the painful details of the Judgment to novices or seculars.[194]

Understanding of the deeper meaning of Scripture is gained through the intellective power of the νοῦς.[195] Since the νοῦς is the *locus operandi* of διάκρισις, διάκρισις plays an important role in discerning the meaning of the text.[196] Evagrius demonstrates διάκρισις of Scripture in selecting texts to be used antirrhetically against λογισμοί in his *Antirrheticus*.[197] Furthermore, any monk tackling a given λογισμός would need διάκρισις to discern both the nature of the λογισμός attacking him and which recommended text to use against it. Evagrius' adoption of Origen's

---

192   'The good man is he that pities and lends: he will direct his affairs with judgment (ἐν κρίσει).'

193   *Schol.* 4 in Ps. 111:5 (LXX) [Pitra, 111.5; *PG* 12.1572]. Cf. *gnos.* 24: 'Pay heed to yourself that you never, for the sake of profit, well-being or passing glory, talk of anything secret and (so) are thrown out of the holy precincts, as he who sold pigeon chicks in the temple [Mt. 21:12-13].' Origen similarly advises caution in selecting to whom, when and how to relate spiritual mysteries (*hom. in Num.* 27.12).

194   *Gnos.* 36. Cf. Origen, *cont. Cels.* 6.26. The monk should keep in mind the Last Judgment and the punishments of hell to help himself escape λογισμοί and strive for Heaven and its rewards (*rer. mon. rat.* 9).

195   *Schol.* 1 in Ps. 137:1 (LXX) [Pitra, 137.1]: ὁ νοῶν τὴν δύναμιν τῶν ψαλμῶν ('he who perceives with the mind the meaning of the psalms'). Evagrius does not regard the interpretation of Scripture as an intellective process alone; God teaches the monk through the words of Scripture and reveals to him the nature of existence (*KG* S² 2.73).

196   The search for the veiled meaning of Scripture has marked similarities with Origen (see above, pp. 34-35). Cf. Basil the Great's comment on Ps. 48:6 (LXX) that intelligence (σύνεσις) operating in the νοῦς discerns (διακρίνω) the words of Scripture as taste does food (quoting Job 12:11; *reg. brev.* 279).

197   *Antirr.* prol.; cf. *ep.* 4.1. These antirrhetic texts are generally taken literally and used to encourage the monk to hold to his discipline against the temptations he faces and so advance towards his goals.

teaching on the three books of Solomon to educate the monk in Ethics, Physics and Enoptics[198] so that he can advance towards his goals is applied to discerning the meaning of Scripture:

> He who widens his καρδία through purity will discern [νοήσει] the words of God, which are πρακτική, φυσική and θεολογική. For all diligent study concerning Scripture is divided into three parts: moral [ἠθική], φυσική and θεολογική. To the first relates Proverbs, to the second Ecclesiastes and to the third the Song of Songs.[199]

Thus, like Origen, Evagrius points to the need to develop an understanding of the specific value of each of these three books in order to discern the meaning of Scripture generally. They enable the monk to determine whether a text is to be understood allegorically, literally or theologically and to which stage (πρακτική, φυσική or θεολογική) they apply.[200] By using νοέω ('perceive with the mind') to describe how the καρδία perceives the meaning, Evagrius locates the process of discernment (or διάκρισις) of meaning in the νοῦς. Διάκρισις is thus the tool by which the monk interprets and applies Scripture to his life for the purposes of spiritual progression towards his goals. It enables him to teach Scripture appropriately as well as to use it to counter λογισμοί in his own life.

Διάκρισις and Revelation

Evagrius teaches that, even if they cannot see them, people are surrounded by angels and demons:

> The angels see men and demons; men are deprived of the sight of angels and demons, and the demons only see men.[201]

There is a hierarchy of visual ability here which encourages the individual to value the watchful care of angels. Similarly, Evagrius also describes a hierarchy of providential care: God mediates his care through Christ then through angels,[202] but the demons oppose the angels not wishing human beings to be saved.[203] His view of the opposing roles and influences of the angels and demons can be demonstrated by the following:

---

[198]   See above, p. 47.
[199]   *Schol.* 247 in Prov. 22:40. Cf. *prak.* 1.
[200]   *Gnos.* 18.
[201]   *KG* 6.69. Cf. *antirr.* 4.27.
[202]   *Schol.* 38 in Eccles. 5:7-11.
[203]   *Schol.* 7 in Ps. 16:13 (LXX) [Pitra 16.7; *PG* 12.1221].

Angels guide the ψυχαί of the righteous, but demons shall seize the ψυχαί of the evil.[204]

An angelic dream cheers a καρδία, but a demonic dream throws it into confusion.[205]

Thus in addition to discerning the human, angelic or demonic origin of λογισμοί,[206] the monk needs to discern the respective influences of angels and demons. He also needs to determine his own spiritual condition, since this affects their influence on him. Angels guide and support the pure monk, but demons seek to distract him if he is impure. Thus when the monk examines his λογισμοί this process requires that he understand how angels and demons affect his world and how he is unable to influence theirs,[207] that is to say, he needs to discern how the spiritual realm operates and interacts with him. A pure monk that has attained ἀπάθεια does not suffer from dreams that derive from memories aroused by demons, but memories may still come from himself or from angels and so he needs to distinguish between these and respond accordingly.[208] Similarly, demons may seek to terrify him with false prophecy[209] or perhaps deceive him by appearing to him in human guise[210] and so he needs discern the spiritual background to his experiences. Evagrius esteems angels for their ἀρετή[211] and equates the monk whose νοῦς has attained ἀπάθεια with the incorporeal angelic state.[212] Thus as a monk develops ἀρεταί and approaches his proximate goal, he becomes more like the angels. Accordingly, Evagrius calls monks to imitate angels and become their equals in true prayer and the desire to see God.[213] This would not only require discernment of the nature of angels but also of what should be understood by imitating them, as John Kolobos discovered to his cost.[214] It follows, then, that the monk needs to use διάκρισις to distinguish the guidance of angels from the deceptions of demons, to discern their nature and to determine when something comes from neither but from within himself.

---

[204]   *Ad mon.* 23.
[205]   *Ibid.* 52.
[206]   See above, pp. 58-59.
[207]   Περὶ Λογ. 19.
[208]   *Ibid.* 4.
[209]   *Antirr.* 4.53.
[210]   *KG* 1.22.
[211]   *Ibid.* 5.47.
[212]   *Ibid.* 1.85; cf. 1.68.
[213]   *De orat.* 39, 113.
[214]   John Kolobos 2 (discussed further below, p. 133).

Διάκρισις and Prudence (Φρόνησις)

Φρόνησις carries the sense of intellect, understanding, wisdom and opinion,[215] as well as thought, sense and judgment, while its cognate φρονέω can mean to feel by experience and consider or ponder,[216] as such it touches on the meaning of διάκρισις (judgment and choice). While φρόνησις and διάκρισις are clearly not synonymous, the similarities in meaning and the contexts in which Evagrius uses φρόνησις suggest a close relationship. This suggestion is confirmed by his remarks in his fourth letter:

> For just as φρόνησις delivers right judgment of deeds, in the same way διάκρισις is believed [to judge rightly] the fantasies concerning the mind [διάνοια], distinguishing between [διακρίνω] holy and profane, and pure and impure λογισμοί.[217]

Furthermore, φρόνησις, like διάκρισις, is said to be the means by which the monk weighs how to use good and evil things, which respectively produce ἀρεταί and vices:

> According to their use things which are good and evil produce ἀρεταί and vices; but it remains for φρόνησις to use them either way.[218]

Evagrius opens a discussion on almsgiving by saying 'you must be prudent [φρονέω] in charity'[219] and goes on to explain that monks are to avoid being deceived by demons[220] into the λογισμοί of avarice and vainglory. This is how διάκρισις is used to weigh motives, overcome deceit and counter λογισμοί. Furthermore, describing wisdom as θεωρία of the corporeal and incorporeal, Evagrius says that wisdom consists of φρόνησις, γνῶσις, instruction and intelligence.[221] The close link between wisdom, γνῶσις and διάκρισις has already been noted[222] and encourages a close association of φρόνησις with διάκρισις. Φρόνησις is an ἀρετή acquired, along with wisdom and intelligence, by the righteous whose νοῦς is unclouded by sin.[223] It produces ἀπάθεια[224] and is closely associated with the acquisition

---

215 Lampe, pp. 1490-91.
216 L&S, pp. 1955-56.
217 *Ep.* 4.4.
218 *Prak.* 88.
219 *Rer. mon. rat.* 4; cf. *ad virg.* 36.
220 Cf. *ad mon.* 123: 'Wisdom recognises the dogmas of demons, but φρόνησις searches out their craftiness.' Cf. *ep.* 4.4.
221 *Schol.* 88 in Prov. 7:4.
222 See above (pp. 45-47 and nn. 47 and 52) on Περὶ Λογ. 26.
223 *Schol.* 8 in Prov. 1:13.

of γνῶσις, ἀρεταί, right doctrine and wisdom.[225] Thus, like διάκρισις, φρόνησις is used of making right decisions, discerning natural and spiritual things, of determining true doctrine and of assisting the monk towards his goals. For Evagrius, φρόνησις derives from ἀρετή in the reasoning (λογιστικός) part of the ψυχή and its task is to conduct the campaign against vice and defend ἀρετή.[226] Similarly, φρόνησις is said to be an essential guide to the ψυχή in its battle against the demons and the acquisition of wisdom and ἀνάπαυσις.[227] This again is strikingly similar to the role of διάκρισις as it guides the monk in his fight against the demons and λογισμοί, and helps him to weigh and use different situations to achieve his goals. Φρόνησις is further said to derive from fear of the Lord, which is itself born of faith in Christ and guardian of the ψυχή:

Fear of the Lord will preserve the ψυχή and good self-control will strengthen it.[228]

Fear of the Lord produces φρόνησις and faith in Christ grants fear of God.[229]

This association of φρόνησις with the guarded ψυχή, self-control (a necessary part of πρακτική) and faith again has great similarities with the functions of διάκρισις. Finally, just as διάκρισις is highly valued in the apophthegms,[230] so also is φρόνησις in Evagrius: 'Γνῶσις of wisdom is above gold; and γνῶσις of φρόνησις is above silver.'[231] Φρόνησις is one

---

[224] *Ad mon.* 68; cf. 105.

[225] *Schol.* 64 in Prov. 5:18. Cf. *ad mon.* 125 where heretical doctrines are described as 'angels of death' and 126: 'There is no φρόνησις and there is no wisdom in their words.'

[226] *Prak.* 89. Evagrius describes the monk as an athlete or combatant (ἀγωνιστής) in *de orat.* 92 (cf. 106). This widespread image, which is also used by Origen (e.g. *cont. Cels.* 1.69; 6.72; *exhort. ad mart.* 18) and in the apophthegms (e.g. Arsenius 15; Nau 34, 172, 215, 406), is picked up by Cassian (*inst.* 5.12-19; 8.22; 10.5; 11.19; 12.32; *conf.* 7.20; 13.14).

[227] *Prak.* 73; ἀνάπαυσις is a rest associated with heaven and union with God.

[228] *Ad mon.* 4.

[229] *Ibid.* 69.

[230] See chapters 4 and 5.

[231] *Schol.* 146 in Prov. 16:16. In ancient Egypt during the Old Kingdom (2686-2181BC) silver was a rare import more highly valued than gold, however by the Middle Kingdom (2055-1650BC) increased availability made silver less valuable than gold. (I. Shaw and P. Nicholson (eds), *British Museum Dictionary of Ancient Egypt* (London: British Museum Press, 1995), pp. 270-71). During Late Antiquity there was a scarcity of silver in Egypt (Egypt had its own coinage minted in Alexandria and the silver content in coins was gradually reduced during the period)

68 Discernment in the Desert Fathers

of the four cardinal ἀρεταί, (the others being courage, self-control and justice[232]) which Evagrius says he learnt from Gregory of Nazianzus[233] and which need to be kept complete and in balance.[234] Since διάκρισις will be seen to be regarded as overarching and first among all the ἀρεταί[235] it may be said to govern φρόνησις and keep it in balance with other ἀρεταί. Thus φρόνησις, while part of διάκρισις, is used by Evagrius to serve in place of διάκρισις and on this basis his understanding of the role of διάκρισις is in keeping with that found elsewhere in the monastic literature.

The Guarding and Guiding Role of Διάκρισις

Διάκρισις is used to guard and guide the inward state and outward activity of the monk. For example, if a monk has wronged another he needs to discern his attitude towards that person and his own status before God and to be guided towards reconciliation with the person he has wronged:

> If he who needs nothing and is impartial did not accept the one who approached the altar with a gift until he was reconciled to his neighbour who was grieved by him [Matthew 5:23-24], consider how much guarding [φυλακή] and διάκρισις we need, if we are to offer incense at the intellectual [νοητός] altar acceptable to God.[236]

The saying before this focuses on the need of a pure νοῦς for true prayer and here the offering of prayer made within the νοῦς (νοητός) requires the use of διάκρισις as a guard and guide. The monk, using the counsel of διάκρισις, is thus encouraged to reflect on how to maintain good relations with others, to maintain a watch (φυλακή) over himself and to keep his νοῦς pure so that he can offer true prayer. Given the importance of prayer

---

and the relative bullion value of silver and gold was highly volatile, with gold being more valuable (R. Bagnall, *Egypt in Late Antiquity* (Princeton: Princeton University Press, 1993), pp. 330-32 and R. Bagnall, *Currency and Inflation in Fourth Century Egypt* (Bulletin of the American Society of Papyrologists, Supplements 5; Chico, CA: Scholars Press, 1985), esp. pp. 57-62). Thus although silver was more highly prized than gold in ancient Egypt and more scarce in Late Antique Egypt, which might suggest that Evagrius valued φρόνησις more highly than γνῶσις, this cannot be justified given Late Antique bullion values. Evagrius must therefore be adopting the Scriptural estimate of gold being more precious than silver, as does Cassian after him (*conf.* 23.3.2), making γνῶσις, more highly valued than φρόνησις.

[232] Cf. Gregory the Great, *mor. in Iob* 2.49.76; Thomas Aquinas, *Summa Theologiae* 2.1.61.2.
[233] *Gnos.* 44
[234] *De orat.* 1.
[235] Cassian, *conf.* 1.23.1 (see below, p. 84).
[236] *De orat.* 147. Cf. Rom. 12:1-2.

and purity (inward and outward) in Evagrian theology, διάκρισις is given a crucial role here.

The importance of this watchfulness, associated with the role of διάκρισις, is found throughout the Evagrian corpus. For example, the monk is told: 'Watch yourself so that you never drive away any of the brothers by provoking him to anger.'[237] Similar watchfulness is evident in Evagrius' advice to monks mixing with townspeople; they should hold on strongly to self-control because at such times the νοῦς is in danger of being distracted by demons.[238] Evagrius then describes how demons watch the monk seeking to discover his areas of weakness or neglect with a view to destroying his ψυχή, leading him into blasphemy, interrupting his zeal and causing him to abandon prayer.[239] However, by observing his own words and actions the monk is able to discover whether his ψυχή has been affected by λογισμοί.[240] Finally, Evagrius contrasts seculars, who are tempted through material things, with monks who have renounced such things and are tempted through λογισμοί, which he says is a harder battle because it is easier to sin in intent than in deed and the νοῦς is easily moved.[241] This call to constant vigilance,[242] self-control and watchful self-examination in the struggle to maintain purity and against demons and λογισμοί indicates that διάκρισις needs to be exercised continually.

This observational watchfulness using διάκρισις can be illustrated by Evagrius' advice on avoiding the temptation to wander from the cell. He describes at length the activity of a demon he calls the wanderer or deceiver (πλάνος) which he says leads the νοῦς from place to place and person to person drawing it away from γνῶσις of God and making it forget ἀρετή. Monks are told to watch this demon, noting its origin and activity, but to avoid speaking to it (i.e. antirrhetically) or to other monks about it, presumably because this would encourage its activity. Instead, the monk is told to let it carry on inciting him so that he can learn about its deceitfulness in detail and then put it to flight with a mental rebuke, not least because it hates exposure. During such an attack the νοῦς is said to be clouded and so only after the demon has fled is it possible to reflect on what has happened. This close observation makes the monk aware of his weak spots and

---

[237] *Prak.* 25.

[238] *Ibid.* 41.

[239] *Ibid.* 44-46. Cassian (*conf.* 7.15) also says that the demons act on external symptoms. Since demons are created, they may be said to be incapable of creating but rather corrupt what has already been created. See also below, p. 158 and n. 159.

[240] *Prak.* 47. God, however, knows the νοῦς and needs no such indicative symptoms.

[241] *Ibid.* 48.

[242] On the need for constant vigilance see also *de orat.* 138: 'Expect grievous demonic attacks considering how you might keep far from slavery by them.'

therefore better able to counter future attacks.[243] This saying provides a detailed example of how διάκρισις is used to guard and guide the monk. It enables him to identify the nature and origin of a spiritual attack, expose deceit, determine an appropriate response and to observe and reflect on λογισμοί to gain a clearer understanding of himself and of demonic activity.

The problem of wandering mentally or physically is combated by residence in the cell, which in the apophthegms is regarded as essential to πρακτική and spiritual advancement towards the monk's goals.[244] Just as the prudent monk (i.e. the monk with διάκρισις[245]) should take care of 'the tools of his craft'[246] (i.e. his πρακτική) and guard his tongue,[247] that is use διάκρισις to guard his behaviour, he should also use it to watch over the use of his cell. When tempted, the monk should never leave his cell however plausible the pretext[248] because distractions and the resultant temptations will undermine his resolve:

> Do not let distractions (and) desire vanquish your resolution, for "distraction with desire undermines a guileless νοῦς." [Wisdom 4:12] Many temptations come through this. Fear the defeat and be steadfast in your cell.[249]

Frequent absences from the cell are said to rob the monk of ἡσυχία[250] and so he should remain there concentrating his νοῦς on death, judgment, heaven and its rewards so as not to be distracted from his path.[251] However, remaining in the cell is only a general rule and the monk also needs to

---

[243] Περὶ Λογ. 9. Cf. *prak.* 50 re the respective activities of different demons and observation of λογισμοί by monks skilled in πρακτική who thus become more acquainted with demonic cunning and able to resist through knowledge of their activity, something demons hate.

[244] On the cell, see below, pp. 171-75.

[245] See above, pp. 66-68.

[246] *Ad mon.* 79. Bunge describes πρακτική as a true art and science for examining thoughts which, he says, is what Scripture calls διάκρισις πνευμάτων, and for which teaching, experience and self-observation are required. This 'spiritual method' ('*geistliche Methode*'), as he calls it, requires works of πρακτική, including watchfulness, and is a devoted development of the principles that monks found in Scripture (Bunge, *Evagrios Pontikos*, pp. 123-24).

[247] *Ad mon.* 94.

[248] *Prak.* 28.

[249] *Rer. mon. rat.* 6.

[250] *Ibid.* 7, 8.

[251] *Ibid.* 9. Monks are also advised to live as if they were about to die, countering ἀκηδία and maintaining zeal, yet also as those who will live for many years, encouraging self-control (*prak.* 29).

discern when it is better to leave it, for example if he is becoming too attached to it:

> If you admire the cell in which you live, flee, pay it no heed, do not give way to love of it; do everything, accomplish everything, do all you can to be still and at rest, and to become zealous in the will of God and in the battle against the invisible (enemies).[252]

The monk thus needs διάκρισις to discern his relationship with his cell. He uses διάκρισις to discern its purpose and value as well as any potential danger, and so διάκρισις guards and guides him in its use.

Watchfulness extends beyond the external and physical, since the overall object is to avoid or surmount inner obstacles to spiritual advancement. Evagrius illustrates guarding against the hidden dangers of λογισμοί and being guided through them with the metaphor of a hidden reef on which the monk could flounder:

> Vainglory is an underwater rock, if you run into it you lose the ship's cargo. A prudent [φρόνιμος] man hides his treasure and the intelligent monk his labours of ἀρετή.[253]

The prudent monk thus guards the ἀρεταί he has gained and needs to be guided through the unseen perils of λογισμοί.[254] If he fails to be watchful or to rely on angelic assistance he loses γνῶσις of God.[255] However, living as he should, the monk is not only guarded and guided by angels, God makes the νοῦς (where διάκρισις operates) his guide[256] and the Holy Spirit watches over his thoughts to condemn or approve them.[257] The Godhead thus instructs, judges and guides the monk's inner being. Commenting on the judgment (κρίσις) loved by God in Psalm 32:5 (LXX)[258] Evagrius explains that this means someone who is discerning (διακριτικός)[259] and he expounds the διακρίνω text, Psalm 49:4 (LXX), in terms of the Last Judgment.[260] Thus, for Evagrius, διάκρισις is the quality of just and upright

---

[252] *Rer. mon. rat.* 5 (= Athanasius, *vit. mon. inst.* 3). The cell might be left because of the distraction of continual interruptions (Arsenius 32).

[253] *De octo* 16.

[254] To protect his inner life, the monk must also guard constantly against mental images (νοήματα) that would make him prey to passions (Περὶ Λογ. 17).

[255] *Antirr.* prol.

[256] Περὶ Λογ. 3.

[257] *Ibid.* 7.

[258] [Ὁ κύριος] ἀγαπᾷ ἐλεημοσύνην καὶ κρίσιν. ('[The Lord] loves mercy and judgment.')

[259] *Schol.* 4 in Ps. 32:5 (LXX) [*PG* 12.1304].

[260] *Schol.* 3 in Ps. 49:4 (LXX) [Pitra, 49.4].

decision making perfectly exemplified in the ultimate justice of God and by developing διάκρισις the monk imitates God and comes closer to his image and character. The guarding and guiding role of διάκρισις thus operates within the νοῦς in cooperation with God and the monk grows more like God in διάκρισις as he advances towards his goals.

These hidden obstacles, which the monk tackles using διάκρισις with God's help, are seen as the snares of his spiritual enemy. The monk is warned to 'guard against the traps of his enemies' and not be deceived by apparent manifestations of the Divine when engaged in pure and undistracted prayer, since God is transcendent and not to be limited to a vision.[261] Such a distraction, Evagrius says, begins in the νοῦς and it is vainglory to attempt to give the Divine form.[262] For Evagrius, prayer is so valuable that it should not be distracted even by the presence of angels[263] and so he warns monks never to long to see angels, spiritual powers or Christ lest they be deceived by demons.[264] The monk guards against such demonic deceit by calling on God to enlighten him as to the source of a vision and using supplication to drive away anything that does not derive from him.[265] If a monk fails to mount such a guard he is in danger of being deceived into accepting 'smoke instead of light' in his pursuit of γνῶσις.[266] So he is told to stand guard over his νοῦς during prayer and protect it from such perceptions.[267] This need of alert watchfulness to identify the spiritual source of visions and to avoid visualising God, being deceived, falling into vainglory or false doctrine and to guard the νοῦς is the function of διάκρισις in the apophthegms as it guides the monk through his experiences.[268] For Evagrius 'it is impossible for ... the νοῦς enslaved by passions to see the place of spiritual prayer'[269] because it is distracted and so lacks stability. It follows, then, that διάκρισις is needed not only to overcome the passions and facilitate pure prayer, but also to guard and maintain that prayer against unseen dangers.

The need to be watchful and weigh spiritual experience carefully in order to avoid deceit can be seen in Evagrius' understanding of how the demons operate. For example, he warns that demons can sometimes divide into two

---

[261] *De orat.* 67. Monks should not seek any form of vision in prayer (*ibid.* 114).
[262] *Ibid.* 116. This is a warning to be humble as well as a theological statement about the incorporeal nature of God. The same advice to disregard spiritual manifestations is found in the apophthegms where there is a humble reluctance to assume readily that revelations are of Divine origin and so revelations need careful διάκρισις.
[263] *Ibid.* 112.
[264] *Ibid.* 115.
[265] *Ibid.* 94.
[266] *Ibid.* 68.
[267] *Ibid.* 69.
[268] See chapters 4 and 5.
[269] *De orat.* 71.

parties, one driving the other off when the monk cries for help in order to deceive him into thinking his rescuers are angels.[270] Similarly, demons can suggest λογισμοί, encourage the monk to pray against them and then withdraw the attack voluntarily so that he imagines he is victorious over both.[271] Alongside this inward struggle, demons are said to mount outward attacks through relationships with others. For instance, when a monk helps one person another will harm him and the demons use this to incite a sense of injustice that destroys the good he has achieved.[272] Similarly, demons are said to switch from direct attack at night to 'assaults, slanders and dangers' through other people during the day.[273] If his relationships with others are to remain upright, the monk needs to distinguish between the demonic source of an attack and the human agent used to mount it.[274] Such an understanding of what is happening in the spiritual realm and guarding against deceit would require the charism of διάκρισις.

As the monk advances in ἀρεταί he is counselled and guided by his perfected and passionless νοῦς more and more intuitively as a direct result of its perfected condition:

> The one who has established ἀρεταί in himself and is completely united with them no longer remembers the law, commandments or punishment, but says and accomplishes these things as much as his excellent state of mind suggests.[275]

If it is accepted that the νοῦς is *locus operandi* of διάκρισις, it follows that as διάκρισις develops in the νοῦς it too becomes increasingly intuitive. In Plato the highest level of mental activity was νόησις,[276] the realm of pure thought that leads to a vision of ultimate truth. This highest stage is, in a sense, intuitive knowledge, a knowing that no longer requires impressions, empirical evidence or deductive reasoning. Operating, then, within the νοῦς, διάκρισις may be understood as the highest spiritual and intellectual human faculty with which it is possible to sense what is right without the need to analyse or reason. Since διάκρισις is more fully endowed in union with God,[277] it may be said that this intimate knowledge of God transforms

---

[270] *Ibid.* 95.

[271] *Ibid.* 134.

[272] *Ibid.* 137.

[273] *Ibid.* 139.

[274] The monk should 'consider all men as God after God' (*de orat.* 123) i.e. as made in God's image and therefore to be respected; cf. the Anthropomorphite controversy (see above, pp. 35-36).

[275] *Prak.* 70. Cf. *KG* 6.21.

[276] Plato, *rep.* 7.6-7.7, 509d-521b (see above, p. 17, n. 116 and pp. 44-45, 49-50).

[277] See above, pp. 45-47.

the mind of the believer (cf. Romans 12:2) so that he instinctively makes choices in keeping with God's will and nature by using διάκρισις. Διάκρισις thus acts as a constant guide to the monk in all aspects of his spiritual life, growing stronger as he approaches union with God.

Although Evagrius only uses διάκρισις and its cognates on a few occasions,[278] he uses them in a manner consistent with Scripture but reflecting the developing technical sense found in Origen as a charism and ἀρετή used in the mystical search for God. Διάκρισις is described as a Divine gift essential for the monastic life and integral to the exercise of πρακτική and the pursuit and acquisition of ἀπάθεια and γνῶσις, the monk's goals. It is a strategic tool used to discern the presence or absence of γνῶσις and of purity which enables him to weigh not only what is heard and spoken but also to exercise right judgment and decision making in imitation of God. Διάκρισις guards and guides his inward and outward life enabling him to overcome λογισμοί, maintain a pure νοῦς and offer true prayer acceptable to God. It is also essential for the correct interpretation, exegesis and teaching of Scripture and is integral to faith, salvation and the right use of ἀρεταί and γνῶσις. It has an elevated status associated with the Holy Spirit and his activity in the life of the monk. It may also be associated with the spiritual gifts and Evagrius himself was noted for his διάκρισις πνευμάτων as well as διάκρισις λογισμῶν. While the word-group is not used extensively, Evagrius' writings, which he clearly intends should be read with διάκρισις, consistently bear out these same principles, an impression strengthened by the close relationship between διάκρισις and φρόνησις. Thus διάκρισις may be said to be at the centre of Evagrian spirituality.

---

[278] Περὶ Λογ. 26 (*bis*); *de orat.* 147; *tract ad Eulog.* 21, 24; *ep.* 4.4-5; *schol.* 4 in Ps. 15:9 (LXX) [*PG* 12.1216]; *schol.* 4 in Ps. 32:5 (LXX) [*PG* 12.1304]; *schol.* 3 in Ps. 49:4 (LXX) [Pitra, 49.4] (quoted in Bible verse); *schol.* 4 in Ps. 111:5 (LXX) [Pitra, 111.5; *PG* 12.1572]; *schol.* 298 in Prov. 31:9 (= *Expositio in Proverbia Salomonis*, p. 112, ln 13; quoted in Bible verse); *schol.* 20 in Eccles. 3:18 (quoted in Bible verse); *schol.* 16-17 in Job 12:11; and possibly in *epistula ad Melaniam* 2, 3, 7, 17 and 25. Evagrius also uses διακρίνω in two quotations of Prov. 31:9 in *Expositio in Proverbia Salomonis*, p. 76, lln. 13, 17 during a discussion of the critical marks in LXX.

CHAPTER 3

Discretio in John Cassian

It is valuable to consider John Cassian next for a number of reasons. He visited the monks in the Egyptian desert and wrote later of his experiences, was the successor to Evagrius Ponticus and had a significant impact on Western monastic rules,[1] being regarded as an authority on monasticism. A brief overview of his life serves to establish his significance in understanding early monastic life in Egypt.

There can be no straightforward biographical sketch for Cassian because the details of his life are elusive, as uncertain as his name,[2] and can only be arrived at by deduction. He was probably born in the early 360's, but where is uncertain because he only provides vague details.[3] The current balance of opinion is weighted towards Scythia Minor,[4] which as a bilingual region would explain Cassian's skill in both Latin and Greek[5] and therefore his ability to fulfil his expressed intention of presenting Eastern monasticism and theology to a Western audience.[6] Cassian began his monastic life in a cœnobium in Bethlehem[7] with his older close friend and compatriot

---

[1]   For example, Benedict recommends reading the *Conferences* and *Institutes* (and also the *Lives of the Fathers*) and these are assumed to be those of Cassian (*reg. Ben.* 42 and 73). It is worthy of note that Gregory the Great wrote that Benedict's rule was 'conspicuous for its *discretio*' (*dial.* 2.36).

[2]   His contemporaries call him Cassianus (e.g. Gennadius, *de vir. inl.* 62; Sozomen, *HE* 8.26.8), which may have been his given name, but he refers to himself by name only twice and then as Iohannes (*inst.* 5.35; *conf.* 14.9.4), which may have been his monastic name.

[3]   E.g. *conf.* 24.1.3; 24.8.5.

[4]   Reading Gennadius, *de vir. inl.* 62 straightforwardly rather than as a reference to Scetis.

[5]   Cassian frequently quotes from the Septuagint and Greek New Testament, uses Greek terms and could converse in Greek (*conf.* 16.1).

[6]   *Inst.* part pref. 3; Cassian's ability to speak Greek was essential since, he says, no one in Egypt spoke Latin (*inst.* 5.39.3) and his task required Eastern monastic ideas to be translated into Latin (*conf.* part, pref. 6).

[7]   *Inst.* 4.31; 5.24; *conf.* 11.5.

Germanus[8] (c.380AD) where they met the famous Egyptian cœnobitic abbot, Pinufius, who had fled his monastery in order to preserve his humility.[9] Doubtless inspired by this encounter, they soon after gained permission to visit the Egyptian monks,[10] probably in the mid 380's.[11] Cassian's *Institutes* and *Conferences* bear witness to his familiarity with the monastic world of Lower Egypt, but despite his intention to visit the Thebaid it seems unlikely that he visited the Pachomian monks of Upper Egypt.[12] Cassian and Germanus stayed in Egypt until at least 399AD,[13] possibly making a brief return to Bethlehem after their first seven years, before going on to Scetis,[14] a centre of Egyptian monasticism. Cassian provides, along with Palladius' *Historia Lausiaca*, one of the few early first hand accounts of life in Scetis and he appears to have become a member of the community there under the leadership of Paphnutius, calling it *nostra congregatio* ('our community').[15]

Although it is generally understood that Cassian draws extensively on Evagrius and their common master, Origen, he mentions neither by name. For example, while Cassian relates some stories about Macarius the Egyptian, the founder of Scetis, he attributes no conference to him. It is possible that Macarius had died before he and Germanus arrived in Scetis, but it is probable that Cassian preferred not to draw attention to any association with Evagrius, who had trained under Macarius.[16] Cassian and Germanus may then have gone on to Kellia and Nitria, which were as renowned as Scetis for asceticism and often included under the general heading of 'Scetis'. He mentions Kellia and Nitria by name only once,[17] but this may again display some reservation about mentioning places associated with Evagrian controversy. It may be that Cassian neither claims to have met Evagrius nor names him[18] because by the time Cassian wrote anti-Origenist feeling would have made it expedient for him not to highlight

---

[8]   *Conf.* 1.1; 16.1; 24.1.2.
[9]   *Inst.* 4.31; *conf.* 20.1.
[10]   *Conf.* 17.2.2; 17.5.2-3; 20.2.1.
[11]   Cassian's failure to mention Jerome gives good grounds for supposing that they never met and that he left Bethlehem before Jerome founded a monastery there in 386AD.
[12]   *Conf.* 11.1; he makes references to these without claiming to have met them.
[13]   Dated from his discussion of the Anthropomorphite controversy (*ibid.* 10.2).
[14]   *Ibid.* 17.30.2 (omitted from one of the oldest MSS; see Chadwick, *John Cassian*, pp. 15-18).
[15]   *Conf.* 10.2.3.
[16]   Socrates Scholasticus, *HE* 4.23.
[17]   *Conf.* 6.1.3.
[18]   Cassian may be referring to Evagrius when he writes of a brother from Pontus (*inst.* 5.32.1) and Palladius expressly states that he studied under Evagrius (*HL* 12.1; 23.1; 35.5).

his links with Evagrian Origenism. However, his indebtedness to and development of Origenist and Evagrian theology are clearly evident in his works.[19] The Anthropomorphite controversy, brought to a head by Theophilus' Paschal letter in 399AD and discussed in *conf.* 10, had a devastating impact on Origenist monasticism in Egypt and this was probably what prompted Cassian and Germanus to leave Egypt along with other Origenists such as the 'Tall Brothers'.[20] Arriving in Constantinople, Cassian and Germanus were ordained deacon and priest respectively by John Chrysostom[21] and acted as his envoys to Rome[22] until Chrysostom was deposed in 403-404AD. It was during this period that Cassian probably became a recognised authority on monasticism and began to build a large network of ecclesiastical contacts. What Cassian did in the following twelve years or so is uncertain, but it is possible he stayed on in Rome and likely that Germanus died during this period. Eventually, Cassian arrived in Massilia (modern Marseilles) in Gaul, probably in the late 410's, and wrote first the *Institutes*[23] and then the *Conferences* from the mid 420's.[24] He probably died in the mid 430's. Cassian's extensive connections with Eastern and particularly Egyptian monasticism make him a bridge between Eastern and Western monastic thought.

The delay between Cassian's stay in Egypt and writing about it could lend credence to the suggestion that his works do not accurately reflect monastic life there. Indeed, Cassian himself says that his memory of his stay was poor after such a gap in time,[25] but this may equally be an expression of humility since the powerful use of the memory in Antiquity

---

[19] Similarities between Cassian and Evagrius have already been noted in chapter 2 (the influence of Evagrius on Cassian is discussed at length in C. Stewart, *Cassian the Monk*). Cassian is also familiar with a range of monastic writings, including *vit. Ant.*, Antony's letters, *HM*, the traditions behind the *Apophthegmata* and refers (*inst.* pref. 5) to the monastic works of Basil and Jerome.

[20] On the Anthropomorphite controversy, see above (pp. 35-36).

[21] *De inc.* 7.31.1, Gennadius, *de vir. inl.* 62; Palladius, *dial.* 3 (the first historical reference to Cassian and Germanus).

[22] Sozomen, *HE* 8.26.8.

[23] Dedicated to Castor, Bishop of Apta Julia in Gallia Narbonensis from c.419AD.

[24] Cassian's last work (c.430), *de incarnatione domini contra Nestorium.* (written at the command of Leo, archdeacon of Rome), was probably to establish his own anti-Pelagian credentials, but it is generally regarded as a lesser work. In *de inc.* Cassian attacks Pelagianism and Nestorianism, which he links together. In response to the Nestorian doctrine of Christ which separated his Divine and human natures into two persons, Cassian defends the full divinity of Christ and argues in favour of the virgin Mary's title *theotocos* ('God bearer') rather than *Christotocos* ('Christ bearer'), which Nestorius favoured over the former. See also below, pp. 85-86 and n. 78.

[25] *Inst.* pref. 4.

and Late Antiquity should not be dismissed too lightly.[26] He also says that the monastic life is to be lived and communicated through lifestyle as well as words,[27] so it could be argued that he had lived and discussed what he had learnt in the intervening period and that this kept his memory fresh. Furthermore, the geographical, biographical and observational detail and the similarity of thought to the apophthegms lend credibility to his accuracy.

Turning to Cassian's works, the *Conferences* are presented as a record of discussions held with leading figures in Egyptian monasticism. In his prefaces to each part of the *Conferences* Cassian expresses his intention to introduce Gallic cœnobia to the *virtutes* and way of life of the Egyptian anchorites, whose lifestyle he regards as superior to the cœnobitic;[28] he thus intentionally draws on the anchoritic rather than cœnobitic tradition. *Prima facie*, the *Conferences* are simple records of conversations, but Cassian's redactive effort is evident in the sequence of thought running through the work so that it becomes what might be termed a systematic theology of the desert. Such systematisation was the natural result of Cassian writing in response to specific episcopal commissions rather than simply recording anecdotes, like the apophthegms, for the instruction and edification of monks. This conscious redaction is also indicated by the significance Cassian places upon the number of conferences corresponding to the twenty-four elders in the book of Revelation.[29] The sequential development of thought suggests that the subject matter of the opening conferences, viz. *discretio*, is foundational to the spiritual life he is about to describe. While Evagrius and Cassian were the first to intellectualise the theology of desert monasticism and Cassian's discussion of *discretio* has a correspondingly distinct intellectual bias, Cassian's teaching has a much more practical approach than Evagrius.

This more practical approach is evident in the *Institutes*. The first part[30] provides a monastic rule based on the Egyptian model, modified by the practices in Palestinian and Mesopotamian monasteries, but adapted to the cold climate of Gaul.[31] The second part[32] is a detailed examination of how to overcome the eight λογισμοί.[33] Cassian's typically effulgent preface to

---

[26]   Oral traditions often prove to be extremely accurate and memorising books of Scripture and sermons was common practice in this period (cf. also the ability of modern day devout Muslims to memorise the Koran).

[27]   *Inst*. pref. 5.

[28]   *Conf*. part 2, pref. 2; part 3, pref. 1; part 1, pref. 4 respectively.

[29]   *Ibid*. 24.1.1 (cf. Rev. 4:4).

[30]   *Inst*. 1-4.

[31]   *Ibid*. pref. 9; 1.10.

[32]   *Ibid*. 5-12.

[33]   Although Cassian does not use the Greek term λογισμός it has been used in this chapter as a helpful way of referring to the eight principal faults.

Castor compares the bishop's wisdom and discernment to that of Solomon, who similarly sought advice, and he praises Castor's exemplary knowledge and spiritual advancement in *virtues*;[34] he thus implies that Castor exhibits *discretio*.

The importance placed on Cassian's contribution to Eastern monasticism and the understanding of *discretio* in particular is clearly evident. The translation of his work into Greek is unique[35] and he is the only Latin to be included in the Greek Alphabetical Collection, where six of his eight apophthegms derive from the *Institutes*,[36] and four more from the *Conferences* appear in the Greek Systematic Collection, two of them from the conference with Moses 'On *Discretio*.'[37] Photius, writing on Cassian in the ninth century, bears witness to the existence of Greek abridgements of the *Institutes* and *Conferences* and provides three epitomes, two covering the *Institutes* and one the *Conferences*. Importantly for the argument being put forward here, the epitome of the *Conferences* covers *Conferences* 1, 2 and 7; that is, it includes the conference 'On *Discretio*.' Additionally, Photius makes particular reference to Cassian teaching that διάκρισις is 'greater than all the other ἀρεταί ... and the greater gift from above.'[38] Cassian is also the only Latin author to appear in the *Philokalia*, with summaries of *Conferences* 1 and 2 and *Institutes* 5 to 12 on the eight λογισμοί.[39] It would be reasonable to argue that Cassian is presenting Eastern thought on διάκρισις for a Western audience and therefore adapting it to suit a different milieu. However, the fact that his work on the subject is translated into Greek and commended in the East indicates that his thought is faithful to the original concepts and may be used to gain insights into how διάκρισις was understood by the Egyptian Desert Fathers. Cassian is, then, afforded the rare honour of being counted among the Eastern theologians of the desert and his understanding of διάκρισις is rated as one of his most valuable contributions.

---

[34]   *Inst.* pref. 1-3.

[35]   The later 8th century translation of Gregory the Great's *Dialogues* into Greek by Pope Zacharias (d.752) is also noteworthy.

[36]   Cassian 1 = *inst.* 5.24; Cassian 3 = *inst.* 5.25; Cassian 4 = *inst.* 5.27; Cassian 5 = *inst.* 5.28; Cassian 6 = *inst.* 5.29, 31; Cassian 7 = *inst.* 7.19.

[37]   GSC 4.27 = *conf.* 2.11; GSC 5.4 = *conf.* 2.10, 13; GSC 8.12 = *conf.* 18.11; GSC 16.29 = *conf.* 18.15.

[38]   Photius, *Bibliotheca* codex 197.

[39]   G.E.H. Palmer, P. Sherrard and K. Ware (eds), *The Philokalia: The Complete Text compiled by St Nikodemos of the Holy Mountain and St Makarios of Corinth* (4 vols; London: Faber and Faber, 1979-1995), I, pp. 73-108. John Climacus (*scala parad.* 4) also writes of the 'great Cassian' and translates the opening of *conf.* 2.10 into Greek.

Discretio and the Goals of the Monk

Cassian starts his *Conferences* with a discussion with Moses[40] 'On the goal and end of the monk.' While this could be because he holds Moses in high regard,[41] it is the identification of the monk's goals, *puritas cordis* (purity of heart) and ultimately the Kingdom of God, that makes this his natural starting point.[42] This conference ends with a promise to discuss the next natural subject, *discretio*, but Moses says they must also exercise *discretio* by resting before that discussion takes place so that they can listen attentively the next day.[43] Thus, for Cassian, the monk's first step towards achieving his goals is to learn *discretio*.

To attain his goals the monk is required to exercise discipline, determination and attention to detail and this is reflected in Cassian's frequent use of the metaphors of soldier and athlete of (or wrestler for) Christ.[44] The monk's entire effort should reflect a wholehearted inner desire

---

[40]   This Moses began his monastic life as a boy (*conf.* 2.11.1) and so cannot be the famous former robber, Moses the Ethiopian, who became a monk as an adult.

[41]   *Conf.* 1.1.1; cf. *inst.* 10.25.

[42]   *Conf.* 1.4.3. While these goals equate to Evagrius' ἀπάθεια and γνῶσις of God (noted above, p. 46 and n. 60), the degree of equivalence is debatable. For example, Bamberger regards *puritas cordis* as equivalent to ἀπάθεια (J.E. Bamberger, *Evagrius Ponticus: The Praktikos & Chapters on Prayer* (Cistercian Studies Series, 4; Kalamazoo: Cistercian Publications, 1972), p. lxxxvii), but Stewart sees *puritas cordis* as an avoidance of a controversial term, which Cassian also develops beyond Evagrius' ἀπάθεια (Stewart, *Cassian the Monk*, pp. 42-45; so also W. Harmless, *Desert Christians: An Introduction to the Literature of Early Monasticism* (Oxford: Oxford University Press, 2004), p. 391). Both ἀπάθεια and *puritas cordis* may be viewed positively or negatively: ἀπάθεια as an ability to be undistracted or an absence of feeling; *puritas cordis* as a wholesome quality possessed or the absence of evil. While they may be seen as equivalent, there may also be subtle contrast in concept: to remain unmoved by evil (etc.) and to be devoid of evil. However, in Περὶ Λογ. 35 Evagrius contrasts abstinence (actions that prevent sin) with ἀπάθεια (intentionally cutting off λογισμοί), which suggests that he views ἀπάθεια as a positive inward cleansing process not dissimilar to *puritas cordis*. While Cassian's *puritas cordis* may well be a development of Evagrius' ἀπάθεια, they may also be seen as two sides of the same coin, placing slightly different emphases on the same concept. Rousseau also notes that 'Evagrius made more precise distinctions between βασιλεία τῶν οὐρανῶν ['kingdom of heaven'] and βασιλεία τοῦ θεοῦ ['kingdom of God']' than Cassian (P. Rousseau, 'Cassian, Contemplation and the Coenobitic Life', *JEH* 26.2 (April, 1975), p. 123, n. 1).

[43]   *Conf.* 1.23.

[44]   *Miles Christi* ('soldier of Christ'): *inst.* 1.1.1; 1.11.1; 2.1; 5.19.1; 5.21.1; 7.21; 10.3; 11.3; 11.7; cf. 2.3.2; *conf.* 4.12.5; 7.23.2; 8.18.2; cf. 1.1; 3.6.4.
       Athleta Christi ('athlete of Christ'): *inst.* 5.17.1; 5.18.2; 5.19.1; 8.22; 10.5; 11.19.1; 12.32.1; *conf.* 7.20; cf. 4.6.2; 6.16.2; 18.14.5; 19.14.3.

to attain his goals as he trains and fights to attain *puritas cordis* (also identified with holiness and love),[45] which alone prepares him for the Kingdom of God. He needs to be attentive to every detail of his life, discerning the right use of things and choosing between what is useful and harmful to his advancement. He should therefore pay close attention to his purity of heart (*contemplationem cordis mundi fixam*[46]) and use practical disciplines, such as fasting and vigils, to develop and maintain *puritas cordis*.[47] For example, Isaac, in his first conference, compares the soul at prayer rising to God to a feather caught in an upward draft, but just as a damp feather fails to rise so also the soul weighed down by vice and worldly concerns and so it must be purged of these.[48] Similarly, Theonas says that 'voluntary and invisible *puritas cordis*' leads to perfection and monks should not rely on proficiency in outward practical disciplines alone.[49] Monks thus need to discern the value and purpose of practical disciplines for developing inward purity in pursuit of their ultimate goal. This requires monks to be attentive to the detail of both their inward state and the disciplines they use to purify it.

This determined and attentive approach to achieving *puritas cordis* and the Kingdom of God, rejecting all hindrances, is brought out in the conference following that on *discretio*. This conference with Paphnutius 'On the three renunciations' describes how Paphnutius, after he had achieved perfection in all the *virtutes* while living in a cœnobium, went into anchoritic solitude renouncing the company of others in order to advance yet further and 'adhere inseparably' (*inseparabiliter inhaerere*) to God.[50] He defines these three renunciations as of possessions, vice and the visible (i.e. in favour of contemplating God and the invisible). The third renunciation would involve the rejection of human companionship as a distraction from seeking God.[51] By placing this discussion immediately after that on *discretio*, Cassian indicates that monks need to use *discretio* to avoid distractions from their goals.

For the monk John in the nineteenth conference avoiding distraction meant, in contrast to Paphnutius, a return to the cœnobium. This John says he found the desert increasingly crowded and full of the distractions (e.g.

---

[45]   *Conf.* 1.5.2; 1.7.2. Cf. Heb. 5:14 and the strenuous exercise and training needed to gain διάκρισις (see above, p. 7).

[46]   *Conf.* 1.6.1.

[47]   E.g. *conf.* 1.5-7. Even the monk's clothing should act as both a reminder and portrayal of his way of life (*inst.* 1.1-11).

[48]   *Conf.* 9.4-5.

[49]   *Ibid.* 21.36.1.

[50]   *Ibid.* 3.1.2. Cf. Evagrius, Περὶ Λογ. 26, where διάκρισις and γνῶσις, the monk's ultimate goal, are linked to the three renunciations (see above, pp. 45-47).

[51]   Although this appears to contradict biblical teaching on the value of relationships, relating well to others also features prominently in Cassian.

providing hospitality) and the anchoritic life a perilous mixture of ecstatic contemplative experience and of destructive vanity and lax discipline. He says that the fruits of the anchoritic life require a 'peaceful stable mind' and that any loss of *puritas cordis* resulting from a return to cœnobitic life would be mitigated by obedience and not worrying about tomorrow.[52] He also describes how as an anchorite he became so absorbed in contemplation that he was forgetful of his practical disciplines and so had to take practical steps to overcome his forgetfulness.[53] This is a different and more positive kind of distraction in that it is a preoccupation with God, but such forgetfulness could lead to neglect of equally important practical disciplines. Monks thus needed to use *discretio* vigilantly to avoid anything that might distract them from the disciplines that helped them achieve their goals.

Monks thus need to weigh the contrasting benefits and distractions of solitude and community, selecting a personal way of life that will best lead them to their goals. Thus in his first conference Moses says the heart should be fixed on its goal, the mind ever adhering to God and divine things with everything else judged to be harmful.[54] Although human frailty makes it impossible, the monk should nevertheless aim to adhere to God continually and to be inseparably united with him in contemplation. The monk should recognise any distraction as a lapse from the highest good and return his gaze to Christ. Once ignorance of the truth, the kingdom of the devil and vice have been replaced by knowledge and *virtutes*, the Kingdom of God can be established in the monk's heart and so the monk needs to learn to distinguish (*discerno*) between these two kingdoms.[55] With *discretio* the monk is able to identify his goal, remain fixed on it and avoid anything that might hinder his progress towards continual union with God.

The need to adhere continually to God and the ease with which monks can be distracted from contemplation is also discussed in the third conference with Theonas.[56] Monks should be watchful in contemplation, immediately restoring their attention when their minds wander[57] and, struck with compunction, seek God's pardon in humble dependence upon him.[58] Such undistracted contemplation, carried out in an impassive state,[59] arms

---

[52] *Conf.* 19.5-6.

[53] *Ibid.* 19.4.

[54] *Ibid.* 1.8.1.

[55] *Ibid.* 1.13.1-3.

[56] *Ibid.* 23.5. Cf. Evagrius and the 'demon wanderer' (see above, pp. 46-47).

[57] *Ibid.* 23.8.1; the monk should concentrate like a tightrope walker on not deviating from his path (*ibid.* 23.9). He should strenuously bring his thoughts back to God so that his mind rotates around the centre of God's love (*ibid.* 24.6).

[58] *Ibid.* 23.10.1.

[59] Described by Paphnutius (*ibid.* 3.7.3) and familiar from Evagrius' teaching on undistracted prayer and ἀπάθεια.

the monk with *virtus discretionis* ('the virtue of discernment').[60] Theonas says that sin destroys the tranquillity produced by contemplation[61] and that even more advanced monks, who seek to imitate the holiness of angels and adhere constantly to God, can be distracted from what leads to *virtus* and perfection by words and images during psalmody and prayer.[62] Monks should therefore scrutinise their thoughts and consciences aware of their constant need of God's mercy and the purity that comes from contemplating him.[63] *Discretio* thus develops as the monk advances in undistracted prayer and contemplation, since these require *discretio* for self-examination and watchfulness and produce *virtus discretionis*. *Discretio* is thus as much an ability learnt through use[64] as granted through union with God.

Ascent to and union with God is also understood to be developmental and progressive. This can be seen in the three kinds of monastic calling described by Paphnutius in the conference following that on *discretio* and so the monk is effectively encouraged to discern which relates to him. The first is a calling from God, exemplified by God's call on the patriarch Abraham and on Antony to leave everything for him. The second calling comes through human sources, such as the example and inspiration Moses gave to the Israelites, and the third through necessity, such as when the death sentence for murder compelled Moses the Ethiopian to enter the monastic life.[65] These find a parallel in Chæremon's first conference where a disposition for good and love of *virtutes*, a desire for the Kingdom of Heaven and a fear of eternal or temporal judgment are each said to restrain people from vice.[66] However, only the first of these, he says, properly belongs to God and to those who have advanced to the point that they have received the image of God.[67] Chæremon develops this by describing the monk's progression through different degrees of perfection moving from fear (as of a slave), through hope (as a hireling hoping for reward in return for good work) to love (as a son). In this last stage the monk loves God, *virtus* and good for their own sakes, hates sin and impurity, longs to receive in himself the image of God and is devoted to him in his every word and

---

[60] *Ibid.* 10.11.4.
[61] *Ibid.* 23.13.2.
[62] *Ibid.* 23.16.1-2 (cf. wordless and imageless prayer in Evagrius). Cf. Evagrius (above, p. 65) and John Kolobos 2 (below, p. 133). Theonas counters Germanus' earlier assertion that Paul, having reached the heights of perfection, spoke not of his own struggle against sin in Rom. 7 but that of sinners (*conf.* 22.15; 23.1).
[63] *Conf.* 23.17.1-3.
[64] Cf. Heb. 5:14 (see above, p. 7).
[65] *Conf.* 3.3-5; cf. *vit. Ant.* 2. The esteem in which Antony was held is evident in Augustine (*confess.* 8.6.14).
[66] *Conf.* 11.6.1; I have changed Chæremon's order.
[67] *Ibid.* 11.6.3.

action.[68] This hierarchy of vocation and formation and of the monk's progression towards perfection and his goals would require *discretio* of calling and motivations to determine the degree of advancement attained and what yet needs to be achieved.

This self-awareness of one's advancement, gained through *discretio*, is evident in the conclusion of the conference 'On *Discretio*.' Cassian says that Moses had opened his and Germanus' eyes to the way in which they had strayed from *puritas cordis* and needed clear goals if they were to progress further. Cassian here also refers back to the previous conference on the goals of the monk making clear the need of *discretio* to achieve them.[69] *Discretio* is thus the means by which monks come to know their inner condition and measure of advancement and by which they achieve their goals (not least by learning from a senior monk).

Discretio as a Grace and *Virtus*

Cassian concludes his second conference with Moses 'On *Discretio*' by saying that he had taught him and Germanus *discretionis gratia atque virtus* ('the grace and virtue of discernment').[70] *Discretio* is, then, a God given strength, which the monk uses to pursue his goals. When Moses introduces the subject of *discretio* at the end of his first conference, he says:

> *volo vobis adhuc super discretionis eximietate vel gratia, quae inter cunctas virtutes arcem ac primatum tenet, pauca disserere.*[71]

Here the gift of *discretio* is described in terms of excellence (*eximietas*), which is then reinforced by calling it pre-eminent or first in rank (*primatus*) over all the other *virtutes*. *Discretio* is not merely a *virtus* but the supreme *virtus* and the summit (*arx*) towering over them. There is a double sense here: *discretio* overarches the *virtutes* being first in importance and value among them, but it is also supreme and master over them all. Thus Moses again calls *discretio*, later in the chapter, *prima virtus*,[72] suggesting that it is first, foremost and the beginning of *virtus*, and Germanus calls it 'the origin and root of all the *virtutes*'.[73] *Discretio* is thus a Divine gift and charism, the most esteemed, valuable and desirable of all the *virtutes* and essential

---

[68]   *Ibid.* 11.7-13; cf. Antony 32 and the steps leading to perfection described in *inst.* 4.39.
[69]   *Conf.* 2.26.4.
[70]   *Ibid.* 2.26.4. *Ibid.* 10.11.4 also refers to *virtus discretionis*.
[71]   *Ibid.* 1.23.1.; 'I want to explain a little more to you about the excellence and grace of *discretio*, which holds the summit and first place among all the virtues.'
[72]   *Ibid.* 1.23.3.
[73]   *Ibid.* 2.9.

for controlling and governing them. The central importance of *discretio* is thus made very clear.

By contrast Theonas, in his third conference, says that the apostle Paul had achieved perfection in all the *virtutes* and that the *virtus* of Divine contemplation is incomparably superior.[74] However, Theonas draws here on the story of Martha and Mary (Luke 10:38-42) in which Mary chooses contemplation over works and he indicates that monks must make the same choice,[75] perceiving (*decerno*) evils that would draw them away from the chief good of constant union with God.[76] It has already been noted that contemplation requires and produces *discretio*[77] and this exhortation to choose good over evil and contemplation over works, which choice is the function of *discretio*, places *discretio* at the centre of what Theonas regards as the highest *virtus*.

The assertion that *discretio* is a Divine gift with which choices are made draws attention to Cassian's view of the interplay between grace and freewill, which was attacked and parodied by Prosper of Aquitaine who accused Cassian of Pelagianism and of undermining Augustine's teaching on grace and predestination.[78] This controversy centred particularly on *Conference* 13 where Cassian develops his view first put forward in *Institutes* 12 that ascetical effort alone is incapable of leading the monk to perfection; he also needs the grace of God.[79] For Cassian flesh and spirit are at war with each other and, while ascetical effort is valuable, without

---

[74]   *Ibid.* 23.2-3.

[75]   *Ibid.* 23.4.4.

[76]   *Ibid.* 23.11.2.

[77]   See above, pp. 82-83.

[78]   Prosper of Aquitaine, *contra collatorem*. Later, in his final work, Cassian mades it clear that he regarded Pelagianism as a heresy (*de inc. passim*). Pelagianism was an ascetic movement that rejected Augustine's views on predestination and dependence on God's grace as these seemed to abdicate people of personal responsibility, denying all human initiative in salvation and negating the value of monastic ascetic discipline. It took such a positive view of human will that it was held that Christians were capable of sinlessness; Cassian rejects this notion, stating clearly that no human being is sinless (e.g. *conf.* 23.18-20; *de inc.* 1.3.3. See also comments on *conf.* 22 on p. 100, n. 186). He presents a more balanced view which acknowledges constant dependence upon God's grace and help, but stresses the need for human effort through ascetic discipline; against this he also recognises the dangers of failing to depend upon God and of relying purely on human effort. This debate later became known as the Semi-Pelagian Controversy. Cassian sees himself as presenting traditional theology based on practical experience rather than engaging in theological dialectic and the controversy may have arisen as a result of these contrasting approaches (for a fuller discussion see Stewart, *Cassian the Monk*, pp. 76-81). See also above, p. 77, n. 24.

[79]   E.g. *inst.* 12.10; *conf.* 13.1-3.

reliance on grace it can never win integrity and purity;[80] such inner purity is God's gift.[81] Ultimately, however, the interplay between freewill and grace remain for Cassian a mystery beyond human reason.[82] Considering grace and freewill in relation to *discretio*, the monk would need to use his freewill to choose dependence upon God and obedience to him, having discerned the value but ultimate insufficiency of ascetic practice.

Discretio and the Practical Disciplines (Πρακτική)

Throughout the *Conferences* and *Institutes* Cassian draws attention to the practical activities and ascetic disciplines the monks in Egypt used to overcome vice and develop *virtutes*. His lists of these disciplines vary, but generally include: fasting, vigils, work, renunciation, solitude, constant prayer and reading, studying, memorising and meditating upon Scripture.[83] One extended list also includes dress, appearance, bearing, voice, silence, obedience, humility and endurance.[84] Cassian explains that when monks first withdrew into the desert they sought to emulate and improve upon the life of the early church described in Acts 4:32-35 by devoting themselves to Scripture reading, prayer, manual work and fasting.[85] Manual work in the cell, combined with meditation on Scripture,[86] was seen as a means of attaining greater heights of spiritual contemplation,[87] of uniting the spiritual and physical *virtutes* and of guarding thoughts.[88] In Cassian's teaching on the practical disciplines it becomes evident that the monk needs *discretio* if he is to exercise them properly.

---

[80]   *Inst.* 12.10-16 developed in *conf.* 13 *passim.*

[81]   *Conf.* 13.5.4.

[82]   *Ibid.* 13.18.5.

[83]   E.g. *inst.* 12.13; 12.16; *conf.* 1.7.

[84]   *Inst.* 11.3. Cassian's discussion of the dress of the monk and its meaning (*inst.* 1) follows Evagrius (*prak.* prol. 2-8).

[85]   *Inst.* 2.5.1-2. The same point is made in the conference with Piamun. He explains that the gradual introduction of concessions for Gentiles (beginning at the Jerusalem Council, Acts 15) spiritually weakened the Church in contrast to cœnobitic monasticism which maintained the earlier apostolic fervour. Out of the latter grew the anchoritic discipline, beginning with Paul and Antony who withdrew to the desert, in imitation of John the Baptist, Elijah and Elisha, in order to advance in divine contemplation and to do battle with the demons (*conf.* 18.5-6; cf. 18.30. This Paul is the subject of Jerome's *vit. Pauli*, cf. *ep.* 22.36). This reveals something of what Cassian and monks generally understood their origins to be, albeit retrospectively.

[86]   *Inst.* 3.2.

[87]   *Ibid.* 2.12.2.

[88]   *Ibid.* 2.14; *conf.* 10.14.1-2.

Cassian follows Evagrius' distinction between practical and contemplative knowledge, adopting the Greek terms πρακτική and θεωρητική. He defines these respectively as practical (*actualis*) culminating in 'the correction of lifestyle and purification from vices' and '*contemplatio* of divine things and reflection on most sacred notions.'[89] Becoming perfectly *actualis*, Nesteros explains, has two stages: firstly, knowing the nature of vices and how to overcome them and secondly, discerning (*discerno*) the order of the *virtutes* and fashioning the mind according to their perfection.[90] Although Cassian normally translates πρακτική as *actualis*, he defines it more specifically, at the end of a discussion of the Mosaic Law and Gospel perfection, as having 'perfectly mastered *actualis disciplina*'. Monks, living under grace founded upon the Law, are said to reach such perfection 'through the merits of great *virtutes*' and gain understanding through work rather than through debate.[91] The practical disciplines are therefore used to develop inner purity and *virtutes* through experience. However, the understanding provided by spiritual knowledge is also described as a means of analytical and practical *discretio* of what is beneficial:

> Knowledge ... by which we discern [*discerno*] by prudent examination all that relates to *discretio actualis* to see whether it is useful or upright as when we are instructed to judge for ourselves...[92]

Here Cassian comes close to ranking *discretio* among the practical disciplines as well as speaking of it in terms of careful mental or inward analysis. Thus, while *discretio* is necessary for the right use of outward practical disciplines it also has an inward dimension and as such forms a bridge between the inner and outer life of the monk, binding them together and enabling him to perfect *virtutes* and advance towards his goals.

Moses, in his second conference, describes Antony's teaching on the purpose of practical disciplines to bring the monk to perfection but their inadequacy per se to do so. *Discretio* is also needed if the monk is to avoid the dangers of deceit, excessive asceticism and vices and so achieve his goals.[93] Moses then describes *discretio* as the light and eye of the body whereby thoughts and actions, 'which derive from the deliberation of

---

[89]   *Conf.* 14.1.3. Cassian also uses the threefold distinction based on Proverbs, Ecclesiastes and the Song of Songs (*conf.* 3.6.4) found in Origen (*comm. in Cant.* prol. 3; see above, pp. 30-31) and Evagrius (*prak.* 1; *schol.* 247 in Prov. 22:20; see above, p. 47-48, 64).

[90]   *Conf.* 14.3.1.

[91]   *Ibid.* 21.33-34; cf. Antony 8 and parallels; Antony, *ep.* 6.106.

[92]   *Conf.* 14.8.6.

[93]   *Ibid.* 2.2.1-4.

discretio,' are clearly seen and understood. Without the 'eye' and 'light' of
discretio the monk lacks 'true judgment and knowledge'; his mind is
darkened and his inner vision lost, he is unable to see how he should act
and his heart lacks judgment.[94] Moses illustrates this with King Saul who
lacked the 'eye of *discretio*' and so was deceived into error
(cf. 1 Samuel 15) and with King Ahab who, through 'ignorance of
discretio,' regarded his own mercy as superior to God's command
(1 Kings 20).[95] *Discretio* is thus understood to be a means of spiritual
vision and insight that enables the monk to regulate his practical
disciplines, conduct his life, avoid deceit and to increase in knowledge and
understanding as he pursues his goals; without *discretio* he struggles
blindly in the monastic life and is incapable of making sound judgments.

The regulation of practical disciplines using *discretio* can be illustrated
from Theonas' discussion in his first conference of the customary
relaxation of fasting by Egyptian monks during Pentecost.[96] Beginning with
Ecclesiastes 3:1-8 (LXX), he describes how some things are essentially
neutral, being beneficial or harmful depending on whether or not they are
used at the appropriate time and in the right way. However, others are
intrinsically and permanently good or bad, such as the four cardinal (and
indeed other) *virtutes* and vices,[97] and so their nature should be discerned
(*discerno*).[98] Thus if fasting were regarded as an essential good, eating
would be evil and abstinence of no spiritual value, an argument
unsupported by Scripture.[99] Fasting and other practical disciplines, he says,
are recommended rather than commanded in Scripture and so are beneficial
when done but not punishable when omitted. Thus, the monastic
predecessors taught that practical disciplines should be observed
thoughtfully according to the occasion, place, method and time, so that they
would be beneficial rather than harmful. For example, maintaining an
austere fast when hospitality should be shown to a visitor or when
physically weak would make the monk guilty of being inhospitable or of
murdering his body respectively, gaining him neither merit nor salvation.
This would prove a struggle for those seeking human praise through their

---

[94]   *Ibid.* 2.2.5-6; cf. 2.26.4, *inst.* 8.22. Pseudo-Macarius also calls διάκρισις an eye
       that keeps a person from sinning (*hom. H* 4.1; *hom. B* 49.1.1).

[95]   *Conf.* 2.3. Cassian frequently uses 'eye' to describe inner spiritual vision but does
       not develop the doctrine of the 'spiritual senses' found in Origen (e.g. *comm. in
       Cant.* 2.9) or, less categorically, in Evagrius (e.g. *KG* 2.35; see above, p. 50 and
       n. 90) whose general approach is to emphasise the value of spiritual sight.

[96]   Theonas' discussion demonstrates that he has *discretio* of the correct use of fasting.

[97]   *Conf.* 21.12.3-4. For *discretio* used to determine the correct degree of fasting see
       also *ibid.* 21.22.1. Cf. Evagrius on using πρακτική at the appropriate time and
       measure *prak.* 15 (see above, pp. 60-61).

[98]   *Conf.* 21.16.2.

[99]   *Ibid.* 21.13.

fasting. Next, Theonas explains, using Isaiah 58 on the nature of true fasting, that fasting is good and pleasing to God when combined with other works, but futile and hateful to him when combined with the wrong things.[100] Fasting is thus not an end in itself but a discipline or tool that aids the acquisition of other *virtutes*, love and purity of heart and body.[101] By using fasting properly, he says, the flesh is dulled and the peaceful mind reconciled to God, but used improperly it ruins the soul.[102] Conversely, the enjoyment of food is not evil unless it is combined with a vice such as intemperance.[103] The monk should thus use every effort to determine the right time, quality and extent of his fasting[104] and, by implication, of his eating. Theonas concludes with the illustration of the disciples eating with the risen Christ during Pentecost because it was not appropriate to mourn while the Bridegroom was with them (Matthew 9:15).[105] Practical disciplines should thus be used as a means of acquiring *virtutes* and *puritas cordis*, but their use needs to be properly regulated and their nature and purpose understood using *discretio* if they are to be beneficial and not harmful.

Developing this regulated approach to fasting and eating is discussed by Moses in his conference 'On *Discretio*.' In response to Germanus' enquiry about the 'balanced management' (*aequum moderamen*) of abstinence, Moses begins by providing a general rule, based on the example of the elders, on the amount of food to be eaten so that the monk remains able to fast without difficulty, since excessive consumption makes fasting more difficult. He then points out that monks need to be aware of their capabilities, taking into account their age and physical condition. To this self-awareness he adds the need to rely on the *discretio* of others. He illustrates this with the adverse example of a monk, Benjamin, who was 'ignorant of perfect *discretio*' and relied on his own judgment rather than that of the elders and so succumbed to the devil's deceit by prolonging his fasts and saving up his food only to gorge on it when his fast was over. Finally, he provides practical advice on how to fulfil the demands of hospitality by reserving a little food until the end of the day against the possibility of unexpected visitors. This food can then be eaten alone or with guests so that the discipline of fasting and the measured consumption of food are not compromised. For Moses, the most important point is consistency in abstinence, steering a moderate course between excessive eating and fasting. *Discretio* is used to assess personal capacity for fasting

---

[100] *Ibid.* 21.14.
[101] *Ibid.* 21.15; 21.16.2; 21.17.1.
[102] *Ibid.* 21.16.2. E.g. fasting out of rage (*ibid.* 16.19).
[103] *Ibid.* 21.16.3.
[104] *Ibid.* 21.17.1.
[105] *Ibid.* 21.18.2.

and to take both advice and practical measures to ensure a balanced application of practical disciplines.[106]

Cassian also recommends practical measures to help regulate sleep and contemplation. He says Egyptian monks used manual labour to ward off sleep in order to concentrate on spiritual meditation and keep their minds from wandering.[107] They also used vigils after morning office to maintain their spiritual fervour and keep themselves from being corrupted by the deception of their spiritual enemy.[108] It was recognised, of course, that some sleep was necessary for alertness and so an appropriate rhythm of limited sleep was established.[109] Similarly, fasting was relaxed for two days each week during the longer Sabbath vigils to keep monks from becoming too weak[110] and to make the next week's fasts less daunting.[111] This use of *discretio* to regulate eating, fasting and vigils is a major theme in the second conference with Moses.[112] *Discretio* is thus used to avoid excess and distraction, often by identifying simple practical steps that help maintain the disciplines.

An important aspect of this practical and balanced management of the disciplines was discerning when they should be relaxed. In his conference, Abraham relates how a philosopher out hunting was surprised to see someone of John the Evangelist's reputation stroking a partridge. In response John asked why the philosopher did not always keep his bowstring in the nock and was told that the constant tension would ruin the bow. John then pointed out that without occasional relaxation, the spirit is similarly weakened.[113] In Joseph's second conference he addresses the knotty question of whether it is better to relax a personal fast when offered hospitality (thus breaking the rule but maintaining secrecy) or to refuse to eat and so publicise it. He says that the elders, using '*discretio* of spirit', believed it a more sublime *virtus* to keep their practice concealed.[114] Monks should, he says, not be bound by rules but learn to determine when it is

---

[106] *Ibid.* 2.18.1-2.26.3. 'Perfect *discretio*' is needed for fasting (*inst.* 5.3), which should be tailored to the individual (*ibid.* 5.5). Cf. Syncletica 15 and parallels on using διάκρισις to moderate fasting (see below, pp. 142-43) and An Abba of Rome 1 and parallels on διάκρισις of the validity of different personal levels of asceticism (see below, p. 131). Further on hospitality, see below, pp. 220-23.

[107] *Inst.* 2.14.

[108] *Ibid.* 3.5.1.

[109] *Ibid.* 3.8.

[110] *Ibid.* 3.9.

[111] *Ibid.* 3.11.

[112] *Conf.* 2.17-26.

[113] *Ibid.* 24.21. This story appears to combine similar ones found in *acta Ioannis* 56 and Antony 13 (and parallels), which make the same point (see below, p. 149).

[114] *Conf.* 17.23.

more beneficial to relax them.[115] It was understood, then, that practical disciplines needed to be relaxed occasionally if the monk was to persevere in them generally, but this would need to be regulated carefully to keep relaxation from turning into neglect. This would require a means of determining the correct balance, as did weighing the conflicting demands of hospitality and fasting. Practical disciplines are not seen as ends in themselves but useful tools to achieve the monk's goals and so with *discretio* monks are able to use practical disciplines to the best effect, even if this means not exercising them from time to time. *Discretio* is not a legalistic tool by which an individual judges which 'rule' applies in a given situation, but rather an intuitive sense of how to behave appropriately.

Although it was appropriate to relax practical disciplines occasionally, this is seen as quite distinct from being at ease because of material comforts, as the latter is seen as failing in renunciation. Thus Abraham, in his conference, relates how Antony confuted a monk who maintained that there was greater *virtus* in living among others than in the anchoritic discipline. Antony ascertained that the monk was only free from worry and work, and so able to concentrate on undistracted reading and prayer, because he was still supported by his relatives and that his mood waxed and waned with their changing circumstances. Antony explains that this is a failure fully to renounce the world (i.e. family ties and support) and so the monk was losing the reward of his labours.[116] The monk was strong and in no need of charitable support and so he is told to embrace work and poverty, even preferring to live in an inhospitable place, so as to remain undistracted from the pursuit of his goals.[117] Later Abraham explains that the devil uses material possessions to bind the soul, seeking to deceive the monk and separate him from spiritual joy by tormenting him with worldly cares.[118] Only by a complete renunciation of the world can the monk attain the sublime *virtus* of remaining completely unmoved by any persecution or hardship.[119] Theonas, in his first conference, says that while tithing and alms giving are good, they are nevertheless made from what is owned and under the old Law rather than from grace. Gospel perfection, he says, calls for a complete renunciation of all possessions and family ties, even marriage, in order to seek God and be united to him;[120] renunciation, then, is a complete self-giving to God. Thus when Germanus and Cassian confess to Abraham at the start of their conference with him that they struggle with

---

[115] *Ibid.* 17.28.3.

[116] *Ibid.* 24.11; cf. 24.2.1-3. Further on the renunciation of family ties, see below, pp. 211-13.

[117] *Conf.* 24.12; cf. 24.2.3-4.

[118] *Ibid.* 24.24.1-2.

[119] *Ibid.* 24.24.7; 24.25.1 (clearly a description of ἀπάθεια).

[120] *Ibid.* 21.2, 5, 8, 9.

thoughts of returning home and seeing their relatives, he says that this indicates an incomplete renunciation.[121] The degree to which monks renounce family ties is illustrated by Abraham who describes how a monk, Apollo, considered himself so dead to world and family that he said he was unable to help his brother pull an ox from a bog.[122] The renunciation of possessions and family ties is seen as integral to the monk's undistracted pursuit of his goals, but as Moses explains in his second conference it needs to be governed by *discretio*.[123] Monks need *discretio* to discern a correct attitude to possessions and their relatives as well as to distinguish between relaxation that supports their aims and ease that distracts from them.

An important element in the balanced management of practical disciplines is thus learning to discern both the appropriate level of personal asceticism and whether those practices are devalued or invalidated by other factors, such as incomplete renunciation. Furthermore, monks need to discern the lifestyle and practical disciplines appropriate to them and distinguish between good and bad examples of monastic practice. Nesteros, in his first conference, contrasts the different styles of πρακτική chosen by anchorites and cœnobites and stresses the importance of each keeping to their chosen method of striving for perfection. He says that some are tempted to change their practice when they are attracted by the *virtutes* of others, but in doing so suffer loss of *virtus* themselves; thus the practice of another monk may be held up for admiration but not imitation.[124] However, not all monastic lifestyles are considered admirable. Piamun describes four types of Egyptian monk, saying that cœnobites and anchorites should be emulated but not sarabaites,[125] who affect only a pretence of *virtus* and the practical disciplines but fail, for example, to submit to elders, make a true renunciation of possessions or 'accept any rule by proper instruction of *sana discretio*.'[126] By implication, the good examples of monasticism (cœnobitic and anchoritic) are governed by *sana discretio* (healthy *discretio*). The fourth type provides another negative example. They fail to reach perfection because their initial fervour is cooled and they fail to overcome vice; he concludes: '*virtutes* are acquired not by the concealment of vices but by attacking them.'[127] The monk, then, needs to exercise

---

[121]   *Ibid.* 24.1.1-24.2.1.

[122]   *Ibid.* 24.9 (= App 7). Further on monks regarding themselves as dead towards others, see below, pp. 219-20.

[123]   *Conf.* 2.2.3-4; 2.26.4.

[124]   *Ibid.* 14.4-7; cf. Nau 204; GSC 7.43; *VP* 5.7.36; PE 1.40.8.3 p595 and Arsenius 38; *VP* 7.18.2; Budge 1.21 where solitude and life with others are both commended.

[125]   *Conf.* 18.4.

[126]   *Ibid.* 18.7.3.

[127]   *Ibid.* 18.8. Cf. *reg. Ben.* 1 where the fourth type are called Gyrovagi or wandering monks.

discretio to choose between good and bad examples of monastic practice, to select one exhibiting *sana discretio* and then discern the value of persevering in that choice without deviating from it.

Discerning an appropriate monastic practice required the monk to assess his capabilities. In his conference, Abraham addresses the monk's need to gauge 'the measure of his own strength' before choosing which discipline to follow, otherwise he is in danger of being deceived into a way of life that would be injurious to him. He illustrates this with the boy David who, using *prudens discretio*,[128] selected weapons suited to his age before fighting Goliath (1 Samuel 17:38-40). Thus, he says, the monk should weigh the anchoritic and coenobitic practices against each other and select that to which he is best suited.[129] *Discretio* is used to achieve this and to avoid being deceived into selecting a harmful choice.

In choosing an appropriate monastic practice, the monk needs to discern not only the respective benefits and his own capabilities but also his need of proper formation. Cassian sees the coenobitic life as inferior to and a preparation for the anchoritic life,[130] respectively focussing on the external and inward life.[131] The monk John, in his conference, says that in the coenobium a monk learns to overcome his desires and develop contempt for worldly things, but the anchorite alone is able to attain purity of contemplation. The rare Divine gift of perfection (notably achieved by the monks Moses, Paphnutius and the two Macarii) is only gained through equal success in both arenas.[132] This sense of progression from the coenobitic to anchoritic life is evident from the way John calls the coenobium 'the school for juniors' and says he returned to it because he believed himself unequal to the anchoritic discipline.[133] This John thus demonstrates *discretio* of himself, discerning the limitations of his ascetic ability, but to this must also be added its use to maintain a humble self-assessment that does not lightly attempt perfection in both the coenobitic and anchoritic lifestyles.

Discretio and Λογισμοί

Cassian follows Evagrius' identification of the eight λογισμοί throughout his works and particularly in *Institutes* 5-12 and *Conferences* 5, adopting and transliterating the Greek terms for four of them. However, he changes

---

[128]   *Prudens discretio* conveys the sense that *discretio* here is wise, prudent, skilful, intelligent, judicious and even cautious.

[129]   *Conf.* 24.8.

[130]   *Ibid.* 17.10; part 3, pref. 1; 18.16.15.

[131]   *Ibid.* part 1, pref. 1.5.

[132]   *Ibid.* 19.8.3-19.9.1.

[133]   *Ibid.* 19.2.4; cf. 19.11.1.

the order[134] reversing Evagrius' λύπη and ὀργή thereby emphasising the connection between λύπη and ἀκηδία, as shown in the table below:

Evagrius (*prak.* 6)	Cassian (*inst.* 5.3)	
γαστριμαργία	*gastrimargia / gulae concupiscentia*	gluttony
πορνεία	*fornicatio*	fornication
φιλαργυρία	*filargyria / avaritia / amor pecuniae*	avarice
λύπη	*ira*	grief / anger
ὀργή	*tristitia*	anger / grief
ἀκηδία	*acedia / anxietas / taedium cordis*	accidie
κενοδοξία	*cenodoxia / inanis gloria*	vainglory
ὑπερηφανία	*superbia*	pride

Table 1

The need to overcome λογισμοί is clear from Cassian's opening comment as he begins to discuss them: 'they devastate everybody and indwell every person'.[135] When he begins to consider the monk's struggle against gluttony, he speaks of the Egyptian monks having 'a more sublime discipline of self-control and perfect rule of *discretio*.'[136] Thus Cassian leaves no doubt that λογισμοί need to be overcome and that those with *discretio* are best equipped to do so.

In his conference, Abraham identifies the same three parts of the soul as Evagrius (λογικόν, θυμικόν and ἐπιθυμητικόν), makes explicit the susceptibility (implied by Evagrius) of each part to particular λογισμοί[137] and equates them with the three Temptations of Christ.[138] For Abraham the λογικόν is the weakest part of the soul and therefore the first point of enemy attack.[139] When it is attacked by vainglory, which deceives the monk

---

134   See above, p. 55, n. 131.
135   *Inst.* 5.2.1.
136   *Ibid.* 5.3. Cassian goes on to praise Antony's *discretio* (*ibid.* 5.4).
137   *Conf.* 24.15.3-4; cf. Evagrius, *prak.* 86 (see above, p. 56).
138   *Conf.* 24.17.5-6; cf. *ibid.* 22.10.
139   *Ibid.* 24.17.1-2.

into thinking that he has already attained perfection and is able to teach others, he can cure it by 'the judgment of right *discretio* and the *virtus* of humility,' cut off the λογισμός with 'the humility of true *discretio*' and so realise that he still needs a teacher himself.[140] *Discretio* thus works with humility to overcome the λογισμός of vainglory and encourage obedience to another. *Discretio* is also presented as the first line of defence against attacks by the λογισμοί and therefore essential to achieving *puritas cordis*.

This need of *discretio* to overcome λογισμοί is also evident from the conference with Sarapion on the eight λογισμοί because it begins by noting that Sarapion was particularly endowed with *gratia discretionis* ('the grace of *discretio*').[141] Sarapion says that the monk should conduct his campaign against λογισμοί by first identifying the vice with which he struggles most, then concentrate a watchful mind on it, use the practical disciplines against it and when it is overcome go on to defeat other lesser λογισμοί that remain.[142] *Discretio* thus unites inward and outward effort to produce a measured and tactical attack on λογισμοί that does not overstretch the monk by tackling them all at once or dividing his efforts.

Although the monk should use *discretio* to identify and tackle the most threatening of his λογισμοί, he should also be aware that he cannot avoid being attacked by them and that he has a choice about whether to allow their influence. Hence Moses, in his first conference, says:

> It is indeed impossible for the mind not to be disturbed by thoughts, however it is possible for all who are zealous to receive them or reject them.[143]

The mind, he says, has the power to choose which thoughts to admit, rejecting λογισμοί with zeal or consenting to them through negligence.[144] Like Evagrius, three sources of thoughts are identified (God, the devil and the monk himself)[145] and the monk should determine their origin and his response by carefully examining his thoughts using sagacious and most prudent *discretio*.[146] Moses explains that *discretio* is necessary for four things: distinguishing the genuine; identifying false thoughts; determining

---

[140] *Ibid.* 24.16.

[141] *Ibid.* 5.1.

[142] *Ibid.* 5.14. Cf. the διάκρισις apophthegm Nau 219 and parallels (see below, p. 155). Theonas says that monks should not seek to be purified of a vice merely because it preoccupies and disturbs the thoughts, but because without doing so others will also attack (*conf.* 22.3.7).

[143] *Conf.* 1.17.1. Cf. GSC 10.81 and parallels (see below, p. 155).

[144] *Ibid.* 1.18.2-3; cf. GSC 5.23; Nau 169; *VP* 5.5.19; *VP* 3.13; PE 1.21.6.4 p307; Budge 1.575 (see below, p. 112, n. 255). Evagrius says the same (e.g. *prak.* 6).

[145] *Conf.* 1.19.1; cf. *ibid.* 4.3; Περὶ Λογ. 8.

[146] *Conf.* 1.20.1.

erroneous theology; and weighing counterfeit ideas. *Discretio* and continual scrutiny of the recesses of his heart enable the monk to distinguish between what is genuinely of God and what is counterfeit and so defend himself against spiritual attack.[147] By placing this statement that *discretio* is a necessity for monks at the start of his conferences in the section on the monk's goals, Cassian makes it a fundamental ability for monastic life and practice. When Cassian and Germanus confess to Abraham, in their conference with him, that they struggle with their thoughts,[148] he also advises them to 'have a constant watchful care over the purity of the inner man' and to avoid places that would distract their minds. Using the metaphor of a fisherman, he tells them to watch the thoughts of their hearts and, with wise *discretio*, choose which to catch and which to disregard as evil and harmful.[149] Although such constant watchfulness is very demanding, he says monks need to remain in their cells and learn to resist λογισμοί[150] and to cut them off if they are to attain perfection.[151] *Discretio* thus enables the monk to examine his thoughts closely to determine which are from God and choose which to eradicate. This potentially intensely introspective use of *discretio* needs to be set against the way *discretio* is not used legalistically but intuitively,[152] so that *discretio* becomes a means of knowing or sensing whether thoughts are right or wrong.

Just as *discretio* should be used to determine the origin of λογισμοί and whether to consent to them, it is also used to identify the nature of things and how to use them. When Germanus and Cassian express concern over why God allowed the murder of Palestinian monks by Saracens,[153] the monk Theodore identifies three types of thing in the world: 'good, evil and indifferent.'[154] He says that *virtus* of the soul is good, that sin and consequent separation from God is evil and that indifferent things can result

---

[147]   *Ibid.* 1.22.

[148]   *Ibid.* 24.1.2.

[149]   *Ibid.* 24.3.

[150]   *Ibid.* 24.4-5.

[151]   *Ibid.* 24.23.1. Pinufius, discussing repentance and forgiveness, stresses the need to 'drive the disposition towards (sins) from our hearts' (*ibid.* 20.5.1; cf. 20.11.1). The monk should no longer dwell on past and forgiven sins, but die to vices and so flourish in *virtutes* and concentrate on future joys (*ibid.* 20.8.11). Such recollection only distracts from contemplation and destroys *virtutes*, since it is impossible for the mind to concentrate on good things when it is preoccupied with the shameful (*ibid.* 20.9.1, 4). Rather the monk should have 'an appetite for *virtutes* and a desire for the Kingdom of Heaven' (*ibid.* 20.10) and for '*puritas cordis* and the perfection of apostolic love' (*ibid.* 20.12.4).

[152]   See above, pp. 90-91.

[153]   *Conf.* 6.1.

[154]   Cf. Theonas' identification of good, bad and neutral things (*ibid.* 21.12.3-4; see above, p. 88).

in either good or evil depending on the 'disposition and decision of the user.'[155] Evil and sin cannot, he says, be imposed on someone who is 'unwilling and resistant,'[156] in other words evil is a matter of consent or, as he says later, someone's reaction to an action.[157] Similarly, Serenus in his first conference says that the monk suffers inner struggles when his spiritual enemy incites him to sin, but that enemy cannot force him to do evil because he has the '*virtus* to refuse or the freedom to acquiesce.'[158] He says that the νοῦς, which Cassian translates as *mens*, is readily distracted but has the power to resist the 'enemy's suggestions'[159] and that monks 'are able to subject hostile disturbances and vices to (their) authority and *discretio*'. They have the 'power and *virtus*' to command evil suggestions to go and the good to come and so enjoin their bodies to live uprightly.[160] Cassian speaks elsewhere of the illuminating power of 'the mind [*mens*], that is the νοῦς or reason, which scrutinises the thoughts and *discretio* of the heart'.[161] *Discretio* is therefore the faculty, power and *virtus*, used by the νοῦς to distinguish between good and bad things externally and internally, to battle against what is evil and to choose an appropriate reaction, particularly consent or rejection. Like Evagrius, then, Cassian places *discretio* in the highest spiritual faculty and centre of being making it a central function in the monk's life.[162]

The use of *discretio* to distinguish between good and evil is understood to be a work of cooperation between the monk and the Holy Spirit using Scripture.[163] In his first conference Serenus speaks of the Word of God as the sword of the Spirit (Ephesians 6:19) and interprets this using Hebrews 4:12 saying it is the '*discretor* of the thoughts and intentions of the heart' which 'divides and cuts off what is carnal and earthly in us.'[164] Later he answers Germanus' concern that, but for the grace of God, the difference between thoughts inspired by demons and by human will 'can hardly be distinguished [*discerno*]'[165] by explaining that since God alone is incorporeal, he alone is able to penetrate 'all spiritual and intellectual

---

[155] *Conf.* 6.3.1-2.

[156] *Ibid.* 6.4.1.

[157] *Ibid.* 6.6.4.

[158] *Ibid.* 7.8.1-2; cf. 8.19.2 where demons are said not to be capable of affecting a monk's soul unless he is devoid of 'every holy thought and spiritual contemplation.'

[159] *Ibid.* 7.4.2. On the easily distracted νοῦς see Evagrius, *prak.* 48 (above, p. 69).

[160] *Conf.* 7.5.2-3.

[161] *Inst.* 8.10.

[162] See above, pp. 49-50.

[163] *Discretio* and Scripture in Cassian is discussed further below (pp. 107-11).

[164] *Conf.* 7.5.7.

[165] *Ibid.* 7.9.

substances', again using Hebrews 4:12 to support this.[166] Thus in order to distinguish between good and evil thoughts, the monk is dependent upon God and Scripture. Similarly, when Chæremon, in his second conference, describes true chastity as a state where body and spirit are no longer at war with each other,[167] he says that *discretio* stands at the boundary between the two enabling the monk to discern his thoughts and actions in a just and balanced way that avoids deceit. This is achieved through 'long experience and *puritas cordis*' and the guidance of God's Word, *discretor* of thoughts and intentions (Hebrews 4:12).[168] Perfect chastity is distinguished (*discerno*) from continence in that it no longer fights carnal desire but detests it, seeking purity instead.[169] Thus, although *discretio* is developed by using it, it is also used in reliance upon God and Scripture. *Discretio* provides a bridge between the inner and outer life, standing as guardian over both and uniting them so that inward and outward purity are in harmony. Integral to that process is using Scripture under God's guidance to determine the nature and origin of thoughts, to advance in purity and to gain a realistic assessment of purity attained.

This need for purity and integrity of body and spirit can be illustrated from Joseph's first conference on friendship[170] and how to deal with anger and disputes. He says that it is insufficient to resolve a dispute over something trivial by only dealing with the presenting problem; inner anger needs to be addressed as well.[171] Failure to resolve inner anger is dangerous, he says, and may result, for example, in a deterioration of relationship with others and with God.[172] Both the external act and the inner intention need to be examined and monks should match their outward action to their inward disposition;[173] anger should 'be controlled by the guidance of *discretio*'.[174] Monks should aim, then, at a unity and integrity of body and spirit where actions and thoughts are examined, guided and governed by *discretio*.

---

[166]   *Ibid.* 7.13.2-3. Thus demons cannot see the monk's thoughts but are said to be keen observers of his outward behaviour and tempt him accordingly (*ibid.* 7.15). Similarly, in Macarius the Egyptian 3 (see also: GSC 18.13; *VP* 5.18.9; *VP* 3.61; *VP* 7.1.8; PE 1.20.3.9 pp268-9; Ch181; Am230.1; Dorotheos, *doctr.* 5.65; cf. Nau 488; PE 3.9.2.8 pp99-100) Satan is described as experimenting with different temptations until the monk succumbs.

[167]   Cf. *conf.* 4.12.3.

[168]   *Ibid.* 12.8.1-2.

[169]   *Ibid.* 12.11.1.

[170]   This is poignant as it is addressed to two friends, Germanus and Cassian.

[171]   *Conf.* 16.8-9.

[172]   *Ibid.* 16.15-16.

[173]   *Ibid.* 16.22.1-2.

[174]   *Ibid.* 16.27.1.

Cassian thus understands *discretio* as a means of guarding against λογισμοί and as a weapon to overcome them. *Discretio* enables the monk to watch over his thoughts, to determine their nature and origin, and to choose which to accept and reject. It is the power to distinguish between good and bad things, actions and thoughts and to choose how best to respond to them. By using *discretio* in conjunction with the practical disciplines, humility, obedience, dependence upon God, who knows the monk's inner self, and Scripture, the monk is able to examine and govern his inner and outer life bringing them to purity and harmony.

Discretio and Self-knowledge

The monk's examination of thoughts is closely related to his understanding of his inner condition. Origen says that self-knowledge is to 'master *discretio* of everything that should be done and be avoided,'[175] focussing particularly on *virtutes*, vices and the avoidance of deceit. This is reflected in the third conference with Theonas who says the sharp spiritual eyes of the more perfect are able to see every small inner imperfection, but those blinded by vice are incapable of seeing their inner faults.[176] Later he says that as the mind advances towards 'purity of contemplation' it is increasingly capable of seeing its impurity mirrored in its purity.[177] Thus as the monk advances towards his goals, he becomes progressively more aware of his inner state and what remains to be purified.[178]

The monk gains this growing awareness of his inner condition through the conflict between his flesh and spirit. Daniel, in his conference, describes how the spirit in this conflict acts as 'a most diligent pedagogue' teaching the monk that the 'gift of purity cannot be possessed except by the grace of God alone.'[179] Daniel explains that this conflict arises from the passion of the flesh for vice and the spirit for *virtus*, centring on not being able to do what one wants to do. Between the two lies the will or choice (*voluntas*).[180] He then says:

---

[175] Origen, *comm. in Cant.* 2.5.16. Cf. Cassian, *conf.* 2.2.5.
[176] *Conf.* 23.6.
[177] *Ibid.* 23.19.2.
[178] A similar progression is found at the start of John Climacus' discussion of discernment (*scala parad.* 26): in beginners discernment is self-knowledge, next it is the spiritual ability to distinguish between good and evil and finally in the perfect it is God given knowledge. In general, he says, discernment is a sound and constant understanding of God's will found in those who are pure in heart, body and speech.
[179] *Conf.* 4.15.
[180] *Ibid.* 4.9.2; 4.12.1. Cf. Gal. 5:17.

To discern [*discerno*] the divisions and threads of questions is the role of the intellect, and the greatest role of intelligence is to know what you do not know.[181]

Discretio is thus the operation of freewill in the intellect, choosing between *virtus* and vice, but it is not merely a means of knowing, it is also an awareness of ignorance. Daniel says that monks will fail to progress if they rely on modifying their outward behaviour alone, they must also 'apprehend (their) spiritual state'.[182] Thus, *discretio* lies at the border between flesh and spirit enabling monks to resolve their conflicting drives[183] and bring them into harmony by learning from their experiences, determining the limits of their knowledge, increasing their self-knowledge and applying these to develop inward as well as outward purity. It is, therefore, *discretio* to use knowledge and awareness of ignorance not for information but for transformation; *discretio* guides the monk in the practical development of purity.

The need to correct exterior behaviour before attempting to purify the interior life could easily be neglected. For example, the monk John, in his conference, speaks of monks drawn to the anchoritic life without first learning to overcome their vices in the cœnobium. As a result they found the solitary life as distressing and difficult as living in community because they had failed to discern the purpose of withdrawal into the desert.[184] This suggests that monks need to know themselves accurately, the extent to which they have overcome their vices and particularly how stable and resilient their inner state is. Such neglectful monks are said only to have suppressed the external manifestations of their faults and not eradicated the dispositions behind them. Thus they need to discern (*deprehendo*) the difference from the indications of those vices still rooted in their hearts[185] using *discretio*.[186] Thus monks separated (*discerno*) from ordinary human

---

[181]   *Conf.* 4.9.1. Cf. Antony 17 (see also: GSC 15.4; *VP* 5.15.4; PE 4.17.1.13-14 p314; Budge 1.551) where the wisest monk claims not to know the meaning of a Scripture text. Cf. also Plato, *rep.* 7.6-7.7, 509d-521b on the role of the intellect (see above, p. 17, n. 116).

[182]   *Conf.* 4.19.2.

[183]   See above, p. 98.

[184]   *Conf.* 19.10.

[185]   *Ibid.* 19.12.

[186]   *Ibid.* 19.13.1. Theonas says, 'even if someone has ascended the splendid summit of *virtutes* ... nevertheless he should know he cannot be without sin' (*ibid.* 22.7.2.) since Christ alone is sinless (*ibid.* 22.9.1-2) and resisted the wilderness temptations presented by the 'author of deceit' (*ibid.* 22.10.1) and so monks should not be deceived into claiming they too are without sin (*ibid.* 22.12.3). *Discretio* thus enables monks to recognise their sin and avoid the devil's deceit. See also above, p. 84, n. 78.

life, need to be their own 'severest censor' and overcome what motivates them to vice with humility, constant meditation, self-reproach, ascetic acts and compunction.[187] This use of *discretio* as a severe censor is evident from this same John's rhetorical question:

> What ... is more destructive or what more loathsome, than that someone should lose the evidence of integrity and the rule and discipline of proper *discretio* and, sane and sober, perpetrate things for which even someone drunk and senseless would not be pardoned?[188]

Discretio is thus disciplined self-examination that results in an accurate self-assessment of capability and vulnerability. Unless monks use *discretio* to read their own condition they are in danger of advancing too quickly (e.g. from cœnobitic to anchoritic life) and of failing to determine whether they have controlled their λογισμοί or eradicated them.[189] Monks need *discretio* to gain self-knowledge and to maintain their integrity.

Discretio and Prayer

In the second conference with Isaac, Germanus rues how readily he is distracted from prayer and contemplation, which needs to be learnt like any natural art or discipline.[190] Isaac explains that such self-examination using discernment (*discerno*) indicates that he is approaching purity in prayer.[191] Thus the monk requires *discretio* if he is to pray and contemplate effectively. Like Evagrius, Cassian regards pure prayer as wordless and imageless,[192] and speaks of 'fiery prayer', a rarely achieved state beyond understanding in which the monk is immersed in Divine light.[193] Such pure prayer is reached progressively through four levels which Cassian bases on 1 Timothy 2:1. Cassian's highest level is thanksgiving, a wordless contemplation of God's beneficence,[194] but the levels can only be comprehended with 'great purity of heart and soul and the inspiration of the

---

[187] *Conf.* 19.14.1-5.

[188] *Ibid.* 19.14.6. Cf. *sana discretio* in *ibid.* 18.7.3 (see above, pp. 92-93).

[189] Cf. Abraham 1 and parallels (see below, pp. 151-52).

[190] *Conf.* 10.8.

[191] *Ibid.* 10.9.1-2.

[192] *Ibid.* 10.5.3; 10.11.6; cf. Evagrius, *de orat.* 11, 66, 114, 117. The Anthropomorphite controversy distressed Sarapion because he was no longer permitted a mental image of God in prayer (*conf.* 10.3.5; see above, p. 36).

[193] *Conf.* 9.25; cf. Evagrius, *antirr.* prol. (light of Trinity); *skem.* 2, 4; Περὶ Λογ. 39 (sapphire light); see above, pp. 53-54.

[194] *Conf.* 9.9-14.

Holy Spirit.'[195] This suggests that pure prayer is attained by using *discretio* both to grow in purity and to understand prayer at each level. There is understood to be a reciprocity between constant prayer and 'bodily labour' (i.e. practical disciplines) or *virtutes*, since they serve to perfect each other.[196] Thus, for example, in his conference 'On *Discretio*' Moses says that for pure prayer to be achieved a moderate regime for the discipline of fasting needs to be established.[197] *Discretio* is understood, then, to be woven into the fabric of prayer. It is needed to attain purity and regulate practical disciplines so that pure prayer can be progressively perfected, but the reciprocity Isaac indicates suggests that *discretio* is also developed through prayer.

This development of *discretio* through perfect and impassive prayer is also associated with the use in prayer of Scripture, particularly the psalms. Scripture and psalmody enable the monk to express his inner state, progress to a higher understanding of Scripture and the nature of things as well as breaking away from a dependence on images and words in order to concentrate the mind more fully on God.[198] Cassian promotes 'the rule of canonical prayers and psalms' based on the Eastern model[199] and the use of brief, repeated ejaculatory prayers using, for example, Psalm 69:2 (Vg): 'O

---

[195]   *Ibid.* 9.8.1. Origen similarly categorises prayer using 1 Tim. 2:1 (*de orat.* 14.2) but Cassian departs from Evagrius who does not consider Cassian's highest level, εὐχαριστία (thanksgiving), at all. Cassian is also very similar to Origen in his discussion of the Our Father (*conf.* 9.18-23; Origen, *de orat.* 22-30), for example: adoption as sons of God; gaining understanding of God; petition for the interior reign of Christ; heavenly submission to the Divine will; spiritual interpretation of ἐπιούσιος; a shift to the practical life in relation to forgiveness; and the value of temptation. Cassian concludes that the Our Father emphasises eternal rather than transitory needs and leads the monk towards a higher state of prayer (*conf.* 9.24-25; cf. the progress towards spiritual perfection in Origen, *de orat.* 25.2).

[196]   *Conf.* 9.2.1-2.

[197]   *Ibid.* 2.22; cf. *inst.* 5.9. Cassian says that his *Institutes* concentrates primarily on the exterior life of the monk and the *Conferences* on the interior state of the monk in prayer (*conf.* part 1, pref. 5; *inst.* 2.9).

[198]   *Conf.* 10.11.4-6. Cassian notes the varied number of psalms used in the offices of different regions and the competitive attempts by some to exceed thirty or even sixty (*inst.* 2.2.1; 2.5.4). However, in Egypt the number was set at twelve after a monk miraculously vanished after singing the twelfth (*inst.* 2.5.5; cf. Pachomius and the rule of the angel in *HL* 32.6) to which they added either two New Testament passages or one from each Testament for those eager in the study of Scripture (*inst.* 2.6). Since Egyptian monks were more concerned to understand the meaning than to recite a great volume of Scripture these twelve psalms were sung a few verses at a time (*inst.* 2.11.1-2). This suggests *discretio* in the use of psalmody and Scripture in that they chose to limit their practice in order to gain understanding.

[199]   *Inst.* 2.1; cf. Evagrius, *de orat.* 82, 83, 85, 87.

God, turn to my aid; O Lord, make haste to help me!'[200] By ruminating on this verse the monk is able to establish a watchful guard over his heart and defend himself from demonic attack, using the verse antirrhetically.[201] Such repetitive prayer enables the monk to cling more closely to God and counter demonic distractions during prayer,[202] but he should also rid his heart and mind of all potential distractions before praying.[203] *Discretio* provides the monk with the means to examine and rid himself of these distractions as well as to use Scripture during prayer to defend himself effectively against demonic assault. The careful regulation of Scripture used, the discernment of meaning and especially the use of psalms to express the inward state and to advance in understanding all support the impression that *discretio* lies at the heart of prayer.

Discretio as Counsellor and Guide

The second conference with Joseph provides an example of how *discretio* was used to arrive at a decision; a problem is submitted to an elder and to Scripture rather than relying on personal judgment alone. The *mise en scène* was a struggle facing Cassian and Germanus about whether to keep their promise to their superiors and return to their cœnobium in Palestine, which return they believed would be detrimental to their spiritual advancement, or renege on their promise and remain in Egypt where they had found the monastic ideal they sought.[204] Joseph says that promises should not be made hastily as monks are bound to keep them,[205] but an incautious promise may be broken in order to pursue the monk's goal of a pure heart.[206] The ethical uncertainty of such a breach is not ignored. Lying is likened to hellebore:[207] potentially deadly to the healthy but beneficial to

---

[200]   *Conf.* 9.36.1; 10.10.2; cf. Evagrius, *de orat.* 98, 151; Περὶ Λογ. 34; Augustine, *ep.* 130.10.20; Benedict, *reg. Ben.* 20. Around half of the Scripture texts used by Evagrius in *Antirrheticus* for antirrhetic prayers against specific λογισμοί derive from the psalms. This use of Ps. 69:2 (Vg) by Cassian is a significant step towards the monastic and Orthodox use of the Jesus Prayer.

[201]   *Conf.* 10.10.3-15.

[202]   *Inst.* 2.10.3.

[203]   *Conf.* 9.3.4. Cf. the simile of the feather earlier (p. 81): sin weighs down the soul keeping it from rising to the heights of spiritual contemplation (*conf.* 9.4.1-9.5.2), thus the monk needs to weigh up with *discretio* whether there is anything within him that prevents him praying.

[204]   *Ibid.* 17.2. Cassian may have written this conference as an *apologia pro vita sua* that justified his decision to remain longer in Egypt.

[205]   *Ibid.* 17.8.1.

[206]   *Ibid.* 17.14.3.

[207]   Hellebore was used in antiquity to treat mental disorders (Hippocrates, *de diaeta* 1.35) and as a purgative, although in greater doses it is poisonous

someone with a fatal condition.[208] Thus lying is said to be permissible *in
extremis*, but needs to be used carefully. Using the example of 'the more
sublime *virtus*' and 'humble lie' of concealing personal abstinence when
eating with others, Joseph contrasts the obstinate determination of
Palestinian elders who follow their own will and Egyptian elders who act
according 'to the judgment and *discretio* of the Spirit'.[209] Using Scriptural
examples, Joseph argues that when circumstances change it is not always
possible to do what the mind has decided.[210] Thus monks should not hold
obstinately to their decisions, which is to be without *discretio*,[211] but use
discretio to select what is useful.[212] Thus, while monks should hold
unswervingly to such 'principal commands' as love, chastity and faith, they
should have a light hold on 'bodily exercises' (i.e. practical disciplines) and
not keep to them so rigidly that they cannot let them go in order to do what
is more beneficial.[213] *Discretio*, then, is not legalistic but used with great
flexibility to re-examine or even reinterpret earlier decisions in order to
advance towards God. It is used to weigh up what will be beneficial to the
monk's progress and guides the monk through difficult choices about
courses of action that appear equally wrong in the light of earlier promises
and commitments.

Less controversially than the re-evaluation of promises, *discretio* is also
used to steer a course between extremes of asceticism. For example
Theonas, in his first conference, says that *discretio* should be used to guide
the monk between excessive abstinence and indulgence:

> If we weigh out everything that we do with the reasonable examination of
> the mind and from our *puritas cordis* not the judgments of others, but we
> always consult our conscience, it is certain that this interval of recreation
> is unable to injure a just rigour, if only, as has been said, the uncorrupted
> mind weighs carefully the impartial measure of indulgence and
> continence on a proper scale and similarly on the other side chastises
> excess, and it distinguishes with true *discretio* whether the weight of
> pleasures presses down our spirit or in truth a greater austerity of
> abstinence brings down the other part, that is the body, either crushing or

---

(Gellius, *noctes Atticae*, 17.15; Horace, *ep.* 2.2.137; Seneca, *epistulae morales ad
Lucilium* 10.83.27). Cf. Dorotheos, *doctr.* 9.102.

[208] *Conf.* 17.17.1, 3.

[209] *Ibid.* 17.23.1; cf. Eulogius 1 and parallels (see below, p. 169).

[210] *Conf.* 17.25.5-6. However, lying is also condemned in Scripture and said to cut a
person off from God (Pss 12:2-3; 101:7).

[211] *Conf.* 17.26.

[212] *Ibid.* 17.25.9.

[213] *Ibid.* 17.28.

raising that part, which it has perceived either to be raised or weighed down.[214]

Discretio operates within the reasoning mind[215] providing the monk with the means to moderate his fasting and, by implication, his other practical disciplines. It acts as an accurate and impartial balance in which matters are weighed and as a 'true judge' of the monk's inner purity. However, *discretio* needs to be maintained by a 'constantly circumspect heart' so that the monk is not led astray, but can keep himself from extremes[216] by using *discretio* like a rudder.[217] Moses, in his conference 'On *Discretio*', also describes how *discretio* is used to guide the monk between the detrimental extremes of fasting and overeating and of excessive vigils and, by implication, over indulgence in sleep.

> Therefore with every effort the good of *discretio* must be acquired by the *virtus* of humility, which can keep us uninjured from both extremes. For truly there is an old aphorism: ἀκρότητες ἰσότητες, that is extremes are equals.[218]

He explains that monks not 'deceived by gluttony' may fall into 'immoderate fasting' and so they need to 'walk between either extreme by the guide of *discretio*,'[219] which enables them to 'advance with balanced [*aequalis*] rigour'.[220] *Discretio* is thus used to identify extremes harmful to the monk's spiritual state and his progress towards his goals and to guide him safely between those extremes. Since the acquisition of guiding *discretio* is said to require the *virtus* of humility, it follows that a humble

---

214   *Ibid.* 21.22.1. *Discretio* here carries the same senses of weighing, examination and choice associated with διάκρισις.

215   As Evagrius (see above, pp. 49-50).

216   *Conf.* 21.22.2-3.

217   *Ibid.* 21.22.5 (*moderamen discretionis*. Cf. *ibid.* 2.18.1 re *aequum moderamen* of abstinence; see above, p. 89).

218   *Ibid.* 2.16.1. B. Ramsey, *John Cassian: The Conferences* (Ancient Christian Writers 57; New York: Paulist Press, 1997), p. 111 notes that the origin of this Greek maxim is unknown. However, it is defined in Aesop (6th century BC): 'Great riches and great poverty have equal ἀνάπαυσις [rest] from cares' (*proverbia* 81). It is also used by the commentator on Aristotle, Alexander Aphrodisiensis (2nd-3rd century AD) when explaining how cold snow burns (*problemata* 4.24) and by Epiphanius Constantiensis (c.315-403AD) in his discussion of the Collyridian heresy when explaining the equal harm done by extremes of honouring and disparaging the virgin Mary (*adversus haereses* 79.1).

219   *Conf.* 2.16.2. Cf. Aristotle (*eth. Nic.* 2.6, 1106b-1107a) who says that virtue finds the mean between the evils of excess and deficiency.

220   *Inst.* 5.41.

submission to the counsel of *discretio* is called for. This almost gives *discretio* the counselling role of the Holy Spirit, although, unlike the Holy Spirit, *discretio* can be misled. Thus Cassian comes close to personifying *discretio* as a pilot or judge that can be deceived. However, this is countered by making *discretio* an activity of the reasoning mind and therefore an analytical and ultimately intuitive ability to moderate practical disciplines and so make them effective tools for spiritual advancement. The need for *discretio* to be constantly maintained further suggests that it requires constant use and practice to be effective, indicating that it is more rudder than helmsman. The monk thus steers his course on his spiritual journey with *discretio*.

As monks advance in experience and develop their skill in *discretio* they are more capable of exercising their ability to make reasoned and intuitive decisions and to moderate their lives more effectively with it. When Moses, at the end of his first conference, speaks of *discretio* in superlative terms,[221] he says that 'the best counsellors of *discretio*' should evince 'diligence of mind' and patience when they discuss that 'mother of moderation'. He thus says that *discretio*, which in part consists of moderation, dictates that they limit how long they speak and rest before continuing.[222] When the discussion continues in the second conference, he says he will show how 'to aspire to and develop [*discretio*] by considering its merit and the dignity of its grace.' *Discretio*, he says, is 'no mean *virtus*' and it can only be acquired if human effort is united with Divine generosity. Thus he lists the spiritual gifts in 1 Corinthians 12:8-11 stressing the Divine source of *discretio* and the monk's need to 'possess *discretio spirituum* [discernment of spirits] rising up in himself' if he is to be guided and not go astray.[223] Teachers and counsellors can thus only counsel if they themselves have the counsel of *discretio*, given by God and learnt through using it. Put another way, if monks are to guide others, they need to be guided by *discretio* themselves and they pass on their experience of how to use the spiritual gift of *discretio* to govern the monastic life.

As the monk develops *discretio* through experience and practice, he is able to use it to govern his life and progress towards his goals more and more effectively. Thus Moses, in his second conference says *discretio* is 'the lamp of the body ... the government of our life ... counsel ... guidance,' in it 'rests wisdom ... understanding and sense.' It is 'solid food' that gives the monk '*discretio* of good and evil' (Hebrews 5:14) and is so 'useful and necessary' to him that Moses compares it to the Word of God as '*discretor* of the thoughts and intentions of the heart' (Hebrews 4:12). Moses says that 'without the grace of *discretio* no *virtus* can be perfectly

---

[221] *Conf.* 1.23.1 (see above, p. 84).
[222] *Conf.* 1.23.3.
[223] *Ibid.* 2.1.2-4.

achieved or endure', but *'discretio* guides the fearless monk with a fixed step towards God and continually preserves uninjured the aforesaid *virtutes'*. With *discretio* the monk may attain the heights of perfection 'for *discretio* is the mother, guardian and regulator of all the *virtutes*.'[224] This emphatic statement of the supreme value of *discretio* is quite breathtaking. It is equated with Scripture and said to be essential for the monk's ascent to God as it regulates and controls the whole of the monk's life. There would appear to be a danger here of over dependence on *discretio* such that it begins to replace Scripture and the Holy Spirit as the monk's counsellor and guide. However, this is countered by the repeated emphasis on dependence upon God, constant recourse to Scripture and frequent warnings against pride in personal ability. Nevertheless, it is clear that for Cassian *discretio* is central and vital in the monk's spiritual life.

Discretio and Scripture

Given the equation of *discretio* with Scripture and the potential danger of *discretio* replacing it in importance, the relation between the two requires investigation. *Discretio* is used to interpret Scripture and discover its deeper meaning. In his second conference Serenus explains that while the meaning of some Scripture is clearly evident to all, other parts have hidden spiritual meanings that only those 'devoted to *virtus* and prudence' can understand;[225] although the Holy Spirit has concealed these meanings, they can be discovered through meditation.[226] Thus Nesteros, in his first conference, says that monks should commit themselves to meditating on the Scriptures in order to discover the 'spiritual and divine' in them[227] and that good speaking abilities are no indication of such perceptiveness.[228] Similarly, Paphnutius speaks of the need of God's instruction and enlightenment rather than merely reading words.[229] Cassian reports that Theodore said that the monk wishing to understand Scripture should not study commentaries but:

> ...engage every activity of the mind and intention of the heart towards cleansing carnal vices, when these have been driven out and the veil of the passions has been lifted, immediately the eyes of the heart instinctively contemplate the mysteries of the Scriptures.[230]

---

[224] *Ibid.* 2.4. Cf. Benedict, *reg. Ben.* 64.
[225] *Conf.* 8.3.1-2.
[226] *Ibid.* 8.4.1.
[227] *Ibid.* 14.13.1.
[228] *Ibid.* 14.9.7; 14.16.1.
[229] *Ibid.* 3.14-15.
[230] *Inst.* 5.34.

Thus sin and λογισμοί cloud the monk's inner eye to the deeper and veiled meaning of Scripture. However, he is able to access that meaning by eradicating λογισμοί, purifying the heart, developing *virtutes* and dedicating himself to meditation in dependence upon God rather than upon reading, skill or education. Since *discretio* is required for each of these processes and because there is an implicit need of discernment in determining this deeper meaning, *discretio* is therefore necessary for understanding Scripture.[231] The impression that *discretio* is necessary for interpreting Scripture is confirmed by a negative example provided by Joseph in his first conference where he speaks of those who fail to discern (*discerno*) what a passage means.[232]

Discerning the meaning of Scripture correctly was important for avoiding false doctrine. Moses in his first conference says that *prudentissima discretio*[233] is therefore needed to guard against being deceived into false doctrine arising from the 'corrupt interpretation of Scripture'. He compares this to 'approved moneychangers' weighing and testing coinage to determine whether they are genuinely gold (pure gold equating to Scripture), just as διάκρισις is used of testing gold and weighing the clouds in Job 23:10 and 37:16 respectively.[234] In the next

---

[231] Origen similarly speaks of the meaning of Scripture being hidden by a veil over the heart but lifted on the advent of Christ and conversion to him (*de prin.* 1.1.2; 4.1.6; *cont. Cels.* 6.70; *comm. in Cant.* 3.11; cf. Basil the Great, *de spiritu sancto* 21.52). The veil over the heart is lifted as God's gift to those who make every effort and pray for understanding and so are able to exercise διάκρισις of good and evil (*cont. Cels.* 4.50). There are also veiled mystical meanings behind the historical account of creation (*de prin.* 3.5.1) and the created order (*comm. in Cant.* 3.12). Origen also contrasts the Jewish literal and Christian spiritual understanding of Scripture (*hom. in Gen.* 6.1). Clement of Alexandria speaks of a veil of allegory and mystic veil over knowledge of God which, when lifted, allows διάκρισις of good and evil, *inter alia* (*strom.* 5.9-10; cf. Arnobius, *adversus gentes* 5.35; 5.41). Augustine writes frequently of the veiled meaning of Scripture: the veil over the Old Testament (*enarr. in Ps.* 118, *sermo* 26.8) is made void in Christ (*de utilitate credendi* 3.9), removed on conversion to him (*enarr. in Ps.* 7.1) and may be lifted to reveal the inner meaning by the pious using the eye of the heart (*enarr. in Ps.* 34 *sermo* 2.3). By contrast, much later, John Calvin speaks of Scripture as spectacles that restore vision of God and therefore revelatory rather than obscure (*Institutes of the Christian Religion* 1.6.1; 1.14.1).

[232] *Conf.* 16.17.3.

[233] Most wise / prudent / skilful / intelligent / judicious / cautious *discretio*.

[234] *Ibid.* 1.20. In Late Antique Egypt the precious metal content of coins was gradually reduced and so coins needed to be assayed to assess their value. The production of copy coins (by stamping and plating) was also widespread, with one major outbreak of copying occurring in fourth century Egypt, making the detection of imitations necessary (Bagnall, *Currency and Inflation*, pp. 53-54; C. King, 'Roman Copies', in C.E. King and D.G. Wigg (eds), *Coin Finds and Coin Use in the Roman World,*

conference 'On *Discretio*' Germanus repeats the 'become approved moneychangers' agraphon when he expresses his desire to learn *discretio* so that he can test 'what is true and from God or false and diabolic.'[235] *Discretio* is used, then, to weigh and test doctrine and Scripture interpretations so that deceit can be avoided.

Discretio was also needed to determine the type of Scripture interpretation that should be used. For example, Serenus says that Scripture can be understood historically, allegorically or both. While allegorical interpretations, he says, can yield deeper spiritual meanings that feed the monk's spiritual inner man, he can be led astray by a literal interpretation. He illustrates this from the way the injunction to take up one's cross (Matthew 10:38) led strict and zealous monks who nevertheless lacked knowledge (Romans 10:2) to carry wooden crosses, an act which brought ridicule rather than edification.[236]

Nesteros, in his conference on spiritual knowledge, expands the division of Scripture interpretation to four levels. He explains that θεωρητική consists of *historica interpretatio* ('knowledge of past and visible things') and the three elements of *intellegentia spiritalis*: *tropologia*; *allegoria*; *anagoge*. He understands *allegoria* to be a revelation of spiritual mysteries hidden and prefigured in *historica*, *anagoge* to be the deeper heavenly secrets beyond those mysteries and *tropologia* as 'the moral explanation relating to the purification of life and practical instruction'.[237] He goes on to say that *tropologia* is knowledge 'by which we discern [*discerno*] by prudent examination all that relates to *discretio actualis* to see whether it is

(Studien zu Fundmünzen der Antike 10; Berlin: Gebr. Mann, 1996), pp. 237-63). On the agraphon 'become approved moneychangers' and coin impresses see below, p. 157, n. 153.

[235] *Conf.* 2.9. Waaijman uses this agraphon to distinguish four components in the action of discernment in Cassian: determining difference (e.g. good and evil), meaning, a course between extremes and spiritual progress (K. Waaijman, 'Discernment: Its history and meaning', *Studies in Spirituality* 7 (1997), pp. 5-41).

[236] *Conf.* 8.3.4-5. Cf. the zealous literal interpretation of Mt. 19:12 that led some to castrate themselves (GSC 15.111; Nau 334; *VP* 5.15.88; PE 1.45.1.75 p656; Ch155; Budge 1.524) as Origen was said to have done (Eusebius, *HE* 6.8.1-2; Jerome, *ep.* 84.8).

[237] *Conf.* 14.8.1-3. De Lubac also identifies a fourfold division of Scripture in *conf.* 8.3: a loftier interpretation than the literal sense; allegorical; combined literal and allegorical; and historical (for the less able). Discussing Nesteros' fourfold division in *conf.* 14.8 de Lubac notes that although Cassian regards them as successive interpretations necessary for gaining a full understanding of Scripture, Cassian does not hold rigidly to the order and insists that different texts fall into different categories (H. de Lubac, *Medieval Exegesis: The Four Senses of Scripture* (trans. M. Sebanc; 2 vols; Grand Rapids: Ressourcement, 1998), pp. 134-37).

useful or upright'.[238] The interpretation of Scripture was thus understood to require careful discernment both of the type of interpretation that should be used and the different levels of meaning a passage carried. The deeper spiritual meaning was the most valued for personal spiritual development and so monks needed to guard against misguided literal interpretations. However, *discretio* of that meaning was intended for practical purposes rather than knowledge for its own sake. *Discretio* is thus presented not only as a practical discipline and mental process,[239] but also as a spiritual exercise to gain spiritual knowledge.

For Nesteros the interpretation of Scripture using *discretio* to gain spiritual knowledge begins with humility of heart. The monk should, with a pure heart, memorise, continually repeat and meditate upon Scripture,[240] since a mind full of Scripture cannot be filled with λογισμοί. Such undistracted reflection upon Scripture reveals its most hidden meanings[241] and through it the monk grows in understanding of them as he grows spiritually.[242] Since the mind cannot be devoid of thoughts, if it is not occupied with spiritual matters it will be occupied with whatever else it has learnt in the past.[243] Furthermore, a monk with an unclean soul and heart can neither teach nor acquire spiritual knowledge.[244] Nesteros also emphasises the need to weigh carefully the opinions of others and not be taken in by those who seem to possess knowledge but lack purity.[245] Finally, he details the process of acquiring spiritual knowledge: seek practical perfection, expel carnal sins, grow in spiritual *virtutes* and so attain to the light of knowledge or perfection.[246] Discerning the meaning of Scripture and gaining spiritual knowledge is once again shown to be for practical application to life.[247] While *discretio* is not used in this part of Nesteros' discussion, the different elements he describes are each said elsewhere to require *discretio*. The regulation of thoughts and practical disciplines associated with the use of Scripture, self-examination and the eradication of λογισμοί and distractions, the assessment of teachers and

---

[238]   *Conf.* 14.8.6.
[239]   See above, p. 87.
[240]   Cf. practice of *lectio divina.*
[241]   *Conf.* 14.10.
[242]   *Ibid.* 14.11.1.
[243]   *Ibid.* 14.13.2.
[244]   *Ibid.* 14.14.
[245]   *Ibid.* 14.16.1, 4.
[246]   *Ibid.* 14.16.3.
[247]   Cf. the διάκρισις apophthegm Nau 228 and parallels which bemoans the decline over several generations of monks from applying Scripture in life, through memorising it, to simply possessing copies of it. Similar expressions of decline over three generations of monks are noted elsewhere (e.g. John Kolobos 14, Ischyrion 1, Poemen 166). It is διάκρισις to apply Scripture in life.

their doctrine, and choosing to apply what has been learnt all require *discretio*. Without *discretio*, then, monks cannot use or interpret Scripture effectively.

Discretio **and Revelation**

In his second conference Nesteros discusses spiritual gifts (particularly healing and exorcism) and their threefold nature: evidence of personal sanctity; edification of the Church; and demonic counterfeits that bring religion into disrepute and engender pride in the user.[248] This implies the need of *discretio* to distinguish between these different types and particularly between the true and counterfeit. The counterfeit should be discerned by observing whether the thaumaturge has 'driven out all his vices and emended his behaviour'. That this requires *discretio* can be deduced from the subsequent list of spiritual gifts cited from 1 Corinthians 12:8-10. Although he stops short of *discretio spirituum*, he clearly intends its inclusion both by his use of *et reliqua* ('and so on') at the end of the quotation[249] and his repeated references to exorcism and demonic counterfeit miracles throughout the conference. For Nesteros the virtuous and corrupt are equally capable of performing miracles and so it is not thaumaturges that should be admired but 'the fruits of their *virtutes*'.[250] This leads him to emphasise the importance of humility and love in the exercise of spiritual gifts (thus avoiding pride and vainglory)[251] and he regards it a far greater miracle to eradicate personal vice and achieve inward *puritas cordis*.[252] Spiritual gifts and thaumaturgy are thus seen as of less spiritual value than *puritas cordis* and the eradication of λογισμοί.[253] The general implication is that *discretio* is needed for the exercise of spiritual gifts and for discerning the spiritual status both of a monk exercising them and the monk's own state if he aspires to the same.

Monks were not only to use *discretio* to discern what laid behind spiritual gifts and the spiritual status of those exercising them, they were

---

[248]   *Conf.* 15.1.2-5.

[249]   *Ibid.* 15.2.2. Nesteros equates 'practical knowledge' with the purity of love, which he says is above all the spiritual gifts (1 Cor. 12:30b; 13:8). This would make the gift of *discretio spirituum*, elsewhere said to be among the greatest of the gifts (*conf.* 2.1.3-4), subordinate to love (although later Bernard of Clairvaux (*serm. in Cant.* 49) would say that *discretio* moderates love). The key to this would appear to lie in knowledge and pure love being associated with the monk's goals, to which *discretio* leads him, and the need to exercise *discretio* with charity.

[250]   *Conf.* 15.6.1-2.

[251]   *Ibid.* 15.7.2-5.

[252]   *Ibid.* 15.8-9; 15.10.5.

[253]   Cf. Agathon 19 and parallels: 'Even if an angry man raises a corpse, he is not acceptable before God.'

also to use it to determine the nature and origin of visions and revelations and to decide how to respond to them. For example, Nesteros relates how Paphnutius failed to discern the extent of his own progress and was prompted by an angelic vision to re-examine his inward state, whereupon he concluded that it was a 'greater *virtus* and sublimer grace' to overcome lust personally than to be delivered by Divine miracle.[254] The monk is called to be constantly on his guard so that he can distinguish between the malevolent and benevolent influences of demons and angels since one of each is understood to vie for his attention and he must decide to which he will consent.[255] When confronted by spiritual phenomena *discretio* should be used to determine whether their influence is malign, thus Moses, in his first conference, says that *discretio* acts as a watchman that guards against demonic deceit:

> The devil deceives when he is concealed in the appearance of sanctity. "But he hates the sound of the guardian," [cf. Proverbs 11:15b (LXX)] that is the power of *discretio* which comes from the words and advice of the elders.[256]

Discretio, learnt from more experienced monks, thus not only maintains a watch for dangerous deceit, possessing it is understood as a defence in itself. Moses then illustrates the guardian role of *discretio* by describing how John of Lycopolis eventually perceived through *discretio* that he had been deceived by the devil into a spiritually harmful excessive fast.[257] The failure here to detect the deceit immediately underlines the requirement to use *discretio* constantly if the monk is to avoid becoming so preoccupied with ascetic practice that he fails to discern whether it is divinely inspired. Without *discretio* monks are unable to see through spiritual deceit.[258]

Discretio is not only used to avoid demonic deceit, it is also used to discern when God is at work on his behalf. With *discretio* the monk can

---

[254]   *Conf.* 15.10.

[255]   *Ibid.* 8.17; 13.12.7; cf. Hermas, *Mandates* 6.2. Cf. Origen (see above, pp. 33-34) and Evagrius (pp. 64-65). Nau 169 (see above, p. 95, n. 144 for parallels) provides an excellent example of a monk caught between the conflicting messages of an angel sent to assist him and 'the spirit of lust' to which he consents.

[256]   *Conf.* 1.20.8.

[257]   *Ibid.* 1.21.1; the metaphor of counterfeit coins is again used. Other examples of demonic deceit in relation to πρακτική and spiritual phenomena are found in *ibid.* 9.6 (labour and demonic presence) and *HM* 1.45-58 (John of Lycopolis describes how a monk became so complacent when God miraculously provided him with bread that he neglected his πρακτική and so fell prey to λογισμοί; he only realised his error when teaching others how to avoid 'the snare of the devil'.).

[258]   *Conf.* 1.22.1. Cf. *vit. Pach.* G¹ 87 (Pachomius uses διάκρισις to distinguish between evil and holy spirits when a demon appears claiming to be Christ).

understand the nature of God's provision and intervention. For example Moses, in his second conference, describes how two monks, 'insufficiently motivated by cautious *discretio*', decided to cross the desert relying only on God to provide them with food. Weak with hunger, a murderous barbarian tribe unexpectedly offered them food. One monk, assisted by *discretio*, recognised that the two had acted 'rashly and incautiously' and so accepted the food as Divine intervention and provision, whereas the other, 'continuing in his foolish presumption and thoroughly ignorant of *discretio*,' failed to discern this and so died.[259] Lack of *discretio* is thus seen as foolishness, whereas, by implication, *discretio* is wisdom or an intuitive understanding of what is encountered and how best to react. Moses continues with further adverse examples of the need of *discretio* to understand spiritual phenomena and detect deceit. One monk was so deceived by the innumerable revelations of a demon appearing as an angel that he attempted to sacrifice his son in imitation of Abraham.[260] Another was similarly deceived by 'diabolic revelations and visions', many of which were true, so that eventually he became a Jew. With these two examples Moses stresses 'how destructive it is not to have the grace of *discretio*.'[261] *Discretio* is thus seen as essential for distinguishing between divinely and demonically inspired visions and revelations. *Discretio* is thus also regarded as necessary for Christian living and as providing insight born of experience, but it is capable both of neglect and loss, and of recovery. It therefore requires constant use if a monk is to be aware of how best to act in a given situation and of the spiritual background to an event.[262] Such continual use and percipience suggests that *discretio* is a skill that can be employed almost without thinking, like an artisan who, through long experience and practice, can perform a complicated task without apparently needing to think about it.

---

[259] *Conf.* 2.6.

[260] *Ibid.* 2.7; cf. Evagrius, *de orat.* 94 (alertness to demonic visions and dependence upon God to avoid deceit).

[261] *Conf.* 2.8; cf. 8.16 (demonic vision of a real event). A more positive example is provided in Antony 12 and parallels (discussed below, pp. 184-85): monks sought advice regarding the source of their visions and Antony, wishing to show them that they were being deceived by demons, said the demons had told him their donkey had died on the way to see him. Banquo's comment in *Macbeth* is apposite: 'And oftentimes, to win us to our harm, / The instruments of darkness tell us truths, / Win us with honest trifles, to betray's / In deepest consequence.' (Shakespeare, *Macbeth*, Act 1, Scene 3).

[262] The need to discern any deeper spiritual significance in an everyday event can be illustrated from Pachomius who rebuked a cook who stopped preparing meals for monks who were fasting because he had failed to discern that by so doing he had removed the opportunity to choose and thereby robbed them of their spiritual reward (*Paralipomena* 8.15-16).

Discretio and the Teacher / Disciple Relationship

Cassian's expressed intention in writing his *Institutes* is to pass on what he had learnt 'concerning the correction of our morals and the achievement of a perfect life' from the elders, fathers and customs of Egypt and Palestine (which he regarded as survivals of apostolic teaching) so that Gallic monasticism could be founded upon it.[263] He understood that the Egyptian monks were continuing the monastic life taught to them by their forebears.[264] Within a monastery monks were not allowed to direct their own lives or those of others until they had become accomplished in the practical disciplines and learnt obedience and humility.[265] Monks who had failed to learn from their forebears and set themselves up as superiors without having first been novices, he says, relied on their own judgment, with the result that different and inappropriate rules arose in different places.[266] From the start, then, Cassian demonstrates the importance of subjecting monastic formation (corporate and personal) to established tradition and worthy superiors. Personal judgment is considered potentially unreliable and so monks are told to submit with humble obedience to more senior and experienced *confrères*.[267] Such humble obedience to and reliance upon tradition, others and their judgment is understood to be an expression of *discretio*.

In his conference 'On *Discretio*' Moses justifies such humble obedience to another from the example of Paul and Ananias (Acts 9:1-19). He says Christ instructed Paul to learn 'the way of perfection' from Ananias rather than directly from God in order to avoid any 'bad example of presumption' whereby monks suppose that God alone should teach them rather than their elders. Moses thus sees it as a Dominical requirement that monks be taught by their elders and not rely on their 'own judgment and *discretio*'.[268] Similarly Joseph, in his first conference, understands that a foundation of true friendship is mutual submission to each other's wills, since this removes any cause of divisive disputes and results in that evangelical fraternal love which will distinguish (*discerno*) the monk from other people.[269] By refusing to rely on personal judgment and obeying others instead, monks are said to avoid diabolic deceit.[270] For example, by

---

[263] *Inst.* pref. 8.
[264] *Ibid.* 2.3.1.
[265] *Ibid.* 2.3.1-4.
[266] *Ibid.* 2.3.5; e.g. the competitive reading of numerous psalms (*ibid.* 2.5.4).
[267] Although senior monks are frequently referred to as 'old men' or 'elders', these terms refer to their greater experience in the monastic life rather than their physical age.
[268] *Conf.* 2.15.
[269] *Ibid.* 16.6. Cf. Jn 13:35.
[270] *Conf.* 16.10.

submitting themselves to the examination of more mature *confrères*, Satan, who can appear as an angel of light (2 Corinthians 11:14), will be unable to darken their thoughts and knowledge. He concludes that for a monk 'the essence of true *discretio* rests in the judgment of another rather than in his own.'[271] Such obedience requires humility, since even the most knowledgeable and intelligent can be deceived and the slower witted can be more perceptive.[272] The frequent encouragements to learn and use *discretio* thus need to be seen against this background of relying on the *discretio* of others, particularly during monastic formation. It is in the teacher / disciple relationship that skill in *discretio* is learnt, but it is also *discretio* to live in humble obedience to others, particularly in the cœnobium.

The necessity of obedience to a senior monk during monastic formation is an important theme in Cassian's fourth institute 'On the formation of renunciants.' Noting the strict observance of obedience in a cœnobium at Tabenna, Cassian says that the perseverance, humility and obedience of the monks there were built on a foundation of renunciation.[273] He describes the harsh tests of vocation and removal of all possessions before a new novice was accepted into the cœnobium, since it was understood that only with complete renunciation could a monk acquire the *virtus* of humility and obedience.[274] Renunciation and humble obedience are closely linked since the latter requires a renunciation of personal will to the will, judgment and *discretio* of another.[275]

From the outset novices were placed under the authority of older monks, first to learn humility and then, under a new novice master (himself under the authority of the abbot), to learn obedience and how to overcome λογισμοί.[276] Novices were taught not to rely on their own *discretio* in the matter of λογισμοί lest they be deceived by the devil. Instead, they were taught to reveal their thoughts to their superior and 'be defended by the *discretio* of the elder;' being ashamed to reveal a thought is seen as a sure sign that it is diabolic.[277] Obedience and exposure of thoughts to a senior

---

[271] *Ibid.* 16.11.

[272] *Ibid.* 16.12; cf. *reg. Ben.* 3 where it is understood that God sometimes reveals what is best to the young, and presumably inexperienced.

[273] *Inst.* 4.1-2.

[274] *Ibid.* 4.3. Cf. 4.32; *vit. Pach.* G¹ 6; Pachomius, *Praecepta*, 49; Macarius the Egyptian 4 (GSC 7.14; VP 5.7.9; PE 2.3.8.1 p96; Ch38; Budge 2.221).

[275] Cf. *conf.* 24.23.4; 24.26.14. Surrendering the will is regarded as a means to perfection (*inst.* 5.28; Cassian 5; GSC 1.15; VP 5.1.10).

[276] *Inst.* 4.7-8. *Ibid.* 5-12 deals with overcoming λογισμοί. Other monks are also expected to respect and support the rebuke of a monk by his superior (*ibid.* 2.16). Pachomius also taught the submission of questions (*vit. Pach.* G¹ 95) and the confession of temptations (*ibid.* 96) to the διάκρισις of an elder.

[277] *Inst.* 4.9; cf. Poemen 93 (and parallels) and 101 (VP 3.177; PE 1.20.3.3 p267; Budge 2.138). See also *inst.* 4.39.2-3 (renunciation of personal *discretio* in favour

monk are thus used to develop the novice's inner life and train him in the use of *discretio*. Until he had learnt *discretio* the monk was dependent on others for it.

Cassian, like the apophthegms, provides examples of the extreme obedience of novices and disciples. This arises from the understanding that obedience was more valuable than work or meditation.[278] Novices were required to gain permission to carry out even the most trivial actions and would, as if commanded by God himself, attempt impossible or futile tasks without hesitation if asked to do so.[279] The unhesitating nature of their obedience is significant given that διάκρισις can convey wavering between two courses of action; it is *discretio* to respond immediately with obedience. By renouncing personal will and relying on the *discretio* of a superior, the monk learns humility and obedience to God (i.e. by obeying his superior).

The development of true *discretio* through humility and obedience is expressed in Moses' reply to Germanus when he asks how *discretio* may be acquired: *vera discretio non nisi vera humilitate conquiritur*.[280] The use of *conquiro* indicates the need to search for *discretio* diligently using humility. Although according to Cassian reliance on the *discretio* of a superior is one of ten signs of humility in the formation of monks,[281] humility and obedience are also used to gain *discretio*.[282] Monks are thus required to seek and learn *discretio*, at first from their superiors and later by seeking exemplars of *discretio* and humbly learning from them.

On the authority of Antony the Great, Cassian says in his *Institutes* that once a monk has become accomplished in *discretio* he is capable of embarking upon the more advanced anchoritic life.[283] He should then seek to learn different *virtutes*, especially *discretio*, from those monks

---

of a superior's judgment as the third of ten signs of true humility) and *conf.* 2.24 (ignorance of perfect *discretio* in relation to fasting as dependence on personal judgment and rejection of the judgment and tradition of the elders).

[278] *Inst.* 4.12; cf. Mark 1 (GSC 14.11; *VP* 5.14.5; *VP* 3.143; PE 1.35.5.2 pp516-517; Budge 1.240).

[279] *Inst.* 4.10 (cf. Antony 38; GSC 11.2a; *VP* 3.176; PE 1.20.3.5a p267); *inst.* 4.24 (cf. John Kolobos 1; GSC 14.4; *VP* 5.14.3; PE 1.33.4.3 p487; Am347; Budge 2.271; Sulpicius Severus, *dial.* 1.19). Similar tasks testing obedience are described in *inst.* 4.25-30 (see also below, pp. 191-92). Novices would also submit to corrective physical abuse from their superiors with forbearance (*conf.* 19.1.2-3; cf. John the Disciple of Paul 1; GSC 14.5; *VP* 5.14.4; *VP* 3.27; PE 1.34.4.2 p507; Budge 1.238).

[280] *Conf.* 2.10.1; 'True *discretio* is not sought / acquired except by true humility.'

[281] The important interplay between submission / obedience and the novice not relying on his personal *discretio* is seen in ten signs of true humility leading to perfection in the formation of a monk (*inst.* 4.39).

[282] *Conf.* 2.10.2-3.

[283] *Inst.* 5.4.1.

particularly accomplished in each of them (understanding that no one person is perfect in every *virtus*), gathering this 'spiritual honey' like 'a most prudent [*prudentissima*] bee'.[284] This passage not only lays particular stress on the importance of learning *discretio*, it also demonstrates that *discretio* should be used to identify the best exemplars of each *virtus* and in humility learn from their example and apply it to one's own life. Life as an anchorite is thus understood to be a continuing learning process for which *discretio* is required.

This continuing education and development is seen as part of the monastic life however advanced a monk may be and so senior monks are also found submitting to the *discretio* of others and exposing their thoughts to them. For example, when Theonas, in his second conference, discusses whether nocturnal emissions should exclude a monk from the Eucharist, he first explains how these may derive either from sin or be involuntary and prompted by the devil, in which latter case the monk may be deceived into believing that he is at fault and should not take communion. He then uses the διακρίνω text that institutes the Eucharist (1 Corinthians 11:27-29) to emphasise the need to distinguish it from ordinary food and to judge oneself rightly. Finally, he describes an experienced monk, noted for his 'chastity of heart and body through great circumspection and humility', who frequently suffered such emissions prior to communion and so absented himself from it. This monk submitted himself to the examination of his superiors who weighed his case, found him to be the innocent victim of demonic deceit and advised him to take communion rather than refrain from it in order to be healed.[285] Disclosures to *confrères* could thus be of very private matters and, no matter how advanced the monk might be, exposing his life to the scrutiny of others was held to be vital to further advancement. It may be said then that the more advanced a monk became in the practice of *discretio* the more he might be prompted to rely on the *discretio* of others for an objective evaluation of his life.

A further example of a senior monk placing himself under the authority and *discretio* of others is found in the conference with the monk John. Cassian describes his surpassing humility, which he calls 'the mother of all the *virtutes*'.[286] Since Cassian elsewhere similarly describes *discretio*, albeit in slightly different language (*generatrix* rather than *mater*),[287] a close association between humility (and therefore obedience to others) and

---

[284] *Ibid.* 5.4.1-4; cf. *vit. Ant.* 3; Jerome, *ep.* 125.15 (Rusticus is advised not to rely on his own judgment (*arbitrium*), but to submit to a father in a monastery just as bees have a leader).

[285] *Conf.* 22.5.1-22.6.4; cf. 2.10.2-3 (submissive exposure of thoughts to the *discretio* of a superior in order to avoid demonic deceit).

[286] *Ibid.* 19.2.1.

[287] *Ibid.* 2.4.4.

discretio is indicated. Cassian also describes obedience as *inter ceteras virtutes primatum tenet*, that is, in the same terms as he describes *discretio* elsewhere.[288] For Cassian, then, humility, obedience and *discretio* are very closely related, an observation confirmed by the repeated emphasis laid on all three and the expressed need of humility and obedience to gain *discretio*.[289] Humility and *discretio* of his own inner state and ability prompted the monk John of *conference* 19 to return to the cœnobium and live in obedience to others even though he was a highly experienced monk.[290] Thus, experienced monks exercised *discretio* up to a point, judging themselves and their own inner state, but were also willing to submit themselves in humble obedience to the *discretio* of others when they discerned the need to do so. *Discretio* is thus a natural partner with obedience and humility and by using *discretio* in conjunction with them monks were able to advance their own inner purity.

Notwithstanding Antony's apian example[291] and the acquisition of *discretio* through humble obedience of novitiates to a cœnobitic superior, monks generally (particularly the less experienced) are encouraged to find a senior *confrère* and live under his authority. Selecting such a teacher in itself requires a measure of *discretio*. In his conference 'On *Discretio*' Moses warns against regarding age and grey hair as a sign of a worthy superior; the devil can equally deceive zealous young monks and older ones that these are indicative of a 'mature way of life'. Moses illustrates this with the story of a young monk who revealed his thoughts to an unworthy superior. He was treated severely and inappropriately, and told he was no longer worthy of being a monk. A third monk, Apollo, intervened encouraging the disciple to return to his cell and reminding him of God's mercy. Apollo, presented as a worthy superior, demonstrated humility and self-exposure by confessing his own struggle with the same thoughts. Apollo also corrected the older monk using a mixture of prayer (particularly for Divine intervention), counsel and Scripture. Apollo represents the percipient use of *discretio* by a worthy superior to assess the inner condition of others and to discern how best to correct them without being judgmental. For Moses, the existence of bad examples does not diminish the need for monks to rely on the judgment of others.[292] The teacher / disciple relationship is built upon *discretio*. Disciples need it to choose a teacher and would be teachers need it to discern their own spiritual status.

---

[288]   *Inst.* 4.30.1; *conf.* 1.23.1 (see above, p. 84).
[289]   *Conf.* 2.10.1.
[290]   *Ibid.* 19.1-2. Cf. similar accounts in: *ibid.* 20.1-2; *inst.* 4.30-32 (Pinufius); *HL* 18.12-16 (Macarius of Alexandria).
[291]   *Vit. Ant.* 3.
[292]   *Conf.* 2.13. By contrast grey hair in Scripture is a sign of a righteous life (Prov. 16:31). See also below, pp. 194-95.

Disciples learn *discretio* from their teachers who, through *discretio* have insight into the spiritual needs of the disciple and into how best to encourage their spiritual growth. Just as it is *discretio* for disciples to expose their thoughts to their teachers, *discretio* may also counsel teachers to expose their own struggle to their disciples in order to help them. Without *discretio*, used with humility, the teacher / disciple relationship breaks down.

This adverse example of the teacher corrected by Apollo draws attention to the need for senior monks to assess their own inner condition with *discretio* before attempting to instruct others. For example, when age and experience encourages them to teach they should beware the seduction of vainglory, which leads them to teach impure people. Older monks need *discretio* to discern not only when and to whom they should teach spiritual things but also their motivation in doing so.[293] Thus Theonas warns monks against laying heavy burdens on others that they are personally unable to bear and against seeking human praise by pretending greater asceticism than they practice.[294] Hence, the centenarian Chæremon, in his first conference, is conscious that he is no longer able to practice what he would teach and so is reluctant to instruct Cassian and Germanus[295] (this provides a further example of *discretio* linked with humility). Older and more experienced monks (such as Heron, a monk of fifty years standing) are seen to be capable of relying on their own judgment and failing to submit to the counsels of other monks or the traditions of the elders and so are said to lack *virtus discretionis*.[296] Years of experience are thus no guarantee of *discretio* and therefore no protection against demonic or self-deceit, since these require *discretio*. Would be teachers need *discretio* to examine their motives and spiritual condition to gain a realistic assessment of their capabilities and of whether it is appropriate for them to instruct others. With *discretio* they are able to moderate their teaching and keep it from being too harsh. However senior a monk may be and however capable a teacher, it is understood that *discretio* means that a monk remains humble and teachable because, like his disciple, the teacher is still *en route* to his goals and perfection.

Discretio and Balance

In teachers particularly, then, balance and integrity between the inner and outer life was an important requirement, but it is seen as necessary for all

---

[293] *Conf.* 14.17. Cf. *Schol.* 4 in Ps. 111:5 (LXX) [Pitra, 111.5; *PG* 12.1572] (see above, p. 63).

[294] *Conf.* 21.22.6-7.

[295] *Ibid.* 11.4.

[296] *Ibid.* 2.5.1-2.

monks. Antony is said to have emerged from twenty years of solitude physically and spiritually 'completely balanced,'[297] and integrity of heart, speech and body is understood to be essential.[298] Cassian speaks of interior purity being evident in exterior behaviour when he says that 'the chastity of the interior man is discerned [*discerno*] by the perfection of this *virtus* (of overcoming gluttony).'[299] Elsewhere he speaks of how Egyptian monks 'exercising equally the *virtutes* of the body and spirit, balance [*exaequo*] the labours of the exterior man with the spiritual gain of the interior,' but says it is 'not easy to discern [*discerno*]' which came first.[300] Inward and outward purity are, then, inextricably linked, they develop together and should be kept in harmony if the monk is to advance spiritually. Thus Theonas says both inward *puritas cordis* and outward abstinence are required when he speaks of 'the gift of integrity.'[301] The monk's guiding light in finding this balance is *discretio* and so Cassian (thinking particularly of steering between the dangerous extremes possible in eating and fasting) can say, '*discretio* is useful and prudent [*prudens*], causing the monk always to advance with balanced [*aequalis*] rigour.'[302] It is understood that inner purity, words and actions should correspond to each other and not only can the quality of this integration be discerned using *discretio*, *discretio* also guides the monk in developing this well-balanced life.

For Cassian, then, *discretio* touches every aspect of the monk's inner and outer life. He lays considerable stress on its necessity for achieving the monk's goals of *puritas cordis* and the Kingdom of God, so much so that his contribution to the understanding of *discretio* was highly valued in the East. He repeatedly stresses its superiority and its necessity for developing and governing *virtutes* and practical disciplines. *Discretio* is needed for gaining insight and knowledge of the spiritual realm and provides the monk with the ability to detect demonic deceit. It operates within the mind and reason providing him with the ability to make right choices and to examine and understand his inner state. It thus guides and counsels him in all his decision making so that his inner and outer life become balanced. The monk needs to learn *discretio* and how to use it effectively; it must be

---

[297]   *Vit. Ant.* 14.

[298]   Gregory 1 (GSC 1.3; Nau 3; *VP* 5.1.3; PE 2.45.5.2 p553; Budge 2.29); cf. Poemen 63, 164, S1 and parallels. For the importance of the integration of life and words in Scripture and the Apostolic Fathers see e.g. Mt. 23:3; Rom. 2:21-23; 1 Jn 3:18; Ignatius, *ep. to the Ephesians* 15.1 (cf. Felix 1; GSC 3.36; *VP* 5.3.18; PE 1.18.5.2 p239).

[299]   *Inst.* 5.11.1. Cf. Tithoes 3 and Budge 2.92; other parallels (GSC 11.13; *VP* 5.11.27; *VP* 7.32.2; PE 4.24.1.6 p419) omit the reference to eating.

[300]   *Inst.* 2.14.

[301]   *Conf.* 21.36.

[302]   *Inst.* 5.41. Plato (*rep.* 9.11 591c-d) also speaks of the need to keep the body and ψυχή in harmony.

sought, maintained and used constantly. Without it he struggles blindly in his spiritual life and lacks wisdom. Cassian understands that *discretio* is essential for the monastic life and the search for God.

Cassian's use of the word-group reflects both the Scriptural meaning and the emerging technical sense, found in Origen and Evagrius, for a charism integral to the mystical search for God. However, Cassian also marks the beginning of a shift away from considering *discretio spirituum* / διάκρισις πνευμάτων, where the spirits or demons are regarded as personal, to addressing the concept of *discretio* / διάκρισις of inward πάθη or λογισμοί.[303] *Discretio* at once takes on a more general sense of discernment needed by everyone in every aspect of the spiritual life, rather than an extraordinary spiritual gift occasionally used, and a more specialised sense for facilitating the mystical search for God.

Cassian's record of monastic life in Egypt is an intellectual analysis providing a theology of the desert. Although his approach is far more practically based than that found in Evagrius, his intellectual approach gives his understanding of *discretio* an intellectual bias. For Cassian, *discretio* emerges as a skill in reasoning and mental analysis; it is deliberative and rational. With *discretio* the monk is able to remain focused on his practical disciplines, contemplation and goals; he uses it to control every part of his life. The use of *discretio* for constant self-examination and self-criticism make it a potentially highly demanding and introspective ability. Its use to evaluate questions, arguments, doctrines, Scriptural interpretation, personal knowledge and the lives, motives, words and advice of others further suggests that he understands *discretio* as intellective and noetic. Even when he applies *discretio* to determine the background to spiritual phenomena it is possible to see its operation as a mental skill. This is also suggested by his descriptions of *discretio* in terms of wisdom, sane and sober rule, true judgment, the reasoning mind, understanding and sense. It is a skill that can be learnt by human effort although there are indications that this skill can become a more intuitive spiritual ability. The repeated stress on continual watchfulness in every aspect of thought, word and action suggest an intense, joyless and tiring approach to faith and practice based more on human effort than on grace. There is therefore a potential danger in his understanding of *discretio* in that it could be seen as a purely human ability of which a monk might consider himself so accomplished that he becomes proud of his prowess, despite the repeated warnings not to rely on personal judgment but on the *discretio* of others.

Cassian's bias towards a more noetic and reasoning understanding of *discretio* may be attributed to his intellectual and academic approach to his

---

[303] For a discussion of this shift in focus in the Early Church see J.T. Lienhard, '"Discernment of Spirits" in the Early Church', *Studia Patristica* 17.2 (1982), pp. 519-22.

subject. This is in sharp contrast to the Egyptian monks who, with a few notable exceptions (e.g. Arsenius and Evagrius), were uneducated. For all that Cassian's theological reflections may constitute a fair reflection of their lives, he is nevertheless presenting a carefully considered argument and case for how their lifestyle should be understood and put into practice. While his theology is distinct from Neo-Platonism, he remains a man of his time and reflects the academic worldview of his day as he formulates his theology of the desert. For example, like Evagrius he speaks of the need for constant reasoned introspection and striving towards wordless, imageless and light filled union with the Divine. However, Cassian does not reflect the dualism of Neo-Platonism and is more concerned with physical considerations than Evagrius. There is frequent stress on the need to keep the physical and spiritual life integrated and in harmony with each other as the monk strives for union with God.

This intellective and noetic view of *discretio* based on human effort and skill needs to be set against Cassian's stress on the need to depend on God. *Discretio* is a spiritual gift and its use is learnt in dependence upon God; monks are told to rely on God and pray for his aid. He closely associates *discretio* with the incisive power of Scripture and the guidance of the Holy Spirit; this indicates that he regards *discretio* as a spiritual faculty but also suggests an inherent danger of depending on *discretio* for guidance rather than God. The stress on constant effort and self-examination is mitigated by calls to relax discipline and be considerate of others. Cassian's *discretio* is not legalistic decision making based on fixed rules, but flexible and capable of being used to respond to new or changed situations. *Discretio* is not used in isolation but in company with others and with their help, so while it may seem preoccupied with the self, it has an outward dimension as well. Although it operates in the mind, *discretio* is presented as a spiritual faculty as well, that forms a bridge between the inner and outer life. These factors are more evident in the apophthegms which fill out and balance the intellectual approach provided by Cassian and Evagrius with a more practical one based on responses to questions and actual situations. The next two chapters address these sayings and provide a fuller impression of how *discretio* / διάκρισις was understood by the Desert Fathers.

CHAPTER 4

The Apophthegms 1 – Διάκρισις in Personal Life

After considering the basis of διάκρισις in Scripture and early philosophy in the Christian Church, monastic exploration of these themes has been examined in two major writers, Evagrius and Cassian. They provide theological reflections on the teaching and lives of the Desert Fathers, but the final corpus of material to be considered is the sayings of the Egyptian Desert Fathers themselves. This material is different in nature from the analytical approach of Evagrius and Cassian. The anchoritic sayings emerged as anecdotes and aphorisms spoken in response to specific situations and questions raised by monks. These sayings, arising from personal experience and instances of spiritual direction, were valued as divinely inspired teaching given by elders skilled in διάκρισις and so were preserved through frequent transmission. These apophthegms are *prima facie* much closer to the original speakers and so clarify the monk's understanding of διάκρισις. This chapter concentrates on διάκρισις in the personal and inward life of monks and the next on how it affected their behaviour towards others. However, this corpus of material presents particular difficulties of definition and it is therefore necessary to summarise the consensus of discussion about the various forms in which it appears.

The origin of the apophthegm collections is far from certain but a broad outline of how they came into existence is possible. It is probable that many of the sayings were first uttered in Coptic and later committed to writing in Greek. Initially they were transmitted orally[1] and these chains of transmission indicate both a living spiritual tradition and an habitual referral to earlier authorities in a desire to preserve the teaching of the monastic founders. Perhaps inevitably this same desire led to the commitment of the sayings to writing, particularly after the dispersal of Egyptian monks from the monastic centre in Scetis following the invasions

---

[1]   Internal evidence indicates the oral repetition of sayings, e.g.: 'Abba Poemen said that Abba Moses asked Abba Zacharias…' (Zacharias 5).

by the barbarian hordes in 407-8AD, 434AD and c.577AD.[2] Many of these monks moved to Palestine and the internal evidence of the great collections[3] suggests that the Greek Alphabetic Collection was compiled here in the early sixth century. Whatever the precise process by which the collections emerged, they do not have the systematic theological approach found in Cassian and Evagrius. Rather the sayings represent gathered *dicta* deriving from real life situations that illustrate the practical application of διάκρισις; nevertheless these *dicta* present a generally consistent understanding of anchoritic life and spirituality in Egypt.

The earliest written collections of sayings were probably compiled very close in time to the original speakers. This impression is supported by references to some of them by Socrates Scholasticus (c.380-450)[4] and Palladius (c.365-425) in his *Historia Lausiaca* suggesting that by the late fourth or early fifth century a collection of sayings was in circulation.[5] The transition from oral to written transmission marks a change in style to a Greek literary genre. While this perpetuated the early tradition it also suggests that it may have become fixed, thereby limiting its development as a living tradition to some extent. However a comparison of the various translations reveals a consistency that suggests translation did not lead to distortion.[6] It is generally agreed that the earliest extant great collection is the Latin Systematic,[7] in which sayings dating from at least the fifth century are ordered under subject headings. This Latin text is a mid-sixth century translation (by the deacon Pelagius and the subdeacon John) of an earlier but no longer extant Greek manuscript.[8] The earliest Greek manuscripts, dating from the ninth to twelfth centuries, provide the much larger Greek

---

[2] The rout of Scetis may be foreseen in Nau 361.

[3] E.g. the inclusion of Palestinian sayings, references to Basil and allusions in Palestinian writings such as the Epistles of Barsanuph and John of Gaza and Dorotheos of Gaza.

[4] *HE* 4.23.

[5] The earliest extant collection (in Ethiopian) dates from the early fifth century and contains only sayings of Egyptian monks, suggesting that the earliest collections derived from an Egyptian milieu.

[6] Gould shares this view (G. Gould, *The Desert Fathers on Monastic Community*, (Oxford Early Christian Studies; Oxford: Clarendon Press, 1993), p. 24, n. 101).

[7] *PL* 73.851-1024. Supplemented by A. Wilmart, 'Le Recueil Latin des Apophtegmes', *RB* 34 (1922), pp. 185-98. The collection is entitled *Adhorationes Patrum* in most MSS but is commonly referred to as *Vitae Patrum* after Rosweyde's edition reproduced by Migne. (The sayings recorded by Pelagius in *VP* 5 are continued by John the subdeacon in *VP* 6. To reflect this continuity, the numeration has been amended in this study to provide a continual sequence so that *VP* 6.1.1 becomes *VP* 5.18.21 and *VP* 6. 2-4 becomes *VP* 5.19-21).

[8] Photius (c.810-895) appears to have possessed this MS or something similar (*Bibliotheca* codex 198).

Systematic Collection, which mirrors the topically arranged Latin Systematic Collection.[9] The Greek *Apophthegmata Patrum* or *Paterikon*, based on that published by Cotelier and reproduced by Migne,[10] arranges the sayings in alphabetical order according to the name of the speaker or main character. The prologue to this work refers to a second section of anonymous sayings, the first part of which was published by François Nau (based on MS *Coislin 126*) later supplemented by Guy (particularly from MS *Berlin 1624*).[11] All of these collections have been analysed in the course of this study along with the Latin supplements attributed to Rufinus,[12] Paschasius,[13] Martin of Dumio[14] and Palladius,[15] the Sahidic Coptic translation collated by Chaîne[16] and the Bohairic Coptic edition published by Amélineau.[17] Budge's translation of the seventh century

[9]   Rediscovered by J.-C. Guy, *Recherches sur la Tradition Grecque des Apophthegmata Patrum* (Subsidia Hagiographica 36; Brussels: Société des Bollandistes, 1962), pp. 117-200). Greek critical edition of GSC (with French translation): J.-C. Guy, *Les Apophthegmes des Pères: Collection Systématique* (SC 387, 474, 498; Paris: Cerf, 1993-2005).

[10]   *PG* 65.71-440; supplemented by Guy, *Recherches*, pp. 13-58.

[11]   F. Nau, 'Le Chapitre Περὶ 'Αναχωρητῶν 'Αγίων et les Sources de la Vie de Saint Paul de Thèbes', *ROC* 10 (1905), pp. 387-417 and F. Nau, 'Histoire des Solitaires Égyptiens', *ROC* 12 (1907), pp. 43-69, 171-89, 393-413; *ROC* 13 (1908), pp. 47-66, 266-97; *ROC* 14 (1909), pp. 357-79; *ROC* 17 (1912), pp. 204-11, 294-301; *ROC* 18 (1913), pp. 137-46; Guy, *Recherches*, pp. 59-115. Supplemented by: J.-C. Guy, 'La collation des douze anachorètes', *Analecta Bollandiana* 76 (1958), pp. 419-27; J.-C. Guy, 'Un dialogue monastique inédit', *RAM* 33 (1957), pp. 171-88; J.-C. Guy, 'Un entretien monastique sur la contemplation', *Recherches de science religieuse* 50 (1962), pp. 230-41; and M. Jugie, 'Un apophthegme des pères inédit sur le purgatoire', in *Mémorial Louis Petit. Mélanges d'histoire et d'archéologie Byzantines*, (Archives de l'Orient chrétien 1; Bucharest: Institut français d'études byzantines, 1948), pp. 245-53.

[12]   *VP* 3 (*PL* 73.739-814).

[13]   *VP* 7 (*PL* 73.1025-1066). Freire has also edited a critical edition of Paschasius (J.G. Freire, *A versão latina por Pascásio de Dume dos Apophthegmata Patrum* (2 vols; Coïmbra: Instituto de Estudos Classicos, 1971).

[14]   *Ægyptiorum Patrum Sententiæ* (MD; *PL* 74.381-394).

[15]   *Palladii Lausiaca* XX (App; *PL* 74.377-382).

[16]   M. Chaîne, *Le Manuscrit de la Version Copte en Dialecte Sahidique des 'Apophthegmata Patrum'*, (Bibliothèque d'études coptes 6; Cairo: L'institut français d'archéologie orientale, 1960).

[17]   É. Amélineau, *Monuments pour servir à l'histoire de l'Égypte chrétienne: Histoire des monastères de la Basse-Égypte. Vies des saints Paul, Antoine, Macaire, Maxime et Domèce, Jean le Nain, et autres* (Annales du Musée Guimet 25; Paris: E. Leroux, 1894).

Syriac collection[18] and the eleventh century Greek anthology of Paul Evergetinos[19] (particularly where there is no published Greek text) have been used only for cross-reference purposes. Other cross-references are noted as they occur. Since Palestine was a natural focus and meeting point for Christians and monks from many countries, this probably accounts for the collections being translated into many other languages[20] and being taken to other countries. However, the precise relationship between these different translations is far from clear, although it is generally acknowledged that the original was Greek. The Egyptian origin and original compilation in Greek indicates the importance of focussing this study on the place of διάκρισις in the life and thought of the Desert Fathers primarily on the Egyptian material in Greek and the translations from Greek into Latin.

The importance of διάκρισις in all these collections is immediately apparent. By far the longest sections in the Greek and Latin Systematic Collections are those concerned with διάκρισις / *discretio*,[21] and ten per cent of the sayings in the Sahidic collection reproduced by Chaîne[22] are elsewhere identified as relating to διάκρισις / *discretio*. The importance of the subject is indicated, then, both by the number of sayings included in these sections, their more or less central position in the Greek and Latin Systematic Collections, which also begin and end with small clusters of sayings on διάκρισις / *discretio*. While these collections are later written redactions of earlier oral material, the sayings identified by the redactors as relating to διάκρισις / *discretio* indicate how it was understood at an early stage. Furthermore, every apophthegm is capable of interpretation in

---

[18]   E.A. Wallis Budge, *The Paradise or Garden of the Holy Fathers being Histories of the Anchorites Recluses Monks Coenobites and Ascetic Fathers of the Deserts of Egypt between A.D. CCL and A.D. CCCC circiter Compiled by Athanasius Archbishop of Alexandria, Palladius Bishop of Helenopolis, Saint Jerome and Others* (2 vols; London: Chatto & Windus, 1907), II.

[19]   Paul Evergetinos, *Εὐεργετινός ἤτοι συναγωγή τῶν θεοφθόγγων ῥημάτων καί διδασκαλιῶν τῶν θεοφόρων καί ἁγίων πατέρων* (4 vols; Athens: Κληρονομοι Ματθαιου Λαλλη, 1997-2000).

[20]   Sahidic and Bohairic Coptic, Syriac, Aramaic, Armenian, Georgian, Arabic and Ethiopian translations are all extant.

[21]   193 in GSC (GSC 10.122 does not exist and appeared in Guy's critical edition by mistake) and 121 in the Latin Systematic Collection (taking into account the additional sayings provided by O. Chadwick, *Western Asceticism*, (The Library of Christian Classics 12; London: SCM Press, 1958)). The διάκρισις section in the Anonymous Collection (Nau 216-253; 37 apophthegms) broadly relates to *VP* 5.10.78-114 and a little more loosely to GSC 10.100-191.

[22]   Ch52-72, 85, 86, 134, 135, 200, 268 (i.e. 27 of 272 sayings). However, none of these sayings contain the key word-group either because the words do not appear in the parallels or because of lacunae.

relation to διάκρισις, whereas the same cannot be said of other key themes such as hospitality. Since over 6,000 apophthegms have been analysed in the course of this study, by and large only those using διάκρισις, *discretio* and their cognates (together with their parallels) and those included under a διάκρισις / *discretio* subject heading are discussed here.[23]

With regard to διάκρισις / *discretio*, the sayings may be divided into four classes:

1. Apophthegms using the key words and listed by the editor under a διάκρισις / *discretio* section heading.
2. Apophthegms using the key words but listed under a different section heading.
3. Apophthegms listed under a διάκρισις / *discretio* section heading but not using any of the key words.
4. Apophthegms neither using the key words nor listed under a διάκρισις / *discretio* section heading.

For the purposes of this study the first class is clearly the most significant; taking into account the parallels there are only eleven distinct sayings in this group.[24] The second class, again taking into account the parallels, consists of forty or more sayings.[25] As these first two classes specifically refer to the word-group under consideration, they are particularly helpful for understanding the meaning of διάκρισις. The third class is clearly very important for appreciating how διάκρισις was understood at an early stage. Since all of the different subject areas identified by the Systematic Collections' section headings are covered by the first three groups, this serves to demonstrate how διάκρισις may be used to analyse and interpret sayings included in the fourth class.

The sayings in the first class of apophthegm above indicate the significance of διάκρισις in all aspects of the monk's life and spiritual endeavour. Διάκρισις governs every aspect of the monk's inward and outward behaviour.[26] It is essential for the correct use of πρακτική in the

---

23 All apophthegms containing διάκρισις, *discretio* and their cognates and those listed under a διάκρισις / *discretio* heading together with their parallels are fully cross-referenced in the table in Appendix 2.

24 GSC 10.1; 10.12; 10.37; 10.88; 10.100; 10.105; 10.110; 10.135; 10.137; 10.178; Nau 225 (for parallels see Appendix 2).

25 Mius 2; Poemen 154, 170; GSC 1.13, 1.20, 1.23, 1.33, 2.35, 4.76, 5.4, 5.38, 5,47, 8.4, 8.32, 9.16, 11.41, 11.58, 14.18, 15.129, 15.130, 16.30, 21.9, 21.25, 21.62; Nau 53, 132A, 417, 451, 635 (?), 641 (?); *VP* 3.20, 3.75, 3.130; MD 39, 108; App 4; QRT 5 (see below, p. 163, n. 178); Am22.3, 96.2, 326.1, 338.3, 370.2 and parallels.

26 Nau 225; GSC 1.32; *VP* 5.1.22; Budge 1.596b, 2.436.

monk's pursuit of his goals,[27] which necessarily incorporates humility and charity.[28] It enables the monk to identify the level of πρακτική appropriate to him[29] as well as the way of life best suited to him.[30] With διάκρισις the monk is able to remain impassive (ἀπάθεια) in the face of provocation and sensitive to the importance of orthodoxy and union with God.[31] Διάκρισις also makes it possible for the monk to discern the origin of thoughts and ideas, that is whether they derive from a Divine or demonic source,[32] and to interpret spiritual revelations.[33] Furthermore, it is as vital to the disciple / teacher relationship and obedience to one another[34] as it is to all relationships with others and the demands of hospitality.[35] In short, διάκρισις is presented as a tool essential to the monk's whole way of life and he needs to learn how to use it properly.[36]

This need of διάκρισις to govern every aspect of the monk's inward and outward life is clearly expressed in an apophthegm from the first class noted above:

> An old man said, "The life of the monk is: [GSC and *VP* add: work] obedience, meditation, not to judge, not to slander, not to grumble, for it is written, 'You who love the Lord, hate evil.' [Psalm 96:10 (LXX)] For the life of the monk is: not to indulge in wrong-doing; not to see evil with his eyes; not to be a busybody; not to listen to strange things; not to steal with his hands, but rather to give; not to behave arrogantly in the heart; not to be evil in his λογισμός; not to fill his belly; but to do everything with διάκρισις, in these things is (the life of) the monk."[37]

Most of the key themes and concerns of the monastic life are encapsulated in this saying: work, obedience, non-judgment, control of the tongue (and

---

27 Antony 8; GSC 10.1; *VP* 5.10.1; PE 3.31.1.1 p372 (διάκρισις section); Budge 1.296 (on watchfulness – this section equates to those on διάκρισις / *discretio* in the Greek and Latin Systematic Collections); Antony, *ep.* 6.106; cf. Poemen 106.

28 GSC 10.135; Nau 222; *VP* 5.10.91; Budge 2.31a.

29 An Abba of Rome 1; GSC 10.110; *VP* 5.10.76; PE 4.46.1.1-16 pp643-644. Cf. Arsenius 36; PE 4.46.1.17-21 p644; Budge 1.450; Bars 191.

30 GSC 10.178; Nau 70; PE 4.5.2.23 p99.

31 Agathon 5; GSC 10.12; *VP* 5.10.10; *VP* 3.21; PE 2.2.6.1 p56; Budge 1.183.

32 Syncletica 15; GSC 10.105; *VP* 5.10.72; *vit. Syn.* 100.

33 GSC 10.137; Nau 404; PE 1.15.4.3 p210.

34 GSC 10.100; Nau 217; *VP* 5.10.85; PE 1.21.1.2 p285 (section on referring λογισμοί to the διάκρισις of the Fathers); cf. Cassian, *conf.* 2.13.4-12.

35 John Kolobos 7; GSC 10.37; *VP* 5.10.28; Budge 2.131.

36 Poemen 52; GSC 10.88; *VP* 5.10.59; PE 3.31.1.2 p372 (διάκρισις section); Budge 2.134; Ammonas, *apoph.* 14.

37 Nau 225. See also: GSC 1.32; *VP* 5.1.22; Budge 1.596b, 2.436.

by implication interpersonal relationships), rejection of sin and evil in thought, word and action, and control of λογισμοί, mind and body. The climactic position of διάκρισις at the end of the saying reinforces its overarching role in achieving all the monk's aims. Two much more succinct apophthegms make the same point with even greater impact. In one the work of the monk is simply summed up as διάκρισις[38] and in the other διάκρισις is said to be 'greater than all the ἀρεταί' the Latin parallel to which is even more emphatic: '*discretio* is the absolute greatest of all the *virtues*.'[39] In both the Latin and Greek Systematic Collections these two apophthegms are placed in the final sections, which represent a summary of all that has gone before thus indicating that διάκρισις is to be understood as the most highly prized and desirable of the ἀρεταί. Furthermore, in the Paul Evergetinos anthology these two sayings are grouped with Antony 8 and Poemen 52 (along with others from the διάκρισις / *discretio* sections in the Systematic Collections), both from the first and most significant class of apophthegm described above, under a chapter heading which again stresses that διάκρισις is the greatest of the ἀρεταί and essential to the conduct of faith. This reflects the status of *discretio*, found in Cassian's first conference with Moses, as the supreme *virtus* overarching all the *virtutes* and first in both importance and value among them.[40] On the evidence of these apophthegms there can be little doubt that διάκρισις was understood by Egyptian anchorites to be of central importance in the conduct of the spiritual life.

This importance can be demonstrated from Poemen who describes διάκρισις as one of three fundamental ἀρεταί used by the ψυχή as guides, instruments or functions:

Abba Poemen said, "To keep guard, to pay attention to oneself and διάκρισις, these three ἀρεταί are the guides [GSC: tools; *VP*: works] of the ψυχή."[41]

However, in both the Greek and Latin versions of this saying διάκρισις / *discretio* is distinguished from watchfulness and self-examination by using a noun rather than another infinitive. Although this could be stylistic it is

---

[38] Ἠρωτήθη γέρων· Τί ἐστιν τὸ ἔργον τοῦ μοναχοῦ; Καὶ ἀπεκρίθη· Διάκρισις. ('An old man was asked, "What is the work of the monk?" He replied, "Διάκρισις."') Nau 93. See also: GSC 21.9; *SP* 6; PE 3.31.1.3 p372 (διάκρισις section); Budge 2.313.

[39] Nau 106 (Εἶπεν γέρων· ὅτι μεῖζον πασῶν τῶν ἀρετῶν ἐστιν ἡ διάκρισις.); *SP* 20 (*Ait senex: Omnium virtutum discretionem esse permaximam.*). See also: GSC 21.25; PE 3.31.1.4 p372 (διάκρισις section); Budge 2.201; 2.281.

[40] Cassian, *conf.* 1.23.1 (See above, p. 84).

[41] Poemen 35. See also: GSC 1.20; *VP* 5.1.12; Budge 1.367 (on watchfulness).

more likely that διάκρισις has been placed last and as a noun for emphasis. Διάκρισις is thus regarded as superior to watchfulness and self-examination and this is confirmed by the understanding that they are expressions of διάκρισις, as will be shown below.[42] Διάκρισις is thus presented as a function of the ψυχή, which uses it to protect and inspect the spiritual and mental life of the monk. Furthermore, in the Systematic Collections this apophthegm is placed centrally or near centrally in the introductory section on perfection,[43] which draws attention to the most important elements of the monastic life. If this positioning was intended as emphatic, it further suggests that διάκρισις was regarded as a foundational ability required of monks. This impression is confirmed in two ways. Firstly, the word-group is used repeatedly in these introductory sections: six times in Greek and five in Latin. Secondly, cross-referencing these introductory apophthegms reveals that 22% (8 of 37) of the Greek sayings and 30% (7 of 23) of the Latin sayings are διάκρισις / *discretio* apophthegms, a higher proportion than in any other section.[44] Διάκρισις is therefore seen as a fundamental requirement of the monastic life.

Διάκρισις and Union with God

These sayings indicating the essentiality of διάκρισις do not stand alone as abstract statements, rather they summarise the place διάκρισις had in the spiritual teaching of the desert. The apophthegms as a whole provide practical teaching given in response to actual situations that would enable monks to achieve their goals of personal purity and union with God. The spiritual teaching of Evagrius and Cassian provide a theological reflection on this practical teaching and identify the monastic goals more precisely as firstly ἀπάθεια or *puritas cordis* and ultimately as γνῶσις of the Holy Trinity or the Kingdom of God.[45] As would be expected, if their theological interpretation is regarded as accurate, the underlying thought of monastic goals in the apophthegms is the same. Since all the monk's effort is directed towards achieving these goals, it is helpful to consider these next.

In Greek Systematic Collection an anonymous monk asserts that, 'γνῶσις of God is sufficient for the health of the ψυχή.'[46] This gnomic saying is somewhat Evagrian in style and conveys a similar idea to *Praktikos* 56: 'ἀπάθεια is the health of the ψυχή and γνῶσις its food'. In the Evagrian saying γνῶσις keeps the ψυχή in ἀπάθεια and therefore healthy, and so the Greek Systematic Collection apophthegm represents an

---

42   See below, pp. 166-71.
43   Latin: 12 of 23; Greek 20 of 37.
44   See Appendix 2.
45   See above, p. 80, n. 42.
46   GSC 10.141.

abbreviated form of this expressing the same concept. Since the Greek Systematic Collection saying is intended to explain διάκρισις, the monk's progress towards his goals is understood to require διάκρισις.[47] Furthermore, since γνῶσις conveys the senses of enquiry and judgment as well as of knowledge and insight, διάκρισις, as the ability to weigh matters and make choices, is presented as closely related to the monk's ultimate goal. Thus it is not only διάκρισις to discern that the health of the ψυχή resides in γνῶσις of God, διάκρισις is also a significant element of that goal.

In addition to associating διάκρισις with γνῶσις or union with God, it is also equated with being filled with the Holy Spirit, suggesting that to be accomplished in διάκρισις is to be indwelt by God. This can be seen in a saying that contrasts the former and present lives of a Roman and an Egyptian monk.[48] The Roman lived relatively comfortably by monastic standards and compared to the Egyptian, but far more austerely than when he had been a wealthy imperial courtier. The Egyptian, however, now lived more comfortably than he had as a shepherd, despite his greater austerity. This apophthegm draws out the meaning of διάκρισις in several ways. The Roman discerns the Egyptian's struggle to understand this disparity (and therefore his lack of διάκρισις) and encourages him to discern that their ways of life are equally valid. However, the saying's main stress is on the Roman's perceptiveness (he is twice called διορατικός) and it concludes significantly by describing him as 'a διακριτικός [*VP*: *discernens*; 'discerning'] man, full of the sweet smell of the Holy Spirit.' If expertise in διάκρισις is understood to be in some way equivalent to the indwelling of the Holy Spirit, this suggests not only that διάκρισις was regarded as fundamental to union with God but also that endowment with the Holy Spirit was closely associated with the operation of the intellect and the ability to reason and analyse. The biblical basis for seeing διάκρισις in this way may be from the fourth Gospel where the Holy Spirit is described as a Comforter or Counsellor who reminds believers of Christ's teaching and provides understanding of everything (John 14:26) while making them aware of sin, guiding them into the truth and revealing God's will to them (John 16:5-15). It will be shown that these properties of the Holy Spirit are

---

[47] Pseudo-Macarius understands that the ψυχή needs both διάκρισις and γνῶσις in order to serve God (*hom. H* 15.5; *hom. B* 54.7.1).

[48] An Abba of Rome 1. See also: GSC 10.110; *VP* 5.10.76; PE 4.46.1.1-16 pp643-644. Cf. Arsenius 36; PE 4.46.1.17-21 p644; Budge 1.450; Bars 191. The Roman monk is almost certainly Arsenius; the story is very similar to Arsenius 36 and PE places the two apophthegms together. The equation of the Holy Spirit with *discretio* is also evident in the comment that Nonnus preached as one filled with the Holy Spirit and without *indiscretus* (James the Deacon, *vita sanctae Pelagiae meretricis* 6).

also used to describe διάκρισις elsewhere[49] and given the equation of the two in this apophthegm, διάκρισις may be understood as the way in which the Holy Spirit operates in the life of the believer and learning to use διάκρισις as learning to allow the Holy Spirit free reign.

This sense of διάκρισις as the indwelling of the Holy Spirit, however, is not seen as a realised eschatology, but as an awareness of present holiness. Rather in his ascent to God the monk is urged to contemplate the purity of his present spiritual condition rather than his future destination, heaven. In an apophthegm that also demonstrates the use of διάκρισις for interpreting Scripture,[50] monks enquiring about heaven are rebuked (somewhat obliquely) for failing to discern that they had not yet purified themselves from sin. When they asked what 'heaven is not pure in God's sight' (Job 15:15) means, Zeno declared that his enquirers had 'abandoned their sins and are examining heavenly matters.'[51] This points to the need of διάκρισις to gain self-awareness of present impurity and humility as well as to seek purity instead of succumbing to a presumptuous zeal that reaches beyond current spiritual attainment to an understanding of higher spiritual reality for which the monk is not yet ready. Thus by using διάκρισις to gain an accurate self-assessment of personal impurity or sin a monk can move on to a fuller knowledge of God. It is by knowing themselves that monks can know God or, in more doctrinal terms, only the repentant sinner striving for righteousness can approach God.

Such excessive or misguided zeal for attaining the ultimate goal of union with God was seen as a threat to achieving it. Two apophthegms, placed consecutively in four of the collections and included in the διάκρισις / *discretio* sections of three of them, demonstrate that such zeal was regarded as a particular struggle encountered by young and inexperienced monks. In the first, a monk, immediately he took the cowl, announced that he was an anchorite and his more experienced *confrères* made him visit all the brethren to say, 'Forgive me, for I am not an anchorite, but a novice.'[52] The novice had failed to use διάκρισις to understand his true spiritual and monastic status. The next saying develops this with the advice:

---

[49]   See below on διάκρισις as guide (pp. 179-80) and as the means of interpreting Scripture (pp. 180-84). Cf. Cassian (see above, pp. 105-106).

[50]   Discussed further below, pp. 180-84.

[51]   *VP* 5.10.22. See also: Zeno 4; GSC 10.27; PE 4.17.1.1-2 p312. Zeno's exegesis is doctrinal: God alone is pure therefore heaven cannot be.

[52]   Nau 243. See also: GSC 10.172; *VP* 5.10.110; PE 1.41.1.1 p600; Ch70; Budge 2.422.

If you see a younger man climbing towards heaven by his own will, seize his foot and cast him down from there [*VP*: to earth], for it is useful to him [*VP*: it does not set him free].[53]

Monks are thus enjoined to watch over their less experienced brethren to discern when they arrogate advancement and the inexperienced are warned to guard against presuming that they have progressed further than is the case. Διάκρισις thus provides insight into the degree to which a monk has progressed towards his goals, both personally and in the lives of others. It also enables the monk to distinguish both between merely living in solitude and true anchoritic life, and between seeking to ascend to God by his own effort (e.g. through excessive πρακτική) and doing so in dependence upon God. Finally, διάκρισις enables a senior monk to correct the behaviour of a disciple and help him to pursue his goals.[54] Διάκρισις is used to understand and deal with one's present spiritual condition as a preparation for achieving union with God.

In order to prepare himself and make progress towards his goal, it is understood that the monk needs to commit himself to the disciplines of πρακτική. For example, with youthful but misguided zeal, the young John Kolobos announced to his older brother, 'I wish to be free from care, like the angels ... who do not work but continually serve God' and then went off into the desert. When John returned a week later his brother (effectively using διάκρισις to know how best to correct John) pretended not to know him, saying, 'John has become an angel and is no longer among men.' He left John outside in distress until the next morning and then told him, 'You are a man and you need to work again in order to grow.'[55] Immaturity in the monastic life and therefore a less developed ability to exercise διάκρισις can urge the monk to rush unsuccessfully towards his ultimate goal. Work (and other πρακτική) is regarded as essential to the pursuit of this goal and is understood to nourish the monk, enabling him to grow (τρέφω) spiritually; it cannot therefore be bypassed. It is thus διάκρισις to recognise the necessity of πρακτική for making spiritual progress.

---

[53]   Nau 244. See also: GSC 10.173; Nau 111; *VP* 5.10.111; PE 3.29.3.2 p346; Ch71; Budge 2.504; Bars 693.

[54]   Further on the teacher / disciple relationship, see below, pp. 189-202.

[55]   John Kolobos 2. See also: GSC 10.36; *VP* 5.10.27; *VP* 3.56; PE 2.3.5.7 p89; Budge 2.70. (PE and Syriac draw attention to John's youth at the time). Cf. Matoes 1; GSC 7.16; *VP* 5.7.11; PE 3.31.1.16 p373 (διάκρισις section); Budge 2.147 where light continual work is preferred to and distinguished from heavy work that is quickly completed or abandoned (identified by Migne (*PL* 74 index p. XXXIII) as relating to *discretio*). It is significant that when John Kolobos was called into the desert, it was described as 'the place where the angelic life (and) all education in angelic piety is found.' (Am326.1).

The idea of heaven is not entirely absent from making spiritual progress, but reaching his goal requires the monk to work steadily at his πρακτική and not circumvent this process. Thus the important monastic goal of ἀνάπαυσις, a rest associated with heaven and union with God, may be enjoyed in part in the world as a product of renunciation and πρακτική:

> An old man said, "Even if the saints have toiled here below, they have yet received a portion of ἀνάπαυσις already." He said this because they were free from worldly care.[56]

While this saying expresses that it is διάκρισις to attain the goal of ἀνάπαυσις through πρακτική, it also demonstrates a distinction between fully and partially attaining that goal. There is a danger of confusing the partial with the full and of thinking that personal effort in πρακτική alone fully achieves this goal, so that 'many take ἀνάπαυσις before God grants it to them.'[57] This is not only to lose sight of dependence upon God for the goal, it is also to become so pre-occupied with the goal that the process by which it is attained is also forgotten or neglected. Διάκρισις is to apply oneself to the work of πρακτική by which the goal is gained and not to focus on the goal itself which only results in failing to achieve it. Hence: '(Poemen) said: "If we pursue ἀνάπαυσις, the grace of God flees from us; but if we flee it, it pursues us."'[58] The monk with διάκρισις thus works steadily and waits patiently for God to grant the goal, allowing it to emerge gradually in his life.

This very practical approach, however, does not indicate a passive lethargy. While misguided zeal and over dependence on personal effort are discouraged, monks are nevertheless urged to make every effort in their ascent to God and to apply themselves with assiduity to their πρακτική. For example, a monk concerned about his negligent approach to saying the synaxis is told 'love towards God shows itself when one does the work of God with all possible application, compunction and undistracted thought [λογισμός].'[59] Love for God and seeking him is thus expressed in wholehearted dedication to serving him and the monk should discern in any neglect a diminution in that commitment. This single minded devotion to seeking God and salvation requires effort, thus Isidore says, 'If you passionately desire salvation, do everything that leads to it'[60] and Poemen

---

[56]   Nau 235. See also: GSC 10.161; *VP* 5.10.103A; *VP* 7.28.3; PE 1.24.2.1 p340; PE 4.5.2.31 p99.

[57]   Theodore of Pherme 16. See also: GSC 10.35; *VP* 5.10.26; PE 1.41.1.3 p600; Budge 2.87.

[58]   GSC 10.80.

[59]   GSC 10.186. See also: Nau 395. Cf. MD 41; Budge 1.497.

[60]   Isidore the Priest 6; GSC 10.43.

asks, 'What is the use of setting yourself to a profession and not learning it?'[61] The parallels to this latter saying in *Vitae Patrum* 7 and *Ægyptiorum Patrum Sententiæ* stress that a monk should learn to complete the work he has begun, which reflects Christ's caveat in Luke 9:62.[62] Διάκρισις is therefore learning to do all that is necessary to achieve union with God and persevering in it. This endeavour encompasses inward devotion as well as exterior activity. Through his inward devotion to seeking God the monk is able to resist attacks from his spiritual enemy and so draw closer to union with God.

> One of the fathers said, "It is essential that man should have an interior occupation [*VP* 5: a work in the cell]. Thus if he [PE: his νοῦς] devotes himself to a work of God, the enemy visits him from time to time but he does not find a place to dwell. On the other hand, if he is controlled by the captivity of the enemy, the Spirit of God often visits him, but as we do not leave him room, he withdraws because of our evil. [*VP* 3 adds: If however he is sought again from a whole heart, he will return quickly.]"[63]

While the *Vitae Patrum* 5 parallel relates this saying to work in the cell it does so without diminishing the interior nature of the monk's devotion to serving God, which the Evergetinos version identifies as a work of the νοῦς and *Vitae Patrum* 3 says should come *ex toto corde* ('from a whole heart'). The monk with διάκρισις thus sets his entire being on seeking union with God and guarding against the encroachment of evil. The emphasis on heart, νοῦς and learning suggests a reasoning, analytical and noetic approach to seeking God, but this is counterbalanced by the love for God it is understood to express. Interior commitment is outwardly expressed in πρακτική and, as the monk comes closer to union with God, the two are brought increasingly into harmony and balance by διάκρισις.

Another way in which the monk's undivided determination to seek God in his inner and outer life can be seen is in renunciation; an outward rejection of material possessions and inward rejection of acquisitiveness and greed.[64] Possessions and the desire to have them are seen as a distraction from seeking and knowing God. Thus Syncletica contrasts merchants who are always looking for how to make more money with monks 'who have nothing of what is sought but wish to acquire everything

---

61   Poemen 128; GSC 10.56. See also *VP* 7.27.2; MD 102; Budge 2.288.
62   'No-one who puts his hand to the plough and looks back is fit for service in the kingdom of God.'
63   Nau 241. See also: GSC 10.168; *VP* 5.10.108; *VP* 3.179; *VP* 7.26.3; PE 4.7.3.2 p200; Ch67.
64   The simple clothing, diet and accommodation that resulted from such renunciation are described in Ch254.

through the fear of God.'[65] The *Vitae Patrum* parallel stresses that monks do not desire even necessities because they fear God; their complete renunciation of all possessions is expressive of their desire for God alone. The desire to be right before God is brought out in Arsenius' dying words: 'Do not trouble to give alms[66] for my sake, for if I have given alms myself, I am able to find it.'[67] The *Vitae Patrum* 3 parallel (and to some extent the Evergetinos version) combines this saying with Arsenius 40 and 41, describing Arsenius' anticipation of the Last Judgment and tears for his sins. He is thus presented as entirely focussed on being right before God and preparing himself for union with him, conscious of the reward that might await him for his acts of charity in life. Arsenius was aware of his faults but assured that if there was any good in him, he would be rewarded for it. Διάκρισις was used to gain awareness of one's inner condition and to conduct life with self-giving to God in anticipation of heaven.

As well as the *virtus* of dispossession, the life-long commitment of the monk to this way of life also involved humility. It was understood that monks needed to protect any progress they made towards their goals, and διάκρισις enabled them to maintain this effort.

> The same (elder) said, "Man must make efforts until he possesses Jesus. Once he has attained him he is no longer in peril. However he must still make efforts to recall the difficulty caused by the effort, he guards himself in all respects out of fear of losing the fruit of such great efforts. That is why God made the children of Israel wander for forty years in the desert: so that the memory of the difficulties of the journey would prevent them from going back."[68]

Διάκρισις is to guard with humility any advances made. Recollecting the effort expended in achieving this progress would act as a psychological deterrent to relapsing and falling away from union with God. However, διάκρισις is also a humble awareness of frailty: the monk has overcome weakness and sin, and although salvation may be his, he still needs to defend himself.

This awareness of the need for defence of spiritual goals is evident in a saying concerning Agathon.[69] Hearing of his 'great διάκρισις' some monks decided to test his temper, accusing him (presumably falsely) first of anger

---

[65] Syncletica 10. See also: GSC 10.101; *VP* 5.10.70; *VP* 5.21.24; *vit. Syn.* 37.

[66] Or possibly an ἀγάπη meal for the dead.

[67] Arsenius 39. See also: GSC 10.10; *VP* 5.10.9; *VP* 3.163a; PE 4.37.4.1 p557; Budge 1.502.

[68] GSC 10.130. See also: *VP* 3.180; *VP* 7.28.1.

[69] Agathon 5. See also: GSC 10.12; *VP* 5.10.10; *VP* 3.21; PE 2.2.6.1 p56; Budge 1.183. Cf. responses to anger in Poemen 118 (see below, p. 137).

and pride and then of talking nonsense and slander. Agathon accepted both accusations with equanimity, remaining impassive in the face of provocation and declaring that they were 'an advantage to his ψυχή,' doubtless because they challenged him to greater purity. However, when they accused him of heresy[70] he denied it, saying 'heresy is a separation from God and I do not wish to be separated from God.' The monks were 'amazed at his διάκρισις and departed edified.' Agathon demonstrated his commitment to his ultimate goal of union with God by denying the last accusation, whereas he showed that he was committed to his proximate goal, ἀπάθεια, by accepting the first two without demur. The accusations were weighed with διάκρισις and Agathon discerned both how to use those which were spiritually helpful and the inherent danger of acceding to the third accusation. He also used διάκρισις to teach his accusers about the monk's goals, humility[71] and the supreme importance of maintaining a relationship with God. With διάκρισις the monk is constantly conscious of his goals and determined to defend them.

In the apophthegms the monk's life and behaviour are frequently portrayed as a search for purity in preparation for full union with God; such purity is sought using διάκρισις. For example, monks are told to pray for purity of heart rather than the approbation others[72] and also, a simple life in which the monk does not regard himself too highly is said to eradicate evil λογισμοί.[73] Humility thus both expresses and helps develop inward purity. Διάκρισις is to seek such humility and purity, since without them even the gift of thaumaturgy is regarded as worthless: 'Even if an angry man raises a corpse, he is not acceptable to God.'[74] Διάκρισις is to overcome λογισμοί[75] in the pursuit of purity and thereby be acceptable to God and capable of union with him.

Works of πρακτική combined with strong faith are understood to facilitate, express and maintain this inner purity:

---

[70] Αἵρεσις in antiquity referred to a chosen system of philosophical thought, but in the early Church it developed a negative sense referring increasingly to theological error condemned by the Church, which often in the course of rebuttal led to the development of orthodox doctrine.

[71] Agathon's humility is evident in his lack of concern for his reputation. The longer *VP* 3 version replaces *discretio* with '*virtus* of humility and patience' suggesting that *discretio* incorporates these two qualities.

[72] Sarah 5; GSC 10.108; *VP* 5.10.74; PE 3.25.1.4 p289; Budge 2.75; Bars 237. Seeking the approbation of others would be vainglorious and require penitence.

[73] GSC 10.28. Cf. Poemen 36.

[74] Agathon 19. See also GSC 10.16; *VP* 5.10.13; PE 2.35.1.1 p439; Budge 1.484 (on humility).

[75] Further on διάκρισις and λογισμοί see below, pp. 150-66.

An elder said, "It is impossible for one who thinks rightly and lives [*alph.*: labours] piously to be abandoned and to fall into shameful errors or the distraction of demons."[76]

Διάκρισις unites inward faith with outward actions[77] and guards the monk against impurity. Similarly ἀπάθεια, the monk's proximate goal, is understood to be achieved through πρακτική regulated by διάκρισις:

> Another [*VP*: Evagrius] said, "One of the fathers used to say a more austere and regular diet bound up with ἀγάπη leads the monk more quickly into the harbour of ἀπάθεια."[78]

The triple repetition of this saying in the Greek Systematic Collection attests to the value placed upon the use of διάκρισις to regulate πρακτική[79] so that purity and ἀπάθεια could be achieved. Essentially, then, διάκρισις is used to protect the monk as he attains a state of ἀπάθεια, to remain impassive, unresponsive and unmoved by any provocation. Because of his humility, the ἀπάθεια of the monk is not that of the Stoic, but part of his way to union with God. Thus, Macarius says the monk should 'be like a dead man, taking account of neither the dishonour of men nor their honour.'[80] Ἀπάθεια is to be as unmoved by injury or flattery as the dead; if the monk is to achieve purity he must not give way to rancour and anger or accept praise which might inflate his ego leading to vainglory and pride. With διάκρισις such dangers and the best way to respond to them can be discerned so that purity may be gained not lost.

Διάκρισις and Ἀρετή

It has already been noted that διάκρισις is the greatest of all the ἀρεταί,[81] governing them and helping the monk to develop and maintain them in his

---

[76] GSC 10.139. See also Macarius the Egyptian 20b; *VP* 7.38.2b; MD 23b; PE 4.22.1.6b p369; Macarius, *apoph. PG* 34.249; *HL* 47.6; Bars 549; cf. Am166.1.

[77] This is brought out by several longer parallels (*alph.*, *VP*, MD and PE), which stress the value of humility (regarding 'contempt as praise') and renunciation.

[78] GSC 1.4, 10.193, 17.35. See also: Evagrius 6; *VP* 5.1.4; Evagrius, *prak.* 91; Socrates Scholasticus, *HE* 4.23.

[79] Further on διάκρισις regulating πρακτική see below, pp. 141-44.

[80] GSC 10.47. See also: Macarius the Egyptian 23b; PE 3.25.1.3b p289; Am126.1, 214.2; Budge 1.446b (on humility); Macarius, *apoph. PG* 34.252; *HL* 9 (*PL* 74.357B-C). In the longer version of this apophthegm Macarius illustrates the point by instructing a monk first to abuse and throw stones at the dead in a cemetery and the next day to praise them (cf. Anoub 1 where throwing stones at an idol is used to illustrate ἀπάθεια which results in ἀνάπαυσις and peace).

[81] See above, p. 129.

search for God. However, the chief danger of the way of the monk is pride since it is understood that any ἀρετή or πρακτική can be used to gain the approval of others instead of God. Thus, monks are told to use διάκρισις to analyse their motives for behaving in a given way. For example, silence is an ἀρετή that can be used for God or misused vaingloriously to gain renown.[82] To advance spiritually, the monk needs to foster the right ἀρεταί and πρακτικαί, discerning damaging practices and attitudes that will lead him away from his goals, as the following apophthegm demonstrates by contrasting three opposites:

> A brother asked an elder, "Tell me, father, how will I acquire Jesus?" He replied, "Toil, humility and unceasing prayer acquire Jesus. For all the saints from start to finish are saved through these three things. But ἀνάπαυσις, self-will and self-righteousness are obstacles to the salvation of the monk, for nearly everyone is destroyed by them."[83]

Here ἀνάπαυσις, the will (which could be used to set the mind to serving God) and righteousness (δικαίωμα) are all capable of positive interpretation, but they are set in opposition to the approved means of acquiring Jesus and thus carry negative connotations. These can therefore be used inappropriately and harmfully and so διάκρισις is needed to examine and evaluate behaviour and motives. This could be seen as making the ἀρετή of διάκρισις a mental exercise in self-analysis, but the acquisition of ἀρεταί is not seen as a purely intellectual process since they cannot be gained merely through information or education. This is evident from an exchange between the two academics, Arsenius and Evagrius:

> An elder [*VP* and Budge: Evagrius] said to the blessed Arsenius, "How is it that we know nothing [*VP*: have no *virtutes*] from so great an education and wisdom, but these Egyptian rustics have acquired so many ἀρεταί?" Abba Arsenius said to him, "We indeed know nothing from secular education, but these Egyptian rustics have acquired the ἀρεταί by their own hard work."[84]

Διάκρισις discerns the need for perseverance in the daily toil of πρακτική rather than academic expertise if the ἀρεταί are to be acquired. Arsenius exhibits humility in regard to his erudition and so while διάκρισις is often presented as noetic, it should not be understood as being derived from learning but rather from practical experience in the monastic life.

---

[82] GSC 10.184. Cf. GSC 10.75 and parallels.
[83] GSC 10.129.
[84] GSC 10.7. See also: Arsenius 5; *VP* 5.10.5; Budge 2.233; Bars 126.

It becomes apparent, then, that there is an interplay between humility and διάκρισις in which true διάκρισις is expressed in humility.[85] A narrative apophthegm on humility[86] describes a monk who was a slave whose masters had released him to serve God. Nevertheless, he still regarded himself as their slave[87] and brought his earnings to them each year at which time they would refuse it and he would insist or otherwise determine (*discerno*) not to return to the desert. His masters so respected the monk that they allowed him to do as he wished, sending him back to his cell and giving his wages to the poor (*Vitae Patrum* 3). In the longer *Vitae Patrum* 3 parallel the monk explains his eagerness to serve God, with Divine assistance, in the practical disciplines to gain salvation. His humility,[88] both in his servile allegiance to his (former?) masters and in his dedicated πρακτική for God, earned him the respect and love of his masters and *confrères* alike. The Greek versions all stress his profound διάκρισις calling him διακριτικός σφόδρα ('exceedingly discerning'), the Evergetinos version repeating διακριτικός at the end of the saying. While the monk's expression of humility is chosen using διάκρισις, his humility is also an expression of διάκρισις. The humility, obedience and dedication expressed in this apophthegm are brought together in a briefer saying where they are understood as the key practices or ἀρεταί necessary for communal life:

> Abba Poemen said, "(Life in) the cœnobium needs three exercises: humility, obedience and being motivated and having the incentive for the work of the cœnobium."[89]

The inclusion of this saying under the διάκρισις heading indicates that διάκρισις was understood to unite the inward ἀρεταί of humility and obedience with the zealous hard work of outward πρακτική. Humility, obedience and work may be said to be properties of διάκρισις and so διάκρισις acts as a bridge between the inner and outer life.[90]

Elsewhere Poemen identifies three different exercises necessary for the monastic life. This difference probably arises from the saying above relating to cœnobitic life, in which there was a particular emphasis on monks relying on the διάκρισις of a senior monk, whereas the saying below relates to the anchoritic life.

---

[85] As was seen in Cassian (e.g. *conf.* 2.10.1, discussed above, p. 116).

[86] Mius 2; GSC 15.47; *VP* 5.15.31; *VP* 3.17; PE 4.40.5.9-11 p611; Budge 2.169.

[87] Whether he had been manumitted or had refused to accept his manumission is unclear.

[88] Particularly noted at the end of the Syriac version.

[89] Poemen 103; GSC 10.74.

[90] See above, pp. 87, 98, 122.

(Poemen) said, "Poverty, affliction and διάκρισις, these are the instruments of the solitary life. For it is written, 'If there should be these three men Noah, Job and Daniel [*alph.* adds: I surely live, says the Lord].' [Ezekiel 14:14 (LXX)] Noah represents poverty, Job suffering and Daniel διάκρισις. Therefore if these three exercises are in man, God dwells in him [MD adds: supporting him, and driving back every temptation from him and every tribulation coming from the enemy]."[91]

Daniel represents διάκρισις because of his ability to discern the meaning of dreams, which relates to the use of διάκρισις by monks to interpret circumstances and situations of all kinds. Not only does this saying present διάκρισις as an essential tool in the search for union with God, it also presents it as a πρακτική and as much a part of being a monk as renunciation and asceticism. The longer version in *Ægyptiorum Patrum Sententiæ* also draws attention to the support and protection afforded the monk by διάκρισις in the pursuit of his goals.[92] Διάκρισις is thus presented not only as an ἀρετή but as a work of πρακτική as well, a discipline by which the monk can oversee and defend his spiritual life.[93] By operating as both ἀρετή and πρακτική, διάκρισις becomes the means by which the inner and outer life are integrated.

Although the monk uses works of πρακτική to achieve his proximate and ultimate goals, they are not seen as ends in themselves. This is expressly stated in the first apophthegm in the διάκρισις / *discretio* section of both Systematic Collections. By so placing it the redactors show that they understood the use of διάκρισις to govern works of πρακτική to be of the first importance if they were to be effective in bringing the monk closer to God.

(Antony) said, "There are some who wore out their bodies in ἄσκησις, and because they lacked διάκρισις, they are far from God."[94]

---

[91] GSC 1.23. See also: Poemen 60; *VP* 5.1.14; MD 8; Budge 2.193, cf. 2.341.

[92] Cf. Poemen 35 where the ἀρετή of διάκρισις is described as a tool that guards the ψυχή (discussed above, pp. 129-30).

[93] Διάκρισις as both ἀρετή and πρακτική is also evident from John Kolobos 34 (GSC 1.13; *VP* 5.1.8; Am138.2; Budge 2.128. Cf. Poemen 46; PE 3.11.2.1 p126; Am333.1, 407.2; Budge 2.118; Dorotheos, *doctr.* 14.150; Evagrius, *gnos.* 6) which says that monks need a little of every ἀρετή, but then lists both ἀρεταί and πρακτικαί including διάκρισις among them, suggesting that διάκρισις can be either.

[94] Antony 8. See also: GSC 10.1; *VP* 5.10.1; PE 3.31.1.1 p372 (διάκρισις section); Budge 1.296 (on watchfulness); Antony, *ep.* 6.106. Cf. Poemen 106: 'Many of our Fathers became vigorous in asceticism; but in λεπτότης [subtlety] very few.' Migne translates λεπτότης as 'fineness of *discretio*'; cf. index reference in W. Bousset,

The longer parallel in one of Antony's letters stresses that even those with a 'most holy way of life (were) destroyed by *indiscretio*' and so monks should discern the extent of their work or fall to the devil at the moment they think they are nearing God and 'hoping for his powerful light.' Διάκρισις is thus used to keep asceticism from becoming excessive and monks from becoming proud of their ascetic achievements. Conversely, a lack of διάκρισις is spiritually destructive resulting in separation from God. Thus διάκρισις is essential for union with God and for discerning the proper use and value of πρακτική. Similarly, God is said to be found 'in fasts, vigils, works, compassion and above all in διάκρισις,' but those who lack discernment (ἀδιακρισία) achieve nothing despite their extensive fasting, memorisation of Scripture and psalmody because they 'do not have what God seeks: [GSC adds: the fear of God], ἀγάπη and humility.'[95] This saying makes clearer still the superior value of διάκρισις among works of πρακτική and its importance for governing them and so achieving union with God. Πρακτική must be exercised not only in conjunction with ἀγάπη and humility, it is also valueless without διάκρισις.

The use of πρακτική, moderated by διάκρισις, enabled the monk to bring his body and behaviour under the control of his ψυχή so that his inner spiritual nature could grow, as the following saying on fasting demonstrates:

> Abba Daniel also used to say, "As much as the body flourishes, so much is the ψυχή made thin; and as much as the body is made thin, so much does the ψυχή flourish."[96]

However, for such inner spiritual growth to take place, ascetic practice needs to be regulated by διάκρισις to avoid destructive excess. Thus Syncletica speaks of the need for moderation (συμμετρία) in fasting, the monk discerning his personal physical ability and distinguishing (διακρίνω) between divinely and demonically inspired levels of asceticism.[97] The longer *Vitae Patrum* parallel says that extended fasts

---

Apophthegmata: Studien zur Geschichte des ältesten Mönchtums, (Tübingen: Mohr, 1923), p. 187: '*Diakrisis und Tapferkeit*' ('διάκρισις and courage').

῎Ασκησις was a term used in classical Greek for the training of athletes and soldiers, but in Patristic Greek it became a technical term referring to monastic life and practices (cf. Cassian's apposite references to *miles Christi* and *athleta Christi*; see p. 80, n. 44).

[95] Nau 222. See also: GSC 10.135; *VP* 5.10.91; Budge 2.31a.

[96] Daniel 4; GSC 10.22. See also: *VP* 5.10.17; PE 2.15.17.3 p210; Ch54; Budge 1.99 (on fasting); cf. GSC 10.140. *VP* reinforces the point by repetition in very similar terms. Cf. *vit. Ant.* 7: 'the force of the ψυχή is strong when the body's pleasures are weak.'

[97] Syncletica 15; GSC 10.105; *VP* 5.10.72; *vit. Syn.* 100.

followed by gorging result in loss of *virtus* and that to defend himself against spiritual attack the monk must bring his body and ψυχή into harmony:

> Everything extreme is destructive. So do not suddenly discard your armour, lest you be found naked in battle and easily captured; our body is our armour, our soul is the warrior. So take care of both, so that you are prepared for what is necessary.[98]

This caveat against extremes is reminiscent of Cassian's use of the aphorism ἀκρότητες ἰσότητες when he writes of the need to use *discretio* as a guide between extremes.[99] Διάκρισις guides the monk between extremes, weighs spiritual and psychological drives that may encourage him towards πρακτική destructive of the inner life, distinguishes between divinely and demonically inspired ascetic practices, helps him to determine his most spiritually productive course and keeps his inner and outer natures in balance so that they can present an effective defence against spiritual attack. Although this use of πρακτική to bring the body under control could have a negative connotation, the moderation of ascetic practice using διάκρισις protected the monk from activity that was potentially physically and spiritually harmful.

Διάκρισις is thus used to moderate both the duration of fasts[100] and the amount of food consumed. The amount eaten is seen as less significant than whether the monk remains hungry, since constant hunger is regarded as a valuable aid to bringing the body into submission to the interior being:

> An old man said, "There is a man who eats a lot and is still hungry, and another who eats little and is full. He who eats a lot and is still hungry will have a greater reward than he who eats little and is full."[101]

Poemen also regards it as better to eat just a little each day and remain hungry; he says:

> The old men tested all these things, as they were strong, and they discovered that it is good to eat each day, but just a little. They passed on to us this way which is royal and light.[102]

---

[98]   *VP* 5.10.72. See also *vit. Syn.* 100.
[99]   Cassian, *conf.* 2.16.1-2 (see above, p. 105).
[100] Syncletica 15; GSC 10.105; *VP* 5.10.72; *vit. Syn.* 100.
[101] Nau 231. See also: GSC 10.154; *VP* 5.10.99; *VP* 3.48; *VP* 7.1.3; PE 2.18.3.6 p233.
[102] GSC 10.61. See also: Poemen 31; *VP* 5.10.44; *VP* 3.45; PE 2.18.3.1 p232; Budge 1.102. PE and *VP* 5 make clearer the allusion to Mt. 11:30.

The abstemious diet Poemen recommended had been discerned from experience and avoided extremes that would cause the monk to flounder. In the first generation monks used διάκρισις to assess their experiences experimentally and to learn how best to conduct πρακτική, but once an appropriate way of carrying out πρακτική had been discovered, διάκρισις was used by subsequent generations to apply this experience and received wisdom. This lessening of severity based on the experience of monastic forebears is reflected in another διάκρισις saying:

> One of the old men said, "Our fathers entered life by severity, but we, if we are able, enter it by kindness [PE adds: through humility]."[103]

The severity here is seen in general terms and the Evergetinos addition of humility may suggest that the kindness came to be understood in terms of the monk's attitude not only to his body but towards others as well. Nevertheless, the saying expresses a shift in attitude over time towards a less severe asceticism and διάκρισις emerges as an attitude towards the body (and possibly others) that is more considerate of physical capabilities and aware of dangerous extremes.

Many apophthegms arise out of questions concerning how best to exercise works of πρακτική. While these at first appear to describe διάκρισις as an analytical preoccupation with the detail of ascetic activity, they are more concerned with using διάκρισις to establish a balanced and realistic (within the monastic context) approach to πρακτική. Thus, when two monks asked Pambo whether their fasting and diet or work and almsgiving would save them or lead them astray, he explained that none of these make a person into a monk per se: 'The exercises are good, but if you guard your conscience towards your neighbour, then you are saved.'[104] Διάκρισις thus provides the monk with a proper understanding of πρακτική in relation to the inner life and wider relationships, keeping him from going astray, not least by becoming preoccupied with practice at the expense of purpose. In a similar story elsewhere, Pambo declares that two contrasting monastic lifestyles are equally valid, saying twice that 'both are perfect.'[105] Διάκρισις thus discerns that while specific works of πρακτική may differ from monk to monk they can be equally valuable and valid, but they are for a purpose and not an end in themselves.

---

[103]   GSC 10.182. See also: J665; PE 1.44.3.9 p645.

[104]   Pambo 2. See also: GSC 10.94; *VP* 5.10.65; PE 3.2.2.6 p24; Budge 1.376 (on watchfulness); cf. *HL* 14.

[105]   *HL* 14.4, 6. In both Pambo 2 and *HL* Pambo only answers once he feels divinely inspired. The teacher with διάκρισις is understood to have the God given ability to read situations and make decisions upon them.

This discernment of the equal legitimacy of different lifestyles and their concomitant πρακτική is found in other sayings. Notwithstanding the higher value placed on the anchoritic life over the cœnobitic found elsewhere,[106] Cyril of Alexandria could assert there to be 'no difference [διακρίνω], for both are well pleasing to God' when he was asked which was superior.[107] Διάκρισις can thus be used to distinguish between different but equally valid monastic lifestyles either wrongly by discriminating against one or correctly by selecting the discipline most appropriate to the individual. Each monk's πρακτική is personal to him and he must discern the specific discipline that will lead him most readily to his goals. Διάκρισις is therefore not limiting, rather it opens up a range of possibilities for serving God and provides the monk with the means to choose between them. Hence Poemen could describe three different lifestyles as having equal merit:

> Abba Poemen said, "If there are three men together and one is thoroughly still [ἡσυχάζω], one a sick man who gives thanks and another serves with a pure λογισμός, the three are doing the same work."[108]

Once a way of life and πρακτική are chosen circumstances may change and require the monk to use διάκρισις to re-evaluate and revise them if he is to continue to make progress. For example, when Netras moved from solitary to episcopal life where all manner of resources were available to him, he discerned that his altered circumstances threatened his ἡσυχία and dependence upon God. He thus redoubled his ascetic efforts in order not to lose what he had already gained spiritually and to continue his advance towards God. He further discerned that his new circumstances permitted him to exercise a greater austerity than had been previously possible.[109] Netras thus used διάκρισις to determine how best to adjust to new circumstances. Διάκρισις is thus used to determine the way of life and πρακτική best suited to the individual and persevere in them. However, it is also flexible and helps the monk to assess when he must change them in order to achieve union with God.

This use of διάκρισις to introduce flexibility and avoidance of severe extremes in the exercise of πρακτική reveals the nature and purpose of πρακτική further. For example, Poemen teaches that extreme penance (whether for three years or forty days) for 'a great sin' is too much: 'if a

---

[106] E.g. Cassian, *conf.* part 1, pref. 4.

[107] GSC 10.178; Nau 70; PE 4.5.2.23 p99.

[108] Poemen 29. See also: GSC 10.76; *VP* 5.10.52; *VP* 7.36.1; PE 3.18.7.2 p230; Budge 2.237.

[109] Netras 1. See also: GSC 10.50; *VP* 5.10.36; App 18; PE 2.18.3.8 p233; Ch62; Budge 2.410.

man repents with all his heart and intends to commit the sin no more, God accepts him within three days.'[110] Διάκρισις moderates πρακτική and directs the heart so that purity is attained not through excessive effort, which is to lose sight of the purpose of πρακτική, but through dependence upon God. Διάκρισις is not exhibited in extremes of effort but in the regular and steady application of πρακτική, hence an anonymous elder says, 'Let us be zealous to work little by little and we will be saved.'[111] Such zeal could at times be misdirected through lack of διάκρισις so that the monk became biased towards one work of πρακτική or towards more interior and contemplative activities at the expense of work and therefore lose the proper balance recommended. The need to balance the interior and exterior life is aptly expressed in an amusing apophthegm about an overly pious monk who visited Silvanus and his community on Mount Sinai. He decried their work saying, 'Do not work for food that spoils [John 6:27]. For Mary chose the good portion [Luke 10:42]' and so Silvanus caused him to be left in a cell with a book and not called to the communal meal. When the monk complained, Silvanus told him that unlike the other monks who were carnal and so needed to work in order to eat, he was clearly a 'spiritual man' who had no need of food and was satisfied with 'the good portion' like Mary. Silvanus explained to the duly penitent monk, 'Mary needs Martha, for it is through Martha that Mary is praised.'[112] The zealous monk lacked διάκρισις and so failed to understand the purpose of work and the need to balance the interior and exterior life, whereas Silvanus used διάκρισις to discern the monk's problem and how best to teach him. Διάκρισις is to moderate and balance the interior and exterior life and keep them in harmony.[113] It keeps the monk aware that the purpose of πρακτική is for spiritual development; πρακτική is neither worthless nor the sole means of human effort to obtain union with God.

This interplay between the interior and exterior life can be seen in the use of πρακτική to support the work of the ψυχή. Theodore of Pherme discusses the work of the ψυχή and manual work in two apophthegms the second of which explains the first (they are consecutive in three of the

---

[110] Poemen 12. See also: GSC 10.57; *VP* 5.10.40; PE 1.1.4.2 p30.

[111] Nau 387; GSC 10.169; PE 3.31.1.15 p373 (διάκρισις section); Ch68. See also: Budge 1.390a (on watchfulness), which goes on to stress the need to be diligent in daily work and not idle.

[112] Silvanus 5. See also: GSC 10.99; *VP* 5.10.69; *VP* 3.55; PE 2.3.5.2 p88; Budge 2.15. This apophthegm also demonstrates the use of διάκρισις to interpret Scripture and apply it practically (discussed further below, pp. 180-84).

[113] John Kolobos 34 and parallels, and Evagrius, *gnos.* 6 point to the need for monks to practice all the ἀρεταί and πρακτικαί indicating that this is necessary for true balance.

collections). In the first[114] Theodore laments the deterioration in monastic standards: originally manual work was subordinate to the work of the ψυχή, whereas now he found the priorities reversed. In the second[115] he explains the nature of each work and attempts to restore the original order. He defines the work of the ψυχή as everything done in obedience to God's commands, whereas he describes manual work in terms of ill-motivated acquisitiveness or selfishness. His explanatory illustrations describe monks who feel compelled to works of charity but find pretexts for not leaving their own work. Theodore concludes that such failures are to 'neglect the command of God, which is the work of the ψυχή, and do what is subordinate, which is manual work.' These apophthegms describe a perceived loss of διάκρισις over generations of monks. The purpose of πρακτική as a response to and as a means of developing an inner relationship with God had been forgotten. Quite apart from any negative connotations in the motivation to work (e.g. greed), outward activity was believed to have become more important to monks than inward purity, whereas the two should have been kept in harmony. Διάκρισις maintains the integrity and balance between interior purity and devotion to God and exterior activity and πρακτική, ensuring that πρακτική is used to develop the interior life of purity.

This interaction between the interior and exterior life is evident in another pair of sayings that are linked in the Systematic Collections. Asked, 'Which is greater, bodily toil or interior guarding?' Agathon likened these respectively to the leaves and fruit of trees, citing Matthew 3:10 to stress the need to produce good fruit. He concluded that the monk's zeal should be directed towards guarding the νοῦς but that this is protected and adorned by bodily toil.[116] The second apophthegm describes Agathon as 'wise in intellect and self-sufficient in body and ... manual work,' that is, his own life was an example of an inner and outer life unified and supporting the development of each other.[117] The Alphabetical Collection places another saying between these two in which Agathon declares that the ἀρετή requiring greatest toil is prayer, which the monk's (spiritual) enemies seek to disrupt because this alone hinders the monk's progress.[118] Set in the context of the other two sayings this suggests that prayer, an outward activity expressing an inner relationship with God needs to be guarded constantly, not least by works of πρακτική. The pair of sayings reveals that

---

[114]   Theodore of Pherme 10; GSC 10.33; *VP* 5.10.24; PE 3.36.4.1 p470; Budge 2.148, cf. 2.469.

[115]   Theodore of Pherme 11; GSC 10.177; *VP* 7.17.2; PE 3.36.4.2-3 pp470-471; Budge 2.149 (adds a reference to Mt. 5:41 at the end).

[116]   Agathon 8; GSC 10.13; *VP* 5.10.11a.

[117]   Agathon 10; GSC 10.14; *VP* 5.10.11b.

[118]   Agathon 9; GSC 12.2; *VP* 5.12.2; PE 4.9.3.7 p242.

διάκρισις is not only to keep the outer and inner life working in unison, with the former serving the latter, it also guards the νοῦς through πρακτική and interior vigilance.[119]

Διάκρισις, then, enables the monk to determine how much he should exercise a work of πρακτική; but it is also a factor in deciding when and how often to work as well, since failure to determine this can prove harmful:

> Abba Evagrius said, "Reading, vigils and prayer strengthen a shifting and wandering mind. However, hunger, work and solitude quench enflamed desire. Moreover psalmody, long-suffering and mercy repress confused anger. But these should be used at the appropriate times and in due measure. If however they are done at an unsuitable time and without due measure, they are useful for a short time but whatever lasts for a short time will be more harmful than useful."[120]

This saying is typical of Evagrius' concern with the wandering νοῦς and reveals how διάκρισις is understood to guide the monk in the steady, moderate and timely use of πρακτική in order to bring the νοῦς and λογισμοί under the monk's control.

This attention to steady work and the avoidance of distraction is evident in another saying about a monk who at first appears to be cantankerous and disobedient:

> A certain old man lived in the temple in Clysma and did not do the manual work given him, but if someone ordered him he did it [Nau: not even if someone ordered him did he do it]. But when it was time to work on nets he left them and worked on hemp and when they required yarn he worked on linen, so that his νοῦς would not stray and be distracted by manual work.[121]

Hemp (στίππυον) and linen (λινοῦς) can both refer to flax and so if they are intended as synonyms here, then the monk continued to work on the same material regardless of any immediate need or command. By working consistently on the same material, he would be endeavouring to remain undistracted by changing circumstances. Διάκρισις is thus to avoid distractions that would divert a monk from working steadily and consistently as he seeks union with God. With διάκρισις the spiritual

---

[119] The guarding and watching role of διάκρισις is discussed further below (pp. 166-71).
[120] *VP* 5.10.20. See also: GSC 10.25; PE 3.31.1.5 p372 (διάκρισις section); Evagrius, *prak.* 15 (see above, pp. 60-61).
[121] GSC 10.190. See also: Nau 59.

principles behind works of πρακτική can be examined and the monk is able to determine when it is appropriate to do them. Thus another monk defended working on a martyr's feast day because the martyr had also worked on that day by witnessing to God and being tortured.[122] This monk used διάκρισις to look beyond the holy day and weigh its significance to his personal πρακτική. Similarly, for all that the regular times of prayer and psalmody at the synaxis are generally regarded as an important element of daily monastic life, an anonymous saying reveals that it is διάκρισις not to adhere so rigidly to the set hours that the purpose of the synaxis is lost; it is better to say the synaxis late and in private than not all, 'since God is glorified at all times.'[123] By becoming preoccupied with times or practical details, the value and purpose of πρακτική can be lost, but with διάκρισις a monk can distinguish between the reason for πρακτική and the means by which it may be carried out. He is then able, using διάκρισις, to conduct his πρακτική in a considered way that achieves the purpose thereof: developing his spiritual life and relationship with God.

Whereas διάκρισις enables monks to discern when and to what extent they should exercise πρακτική, it also allows them to determine when to suspend it altogether. For example, they may lessen the severity of their discipline to practice hospitality.[124] However, διάκρισις permits an awareness both of personal limitations and those of others and so calls for occasional relaxation of discipline so that monks do not become exhausted and broken. In an anecdote similar to that noted earlier in Cassian,[125] Antony stressed the need of relaxation to a hunter by asking him draw his bow so much that he was afraid it would break. Antony told him:

> So it is with the work of God. If we stretch them beyond measure, the brothers quickly weaken, so it is useful to relax their severity sometimes.[126]

With διάκρισις monks are able to moderate the severity of πρακτική since failure to do so would undermine what πρακτική is intended to achieve. Πρακτική needs to be exercised with διάκρισις if it is to achieve its purpose.

---

[122] GSC 10.114; Nau 86; PE 2.3.4.3 p88.

[123] GSC 10.152; Nau 230; *VP* 5.10.98.

[124] E.g. Nau 229 (and parallels) and Nau 283 (GSC 13.8; *VP* 5.13.7; MD 28; PE 3.42.1.8 p548; Budge 1.440. Hospitality is discussed further below, pp. 220-23.

[125] Cassian, *conf.* 24.21 (see above, pp. 90-91).

[126] *VP* 5.10.2. See also: Antony 13; GSC 10.3; PE 2.18.3.3 pp232-233; Am16.2. Διάκρισις is also used here to determine how best to teach the hunter.

Διάκρισις and Λογισμοί

It seems, then, that the aim of πρακτική is to bring the body under the control of the inner person and to develop inner purity *en route* to union with God. But there is a more interior place for διάκρισις in which an essential part of the purification process is the eradication of λογισμοί. Asceticism was controlled and moderated by διάκρισις which also guarded the monk from becoming preoccupied with πρακτική at the expense of its purpose. Thus when Abba Isaac saw Poemen washing his feet he was struck by the contrast with others who treated their bodies more harshly and asked, 'How have those who bathe their bodies used *discretio*?' Poemen replied, 'We have not been taught to be killers of our bodies but of our passions.'[127] Διάκρισις guides the monk in how to use πρακτική to destroy λογισμοί and so increase in purity.

In order to establish purity, λογισμοί must be cut off or destroyed. In the monastic literature they represent the deepest of three levels of 'evil': sin, temptation and λογισμοί. Sin exhibits itself in outward actions or words, or in inward attitudes such as pride. Temptation operates below this inciting the monk to sin; this may arise from an external stimulus or internal idea. The internal idea or thought is closely related to the deepest level where λογισμοί operate. Λογισμοί are preoccupations, motivations and dispositions, an underlying disposition, proclivity or *penchant* rather than temptations per se. For example, a monk may be disposed towards anger, but unless some provocation stirs this tendency, he does not sin; thus in a sense λογισμοί are understood as a sins waiting to happen, hence the need to eradicate them. If circumstances provoke his tendency to anger (a λογισμός), he struggles with the temptation to be angry and if he loses he gets angry. A useful metaphor would be seed (λογισμός), watering (temptation) and plant (sin). To achieve ever greater purity, the monk works down through the levels, first desisting from sin, then learning not to consent to temptations or his λογισμοί and finally eradicating the motivations or λογισμοί themselves from his innermost being, thus achieving purity at the deepest level. This progression from outward to inward purity is expressed by an anonymous monk speaking about evil λογισμοί: 'just as we have made an end of deeds, let us also make an end of desires.'[128] Διάκρισις is thus to progress towards ever deeper purity in the search for union with God. The importance of this aspect of διάκρισις is further underlined by the fact that both Cassian and Evagrius discuss it so thoroughly.[129]

---

[127] App 4d. See also: Poemen 184; PE 2.18.3.4 p233; Budge 2.166. This is in marked contrast to Dorotheos who said, in response to Palladius' concern that he was killing his aged body in the hot sun, 'It kills me so I kill it!' (*HL* 2.2).
[128] Nau 83, 220. See also: GSC 10.126; *VP* 5.10.89; Budge 1.126a, 2.453a.
[129] See above, pp. 55-62, 93-99.

The eradication of λογισμοί is acknowledged to be difficult if essential. Ammonas says:

> The strait and narrow way [Matthew 7:14] is this: to do violence to your λογισμοί and to cut off your will for God's sake. This is also the meaning of, "Behold we have left everything and followed you. [Matthew 19:27]"[130]

To enter the life of the Kingdom of God and avoid eternal destruction (Matthew 7:13-14) the monk must overpower his λογισμοί by eradicating them and their influence. It is thus διάκρισις to renounce self-will and cut off λογισμοί in favour of inward purity and obedience to God. Similarly, besetting sin is regarded as a spiritual threat that must be defeated, albeit with great effort:

> An elder said, "A habit is changed by much toil, especially when it is long standing. If someone works hard to change it, he is saved; but if he remains in it, he suffers loss."[131]

Any abiding habit is a surrender of control and the longer it is allowed to continue unchecked, the harder it is to overcome. If the monk is to be pure he must place himself under the authority of God not his habits (sinful or otherwise) and so it is διάκρισις to break habits at the earliest opportunity. The amount of effort required to overcome λογισμοί is not underestimated, but it is understood that with the discerning and steadfast use of πρακτική, even the most refractory λογισμός can be overcome.

There is understood to be a clear distinction between eradicating λογισμοί and resisting temptation. This is well illustrated by an apophthegm about the monk Abraham visiting a brother of fifty years' experience who claimed to have 'destroyed fornication, avarice and vainglory' in his life. To test this claim Abraham presented him with three different temptation scenarios based on the three λογισμοί the brother claimed to have overcome. Each time the brother admitted he would 'fight the λογισμός' and so not commit the sin, to which Abraham repeatedly pointed out that each λογισμός was therefore alive but bound.[132] The brother lacked διάκρισις and so had not discerned that his λογισμοί

---

130 Ammonas 11. See also: GSC 10.116; Nau 249; *VP* 5.10.81; PE 1.42.2.3 p622; Budge 2.209; Ammonas, *apoph.* 11. This is also an example of the practical application of an interpretation of Scripture (see below, pp. 180-84).

131 GSC 10.132.

132 Abraham 1. See also: GSC 10.19; *VP* 5.10.15; *VP* 3.117; PE 4.22.1.1-4 p369; Ch52 (partial); Budge 2.115. Abraham also exhibits διάκρισις in both reading the true inner condition of the brother and discerning how best to instruct him.

remained and that he still suffered under their influence. If the monk had overcome his λογισμοί he would have been capable of remaining unmoved by temptation and incitement to sin, being inwardly pure and in a state of ἀπάθεια. Monks thus needed to use διάκρισις to discern inwardly whether they were under the influence of λογισμοί, merely controlling them or had overcome them completely.

Overcoming λογισμοί is understood to be essential for gaining salvation, future perfection and γνῶσις of God. Thus Poemen says, 'The power of God does not dwell in a man enslaved by the passions'[133] and an anonymous monk holds that, 'As long as the body has desires, the ψυχή does not know God.'[134] It is thus διάκρισις to overcome λογισμοί with a view to attaining not only the more immediate goal of purity but also the ultimate goal of γνῶσις of God.

The expression 'cutting off λογισμοί' inevitably lends itself to the metaphor of an axe, which suggests a negative and indeed dualist approach, but the imagery is variously used. For example, the axe may represent λογισμοί and if the monk refuses to take hold of the axe (i.e. entertain λογισμοί) then they cannot have a destructive effect on him:

> Abba Anoub asked Abba Poemen about the impure λογισμοί which the καρδία of man produces and about profane desires. Abba Poemen said to him, "Shall the axe be held in honour without him that chops with it? [Isaiah 10:15 (LXX)] If you do not give them a hand, they will be ineffectual too."[135]

The καρδία is the centre of human existence integrating the physical, intellectual and spiritual aspects of a person's being.[136] Since the λογισμοί are said to originate in the καρδία, it seems they too have both spiritual and psychological dimensions. It follows, then, that using διάκρισις to choose between consenting to λογισμοί and cutting them off is also both a mental and a spiritual exercise. Διάκρισις is a spiritual act of the will that maintains a careful watch over λογισμοί and chooses not to use impure ones.[137] In another apophthegm the demons are cast as the blade of the axe, human will as the haft and the ψυχή as the trees. It concludes: 'so let us give nothing of ourselves to the demons, that is to say our wills, and they

---

[133] GSC 10.79. Cf. Am30.2; Ammonas, *ep.* 12.
[134] GSC 10.140. Cf. Daniel 4; GSC 10.22; *VP* 5.10.17; PE 2.15.17.3 p210; Ch54; Budge 1.99.
[135] Poemen 15. See also: GSC 10.58; *VP* 5.10.41; PE 2.28.7.2 p345; Budge 1.255 (on watchfulness), 1.538 (on humility). Cf. Budge 1.603.
[136] See above, p. 49, n. 77.
[137] Cf. Cassian's metaphor of a fisherman: *discretio* is used to select which thoughts to catch (*conf.* 24.3; see above, p. 96).

will not cut us down.'[138] Thus the demons are understood to be powerless to damage the ψυχή if the monk refuses to bend his will to the incitement of demons or to λογισμοί. Διάκρισις thus controls or directs the will to remain strong against λογισμοί, actively refusing to consent to incitements to sin, thereby protecting the monk's inner life and maintaining its purity; if he does consent, it is his own will that attacks him and not the demons. Elsewhere the demons are said to sing to the ψυχή through λογισμοί in order to entice the monk into a sinful act,[139] but using διάκρισις he is able to see through the alluring deception and resist it. In a third example διάκρισις itself is an axe which the monk must learn to use:

> Abba Poemen also said that Abba Ammonas said, "A man can spend his whole time carrying an axe without succeeding in bringing down the tree; while another, experienced in felling brings the tree down with a few blows." He said that the axe is διάκρισις.[140]

This sweeping statement reaches beyond merely cutting off λογισμοί to the general need of διάκρισις in the life of the monk. It is a spiritual tool given to him to use and it is essential that he become proficient in using it if he is to progress in the monastic life; this is brought out in the Evergetinos version where it is the monk who uses the axe properly who has διάκρισις. These 'axe apophthegms' reveal διάκρισις to be the active use of the mind and will against the influence of demons and λογισμοί, and a skill that needs to be learnt and then used, since possession of διάκρισις alone is insufficient. The simile of the axe is helpful because it explains why διάκρισις is variously called an ἀρετή and a πρακτική. It is both and neither, it is beyond both and controls all ἀρεταί and πρακτικαί. Like the axe to a lumberjack διάκρισις is the essential tool of the monastic 'trade', which must be owned and used with practised skill.

Something of the nature of this active use of διάκρισις can be seen in the final apophthegm in the ἡσυχία section of the Greek Systematic Collection, which is a long panegyric on the nature of ἡσυχία.[141] It begins with the following definition of ἡσυχία, which includes the monk's ultimate goal:

---

138 GSC 10.131; *VP* 7.25.4.
139 GSC 10.84; Nau 661; PE 2.28.7.11 p347; Budge 1.577 (on fornication). The λογισμοί here are almost like the Sirens that lure men to their doom (Homer, *odyssey* 12.39-54, 158-200).
140 Poemen 52. See also: GSC 10.88; *VP* 5.10.59; PE 3.31.1.2 p372 (διάκρισις section); Budge 2.134; Ammonas, *apoph.* 14.
141 GSC 2.35.

Ἡσυχία is to sit in a cell with γνῶσις and fear of God abstaining from remembrance of wrongs and haughtiness. Such ἡσυχία is the mother of all the ἀρεταί and it guards the monk from the flaming arrows of the enemy [cf. Ephesians 6:16] and does not allow him to be wounded by them.

This introduction is followed by twenty-eight statements each beginning with ὦ ἡσυχία and concludes with the injunction, 'Yes, brother, acquire (ἡσυχία) remembering your death.' The central pair of statements (fourteen and fifteen) read:

Oh ἡσυχία, coupled with the fear of God, examiner of λογισμοί and fellow worker of διάκρισις;
Oh ἡσυχία, mother of every good thing, foundation of fasting and bridle of (the) tongue and impeding gluttony;

The themes in the introduction are repeated in this pair of statements: the fear of God, ἡσυχία as the mother of all ἀρεταί or good things and the enemy's darts or λογισμοί. This suggests that this central pair of statements is the focal point of the apophthegm and they draw attention to διάκρισις and the examination or discernment of λογισμοί. Thus διάκρισις and the discernment of λογισμοί are central to the nature and acquisition of ἡσυχία. The guarding role attributed to ἡσυχία in the introduction is widely and closely associated with διάκρισις.[142] A briefer version of this apophthegm omits the ὦ ἡσυχία statements but extends the conclusion thus:

Yes, brother, acquire (ἡσυχία), remembering the departure [PE: remembering always the fear] of your death, that you do not know at what hour the thief comes [Luke 12:39]. Finally, be sober concerning your own ψυχή.[143]

This addition again draws attention to the need for interior watchfulness found in the panegyric's central pair of statements. It also strengthens the emphasis on contemplating one's future death and, by implication, Divine judgment, which suggests the fear of God theme found in those central statements. While it is not possible to say which apophthegm was the original, the same central points are made in both and the shorter saying confirms the emphasis noted in the longer. Thus, διάκρισις is pivotal in the development of ἡσυχία, a prized state of quietude in which the monk is open to God and listens to him. Διάκρισις further enables the monk to keep a constant watch over his inner life and to weigh his λογισμοί, and

---

[142] On watchfulness see below, pp. 166-71.
[143] Rufus 1; PE 4.5.2.12 p97.

promotes fear of God and remembrance of the Judgment thereby keeping him alert to λογισμοί, temptation and sin.

If a monk uses διάκρισις assiduously to observe his inner life he becomes alert to the numerous λογισμοί assailing him and so may feel overwhelmed. A brother thus concerned about the dangers of his many λογισμοί is told by Poemen that he can no more 'prevent λογισμοί from coming' than catch the winds, but he 'can oppose them.'[144] With διάκρισις the monk is not only able to determine which λογισμοί are attacking him, he is also aware that although such attacks are inevitable[145] he is capable of resisting them. Another monk assailed by numerous λογισμοί was told to fight one, not all, of them:

> For all the λογισμοί of monks have a single head. So it is necessary to consider what sort of head this is and fight against that and in this way the λογισμοί are lessened.[146]

In the longer Syriac version weakening λογισμοί by overcoming the principal one is compared to the rout of an enemy in war by bringing down their leader. Using διάκρισις the monk is able to weigh the different λογισμοί, identify which is the most dangerous and defeat it, but without διάκρισις he would attempt to defend himself against every attack and soon be overwhelmed. Thus διάκρισις is used to devise the best strategy to counter λογισμοί. However, the difficulty involved in resisting λογισμοί is not underestimated. For example, when a monk told Theodore of Pherme that a 'brother has returned to the world' he said that the monk should be 'more surprised if (he hears) that someone is able to escape from the mouth of the enemy.'[147] With διάκρισις monks can be realistic about the difficulties they face in renouncing the world, in struggling against spiritual attack and about the risks of failure. Διάκρισις thus provides the monk with

---

[144] Poemen 28; GSC 10.81; *VP* 5.10.55; Budge 2.66; cf. Cassian, *conf.* 1.17.1 (see above, p. 95). Cf. Prov. 30:4; Eccles. 8:8.

[145] Constant assault by λογισμοί throughout life is also indicated by GSC 10.31 and Pseudo-Macarius says that those who have διάκρισις and σύνεσις (understanding; *hom. B* 16.1.10) or are φρόνιμος (intelligent; *hom. H* 17.5) understand that even with the grace of God they are still influenced by λογισμοί. Origen says that the 'adversary' is always present looking for an opportunity to tempt the unwary into sin (*hom. in Luc.* 35.5).

[146] Nau 219. See also: GSC 10.125; *VP* 5.10.88; PE 4.6.1.10 p137; Budge 1.302 (on watchfulness). Cassian makes the same point (*conf.* 5.14; see above, p. 95). Evagrius says it is essential for monks to observe their λογισμοί carefully in order to determine which are the most oppressive and to use this information to overcome them (*prak.* 43; see above, pp. 58-59).

[147] Theodore of Pherme 8. See also: GSC 10.34; *VP* 5.10.25; PE 1.25.1.1 p351; Budge 2.96, 2.501.

a reasoned view of his situation and the means to identify the most effective way to defend himself against spiritual attack.

This identification of different λογισμοί can be illustrated from Antony's first letter. He identifies three principle causes of temptation and sin: natural inclination to which the soul must consent; that which arises from external influence (e.g. excessive eating resulting in gluttony); and temptations by evil spirits. If the soul holds these in check, he says, it is able to progress towards peace with God. He sees this as a work of cooperation with the Holy Spirit in which the monk begins to distinguish (*discerno*) between the afflictions assailing him (he has *discretio* to do so) and the Spirit teaches him how to heal them.[148] *Discretio* is thus closely associated with the work of the Holy Spirit[149] who teaches the monk to use it to identify and attack λογισμοί in his quest for purity and union with God.[150] For Antony, διάκρισις, bestowed by the Holy Spirit, enables the monk to distinguish between different λογισμοί or attacks and incitements to sin from evil spirits:

> Therefore much prayer and asceticism is necessary so that any one who receives through the Spirit the gift of διάκρισις πνευμάτων is able to perceive their characteristics; which are less and which are more evil, and what kind of pursuit each of them exerts, and how each of them is overthrown and cast out.[151]

Διάκρισις is thus a spiritual gift that is used with the help of the Holy Spirit to discern different types of λογισμοί and their respective natures, modes of attack and relative threats to the monk and his purity.

Another way of expressing this idea of διάκρισις is illustrated by reference to well-trained moneychangers who are able to distinguish genuine and counterfeit coin impresses.[152] This metaphor, widely used in monastic literature, is also found in the Greek Systematic Collection:

---

[148]   Antony, *ep.* 1.35-49, 73.

[149]   Cf. above pp. 62-63, 106-107, 131-32.

[150]   Cf. Heb. 5:14 (need for training in διάκρισις to distinguish between good and evil; see above, p. 7).

[151]   *Vit. Ant.* 22; cf. 38, 44 and 88. Cf. also Evagrius, *prak.* 43. Peterson (R.M. Peterson, '"The Gift of Discerning Spirits" in the *Vita Antonii* 16-44', *Studia Patristica* 17.2, (1982), pp. 523-27.) makes a convincing argument that in *vit. Ant.* 16-44 Athanasius presents διάκρισις πνευμάτων as 'the determinative gift by which the monk may advance towards perfection' (p. 526). Significantly, one of Antony's disciples, Pityrion, is said to have inherited Antony's spiritual gifts and was regarded as an authority on διάκρισις πνευμάτων (*HM* 15.2).

[152]   Cf. Cassian, *conf.* 1.20.1; 2.9 (see above, p. 108 and n. 234).

An old man said, "Fast with reason and care. See that the enemy does not have a hand in the business of your fast. I think perhaps the Saviour said concerning this, 'Become approved moneychangers', that is to say know the royal impress precisely, for there are counterfeits. The nature of the gold is the same; but the impresses are different. The gold is fasting, self-control, almsgiving; but the Greeks put on these the image of their tyrant and all heretics honour them. It is necessary to look at them and to flee from them as counterfeits. So see to it that you do not suffer loss by falling unprepared among them. Receive then with security the cross of the Lord impressed on the ἀρεταί, that is to say a right faith with holy works."[153]

Although this is not designated a διάκρισις apophthegm, it does appear in *vita sanctae Syncleticae* between two other διάκρισις sayings found in the Alphabetical Collection[154] which stress the need to use διάκρισις in the first to distinguish between divinely and demonically inspired asceticism and in the second 'to govern the ψυχή'. Thus πρακτική, ἀρεταί and λογισμοί all need to be examined using διάκρισις in order to determine their origin, whether they are good or bad and whether they derive from Divine or evil sources. The monk needs to be prepared or trained in διάκρισις in order to protect himself and his purity.

Monks are therefore taught practical ways in which to weigh up λογισμοί. For example, anger is not regarded as justified if it arises from the arrogance or violence of a *confrère*, but appropriate 'if he separates you from God'.[155] Thus, provocation should be met with ἀπάθεια, thereby

---

[153] GSC 4.102. Cf. *vit. Syn.* 100. The agraphon, Γίνεσθε δόκιμοι τραπεζῖται ('Become approved moneychangers'), is the most commonly quoted extra-canonical Dominical saying in the Early Church. Clement of Alexandria is typical of the interpretations attached to it, saying that it refers to the rejection of the unworthy after careful scrutiny and the retention of the good (*strom.* 1.28.177.2). For a full discussion of the agraphon see: J. Jeremias, *Unknown Sayings of Jesus* (London: SPCK, 1957), pp. 89-93.

On coin impresses it is helpful to note that when in the Gospels (Mt. 22:15-22; Mk 12:13-17; Lk. 20:20-26) Jesus is asked about rendering taxes to Caesar, he asks whose portrait and inscription appear on a denarius. Since a denarius carried a portrait of the Emperor (Tiberius Caesar) and the inscription *divus et pontifex maximus* ('god and chief priest'), it symbolised the Emperor's power and religious claims; the impress on a coin thus makes claims for the one who authorised its issue.

[154] Syncletica 15 (*vit. Syn.* 100) and 17 (*vit. Syn.* 101). See Appendix 2 for other parallels.

[155] Poemen 118. See also: GSC 10.67; *VP* 5.10.47; PE 2.38.5.1 p494; Budge 1.233 (on patient endurance). Cf. the testing of Agathon's temper by false accusations (see above, pp. 136-37). Διάκρισις in relationships with others is discussed in chapter 5.

holding to the proximate goal, but if union with God is threatened anger is justified. Διάκρισις acts, then, as a reliable balance by which the monk can weigh up and determine when λογισμοί are right or wrong and so defend his progress towards his goals.

Διάκρισις is not only used to determine whether a λογισμός is good or evil but also to distinguish between the beneficial or detrimental effects it may have and overcome any ill effect. For instance, while ἀκηδία is understood to lead to discouragement, the monk can achieve ἀνάπαυσις if he discerns what ἀκηδία is and perseveres in good work.[156] Similarly, Syncletica distinguishes between useful and destructive λύπη:

> Useful λύπη is to weep for one's own sins and for the weakness of one's neighbours so as not to lose one's purpose but grasp perfect goodness. But there is λύπη from the enemy, full of unreason, which some call ἀκηδία. So this spirit must be driven off, most of all by prayer and psalmody.[157]

Διάκρισις can thus be used to discern the nature and impact of a λογισμός and then use that knowledge to defeat its influence by determining the most appropriate works of πρακτική to apply.[158]

There is here a significant interplay between the monk's interior psychological make up and what is understood to be the exterior influence of demonic activity in regard to λογισμοί. Satan is said not to know to which λογισμός or πάθος the monk is prone and so scatters them all like seeds watching to see which will take root, nurturing the one to which the monk inclines.[159] The demons are incapable of seeing into the heart of the

---

[156]   Poemen 149; GSC 10.87; PE 3.13.7.10 p171; cf. Bars 500, 613. Irvine provides an interesting study of the relevance of the early Christian understanding of ἀκηδία to modern thinking on the subject commenting that 'the monks were fine psychologists' (I. Irvine, 'Acedia, Tristitia and Sloth: Early Christian Forerunners to Chronic Ennui', *Humanitas* 12.1 (1999), pp. 89-103).

[157]   Syncletica S10. See also: GSC 10.102; VP 5.10.71; vit. Syn. 40.

[158]   With διάκρισις, λογισμοί may also be used to help the monk achieve his goals (see below, pp. 163-64).

[159]   Matoes 4; GSC 10.49; VP 5.10.35; PE 4.21.1 p363; Ch61; Budge 2.248. Λογισμός and πάθος are used interchangeably here suggesting that there is understood to be little distinction between them (this is also the case in GSC 10.38; see below, p. 164). Cf. Evagrius (*prak.* 44) who says that the demons look to see which ἀρετή the monk is neglecting before attacking at this weak spot and Cassian (*conf.* 7.15) who says they act on external symptoms (see above, p. 69 and n. 239). Cf. also Macarius the Egyptian 3 (GSC 18.13; VP 5.18.9; VP 3.61; VP 7.1.8; PE 1.20.3.9 pp268-269; Ch181; Am230.2; Dorotheos, *doctr.* 5.65) in which Macarius meets Satan who is carrying a selection of flasks each containing different foods or temptations knowing that each monk will take at least one.

monk, but the monk himself must use διάκρισις to examine it closely and become aware of his weaknesses if he is to defend himself from attack. However, not all λογισμοί are believed to derive from demonic attack. Less experienced monks who have not yet gained control of their will are said to be tempted by their own inclinations and only suffer demonic assaults once they have advanced in purity. Hence, Poemen (with διάκρισις) disabused one of Agathon's disciples of the mistaken idea that he was being attacked by demons by saying:

> (The demons) do not fight against us as long as we are doing our own will. For our own wills become the demons and it is these that afflict us in order that we may fulfil them. But if you want to see who the demons fight against it is Moses and those like him [*VP* 7 adds: but the wills of our hearts attack us].[160]

By examining their own will and disposition carefully with διάκρισις monks were able to discern whether a λογισμός was inspired by their own will, the influence of demons or God.[161] This illustrates the significant shift noted by Lienhard[162] away from διάκρισις πνευμάτων towards διάκρισις λογισμῶν. There is a psychological internalisation of demonic attack that focusses on the interior influence of the mind and motivations rather than external malignant spiritual influence. Διάκρισις is thus being used to know and modify the self as much as to interpret the spiritual realm and withstand evil forces.

This shift, however, is neither total nor fully perceived as such within the apophthegms. Demons are understood to be personal and to impinge on the life of the monk. For example, when Macarius was near death he was said to have overcome the attacks of demons with the abundant ⲆⲓⲀⲔⲢⲓⲤⲓⲤ God had given him.[163] Λογισμοί are understood to be not merely interior motivations but also the exterior influences of demons. For instance, one apophthegm describes a monk who had sinned with a woman and then returned to his cell where the demons tormented him through λογισμοί suggesting that he was no longer saved and so should return to the world. Discerning that they were seeking to 'destroy him utterly,' he addressed his λογισμοί telling them that he had not sinned and then continued to live as a monk. Meanwhile, God revealed to his *confrère* that he had 'fallen terribly

---

[160] Poemen 67; *VP* 7.25.3. See also: GSC 10.91; *VP* 5.10.62; PE 1.30.1.2 p434; Budge 2.308.

[161] Cf. Budge 2.372 where a monk is told to discern whether his motivation to do something comes from God, Satan or himself.

[162] Lienhard, '"Discernment of Spirits" in the Early Church', pp. 519-22 (see above, p. 121).

[163] Am96.2 (διάκρισις is often transliterated in Coptic as ⲆⲓⲀⲔⲢⲓⲤⲓⲤ).

then triumphed.' When this second monk heard the full story from the first, he declared: 'διάκρισις has crushed the power of the enemy.'[164] The monk's denial of his sin is clearly not intended to portray a lack of repentance and it must be assumed that he had repented and been forgiven to the extent that guilt no longer remained (cf. Psalm 103:12). His opposition of the demonic suggestions is thus an assertion of his faith in God's forgiveness.[165] The story does not regard the struggle to be purely within the psychological makeup of the monk, rather demons are understood to have had a real influence and impact on him. Διάκρισις is seen to operate in a number of ways in this apophthegm: discerning how to respond to the fact of sin and refusing to despair (which would be a denial of forgiveness); determining how to oppose λογισμοί successfully; interpreting Divine revelation and choosing how best to respond to it thereby bringing hope to the monk in despair; and the exposure of λογισμοί to another monk to secure full victory over them. Undoubtedly the key theme here is that διάκρισις is a powerful tool with which monks may defeat λογισμοί, whether they derive from interior psychological or exterior demonic sources or indeed both.

The source of λογισμοί can have, however, a more natural explanation; they can arise from within the monk rather than from demonic sources. Thus when a monk asked Sisoes why he could not rid himself of πάθη he was told: 'Their instruments are within you; give them their ἀρραβών and they will go.'[166] The interpretation of this apophthegm hinges on what is meant by ἀρραβών, familiar in the New Testament as the present earnest or deposit represented by the Holy Spirit guaranteeing salvation and union with God.[167] Ἀρραβών was originally a commercial technical term derived from צְרָבוֹן[168] signifying either a down payment for goods thereby securing a legal claim to them or a pledge that validates a contract.[169] *Vitae Patrum 5* uses *pignus*, a pledge which is restored when the contract has been performed, whereas the parallel in *Ægyptiorum Patrum Sententiæ* uses *arrha*, which again derives from the Semitic word and has the same meaning as ἀρραβών. However, the latter version extends the expression to

---

[164] Nau 50. See also: GSC 5.47; App 16.

[165] This opposition of λογισμοί by addressing them is familiar from Evagrius (e.g. *prak.* 42).

[166] Sisoes 6. See also: GSC 10.98; *VP* 5.10.68; MD 27; PE 4.6.1.5 p136; Budge 2.241, 2.528; Dorotheos, *doctr.* 13.141.

[167] 2 Cor. 1:22; 5:5; Eph. 1:14.

[168] See Gen. 38:17, 18, 20. The Semitic background to ἀρραβών is discussed in C. Stewart, *Working the Earth of the Heart: The Messalian Controversy in History, Texts, and Language to AD 431* (Oxford: Clarendon Press, 1991), pp. 199-203.

[169] Ἀρραβών is used in this way when Or was unwilling to use palm-branches on which others had paid an ἀρραβών (Or 4).

arrha retributionis ipsorum, suggesting repayment of the deposit. Several metaphorical interpretations are therefore possible:

1. ἀρραβών refers to the Holy Spirit; when the monk opposes his πάθη with the Holy Spirit, conscious of his hope of salvation, they will go;
2. the monk should refund the deposit his πάθη have paid him and so free himself of any obligation to them;
3. he should return their pledge because they have served their purpose;
4. he should give them a deposit guaranteeing them full payment later.

The fourth option is unlikely as it would suggest that the brother is in some way still legally bound to his πάθη and so not separated from them. The third option also seems unlikely as there is no inherent suggestion of purpose. The first two options are the most likely: the monk, conscious of the indwelling Holy Spirit and ultimate union with God, should free himself from any obligation to his πάθη by paying them off, as it were. The suggestion is thus that the monk is in some way holding on to his πάθη and not releasing them, but with διάκρισις he can discern that this is the case and cut them out of his life. Just as διάκρισις had provided him with insight into the psychology of his enquirer, so also should monks use διάκρισις not only to identify λογισμοί but also whether they are holding on to those thoughts and passions. Once they have done so, they are able to use διάκρισις to take control and authority over their inner life.

This use of διάκρισις to control the inner life means that the monk must take responsibility for his actions. However, the possibility that λογισμοί might arise from demonic sources opens the way to blaming the demons for sinful activity and abdicating personal responsibility for sin:

> A brother asked Abba Pambo, "Why do the spirits prevent me from doing good to my neighbour?" The old man said to him, "Do not speak thus, otherwise you will make God a liar; but say rather, 'I utterly refuse to be merciful.' For God anticipating this said, 'I have given you power to tread upon scorpions and serpents and upon all the power of the enemy', [Luke 10:19 (Vg)] why then do you not tread upon the unclean spirits?"[170]

Since monks are understood to have the God given ability to defeat demonic assault, they are duty bound to use it. Διάκρισις distinguishes between incitement and consent, the demons / λογισμοί are responsible for

---

[170]   *VP* 5.10.66. See also: GSC 10.95; Nau 383; PE 1.30.1.3 p434.

the former and the monk's will for the latter, thus with διάκρισις the monk chooses not to consent and sin.

However, the monk also needs to discern when it is best to stop opposing λογισμοί. For example, Poemen advises that when a monk is attacked by a 'λογισμός concerning bodily needs' he should deal with it at once the first and second time it comes but should it come a third time he must 'not heed it for it is useless.'[171] Διάκρισις thus directs the monk how best to overcome λογισμοί whether by opposing them or, when this fails, by ignoring them since they cannot exert any influence on him if he refuses to dwell on them. This is because it is understood that some λογισμοί become more difficult to eradicate if they are dwelt upon and not cut off quickly:

> The old men used to say that the λογισμός of fornication is like a strip of [VP adds: brittle] papyrus, so if it is sown in us and we are not won over by it but throw it away from us it is easily cut off; but if, when it is presented, we are softened by it, it is converted into iron and is cut off with difficulty. Thus διάκρισις is needed for this λογισμός, since for those who are won over by it there is no hope of salvation, whereas the crown is in store [cf. 1 Timothy 4:8] for those who are not won over by it.[172]

A λογισμός like lust would lend itself to fantasies that would make it more deeply ingrained in the mind and imagination and therefore harder to dismiss, and so unless it is cut off quickly the monk's inward purity would be rapidly compromised and his hope of spiritual progress ruined. To overcome this λογισμός (and others) the monk needs διάκρισις to recognise and reject it, refusing to consent to its incitement before it can take root in him. Thus with διάκρισις the monk is able to watch and guard his inner life and advance towards salvation, but without it he is spiritually lost. Διάκρισις thus instructs the will so that the monk takes responsibility for his sin and chooses not to consent to incitement to sin; this may express itself in calmly ignoring what his λογισμοί are saying to him.

Having determined the causes and sources of temptation, for which διάκρισις is needed, there is the question of how this is to be applied. Some λογισμοί are regarded as best not tackled by direct attack if doing so will cause them to dominate the monk's thinking. Thus Poemen likens λογισμοί to clothes left in a chest to rot saying that if λογισμοί are not acted upon they too will rot and disappear.[173] The same point is made in the following apophthegm where 'evil λογισμοί produced by demons' are said to suffocate and die (like a snake and scorpion sealed in a bottle) as a result of

---

[171] Poemen 40. See also: GSC 10.83; *VP* 5.10.57; MD 70; Budge 2.231.
[172] Nau 185. See also: GSC 5.38; *VP* 5.5.33.
[173] Poemen 20; GSC 10.59; *VP* 5.10.42; PE 4.6.1.1 p136; Budge 2.162, 2.474.

patient endurance.[174] With διάκρισις the monk is able to recognise when starving λογισμοί of attention is the best way to overcome them. This is particularly the case, according to Poemen, with the λογισμοί of fornication and slander which should not be meditated upon or discussed with others. This demonstrates good understanding and experience of psychology, since such ideas would tend to grow if pondered or debated. Poemen concludes that if the monk wishes 'to discern (διακρίνω) them fully in his heart, he derives no advantage from it; but he who is angered by them will have ἀνάπαυσις.'[175] Διάκρισις can thus be used unwisely to examine λογισμοί inappropriately with a resulting loss of purity. However, properly applied it allows the monk to discern when it is better not to dwell on λογισμοί and so maintain and advance in purity; indeed, it is possible to say from this apophthegm that the monk needs διάκρισις in order to determine how best to use διάκρισις.

Διάκρισις, then, directs the monk how best to address the problems posed by λογισμοί, whether by opposing them, refusing to dwell on them, or by using them to his spiritual advantage.

> An old man said, "It is not λογισμοί entering us that condemns us but using them badly, for it is through our λογισμοί we can be shipwrecked and through our λογισμοί we can be crowned." [PE adds: This saint teaches us to overturn them through contradiction; or to change what we have received from those sources into good things.][176]

With διάκρισις the monk makes a conscious, intellectual (as well as a spiritual) choice about how best to deal with λογισμοί, but that choice here also includes the option to use λογισμοί to achieve some beneficial purpose.

Temptation, trials and, by extension, λογισμοί can, then, be used constructively to train the monk and bring him closer to his goals. Hence Poemen comments: 'Experience is good. That is to say by experience men are more tested.'[177] With διάκρισις monks can use trials or experience (πεῖρα and *experimentum* in these sayings carry both meanings) to develop their spiritual lives. This idea can also be seen in one of the sixty-one additional Greek sayings identified by Guy and noted by Regnault; this saying is also found twice in the Evergetinos anthology.[178] It says that when

---

174 Poemen 21; GSC 10.60; *VP* 5.10.43; PE 4.6.1.2 p136; Budge 2.163.
175 Poemen 154. See also: GSC 5.8; MD 3; PE 2.28.7.3 p345; Budge 2.253.
176 Nau 218; PE 4.6.1.11 p137. See also: GSC 10.123; *VP* 5.10.86.
177 *VP* 5.10.49. See also: Poemen 24; GSC 10.71.
178 QRT 5; PE 1.29.5.6 pp427-428; PE 1.30.1.7 p435. Regnault designates these sixty-one apophthegms QRT (followed by the saying number) to reflect Guy's abbreviations for the MSS in which they were found (Q = *Paris gr. 917*; R = *Paris*

monks first renounce the world they are tempted violently by demons in order to make them blame themselves and give up their vocation. Once the monk has been 'trained by these temptations, he learns perseverance, experience, διάκρισις and finally flees for refuge to God with tears.' Monks are then encouraged to 'endure temptations bravely and patiently, thankful to God for all that happens to (them). For thankfulness to God undoes all the machinations of the enemy.' Διάκρισις is thus not only to use trials as an aid to spiritual growth (physical trials are understood to purify and prepare the monk for the Last Judgment[179]) those same trials also teach the monk διάκρισις, which in turn encourages dependence upon God and gratitude for the spiritual benefits that suffering λογισμοί affords. The value of temptations is succinctly expressed in another apophthegm:

> One of the fathers said, "If the tree is not shaken by the wind, it neither grows nor puts down roots. Similarly the monk, if he is not tempted and endures it, does not become strong."[180]

Experiencing and enduring temptations, trials and λογισμοί are understood to be essential to the monk if he is to grow strong spiritually; they teach him διάκρισις, which enables him to discern their value and use them for spiritual advancement.

In order to use adverse λογισμοί beneficially it was necessary to apply διάκρισις to determine how best to use them (as with πρακτική) and so their treatment varied according to the monk's experience. For example, Joseph of Panephysis gave contrasting advice to Poemen and another monk about how to deal with πάθη or λογισμοί (both terms are used). Poemen was told to 'permit them to enter and fight against them', but the other that he should 'not permit the πάθη to enter at all, but cut them off immediately from the first attack.' He later explained to Poemen:

> If the πάθη enter you and you exchange blows with them, they make you more proven ... but there are others for whom the approach of the πάθη is no use and so they must cut them off immediately.[181]

Thus although a monk may gain experience and spiritual advancement through engaging his λογισμοί, not all monks were capable of doing so.

---

gr. 914; T = *Athens 500*). L. Regnault, *Les sentences des Pères du désert: Troisième recueil et tables* (Solesmes: Abbaye Saint-Pierre de Solesmes, 1976), pp. 109-21; Guy, *Recherches*, pp. 121-24.

[179]   GSC 10.6; Nau 568; PE 3.19.3.1 p240.

[180]   GSC 10. 185. See also: Nau 396; PE 3.33.7.4 p427.

[181]   GSC 10.38. See also: Joseph of Panephysis 3; *VP* 5.10.29; PE 4.6.1.18-21 p138; Budge 2.210; Bars 432.

Διάκρισις, then, is needed for assessing the experience and capabilities of oneself and of one's disciples and for determining how best to counter λογισμοί. This assessment of spiritual capacity to deal with λογισμοί is developed elsewhere in an illustration about two monks, one more advanced than the other, presented with a desirable object:

> If the λογισμός of the perfect one says, "I want this object", yet he does not dwell on it but quickly cuts it off, he is not defiled. But if he who has not yet come to great measures desires it and though he meditates on the λογισμός he does not take it, he is not defiled.[182]

Monks thus needed to use διάκρισις to determine their personal capacity to resist λογισμοί and the most appropriate way for the individual to deal with them. The concern here is not resisting sin but maintaining personal purity when confronted by λογισμοί. Once the monk has ceased to sin he must learn how to cope with temptation, he may dwell on λογισμοί but should not consent to them. However, as he advances in purity he must learn to cut off λογισμοί without even contemplating their suggestions if he is to remain pure. The more advanced a monk becomes he cannot be content with simply resisting after a struggle, he must cut the thought off earlier. Διάκρισις is thus also used to determine how and whether purity has been maintained. Furthermore, it provides him with a realistic personal assessment of his advancement so that he can conduct his spiritual life at that level and so make further progress in purity. In other words he must work from where he is and not from where he was, just as it was noted earlier that a monk should work from where he is and in view of where he eventually aims to be.[183] It therefore emerges that with διάκρισις monks can be realistic about themselves so that they neither castigate themselves for not doing what they are not yet capable of doing nor fail to conduct their lives at a less advanced level so that they fail to advance in purity.

Resisting λογισμοί to maintain purity may not however always be a simple choice between good and evil but a choice between two apparent evils. In this instance διάκρισις is needed to determine which of the two will damage the monk's purity less.

> A brother asked an elder, "Is it good, father, that I should acquire honour for myself or dishonour?" The elder said, "As for me, I prefer to acquire spiritual honour which pleases God rather than dishonour. If I do a good work and am honoured for it, I can condemn my λογισμός because I am not worthy of this honour; but dishonour comes from evil works and how

---

[182] Nau 216. See also: GSC 10.112; *VP* 5.10.78; PE 4.47.1.9-11 pp649-650; Budge 2.502-503.

[183] See above, pp. 132-33.

can I console my καρδία when men have been scandalised by me? Better then to do good and be honoured than to do evil things and be dishonoured." And the brother said, "You have spoken well, father."[184]

Dishonour might seem the *prima facie* choice as it could potentially promote humility. However, the elder discerned that dishonour only arises from sin whereas being praised for good works arouses a λογισμός (vainglory or pride) which he could readily counter by reminding himself that he was not worthy of such praise. Διάκρισις can therefore be used to weigh different courses of action in order to discern the least harmful or most beneficial to purity. With the percipient use of διάκρισις it is possible to determine the implications of actions, foresee potential future problems and devise a strategy to counter them.

Watchfulness

There is a more theological aspect to διάκρισις that concerns the monk's relationship with God and this can be summarised in the word 'watchfulness'. This concept is found extensively in Scripture[185] and is evident throughout the apophthegms, particularly in the examination of λογισμοί and conduct of πρακτική discussed earlier. The monk needs to do all he can to avoid sin, which is destructive of his relationship with God, and so he is urged to 'be diligently zealous not to sin lest he outrage God who lives with him and drive him away from his ψυχή'.[186] The monk should thus use διάκρισις to maintain a constant watch over his behaviour in order to preserve his purity and relationship with God if he is to progress

---

[184]   GSC 10.153. See also: Theodore of Eleutheropolis 1; Budge 2.19.

[185]   For example, judges (Ezek. 44:24) and leaders (Zech. 3:7) of God's people are able to judge and lead with διάκρισις if they guard God's commands since watchfulness is needed for leading God's people (Acts 20:28; 1 Tim. 6:20; Heb. 13:17). Believers are enjoined to guard against greed (Lk. 12:15), error (2 Tim. 4:15; 2 Pet. 3:17), Satan (Lk. 11:21), deceit (Mt. 24:4) and against losing the reward for which they have worked (2 Jn 1:8). They should keep God's commands (Ps. 118 *passim*; Rom. 2:26), that is obey them (Lk. 11:28), with the help of the Holy Spirit (Ezek. 36:27). Wisdom, counsel and understanding guard believers (Prov. 2:10-11; 5:1-2) and so they should guard instruction so as not to sin (Prov. 19:27) and guard against sin (Job 36:21; Ps. 17:24). They should guard the ψυχή (Dt. 4:9, 15) and καρδία carefully (Prov. 4:23) because this brings life (Ezek. 18:21; Prov. 4:13; 7:2) and reward (Ps. 36:34; Prov. 8:34), keep a watch over their speech (Ps. 38:2) and their lives in anticipation of Christ's coming (Mt. 24:42; 25:13). They should also be watchful in prayer (Col. 4:2), not least to guard against temptation (Mt. 26:41). All OT references are from LXX.

[186]   Nau 24. See also: GSC 10.134 (corrupted), 11.82; Nau 650; Budge 1.126, 1.338 (on watchfulness), 1.500c; 2.453.

towards union with him. The human will, however, is understood to be a barrier between God and human beings that needs to be overcome if the monk is to enter more fully into this union:

> (Poemen) also said, "The will of man is a strong bronze wall [cf. Jeremiah 1:18] and resistant rock between him and God. If therefore a man leaves it behind, he also says, 'By my God, I shall leap over a wall, as for my God his way is blameless.' [Psalm 17:30-31 (LXX)] If therefore righteousness is united with the will, the man labours."[187]

The final phrase, κάμνει ὁ ἄνθρωπος (*Vitae Patrum*: *laborat homo*) is ambiguous. Translated positively it suggests that the monk whose will is redeemed is truly capable of serving God. However the phrase can also be interpreted negatively to mean that the monk is sick and suffers, suggesting that he is relying on his own will rather than God for justification. Given that the earlier part of the saying refers to the renunciation of the will and dependence upon God either interpretation is possible. However, since the apophthegm opens with a statement about the division created by the will and the next two sentences each begin, Ἐὰν οὖν ('if therefore'), the saying would appear to offer two contrasting outcomes, dependence and recalcitrance, making the negative translation of the final phrase the more likely (this is supported by the longer version in Dorotheos). In either case the monk needs to use διάκρισις to maintain a constant watch over his will to ensure that it is submissive to God as well as over all his exterior activity and interior life generally.[188]

This vigilant observation of the interior and exterior life is addressed by Silvanus in *Ægyptiorum Patrum Sententiæ* 108. For example, he draws attention to the need for *puritas cordis*, humility (the focus of the *Vitae Patrum* 3 parallel), perseverance in πρακτική and being impassive in the face of provocation, particularly emphasising the importance of non-judgment.[189] He commands the monk: *habeto discretio, discernens temetipsum*, ('hold *discretio*, discerning yourself'); the use of *habeo* here can suggest the habitual use of *discretio*. The *Vitae Patrum* 7 parallel replaces this phrase with Galatians 6:3 (Vg) thereby indicating the need for

---

[187] GSC 10.89. See also: Poemen 54; *VP* 5.10.60; MD 80; PE 1.42.2.1 p622; Budge 2.77, cf. 1.531; Dorotheos, *doctr.* 5.63. Cf. Ammoes 4 (PE 1.45.1.4 p648; Budge 2.225) where Poemen relates that Ammoes exhorted a monk to watch himself and spoke of his own sin as a 'dark wall' between himself and God.

[188] Cf. Athanasius' description of Antony daily preparing himself as if 'to appear before God' by being 'pure in καρδία and ready to submit to the will (of God) and no other' (*vit. Ant.* 7).

[189] Non-judgment is discussed below, pp. 202-11.

a right opinion of oneself and not falling into self-deceit.[190] The watchfulness of *discretio* is thus a constant and habitual self-examination both of the interior life and motives and of exterior behaviour, avoiding any deceitful overestimation of personal spiritual attainment or ability. How such watchful self-examination might work in practice is described in a long apophthegm about a monk who feigned madness so successfully that visitors were not brought to see him by other monks. With διάκρισις Silvanus understood why the monk had been avoided and went to ask him how he lived in his cell. The monk explained that he would sit with two baskets throwing pebbles into the right hand one when he had a good λογισμός and into the left when he had a bad one. If at the end of the day he had more in the right than the left he ate, if not, he went without food.[191] The monk was thus using διάκρισις to keep alert to his inner life and to use a practical means of humbling himself. Διάκρισις has, then, a creative or imaginative quality and enables the monk to find simple practical measures to sustain a watch over his interior life. With watchful διάκρισις the monk has the means to maintain his purity and humility in every aspect of his life.

This comprehensive watchfulness using διάκρισις was also used to ensure that the treatment of others was wholesome.[192] Monks were expected to guard not only their thoughts and actions, but all they heard and said as well, hence: 'The monk must not be a hearer or speaker of scandal, nor be quickly scandalised.'[193] Monks were expected not only to refrain from offensive speech, they were also required to remain impassive to insults and refuse to listen to slanderous remarks. By implication, this last would mean not considering any allegations made, since they had the potential to damage relationships with others. All words then, heard, thought or expressed, needed to be kept under the vigilant eye of διάκρισις. It was therefore necessary that they examine the correctness of their motives before acting in any way.

> An elder said concerning Moses, "When he struck the Egyptian, he looked this way and that and saw no one [cf. Exodus 2:12], that is to say (he examined) his λογισμοί and observed that he saw himself doing nothing wrong, but was acting for God, and so he struck the Egyptian."[194]

This constant use of διάκρισις to examine thoughts, words and actions to determine whether they are right under God would make it intensely

---

[190]   *VP* 3.206; *VP* 7.43.2; MD 108; cf. Am139.2.
[191]   GSC 8.32; Nau 408.
[192]   The different ways in which monks related to each other is discussed in chapter 5.
[193]   GSC 10.159, 21.64. See also: Nau 386; *VP* 5.10.102.
[194]   GSC 10.145; J674.

concerned with the self, were it not used to determine how to treat others and be more considerate towards them.

Διάκρισις can, then, also embrace a more flexible and relaxed approach to people and situations. For example, when Eulogius visited Joseph of Panephysis hoping to learn how to exercise greater austerity, he was disappointed by the generous hospitality he received. Only when Eulogius returned unexpectedly did he discover that Joseph carried out his πρακτική secretly and in what his normal diet consisted. Eulogius had thus failed to discern the relaxation of discipline for the sake of guests and Joseph then:

> taught him διάκρισις λογισμῶν and cut off from him all that was human. So he became accommodating and then ate all that was set before him [cf. Luke 10:8] and he learnt to work in secret.[195]

This apophthegm suggests that Eulogius had been judgmental towards Joseph, considering him less austere than was truly the case, and taking a haughty and vainglorious attitude (the Evergetinos subject heading) towards his host. Only by learning διάκρισις λογισμῶν was Eulogius able to overcome his inner motivations (as the *Vitae Patrum* parallel brings out more clearly), accept whatever hospitality was shown him and not make hasty judgments about others. By accepting that πρακτική should be conducted secretly, the monk is free to accept others without judging them and to remain unconcerned about the opinion of others. Διάκρισις is thus a liberating quality, it is not restrictive but releases the monk to behave contrary to his normal discipline publicly because he is confident in his purity gained through his private works of πρακτική.

The damaging effect of words is not only seen in those spoken or thought of others, those heard are understood to be harmful to the monk's spiritual condition as well. While a monk might, with διάκρισις, refuse to listen to slanderous reports about others, it would be impossible not to overhear bad things sometimes. Watchful διάκρισις was thus needed to guard against the distracting influence of such words by opposing the λογισμοί they aroused. For example, a monk was overheard 'quarrelling with his λογισμοί' and explained the reason as follows:

> I know fourteen books [i.e. of Scripture] by heart, yet I heard one base word outside and when I returned to recite the synaxis all of them disappear and this word alone comes to me.[196]

[195] Eulogius 1. See also: GSC 8.4; *VP* 5.8.4; PE 3.26.8.2-8 pp309-310; Budge 1.322 (on watchfulness). Cf. Cassian, *conf.* 2.26 (above, pp. 89-90); 17.21-23 (above, pp. 103-104). Further on hospitality, see below, pp. 220-23.
[196] Nau 227. See also: GSC 10.149; *VP* 5.10.96; PE 4.8.6.2-4 p224; Budge 1.249 (on watchfulness).

The Evergetinos parallel concludes with the final injunction: 'If we are attentive in prayer, we flee from profane words and blame the wandering νοῦς.' Διάκρισις guards the νοῦς against distraction, defending it against the entry of unhelpful ideas. Should such ideas fix themselves in the monk's mind, it makes him aware of this and directs him to confront any λογισμοί which arise as a result so that neither his inward purity nor his πρακτική suffer.

By using διάκρισις in this way, the monk is able to regulate his outward behaviour. Thus monks are told:

> If our inner man is vigilant, it is possible to guard the exterior man too; but if this is not possible, let us guard our tongue as far as we are able.[197]

This saying is reminiscent of Matthew 12:34[198] and demonstrates how watchful διάκρισις can be used to maintain integrity and harmony between the inner and outer life. At the very least the monk should use διάκρισις to purify his mind and thoughts sufficiently to control his speech, which is the border between inner and outer existence since words express the content of the mind. The adjacent saying in several collections describes a progressive decline into sin beginning with forgetfulness which develops into negligence, then evil desire and finally sin. The remedy offered is for 'the νοῦς (to be) vigilant against forgetfulness' and so, with the help of Christ, it is able to keep itself from falling further.[199] Watchful διάκρισις keeps the inner life from any impurity that would eventually express itself in sinful acts. The first stage towards this interior vigilance is seen as guarding speech which is, as it were, the first outward expression of the interior state. But the eventual aim is to guard the inner life with διάκρισις so that the content of the mind is kept pure and any outward behaviour correspondingly so.

This watchful examination of the interior state using διάκρισις is not passive, it requires a deliberate act of the will. Thus in preparation for the synaxis, Poemen is said to have 'sat quietly alone διακρίνων τοὺς λογισμοὺς αὐτοῦ ['discerning his thoughts'] for about an hour'.[200] This responsible   act   of   personal   preparation   for   worship (cf. 1 Corinthians 11:28) indicates that monks needed actively to use

---

[197]   Nau 239. See also: GSC 10.166, 11.103; Nau 272; *VP* 5.10.106, 5.11.45; Ch65; Budge 2.486.

[198]   'Out of the overflow of the heart the mouth speaks.' Cf. below, p. 197.

[199]   Nau 273; GSC 11.104. See also: *VP* 5.11.46; PE 4.7.3.8 p201; Budge 1.248 (on watchfulness).

[200]   Poemen 32. See also: GSC 11.58; *VP* 5.11.22; MD 32; PE 4.32.2.5 p515; Budge 1.273 (on watchfulness).

διάκρισις for vigilant self-examination and that possession of διάκρισις and the use of it were quite distinct.

The Cell

The use of διάκρισις is also linked to external matters, as for instance, in the fact that the monk's clothing was seen as an aid to watchful διάκρισις. As in Evagrius and Cassian[201] the monk's clothing is understood in the apophthegms to be a constant tangible reminder of his vocation, encouraging him to live up to the ideals of the monastic way of life.[202] Even the choice of clothing required *discretio*:

> Abba Agathon used to control himself, and in everything he was strong with *discretio*, as much in his manual work as in his clothes. For he wore such clothing that nobody noticed whether it was particularly good or bad. [*VP* 7 adds: He also used to say to his disciples, "A monk's clothing is also whatever wards off nakedness and cold, it should be undyed, as the soul may be swollen with boastful pride or vainglory."][203]

With *discretio* the monk chooses clothes that serve purely practical purposes and that neither engender pride in the wearer nor suggest it to others. Just as διάκρισις is used to keep a keen watch over the monk's inner life it is also used to ensure that every detail of his external life, his actions and his appearance, is fully in keeping with his vocation. This close attention to detail with regard to clothes suggests that no aspect of the monk's existence is beyond the remit of watchful διάκρισις.

The external setting, like the clothes of the monk, also needed διάκρισις. His exploration and purification of his inner and outer life was conducted primarily within the cell. For example, Antony regarded it as a lack of ΔΙΑΚΡΙCΙC to leave the cell, since leaving it would only result in a more severe struggle and so he recommended the antirrhetic use of Scripture to overcome λογισμοί that tempted the monk to leave it.[204] The solitude of the desert was seen as 'the place where one weighs hearts and thoughts with ΔΙΑΚΡΙCΙC.'[205] Thus when John Kolobos was asked to describe a ΔΙΑΚΡΙΤΙΚΩC manner in which to examine the thoughts and the movements of the soul, he said it was escape into the cell, like a man climbing a tree to

---

[201]   Evagrius, *prak.* prol. 2-8; Cassian, *inst.* 1. See above, p. 25, n. 191.

[202]   GSC 10.192; Nau 55; *VP* 5.10.115; Budge 2.483a. Cf. Evagrius, *prak.* prol. 2,4,5; Cassian, *inst.* 1.3,4,11; Dorotheos, *doctr.* 1.19.

[203]   *VP* 3.75; '*VP* 7.4A' (*PL* 73.1064D-1066A).

[204]   Am22.3.

[205]   Am326.1.

escape wild beasts, and there pray in dependence upon God.[206] The cell was thus understood to be the setting in which ⲆⲒⲀⲔⲢⲒⳞⲒⳞ was employed and it was ⲆⲒⲀⲔⲢⲒⳞⲒⳞ to remain there.

Monks were repeatedly encouraged to remain in their cells, understanding that this was the place where they were best able to advance towards their goals. Although it nowhere appears under a διάκρισις heading, the importance of the cell is well expressed in Moses the Ethiopian's gnomic saying, 'Go, sit in your cell, and your cell will teach you everything.'[207] Similarly, Antony said that monks away from their cells 'lose (their) interior watchfulness,' just as a fish out of water dies.[208] However, isolation in the cell was not regarded as an end in itself, but the place where the monk worked steadily on his πρακτική as he strived for union with God. Thus when a monk told Ammonas, 'three λογισμοί trouble me, should I either wander in the desert, or go to a foreign land where no one knows me, or confine myself to a cell and meet no one, eating every second day,' Ammonas told him 'rather sit in your cell and eat a little every day, and have the word of the publican [Luke 18:13] continually in your καρδία and you can be saved.'[209] Watchful διάκρισις in the cell meant moderating outward πρακτική and being mindful of personal sin as the monk pursued his goals.[210] This use of διάκρισις within the cell to maintain a constant watchful guard over outward, visible activity and inward, hidden work is brought out elsewhere:

> A brother asked Abba Poemen, "How ought I to live in the cell?" The old man said to him, "Living in the cell, visibly this is manual work, having one meal a day, silence and meditation; but secretly it is making progress in the cell, bearing your own blame wherever you go and neglecting neither the hours of the synaxes nor the secret things. But if you happen to have time without manual work, when you come to the synaxis

---

[206]   Am338.3. See also: John Kolobos 12; GSC 11.40; *VP* 5.11.14A; *VP* 3.208; PE 4.6.1.13 p137; Ch85; Budge 2.211.

[207]   Moses 6; GSC 2.19; *VP* 5.2.9; PE 4.5.2.54 p101. See also: *VP* 3.109a; Budge 1.62.

[208]   Antony 10; GSC 2.1; *VP* 5.2.1. See also: *VP* 3.109b; Am18.3; Budge 1.20; 2.472. Cf. *vit. Ant.* 85. Constant movement from place to place was understood to be as unproductive of ἀρετή as a frequently transplanted tree is of fruit (Nau 204; GSC 7.43; *VP* 5.7.36; PE 1.40.8.4 p595; Ch51 – the only extant words in Ch51 are: ⲁϥϫⲟⲟⲥ ⲚϬⲓ ⲟⲩ...('He said, "A ...''')).

[209]   GSC 10.20. See also: Ammonas 4; *VP* 5.10.16; PE 1.44.3.1 p643; Ch53; Budge 1.447; Ammonas, *apoph.* 4. Cf. the Jesus Prayer used in the Orthodox tradition.

[210]   This apophthegm is also an example of διάκρισις used for insight into the needs of a disciple and inspired instruction. Further on the teacher / disciple relationship see below, pp. 189-202.

complete it calmly. The fulfilment of these things is: keep good company, keep away from bad company. [cf. 1 Corinthians 15:33]"[211]

When the cell is used with διάκρισις it becomes the monk's workshop and laboratory, working physically and examining his inward state. It was where he worked towards perfection and union with God using outward πρακτική and interior disciplines that no one else could see, keeping them in balance. Should there be a break in his labour, διάκρισις counselled him not to be distracted from other disciplines that served to maintain and advance his spiritual condition. However, the cell was not entirely solitary and it was also διάκρισις to develop relationships with upright people who, by implication, would help the monk progress towards his goals or at least not hinder that pursuit. With διάκρισις the cell could be used as the setting for quietly examining the inward and outward life.[212]

Inevitably, perhaps, solitude in the cell could lead to boredom or distraction so that the monk was tempted by ἀκηδία to wander not only in thought but also to visit others.[213] A monk struggling with λογισμοί that encouraged him to visit others was advised not only to examine his λογισμοί and distinguish between the desire to wander because he found his cell incommodious and going off to derive some spiritual profit. His instructor also recommended practical measures he could take to overcome the desire to leave by citing the example of a monk who, when tempted to visit someone, would make a circuit of his cell and then entertain himself as a guest in his own cell. The Syriac version has a different practical suggestion to overcome this wanderlust, making a division in the cell, possibly a second room to make it less cramped.[214] While this apophthegm describes the use of διάκρισις to weigh λογισμοί, it also demonstrates that διάκρισις could be used to develop simple avoidance tactics that would help the monk overcome distraction and maintain the discipline of the cell. Διάκρισις may thus be used almost as a psychological tool to identify a new behaviour pattern that corrects what is believed to be inappropriate thought or action.[215]

Διάκρισις was not only used in the cell, it was used to choose its location as well. This required monks to arrive at a realistic assessment of their abilities. Hence it is said that if a monk should find a place where he was able 'to do good but has not the strength to do it' he should understand

---

[211] GSC 10.93. See also: Poemen 168; *VP* 5.10.64; MD 21; Am37.2; Budge 1.546.

[212] The cell is the place for assiduous watchfulness over the whole being: Ἔσω τήρει φυλακὴν, ἔξω τήρει φυλακήν ('Keep watchful inwardly, keep watchful outwardly.' Poemen 137. See also: PE 3.9.2.4 p98; Budge 1.26).

[213] Evagrius, *prak.* 12.

[214] GSC 10.171; Nau 394; PE 4.6.10.7-8 p191; Budge 2.62.

[215] Cf. modern behaviour and cognitive therapies.

that he will not be able to succeed anywhere else.[216] The cell and its location were intended to support self-examination and the search for God and so the place needed to be chosen with διάκρισις for its potential to promote spiritual advancement. Should a monk find such a place and reject it because he could only get 'the necessities of the body with toil,' he was said not to believe in God's existence.[217] Διάκρισις of cell location thus involved a combination of identifying a place that would enable the monk to make progress and discerning any inward reluctance to endure hardship or failure to rely on God's provision. Using διάκρισις to select a site for the cell was therefore as much an exercise in self-awareness as it was a matter of geography.

Once an appropriate site for the cell had been chosen the monk needed to continue using διάκρισις to make the most of the opportunities for spiritual advancement it afforded:

> An old man said, "If someone dwells in a place and does not produce the fruit of that place, the place will drive him away as he does not do the work of that place."[218]

Using διάκρισις to make the best use of location and circumstances also meant selecting a place where the monk's neighbours would promote and not hinder his progress towards union with God. For example, Poemen said: 'Do not live in a place where you see some are jealous of you, otherwise you will not progress.'[219] There would be a range of potentially detrimental relationships the monk would need to assess with διάκρισις, for example if others respected him he might be tempted by vainglory and pride, if they were jealous of him it might lead to resentment and rancour. So the monk needed διάκρισις to discern the potential of his prospective neighbours to hinder or support the pursuit of his goals and to select the company that would serve him best.

> One of the fathers said, "If a hard worker dwells in a place where there are no other hard workers, he cannot make progress; he can only struggle not to deteriorate. But if a lazy man dwells among hard workers, he makes progress if he is vigilant, and if not he does not deteriorate."[220]

---

[216]   GSC 10.118; Nau 446; PE 1.40.4.1 p576.

[217]   Nau 236. See also: GSC 10.162; *VP* 5.10.103B; *VP* 7.19.5b; PE 1.13.1.3 p188.

[218]   Nau 247. See also: GSC 10.113; *VP* 5.10.79.

[219]   GSC 10.65. See also: Poemen 18; *VP* 5.10.45; PE 1.23.1.4 p332; Budge 1.294 (on watchfulness).

[220]   Nau 251. See also: GSC 10.119; *VP* 5.10.83.

The company of anchorites who shared the same determination to achieve union with God would provide the monk with a supportive, if scattered, community environment and so discernment of the human geography was important. Thus διάκρισις was needed for making the best continuing use of the cell's location which included those that lived nearby.

Διάκρισις and Self-knowledge

The most basic place of διάκρισις in the monastic life, however, is not in external facts but in self-knowledge. Antony begins one of his letters by stressing the monk's need of self-knowledge so that he not only knows and understands his inner nature but also knows God and is prepared for meeting him. This leads Antony directly on to a plea for his readers to acquire *discretio* from Christ in order to perceive Antony's love for them.[221] *Discretio* provides the ability to gain a greater understanding of others here, but Antony also seems to imply that *discretio* is necessary for self-knowledge, which in turn prepares the way for union with God.[222]

One aspect of this use of διάκρισις to gain self-knowledge can be seen in several apophthegms that lament the decline in monastic standards over successive generations of monks. Apart from the way that διάκρισις had been used to detect this decline, the inclusion of these sayings under a διάκρισις heading suggests that monks needed διάκρισις to make critical self-assessments. For instance, Antony noted that the diminishing spiritual strength of monks had resulted in God no longer testing them as once he had, because of their weakness.[223] This suggests that διάκρισις was to be used by monks to discern in the trials and temptations they suffered the extent of their spiritual strength and advancement, an idea supported by the way διάκρισις was used for watchful self-examination in regard to λογισμοί. This impression is further supported by Syncletica who equated greater advancement with harder spiritual struggles: 'So far as combatants advance, so far are they engaged in conflict with stronger opponents.'[224] Another aspect of this decline was the monks' attitude to the Scriptures. The first generation was said to have applied them to everyday life, the next memorised them and the third merely 'wrote them down and put them on

---

[221] Antony, *ep.* 3.1-3.

[222] Evagrius understood that self-knowledge was required for achieving the monk's ultimate goal of γνῶσις of God: 'You wish to know God? First know yourself.' (*sp. sent.* 2). Athanasius provides an explanation of how this is possible: since the ψυχή is made in the image of God, when the ψυχή is purified the Divine image can be seen in it as in a mirror (*contra gentes* 34).

[223] Antony 23; GSC 10.5; *VP* 5.10.4; PE 1.30.1.1 p434; Am17.1; Budge 2.246.

[224] GSC 10.106. See also: Syncletica 14; PE 1.30.1.5 p435; *vit. Syn.* 26.

their window-sills unused.'[225] While this indicates that to use Scripture with
διάκρισις was to put it into practice, it also bids readers discern their own
attitude to the Bible and return to the standards of their monastic forbears,
eschewing nominal faith. A decline in behavioural standards was also
noted. The first monks were said to have gathered to discuss beneficial
things and were thereby 'ascending to heaven,' whereas later they only met
to 'slander and pull one another down into the pit below.'[226] This indicates
that the monk needed to use διάκρισις to assess his own behaviour and
amend it where it fell short of the ideals laid down by his monastic
forebears. These examples provide some indication of how διάκρισις could
be used by monks to hold up a mirror to their actions and attitudes. In it
they could see an accurate reflection of their lives and so correct anything
that fell short of the tradition in which they sought to live.

This accurate self-image gained using διάκρισις included an awareness
of personal capacity for ascetic acts. If the monk failed to use διάκρισις in
this way, he was liable to attempt acts of greater austerity than he was able
only to fail.

> Abba Macarius asked Abba Arsenius, "Is it good not to have any comfort
> in one's cell? For I saw a brother who had a few vegetables and uprooted
> them." Abba Arsenius said, "On the one hand it is good, but it is
> according to the man's capacity [PE adds: that is to say the κατάστασις of
> the ψυχή and advance in ἀρετή]. For if he does not have strength for such
> a way of life [PE adds: that is to say he holds to it perfectly] he will again
> plant others."[227]

Without διάκρισις a monk might attempt to emulate the edifying example
of a *confrère* only to discover that he lacked the same capacity for
asceticism. He would then become unsettled by overreaching his ability and
fall back to his former ascetic regime. While this could be seen as using
διάκρισις experimentally, it would be a failure to use διάκρισις to gain a
realistic opinion of himself and how he should live. The result might well
be disappointment and despair, and so διάκρισις may be said to keep the
monk from these.

This use of διάκρισις to assess an appropriate level of personal
πρακτική can be seen in other apophthegms. For example, when some
Egyptian monks visited their counterparts in Scetis, they were shocked at
the way they ate voraciously. So the local priest, doubtless discerning how

---

[225] Nau 228. See also: GSC 10.191; *VP* 5.10.114; PE 4.15.1.1 p298; Budge 1.250 (on
         watchfulness). Cf. Nau 385 and parallels. Further on διάκρισις and Scripture, see
         below, pp. 180-84.
[226] Nau 238. See also: Megethius 4; GSC 10.165; *VP* 5.10.105; Ch64; Budge 2.259.
[227] GSC 10.9; PE 4.1.15.2 p28. See also: Arsenius 22; *VP* 5.10.7; Budge 2.397.

best to correct the visitors, exhorted everyone to intensify their fasting. Although the monks of Scetis then fasted for a whole week, the priest encouraged the visitors to fast only every other day. At the end of the week the visitors, now eating voraciously themselves, sought forgiveness when asked, 'If you, eating every other day, are so exhausted, how could you be scandalised at the brothers who always observe such asceticism?' They left 'edified by their abstinence' and, by implication, challenged to re-evaluate their own disciplines in fasting.[228] The lack of διάκρισις here is seen to result not only in a judgmental lack of insight into the πρακτική of others but also in a failure to discern a lesser personal capacity to fast until the visitors are forced to re-examine themselves, suggesting that they had learnt διάκρισις through their experience. There was a danger that without διάκρισις monks might also become proud of their ability to fast (or to conduct any other work of πρακτική) and so lose sight of its purpose. Monks are thus warned against such pride and told: 'it is [*alph.* and PE add: more] profitable for a man to eat meat than [PE adds: to fast and] to be arrogant and brag.'[229] Monks thus needed to use διάκρισις to recognise within themselves when they were succumbing to the λογισμός of pride and to modify both their attitude and practice, even to making it less austere. The lack of διάκρισις evident in becoming proud of physical accomplishments is a misinterpretation of personal πρακτική and therefore a failure to understand oneself. Such a misunderstanding is more clearly evident in the lack of humility exhibited by the self-righteous. Only when the monk was aware of his weak and sinful state, that is his lack of purity, was he able to exhibit true humility.

> Abba Poemen said: "I prefer a man who has sinned and has admitted his sin and repented, to a man who has neither sinned nor humbles himself. For, the one who considers himself sinful humbles himself in his λογισμός, while the other considers himself righteous because he is righteous and proud."[230]

This apophthegm contrasts those who knew their weakness and dependence upon God for forgiveness with those who failed to discern that they were sinfully proud of their avoidance of sin. Being capable of desisting from sin was thus seen as an inadequate indication of purity and humility. Monks

---

[228] Nau 242. See also: GSC 10.170; *VP* 5.10.109; PE 3.3.1.2 pp66-67; Ch69.

[229] GSC 10.41; Isidore the Priest 4; PE 3.29.3.1 p346. A helpful study of the composition of the monastic diet based on archaeobotanical evidence is provided by M. Harlow and W. Smith, 'Between fasting and feasting: The literary and archaeobotanical evidence for monastic diet in Late Antique Egypt', *Antiquity* 75.290 (2001), pp. 758-68.

[230] GSC 10.52. See also: Sarmatas 1; PE 1.44.3.5 p644; Budge 1.610.

needed to use διάκρισις to appreciate fully their status before God and the extent to which they had purified their inner being. With διάκρισις the monk was able to examine himself and gain a true and humble opinion of himself (cf. Romans 12:3). Thus when two anchorites tried to humiliate Amma Sarah by telling her not to be conceited in the fact that she, a mere woman, was being visited by them, she replied, 'I am a woman by nature, but not in λογισμός.'[231] This may be seen as an affirmation of biblical sexual equality (e.g. Galatians 3:28), which the anchorites had failed to understand. However, it also reveals Sarah's self-understanding that while she may be regarded as a 'weak woman' by accident of birth, her inner nature was as strong as any man or monk. In the Syriac parallel Sarah says, 'It is I who am a man, and ye who are women,' suggesting perhaps that she was aware of her own greater strength in the pursuit of the monastic life. Διάκρισις thus provided a monk with the ability to look beyond any external aspect of his life (πρακτική, behaviour, outward indications of purity and physical characteristics, even gender) to his inward self and thereby gain a thorough self-knowledge and understanding of his inner life and how it affected his outward behaviour and practice.

Διάκρισις **and Prayer**

Διάκρισις is part not only of self-knowledge and external acts, but also of the essence of monastic life, which is prayer. While διάκρισις is often presented as mental acuity, it was also regarded as a gift of God that was not so much earned as sought and developed through prayer and πρακτική. Hence Antony says that it is through 'much prayer and asceticism',[232] and particularly prayer,[233] that the Holy Spirit's gift of διάκρισις πνευμάτων (1 Corinthians 12:10) is acquired. Such prayer was a personal responsibility that could not be readily abdicated to another, for example in the same way that a monk was expected to call on the διάκρισις of an elder. So when a monk asked Antony to pray for him, Antony refused to do so saying: 'Neither I nor God will have mercy on you unless you make an effort yourself and ask God.'[234] Antony appears to have discerned that the monk was not as committed to prayer as he should have been and needed to

---

[231] GSC 10.107; Sarah 4. See also: *VP* 5.10.73; Budge 2.525. Cf. Elizabeth I at Tilbury on the approach of the Armada: 'I know I have the body of a weak and feeble woman, but I have the heart and stomach of a king, and of a king of England too.'

[232] *Vit. Ant.* 22, cf. 88.

[233] *Ibid.* 38.

[234] *VP* 5.10.3. See also: Antony 16; GSC 10.4; Budge 2.114. GSC presents a slightly different form of this saying by ending: '...if you do not have mercy on yourself and please him.' This suggests that failing to pray for oneself is a failure of both self-concern (as *alph.* and *VP*) and of duty towards God.

correct this, because without praying a monk could neither advance towards union with God nor grow in διάκρισις. There were, however, occasions when monks discerned their own weakness and it was legitimate to seek prayer from another. Such a monk approached a discerning (διορατικός) elder for prayer. The elder responded positively explaining that it was good and Scriptural (James 5:16) to prayer for one another. The nature of the weakness here is unclear, since ἀσθενής might convey either physical or spiritual weakness or sickness. The elder's supporting illustration concerns anointing the sick with oil (James 5:14), which may suggest a physical ailment, but it is also used to show the personal benefit of praying for someone else in that an anointer himself first receives the benefit of the oil.[235] While this apophthegm conveys the use of διάκρισις by a teacher to provide pastoral encouragement it also indicates that διάκρισις in requesting prayer required both a self-knowledge of personal weakness and the discernment of when it was right to do so. Διάκρισις was thus gained and developed through prayer and expressed in praying for others. Naturally any communication from God within that prayer (e.g. a vision or revelation) would also require διάκρισις to understand it.[236]

Διάκρισις as Guide

Once διάκρισις had been gained through prayer and its use learnt from more experienced monks, it became a guide to the monk in his search for union with God.

> (Syncletica) said, 'We must guide the ψυχή with διάκρισις. While we are in the cœnobium, we must not seek our own will [1 Corinthians 13:5] and certainly not be subject to our personal judgment, but be obedient to our father in the faith.'[237]

The cœnobium was understood as a training ground for monks in preparation for the anchoritic life[238] where διάκρισις was learnt from senior monks, but relying on the διάκρισις of others continued in the anchoritic life in the teacher / disciple relationship.[239] The longer parallels of this saying go on to stress renunciation of the world and its resources in

---

[235] GSC 12.14; Nau 635.
[236] On Διάκρισις and Revelation, see below, pp. 184-87.
[237] Syncletica 17. See also: GSC 14.18; *VP* 5.14.10; *vit. Syn.* 101. Pseudo-Macarius also says that the ψυχή possesses a διακριτικός faculty to guide it (*hom. H* 4.3; *hom. B* 49.1.4).
[238] Cf. Cassian, *conf.* 19.2.4: the cœnobium is 'the school for juniors' (see above, p. 93).
[239] See below, pp. 189-202.

favour of abasement and austerity. Directing the ψυχή with διάκρισις meant deferring to the διάκρισις of others, but this does not diminish the significance of using διάκρισις to direct the spiritual life, it merely draws attention to how it worked in practice. Through the renunciation of secular life and personal will the monk was free to be directed in his search for union with God by the διάκρισις of those who had begun to find the way before him.

This suggests a rigorous distinction between the world and the desert. The world was understood to offer little or no spiritual benefit; it was chthonic, whereas the desert was understood to be angelic and spiritually advantageous.[240] The renunciation of the world and self was carried out under God's guidance, which guidance was forfeited if the monk returned to secular life. An apophthegm expressing this is included under a διάκρισις heading,[241] suggesting that not only was it διάκρισις for monks to persevere in their calling but also that διάκρισις could be equated with Divine guidance, which indicates a high theology of διάκρισις.[242] Elsewhere it becomes clearer that this Divine guidance is provided through *discretio*. A monk expressed his concern to Poemen about how his thoughts confused him while he was in his cell. In response, Poemen spoke to him of non-judgment, guarding his speech and *discretio* as the guide of the soul, explaining that the monk needs humbly to abandon himself to God, not seek his own will. Rather, 'sitting in his cell he should watch over his way of life' if he is to be at peace.[243] To the use of *discretio* as a guide for moderating πρακτική and tackling λογισμοί must therefore be added its use to direct every aspect of the monk's life and conduct as he seeks the peace of union with God. This required the monk to renounce his will and give himself to the will of God. Διάκρισις gave practical expression to Divine guidance, which means it was a spiritual quality and art, not just an intellectual activity.

Διάκρισις **and Scripture**

This practical application of Divine guidance, using διάκρισις as a spiritual rather than an intellectual art, is evident in the monastic attitude to Scripture. While Scripture was highly esteemed, there was often a marked reticence to discuss its meaning; it seems their very reverence of Scripture made monks reluctant to inquire into its meaning because, in their humility, they did not feel themselves competent to do so. However, the avoidance of

---

[240] This is the assessment of the desert, and Scetis in particular, in Am326.1.

[241] GSC 10.183; Nau 26; PE 1.15.4.1 p210.

[242] The association of διάκρισις with the role of the Holy Spirit has already been noted in Evagrius (pp. 62-63), Cassian (pp. 106-107) and above (pp. 131-31).

[243] MD 39. See also: GSC 9.11; *VP* 5.9.8; *VP* 3.100; *VP* 7.39.2; PE 3.13.7.7 p170.

debates about Scriptural interpretations was also an aversion for speculative theological dialectics and a preference for practical application. Thus when an esteemed monk visited Poemen and 'began to speak from Scripture about spiritual and heavenly things,' Poemen refused to answer. A mediator asked Poemen to explain his actions and was told:

> (the visitor) is from above and speaks of heavenly things, but I am from below and speak of earthly things. If he had spoken to me about πάθη ψυχῆς ['passions of the soul'], I would have replied, but if about spiritual things, I know nothing about these.

When the visitor heard this he returned to Poemen and instead asked, 'What shall I do, Abba, for πάθη ψυχῆς dominate me.' Poemen then said the visitor had now come as he should and began to help him.[244] Poemen had probably discerned that his visitor was proud of his accomplishments and reputation, and was led by διάκρισις to demonstrate humility in regard to Scripture thereby prompting the enquirer to admit his struggles with λογισμοί. However, this is also an example of the common reluctance to engage in speculative discussions about Scripture as opposed to its practical application to everyday life. It is also possible that the apophthegm is intended to convey the danger of hiding more important issues about the struggle for purity behind pious debate. Thus it is διάκρισις not only to express humility in approaching the interpretation of Scripture, but also to avoid becoming preoccupied with biblical words and meanings at the expense of practical application.[245]

When monks did seek to interpret Scripture, however, they needed to use διάκρισις to ensure that they were not being misled in some way. In an apophthegm that also attests to the monastic devotion to reflecting on the meaning of Scripture, monks are warned that when God does not draw them to its meaning they should guard against false interpretations suggested to them by demons.[246] Διάκρισις was required to discern whence an interpretation derived and so the monk with διάκρισις was to be mindful of his spiritual enemy waiting in readiness to twist the meaning of a text much as Satan tempted Christ in the wilderness (Matthew 4:1-10). The monk was also to be cautious about human interpretations and weigh these too with διάκρισις. Hence one of the fathers said that the Church and heretics used the same two Testaments but interpreted them differently and

---

[244] GSC 10.54. See also: Poemen 8; *VP* 5.10.39; *VP* 3.184; PE 4.17.1.3-8 pp312-314; Budge 2.159. Cf. GSC 10.27 and parallels where Zeno complains about some brothers being more concerned about the interpretation of a passage in Job than about dealing with their sins (discussed above, p. 132).

[245] Cf. Acts 17:21 where the Athenians are said only to be interested in ideas.

[246] GSC 10.164; Nau 646; *VP* 5.10.104; PE 4.17.1.9 p314; Budge 2.79.

so monks needed to ensure that they 'ruminate on good food and not evil.' He explained that 'useful food is good λογισμοί, the tradition of holy teachers (and) good deeds'; the Greek Anonymous Collection and Evergetinos parallels replace 'good deeds' with the reading of the Scriptures. By contrast 'bad food is evil λογισμοί in diverse sins and in the errors of men.'[247] Διάκρισις was therefore needed to distinguish between good and bad Scripture interpretations, to choose to meditate on orthodox doctrine and tradition, and to guard against heterodoxy. Thus διάκρισις kept monks from error and false doctrine.[248]

Διάκρισις was not only important for interpreting Scripture correctly, but also for using it correctly devotionally and for applying it to life. The memorisation of Scripture is widely attested in the apophthegms and, at a time when books were rare and valuable, committing books of the Bible to heart was beneficial practically as well as spiritually. However, when a senior monk heard one brother boast that he had memorised the whole Bible and another that he had copied it out, he was unimpressed. In the longer version of the saying (*Vitae Patrum* 7) the senior monk went on to cite (among other Scripture texts) Romans 2:13 (Vg): 'The hearers of the Law are not just before God, but the doers of the Law will be justified.'[249] Similarly, 'An elder said, "The monk must not only be a hearer but also a doer of the commandments." [Romans 2:13; James 1:23, 25]'[250] Valuable as the memorisation and copying of Scripture might be, it was διάκρισις to make a practical application of Scripture to life. Such a practical engagement with Scripture can be seen in the remark:

> Everyone prays for good things, but those who sincerely partake of the divine word and who are subject to it, acquire them through the ἀρεταί.[251]

With διάκρισις monks could discern the value of Scripture as a revelation of God's will and submit to its direction, and thus be able to advance towards greater purity and union with God. Prayer had the potential to be too passive and so it needed to be combined with the active use of ἀρεταί

---

[247]   GSC 10.151. See also: Nau 645; PE 4.15.1.3 p298.

[248]   Ammonas says that *discretio* is needed for distinguishing between good and evil. It provides the monk with foresight (*prudentia* and *providentia*) and leads him to avoid brethren who follow their own wills and so lack *discretio*, so as not to be led astray by their ideas (Ammonas, *ep.* 4).

[249]   GSC 10.147; Nau 385; *VP* 5.10.94; *VP* 7.41.2; PE 3.29.3.3 p346; Budge 2.250.

[250]   GSC 10.188.

[251]   GSC 10.142. Cf. the epistle of James where the description of heavenly wisdom as ἀδιάκριτος (impartial; Jas 3:17) is followed by a discussion of praying for the right reasons (Jas 4:3).

to ensure that monks lived according to what they understood God's will to be.

The way monks interpreted Scripture reflects the three major interpretative methods of the period. Firstly, biblical figures are used as exemplars of faith,[252] secondly, ethical guidelines are drawn from Scripture passages[253] and finally, there are allegorical interpretations that express deeper spiritual meanings.[254] However one regards the validity of this final method, so favoured by Origen, it would require διάκρισις to discern the veiled spiritual meaning of a given text. One such allegorical interpretation is found in the Greek Systematic Collection's διάκρισις section, but the relevance of that interpretation to διάκρισις is not immediately obvious:

> (An elder) said of the verse in Psalms: "I will set his hand over the sea and his right hand over the rivers," [Psalm 88:26 (LXX)] that it concerns the Saviour: his left hand on the sea signifies the world, and "his right hand over the rivers", these are the Apostles who irrigate the world through faith.[255]

The point would appear to be that monks should discern the sovereignty of God over the world and the global reach of Christ's atonement. This is supported by similar exegeses by Evagrius, who relates the rivers to Christ's 'living water' (John 7:38) and Augustine, who speaks of the subjection of all humankind to Christ.[256] Given the importance placed on the practical application of Scripture this would suggest that monks with διάκρισις were able to discern Christ's presence, control and saving power in the world about them and in their own lives. Furthermore, the saying points to the value of apostolic teaching and therefore Scripture, suggesting that engagement with both was required for entering into a salvific relationship with Christ. Whatever interpretive method was used, the aim was greater purity and union with God and so all the monk's attention needed to be focussed on this objective.

> Some brothers asked one of the fathers, "How is it the ψυχή does not run towards the promises God made in the Scriptures, but turns towards impure things?" The elder replied, "I say it is because it has still not

---

252 E.g. GSC 1.23 and parallels (Ezek. 14:14 (LXX); see above, pp. 140-41).

253 E.g. GSC 10.67 and parallels (Mt. 5:22, 29-30).

254 E.g. *VP* 7.37.4 and parallels (2 Kgs 4).

255 GSC 10.146. See also: J675; Budge 2.98.

256 Evagrius, *schol.* 14 in Ps. 88:26 (LXX) [*PG* 12.1549; *PG* 27.389]; Augustine, *enarr. in Ps.* 88 *sermo* 1.26.

tasted the things from on high and therefore yearns after impure things."[257]

Knowledge of the content of Scripture was thus not seen as sufficient for spiritual advancement. The monk also needed a vital relationship with God in order to appreciate the practical implications of Scripture to his life and to enjoy the blessings Scripture describes. Given that one of the biblical roles of the Holy Spirit is the illumination of Scripture, this suggests that διάκρισις was understood as the means by which he revealed and brought alive its meaning to the monk. Διάκρισις gave access to that meaning, but it also revealed to the monk his spiritual condition, so that by reading Scripture with διάκρισις he was challenged to purify his motivations and to redirect his efforts towards fuller engagement with God. The matter of interpretation thus becomes less significant than that of application and while διάκρισις was necessary for both the aim of the former was to achieve the latter in order to make spiritual progress.

Διάκρισις and Revelation

There is a use of διάκρισις that has always been vital in the spiritual life, that is in relation to visions, dreams and miracles. Διάκρισις provided the monk with insight into theological truths and the spiritual realities underlying them. Thus when Athanasius was asked 'How is the Son equal to the Father?' he replied 'As with two eyes one thing is seen.'[258] This is probably intended as more than an example of the perceptive teaching of the doctrine of the coequality of the Father and Son. It suggests that with percipient διάκρισις a monk was capable of perceiving higher realities beyond the physical realm.

Such percipient διάκρισις was seen as very necessary. Monks are frequently described as encountering spiritual manifestations and they needed to be able to discern whether these derived from Divine or demonic sources. For example, when Antony describes demons appearing to monks and claiming to be angels, he says '*discretio* of good and evil spirits is not difficult when God grants the explanation.'[259] *Discretio* is thus used with God's help to identify the source of a spiritual visitation; this is the understanding of Antony 12 in the epistles of Barsanuph and John. In Antony 12 some brothers went to ask Antony whether their visions were true or came from demons, but Antony asked them how their donkey came to die on their way to see him. When Antony was asked how he knew this, he told them 'the demons showed me' and this convinced them that their

---

[257]   GSC 10.143; PE 1.28.2.4 p404.
[258]   GSC 10.17. See also: Nau 1.
[259]   *Vit. Ant.* 35 (*PL* 73.142D).

own visions had come from demons.[260] Among all the parallels only the Barsanuph and John letter goes on to explain that Antony had in fact received this information from God, but spoke as he did to instruct his visitors. While the weight of evidence is against this interpretation for that occasion (it could be a gloss to put Antony in a more favourable light), it does demonstrate how the ability to discern the origin of visions was regarded as God endowed. All the other versions accept Antony's explanation at face value, which indicates how it was understood that demons were capable of observing events and passing on information about them in order to deceive, disturb or distract monks.[261] In the Systematic Collections this saying appears at the start of the διάκρισις / *discretio* sections between two other Antonine apophthegms relating to the use of διάκρισις to moderate πρακτική. This suggests that the matter of deceit by demons or by misguided human ascetic aspirations was seen as significant to the understanding of how διάκρισις was to be used. If the monk was to avoid any such deceit, he needed to use διάκρισις in dependence upon God to determine the spiritual background to his experiences.

The spiritual realm was thus not seen as entirely positive; there were many spirits, not all of them good. Demons are said to try to deceive monks and to disrupt the teacher / disciple relationship understood as so necessary for spiritual advancement. Since this relationship was one that centred on διάκρισις, in that it was the place where διάκρισις was learnt and where the disciple relied on the διάκρισις of his teacher, such demonic attacks can be seen as an attack on διάκρισις itself. One example of this is very significant because it appears in the διάκρισις section of five collections, indicating that using διάκρισις to determine the nature of a spiritual manifestation and to avoid deceit was regarded as particularly important. In this apophthegm demons masquerading as angels (cf. 2 Corinthians 11:14) attempted to deceive a monk by waking him for the synaxis. The monk reported this to an elder who discerned that it was demonic and so told the monk not to listen to them but rebuke them. The demonic attack then shifted to informing the disciple that this elder had lied to another monk, refusing to give him money saying that he had none. Again the disciple told the elder who admitted that the facts were true, but explained that he had so sinned in order not to cause their ψυχαί greater harm. Finally, the elder told the monk, 'Do not listen to the demons who want to deceive you.'[262]

---

[260] Antony 12; GSC 10.2; *VP* 5.10.2a; PE 4.19.3.1-3 p341 (section on διάκρισις); Am16.1; Budge 2.56; Bars 413.

[261] Cf. *vit. Pach.* G¹ 135 where monks are said to need the keenest possible διάκρισις if they are to avoid being led astray by the devil (cf. *ibid.* 112).

[262] GSC 10.138; Nau 224; *VP* 5.10.93; PE 4.19.3.4-6 pp341-2 (section on διάκρισις); Budge 1.300 (on watchfulness). Further on the disciple / teacher relationship, see below, pp. 189-202.

Διάκρισις is seen here in the insight of the teacher figure and the willingness of the disciple to reveal his struggles to him and rely on the teacher's διάκρισις. The teacher is percipient and capable of discerning both the spiritual condition of his enquirers and the spiritual background to the demonic encounters one of them describes. The concluding exhortation, however, indicates the primary point of the saying: demons deceive monks and they should not heed them. To do this monks needed διάκρισις firstly to determine whether a spiritual encounter was demonic, then to recognise the danger of the deceit and finally to oppose their influence which called for exposure of the demons' activity to another, dependence on the διάκρισις of that other and ultimately ignoring the demons.

There is, however, a far more positive aspect to visions, revelations and miracles. Monks were able to use διάκρισις to discern genuine communications from God and to appreciate when God had intervened in their lives either miraculously or through ordinary events. For example, one narrative apophthegm describes how a monk had fled into solitude after sinning and living with a 'consecrated virgin' for six months. He later explained to a visitor how he had soon after fallen ill in the liver (significantly the seat of the passions) but was miraculously healed by a mysterious stranger who told him he was unable to return to where he had lived before because he was incapable of enduring the attacks of the demons there, something the monk discerned (διακρίνω) was true.[263] Healed of his passions the monk was able to discern and respond to the truth he heard about himself in this encounter with what is understood to be a heavenly messenger. Monks also received revelations and visions from God that challenged them to change. For instance, when a monk heard someone slander a priest, he refused to receive the Eucharist from him. He then heard God's voice telling him, 'Men have taken my judgment away' and received an ecstatic vision in which he was unwilling to drink from the same well as a leper and was asked why not, since the leper was only drawing the water. The monk discerned that the voice and vision were challenging him not to judge others and so he called the priest back.[264] The vision and revelation were identified as Divine and interpreted using διάκρισις and with διάκρισις the monk chose to modify his behaviour. With διάκρισις the monk was able to understand that any such communication from God was not merely for his information but for his transformation and growth in purity. Thus, when a monk took food to his mother during a famine (betraying a failure to renounce all worldly ties and family loyalties) he was challenged by a supernal voice that asked, 'Do you

---

[263]   Nau 132A; GSC 20.15; *VP* 5.20.11; Ch268.

[264]   GSC 9.16; Nau 254; *VP* 5.9.11; PE 4.28.3.5-7 p489. Cf. Mark the Egyptian 1; GSC 9.6; PE 4.28.3.1-4 pp488-489 which makes the same point about non-judgment in the context of demonic activity and Divine vision and voice.

care for your mother or I?' The monk, discerning (διακρίνω) the meaning of the message and its source, replied, 'You, Lord, take care of us' and returned to his cell. Three days later his mother came to tell him that another monk had supplied her with food and so the monk praised God and advanced in every ἀρετή.[265] With διάκρισις the monk was able to discern that God was speaking to him, how to act on what he heard and to recognise that the provision made for his mother derived ultimately from God, even if it was through ordinary charitable means. Διάκρισις thus prompts obedience to Divine revelation with the result that the monk is able to advance in purity. Using διάκρισις to discern in events God's power to provide and protect is also seen in an apophthegm describing the barbarian invasion of Scetis:

> It was said concerning Abba Daniel in Scetis that, when the barbarians came, the brothers fled. The old man said [PE: and he was left behind saying], "If God does not take care of me, why am I alive [PE: why am I sitting here]?" And he passed through the midst of the barbarians and they did not see him. Thus the old man said, "See how God has taken care of me and I did not die. I too ought to do the human thing and flee like the fathers."[266]

Using διάκρισις Daniel discerned that he should rely on God's power to protect him and not just follow the crowd. His miraculous escape is offered as evidence that he had discerned the nature of God correctly, but he then discerned that he should flee like the rest. It is understood that spiritual truths discerned using διάκρισις needed to be given practical expression, but διάκρισις could also suggest prudent responses that did not take this to excess. Not only is διάκρισις necessary, then, for discerning the origin and meaning of visions and revelations and the spiritual background to extraordinary and natural events, it was also used to choose how best to respond to what had been revealed.

It is clear then that the personal life of the monk was governed and directed by watchful διάκρισις. With it he came to know himself and his capabilities accurately and he was able to discern and apply to his life what he understood God required of him. With διάκρισις he could govern and direct all his inward life and outward behaviour towards advancing in purity and achieving union with God. It enabled him to establish a balance between these two sides of his being so that he had integrity and an outward purity expressive of his inward state. However, it also enabled him to discern what was external to himself. Διάκρισις meant he could discern in

---

[265] GSC 10.137; Nau 404; PE 1.15.4.3 p210. Further on renunciation of family ties, see below, pp. 211-13.

[266] GSC 10.21. See also: Daniel 1; PE 3.28.3.1 p332; Ch55; Budge 2.108.

his spiritual and natural environment the potential for deceit and danger as well as for benefit. This use of διάκρισις to manage matters external to the monk involved discerning how best to handle relationships with others and this is addressed in the next chapter.

CHAPTER 5

The Apophthegms 2 – Διάκρισις Towards Others

The previous chapter dealt with the intrapersonal value to the monks of διάκρισις. However, there is another aspect of διάκρισις which is concerned with relationships with others. This is particularly evident in the way monks learnt from others, primarily within the teacher / disciple relationship, but also in the way monks managed interpersonal relationships. This aspect of διάκρισις is addressed in this chapter.

Διάκρισις and the Teacher / Disciple Relationship

The self-knowledge gained by monks, either through examining their lives with διάκρισις or by using it to discern revelations from God, made them aware of those areas of their lives that still required improvement or purification. Διάκρισις thus directed monks to learn from others whose way of life was regarded as superior to their own. For example, when Antony heard a heavenly voice telling him of someone who had achieved more than himself, Antony visited him to learn from his way of life.[1] The much longer Evergetinos parallel not only has Antony declare himself ἀδιάκριτος for not having achieved what the other man had, despite how long Antony had been in the desert, it also goes on to encourage the reader to pay careful attention to the narrative and to understand it with διάκρισις (lit.: μὴ ἀδιακρίτως), which at the end of the apophthegm is defined in terms of humility and of Divine revelation and communication.[2] Διάκρισις is used here to discern and respond to a genuine communication from God. However, it is also used to read in both the life of another and in the apophthegms something that will help the monk improve his πρακτική and progress spiritually. This means that διάκρισις requires both the humility to acknowledge personal shortcomings and to learn from others.

---

[1] This appears to have been Antony's common practice, at least at the start of his formation (*vit. Ant.* 3).

[2] PE 1.45.1.83 pp658-659. See also: GSC 20.22; Nau 67, 490; *VP* 3.130; *VP* 7.15.2; Budge 2.2.

Given the esteem in which Antony was held, this suggests that it was not only inexperienced monks that needed to learn from others. There are, in fact, frequent examples of senior monastic figures consulting each other for advice. One such example occurs in a long narrative apophthegm about a great ascetic who had taken his fasting to such an extreme that he became aware he was in danger of becoming proud. He thus went to consult another renowned anchorite, telling him that he would accept his words as God's. However, when the anchorite told him to buy food and eat, he found it hard to accept the command. Through this struggle he became aware that he had been living without διάκρισις.[3] The monk had thus learnt διάκρισις within a teacher / disciple relationship. Thus as a teacher, John Kolobos is said to have taught ⲇⲓⲁⲕⲣⲓⲥⲓⲥ[4] and taught with ⲇⲓⲁⲕⲣⲓⲥⲓⲥ.[5] Διάκρισις was learnt from others already experienced in the use of it.

The process of learning humble obedience and διάκρισις was understood to begin in the cœnobium. The degree to which a monk renounced his own will there in order to obey his teacher is demonstrated in Poemen's reply to a brother expressing a wish to live in a cœnobium. There, he was told, he would need to 'renounce every relationship and act ... for there you will not have authority over a single little cup.'[6] By relinquishing control of even the most trivial aspects of life and placing himself under the authority of another, the monk gave expression to his willingness to renounce his own will. The purpose of doing so was in order to learn how to obey the will of God instead of personal will by first learning to obey a teacher, regarding his instructions as God's own.[7] Any refusal to go through this process was seen as a hindrance to achieving union with God:

An old man said, "If someone does something following his own will and not according to God, but does it in ignorance, he must certainly come into the way of God afterwards. But he who is attached to his own will contrary to God and does not listen willingly to the others, but believes he knows things himself; such a man reaches the way of God with difficulty."[8]

---

3   Nau 641; PE 3.29.3.5-20 pp346-348.
4   Am370.2.
5   Am333.1.
6   GSC 10.69. See also: Poemen 152; PE 2.6.2.1 p111; Budge 1.629c. It is possible that Poemen discerned a struggle with renunciation and self-will and so made clear the challenge that would face his enquirer.
7   Cf. Nau 641 and PE 3.29.3.5-20 pp346-348.
8   Nau 248. See also: GSC 10.115; *VP* 5.10.80.

Διάκρισις is thus to relinquish self-will and instead obey God's will and the advice of others in order to advance towards God. While a failure to do so through ignorance could be corrected, recalcitrant self-will kept the monk from his goals.

A teacher often tested the extent to which a disciple had renounced self-will by instructing him to do bizarre things, even to break his disciplines. For example, in order to teach him 'perfect obedience' one teacher told his disciple to throw the Bible read at the synaxis into an oven. The disciple, not relying on his own διάκρισις, obeyed without hesitation (ἀδιακρίτως). The fire was miraculously extinguished and the apophthegm uses this to prove that 'obedience is good, for it is the ladder of the kingdom of heaven.'[9] It was thus understood that obedience to another and relying on his διάκρισις made union with God possible. The purpose of using such bizarre commands to teach obedience is noted elsewhere. When a brother (*Vitae Patrum*: Poemen) admitted to Joseph of Panephysis that he had disobeyed his instruction to eat on a fast day he received the following explanation:

> The fathers do not speak straightforwardly to the brothers at first but more twisted things and when they see that they obey and do them, then they no longer tell them twisted things but the truth, knowing that they are obedient in everything.[10]

The disciple can be understood to have failed in his attempt to exercise his own διάκρισις, but the force of the saying concerns the willingness to obey. While some instructions may be more obviously eccentric than others, it was not until a disciple had attained an adequate level of διάκρισις that he was regarded as capable of using it. It may be presumed that a monk who yet lacked sufficient skill in διάκρισις, would not necessarily be capable of assessing whether less odd commands were right or not. Only once a disciple had demonstrated that he was willing to rely on the διάκρισις of his teacher, was he ready to learn how to use it for himself.

---

[9] Nau 53. See also: PE 1.33.4.6 p488. The same unhesitating obedience is displayed by Silvanus' disciple Mark who left the letter omega half written so quickly did he respond to his teacher's call (Mark 1; GSC 14.11; *VP* 5.14.5; *VP* 3.143; Budge 1.240; PE 1.35.5.2 pp516-517). See also above, p. 116.

[10] GSC 10.39. See also: Joseph of Panephysis 5; *VP* 5.10.30. Similarly John Kolobos obediently watered a dry stick (John Kolobos 1; GSC 14.4; *VP* 5.14.3; PE 1.33.4.3 p487; Am347; Budge 2.271; Cassian, *inst.* 4.24; Sulpicius Severus, *dial.* 1.19) and Silvanus' disciple Mark obediently agreed that a wild boar was an antelope (Mark 2; PE 1.35.5.3 p517).

The willingness of a disciple to obey strange commands would require trust, loyalty and respect for his teacher. As the disciple came to value the wisdom and support of his teacher, it was likely that this would promote affection. Such affection, however, would have the potential to diminish respect if the relationship grew too friendly. An appropriate balance between this respect and affection was both achieved with and was an expression of, διάκρισις.

> (Isidore) said, "Disciples must love those who are their teachers as fathers and fear them as rulers; they should neither lose their fear because of love, nor obscure love because of fear."[11]

Only with this proper balance then, could the relationship be productive, since either extreme might make the disciple incapable of or resistant to learning. It follows too that a teacher might be either too harsh or lenient, if the balance was lost. Διάκρισις made possible a moderate course between extremes in their relationship, just as it did between extremes of πρακτική.[12]

One way in which the disciple's respect for his teacher was expressed, was in his silence before his master. Words and speech were regarded as having a potentially destructive power and so the value of silence and the reluctance to speak are frequently indicated in the sayings. Thus a disciple (a young Evagrius in some versions) was encouraged not to initiate discussion but remain silent until his teacher spoke, to which he responded: 'Truly I have read many books but I have never learnt such teaching.'[13] Silence before a more experienced monk was an attitude of humility indicative of a willingness to learn and obey. With such an attitude the disciple was capable of learning διάκρισις.[14] However, he learnt it not through reading but practically and experientially through the wisdom, experience and example of his teacher.

Although a disciple was expected to rely on the διάκρισις of his teacher, there were times when he needed to exercise διάκρισις himself; for instance when he selected his teacher. A negative example of this is found in an apophthegm that describes how a would be disciple told a far more experienced monk that he was searching for a teacher 'according to my will' with whom to live and die, to which the latter replied, 'You search well my lord!' The disciple failed to discern the irony in this response,

---

[11] GSC 10.42. See also: Isidore the Priest 5; PE 1.34.4.1 p507.

[12] See above, pp. 142-44.

[13] GSC 10.24. See also: Euprepius 7; *VP* 5.10.19; PE 2.47.2.3 p574; Ch57; Budge 1.58; Bars 291. Cf. Poemen 45, 139; GSC 4.94, 10.86; Nau 468; *VP* 5.10.58; MD 75; Budge 1.22, 1.313 (on watchfulness), 1.369 (on watchfulness); Bars 698.

[14] Cf. Cassian, *conf.* 2.10.1 (see above, p. 116).

being far too confident of and preoccupied with his own ideas to listen. The experienced monk, discerning the disciple's failure to discern that he was doing anything wrong, then asked whether it would give him ἀνάπαυσις to follow his own will rather than that of his new teacher; the disciple then realised he was being arrogant.[15] A proper teacher / disciple relationship needed to be built on humility and a willingness to obey. A potential disciple thus needed to use διάκρισις to gain an accurate assessment of himself and his willingness to give himself to such a relationship. He then needed to use it to select a teacher that would help him advance and not one that would merely reflect his own ideas.

Another occasion on which a disciple was expected to use his own διάκρισις was when his teacher began to behave badly. One example of how this could happen is found in a narrative apophthegm about how a διακριτικός anchorite came to live near a teacher and his disciple. The teacher provided the anchorite with a cell. The anchorite started to receive visitors seeking instruction and the teacher became jealous, never having had such visitors himself. Although the teacher sent his disciple to the anchorite with increasingly threatening demands to leave, the disciple turned these into enquiries about the anchorite's health. Similarly the anchorite's replies concerning sickness, request for the teacher's prayers and recovered health were reported back as promises to leave. Eventually, the teacher went to drive the anchorite away with a stick, but the disciple ran on ahead and said the teacher was coming to console the anchorite. When the anchorite ran out to meet the teacher with praises for his charity, the teacher dropped his stick and the two embraced. The teacher then discerned that his disciple had not been passing on his messages and, far from rebuking his disciple for disobedience, fell at his feet and said, 'It is you who are my father and I your disciple, for our two souls have been saved by what you did.'[16] Although the explicit reference to διάκρισις relates to the anchorite, the narrative as a whole demonstrates how the disciple had learnt διάκρισις from his teacher so well that he was able to protect him when he failed. The reversal of roles at the end of the story reveals that the teacher discerned how his disciple has advanced beyond him. The διάκρισις of the disciple was understood to have saved the soul of his teacher, but the second soul might either refer to the disciple (his

---

[15] Nau 245. See also: GSC 10.174; *VP* 5.10.112; Ch72; Budge 2.17.
[16] Nau 451; PE 1.37.1.1 pp527-528. See also: *VP* 3.26 (cf. *reg. Ben.* 3: 'The Lord often reveals what is better to the younger.'). This is one of a number of apophthegms that seem to be intentionally humorous. If διάκρισις was being taught with humour in these sayings, then this suggests a lightness of touch that militates against seeing διάκρισις as an intense art. (It is worthy of note that the disciple in Nau 451 could almost be one of the scheming slaves in a comedy by Plautus (c.250-184BC) whose plays were still being staged around 300AD).

διάκρισις led him to disobey a command arising from sinful motivations) or, more probably, the anchorite who sought the teacher's forgiveness for having tried his patience (διάκρισις revealing to him the teacher's true feelings). In either case the saying shows that διάκρισις needed to be exercised by disciples. As they became more skilful in using it, they were able to determine when their teachers were in the wrong and should not be obeyed.

To teach διάκρισις, then, teachers needed to be possessed of διάκρισις themselves. For example, they needed to distinguish those over whom they had authority to teach and correct from those they did not.[17] If a teacher lacked διάκρισις he was understood to be a danger to his disciple. This is well illustrated by an apophthegm in which a disciple went to confess a λογισμός to his teacher who was 'without experience of διάκρισις'. When he asked whether someone suffering such a λογισμός was saved, he was told that such a person had 'destroyed his ψυχή.' The disciple despaired of his vocation and intended to return to secular life, but first he decided to confess his λογισμοί (again in the third person) to Silvanus who was noted for his διάκρισις. Silvanus convinced the disciple from Scripture that repentance, forgiveness and restoration were possible and the disciple went on to become an exemplary monk. Finally, Silvanus visited the teacher and told him what had happened in order to instruct him. The narrative concludes with the comment that it had been recorded so that readers 'may know what kind of danger there is in reporting either λογισμοί or trespasses to those without διάκρισις [lit.: ἀδιακρίτοις].'[18] The inclusion of this saying in so many διάκρισις sections, the repeated use of the word-group, the appearance of a longer version of the story (under the name of Apollo) in Cassian's conference on *discretio*, which itself appears in both Systematic Collections, attests to the value placed upon this apophthegm and the point it made. The teacher lacked the διάκρισις necessary for understanding his disciple's struggle. The disciple used what διάκρισις he had learnt by exposing his λογισμοί to Silvanus and so was saved. Silvanus demonstrated the proper use of διάκρισις in his support of the disciple, his interpretation and practical application of Scripture and his correction of the failing teacher. The reader is bidden to use διάκρισις to appreciate its importance in the teacher / disciple relationship. The story reveals the essentiality of διάκρισις in teaching others, exposing λογισμοί, the proper application of Scripture and in repentance and forgiveness through a practical example. The longer version of this apophthegm[19] comments that

---

[17] Macarius the citizen 2; GSC 10.46; PE 4.49.1.1-2 p664.

[18] Nau 217. See also: GSC 10.100; *VP* 5.10.85; PE 1.21.1.2 p285 (section on referring λογισμοί to the διάκρισις of the Fathers). Cf. GSC 5.4; *VP* 5.5.3-4; Cassian, *conf.* 2.13.4-12 (conference with Moses on *discretio*).

[19] GSC 5.4; *VP* 5.5.3-4; Cassian, *conf.* 2.13.4-12 (see above, pp. 118-19).

physical age is no indication that a monk has διάκρισις. This not only reinforces the importance of disciples using διάκρισις to select teachers with διάκρισις, it also serves to remind teachers that they should examine themselves to determine whether they possess διάκρισις and are therefore capable of instructing others. Only if a teacher had διάκρισις was he able to model it to his disciple. Once he was able to understand his disciple's inner life and struggles with compassion, he could then teach him from personal experience.

The harsh treatment meted out by the teacher lacking in διάκρισις mentioned in the previous paragraph contrasts sharply with the compassionate way exemplary teachers dealt with their forgetful disciples. A disciple was expected to obey his teacher and so he would become distressed if he forgot his instructions. However, teachers with διάκρισις displayed considerable patience and gentleness with disciples who were genuinely trying to advance towards their spiritual goals. For example, one apophthegm describes a monk from Scetis who worked hard at his πρακτική but was not mentally sharp. He decided to consult John Kolobos about his forgetfulness, but despite repeated visits he always forgot the advice he had been given. Eventually he stopped going to see John, explaining when they chanced to meet that this was because he kept forgetting and he did not want to trouble John further. John instructed him to light a lamp and then light others from it. He then had the disciple agree that the first lamp had not suffered in any way from being thus used. John then made his teaching point:

> Similarly, neither is John. Even if the whole of Scetis came to me, it would not keep me from the grace of Christ. Well then, whenever you want to, come, without hesitation [μηδὲν διακρινόμενος].

The apophthegm concludes that the perseverance of both men overcame the disciple's forgetfulness and remarks on how monks in Scetis gave themselves willingly to those in conflict and were prepared to suffer in order to win others to the good.[20] This apophthegm illustrates the use of

---

[20]   John Kolobos 18. See also: GSC 11.41; *VP* 5.11.15; PE 4.41.3.1-6 pp618-619; Ch86 (lacuna); Budge 2.154. John Kolobos also taught from experience, since elsewhere he is said to have been forgetful. On one occasion he repeatedly forgot to fetch, for a brother, baskets he had made and began weaving instead, saying finally that he was too busy for such matters (John Kolobos 30); presumably he was preoccupied with contemplation (John Kolobos 11, 32). On another occasion a cameleer came to take delivery of John's handiwork but John kept forgetting to fetch it because he was so preoccupied with God and could only remember to get it by repeating 'Rope camel, rope camel.' (John Kolobos 31). His distraction, it should be noted, was with God and not from God.

διακρίνω to express uncertainty in choosing between two courses of action. However, it also demonstrates how διάκρισις in the teacher / disciple relationship was expressed in their perseverance and patience. Monks with διάκρισις gave themselves fully to pursuing their goals and were prepared to give themselves as teachers to others in order to help them achieve the same. While the disciple in this apophthegm showed διάκρισις in his readiness to consult John, he later failed to use it by not understanding that John would give himself fully to a struggling disciple who was genuinely seeking to achieve his goals. John's διάκρισις led him to use a visual aid to teach the disciple this very point. This shows a remarkable psychological insight not only into his disciple's mental capacity but also into the power of a practical act carried out by the person under instruction to help them learn and remember.

Another example of such a visual aid technique demonstrates that the very act of asking a teacher for help was purificatory. Here the forgetful disciple was aware of his impurity but asked whether he should keep asking for advice that he could never remember afterwards. The teacher made him rinse one of two empty jars again and again with oil and then caused him to discover that the washed one was the cleaner. The teacher then made his teaching point: 'So it is with the ψυχή, for even if it retains nothing of what it has asked, yet is it cleaner than the one that has not asked at all.'[21] By being made to think about what he had done (as in the previous example) the disciple was able to make his own discovery and was therefore more likely to remember it. The teacher here (like John Kolobos above) discerned that the disciple was genuinely seeking to make progress and so was prepared to teach him. However, the saying reveals that it was understood that the willingness to ask and grow spiritually had in itself a purificatory value. Διάκρισις provided teachers with insight into the spiritual condition of their disciples and how best to help them learn, but they also expressed διάκρισις in a patient, gentle and understanding approach to their disciples. Far from being simply a rigorously intellectual approach to achieving union with God, διάκρισις also had a more tender and understanding aspect.

For teachers to be capable of instructing others with διάκρισις, they needed the experience and integrity to do so.[22] After the first generation of monks it was understood that for a monk to live as an anchorite he needed to be sufficiently prepared and advanced in the monastic life no longer to need the daily instruction of a teacher in a coenobium. Hence:

---

[21]   Nau 223. See also: GSC 10.136; *VP* 5.10.92; *VP* 3.178; PE 1.18.1.2 p231; Budge 2.41.

[22]   Further on the need for all monks to have balance and integrity, see below, pp. 227-29.

An old man said, "He who wishes to dwell in the desert ought to be able to teach, not needing instruction, lest he suffer harm."[23]

A monk needed to have learnt sufficient διάκρισις to be able to discern inwardly that he had attained the level of spiritual strength necessary to cope with the austerity and rigours of anchoritic life, which would otherwise endanger his spiritual condition. The Syriac versions of this saying[24] stress this need for detailed introspection, which would require διάκρισις. This saying indicates that the ability to teach others rested on sound formation, experience in the monastic disciplines and on an ability to exercise διάκρισις.

Should a monk fail to acquire this self-knowledge before becoming a teacher, he endangered his own spiritual condition. The teacher needed therefore to determine whether he had attained sufficient purity and ἀπάθεια before attempting to teach others:

(Poemen) said, "Instructing one's neighbour is for the man who is healthy and impassive [ἀπαθής]; for what is the use of building the house of another and destroying one's own?"[25]

A monk was not necessarily incapable of teaching others if he lacked spiritual advancement, his disciple could still benefit from his instruction. However, if he lacked sufficient διάκρισις of himself he was in danger of damaging any advance he had made and would become increasingly less useful to his disciple. This meant that to teach, a monk needed to be capable of living what he taught and of maintaining his own purity.

(Poemen) said, "A man who teaches, but who does not do what he teaches, is like a stream that waters and washes everyone but is unable to make itself clean; but all filth and impurity are in it."[26]

This saying is linked in *Vitae Patrum* 3 with several others by Poemen all stressing the need to teach the mouth to speak what is in the heart and to get the heart to guard what the tongue teaches (cf. Matthew 12:34b).[27] The teacher thus needed διάκρισις to watch over his inner life as this supplied the words and content of his teaching. Διάκρισις ensured that he

---

[23]   Nau 221. See also: GSC 10.127; *VP* 5.10.90; *VP* 7.19.6; Budge 1.125d, 2.451.

[24]   Especially Budge 1.125.

[25]   Poemen 127. See also: GSC 10.55; MD 79; PE 4.38.3.1 p568; Budge 2.287.

[26]   GSC 10.72. See also: Poemen 25; *VP* 5.10.50; *VP* 3.183a; PE 4.38.3.2 p568. Budge 2.145.

[27]   *VP* 3.183 (see Appendix 2 for parallels); cf. above, p. 170.

maintained his integrity and defended himself against the dangers of teaching before he was ready.

Monks who did not have this integrity and taught before they were ready to do so were also a danger to their disciples. Syncletica said that before monks attempted to teach they needed to have practical experience in the monastic life and inward purity, if not they placed others in danger: 'for in their words they call others to salvation, but in their evil way of life they do ascetics more wrong.'[28] To teach with διάκρισις thus meant having an inner life and outward behaviour that were pure and in harmony. Being capable of saying the right things was not enough, teachers needed to teach by example as well, and so their behaviour needed to demonstrate the veracity of their words. It was διάκρισις to integrate the inner and outer life, and to teach with διάκρισις required an integrity of interior life, words and actions coupled with practical experience.

The teacher, or indeed any monk, was thus expected to teach only what he knew and had put into practice. This was not, however, taken to mean that when a monk became capable of teaching, he no longer needed to learn. On the contrary, it was διάκρισις to be actively engaged in learning:

> Abba Palladius said, "The ψυχή trained according to God ought either to learn faithfully what it does not know or teach clearly what it has learnt. If it is not willing to do either it is sick with madness. For the beginning of apostasy is a surfeit of teachings and a lack of appetite for the word, for which the ψυχή that loves God should always hunger."[29]

It was thus διάκρισις to be earnestly seeking greater knowledge and understanding of God and to pass this on. Failing to do so was to deny the very nature of the ψυχή, which should strive for knowledge of God and union with him. If a teacher became unteachable or had had enough of learning, he became more distant from God and incapable of modelling the search for God to others. There was also an assumption that teaching what had been learnt from personal experience was integral to anchoritic life:

> The necessity for spiritual work, that is why we came here [i.e. into the desert]. For it is very hard to teach with the mouth without doing the work of the body.[30]

The anchorite thus needed διάκρισις to keep his words and behaviour in keeping with each other so that he could teach effectively through his example, which was regarded as more powerful than using words: 'Truly

---

28 GSC 10.104. See also: Syncletica 12; *VP* 5.10.71C; *vit. Syn.* 79.
29 GSC 10.96. See also: Nau 662; *VP* 5.10.67; PE 1.18.1.1 p231; *HL, ep. Laus.* 3.
30 Nau 240. See also: GSC 10.167; *VP* 5.10.107; Ch66.

wise is not he who teaches others by his word, but he who trains by his work.'[31] Διάκρισις was to teach from experience and by example, since such practical training was seen as more trustworthy than words. There was a danger that monks would fall back on oral teaching at the expense of practical training, hence the following complaint:

> (James) said, "There is no need for words alone, for there are many words among the men in this age. But there is a need for work, for this is what is required, not words which bear no fruit."[32]

Whether teaching or not, διάκρισις was to put the monastic life into practice,[33] not merely discuss it, and so teachers were required to teach through example. Thus Poemen advised a teacher on how to train his disciple, who gladly listened to words, thus:

> If you want him to be of use, show him also ἀρετή in work, since someone intent on the word remains idle, but if you show him by work, this will endure in him.[34]

This shows psychological insight because people generally learn more readily from practical demonstrations and by attempting something themselves. To be effective and διάκρισις endowed teachers, monks needed to demonstrate how to put what they taught into practice; something that was only possible if they were living out that teaching in their own lives.

It was not just the method of teaching and quality of the teacher that needed to be tested with διάκρισις, the content of that teaching required it too. Monks were expected to use διάκρισις to test carefully all that they heard and were taught, and only speak and teach what they believed to be true:

> An old man said, "Do not consent to every word and do not agree with it, be slow to believe, quick to speak the truth."[35]

---

[31] *VP* 5.10.75. See also: GSC 10.109; PE 4.38.3.4 p568.

[32] James 4. See also: GSC 10.111; *VP* 5.10.77; Budge 2.52.

[33] Cf. the understanding that Scripture needed to applied to life (see above, pp. 180-84).

[34] GSC 10.73; PE 4.38.3.3 p568.

[35] Nau 234. See also: GSC 10.160; *VP* 5.10.103; Budge 1.33b. The longer Syriac version stresses the need for monks to evaluate every aspect of their life and training.

All monks needed to use διάκρισις to weigh up what they heard and to discern carefully what, when and how long to speak. Thus when a young monk was asked whether silence or speaking was better, he said that to achieve ἀνάπαυσις useless words should be left unsaid and even good speech should not be prolonged.[36] To achieve his goals, therefore, monks needed to exercise watchful διάκρισις over all words heard and spoken. It follows, then, that teachers needed διάκρισις to be careful about what they taught and disciples needed it to weigh what they were being taught. One potential danger of speaking at length was probably the risk that a speaker, whose words were considered valuable and wise, might succumb to vainglory or pride. Another danger lay in the potential for controversy. Thus even when a monk saw or heard something he knew to be true, he was not to report it to his teacher unless he was asked,[37] nor should he report 'spectacles and hearsay' to anyone else because it could lead to controversy.[38] In general, then, it was διάκρισις to remain silent and non-judgmental.[39] When words were spoken, teachers and disciples alike needed διάκρισις to determine the impact of those words and what they conveyed.

A disciple thus needed διάκρισις to evaluate his teacher's instruction, but a teacher would sometimes also leave the decision on how to respond to his teaching to his disciple. This would help the disciple learn how to use διάκρισις and prompt him to examine, with διάκρισις, his motives for seeking advice. For example, a monk asked Poemen how he should use an inheritance he had received. Poemen took a few days to discern how to respond and then presented him with several options. Firstly, the monk could give his inheritance to the Church, but they would only use it for banquets. Secondly, he could give it to a relative, but then there would be no spiritual reward. Finally, he could give it to the poor and be free from anxiety. Several versions of the saying end with Poemen telling the monk, 'Do what you want, it is none of my business.'[40] Given the stress laid on renouncing all possessions in the apophthegms and the dominical command to give everything to the poor (Matthew 19:21), it may be that Poemen's curt conclusion meant that he had discerned his enquirer was looking for a way round what he knew he should do. If so he was seeking to abdicate

---

[36] GSC 10.163; Nau 237; *VP* 5.10.103C; PE 1.38.4.2 pp541-542; Budge 1.340 (on watchfulness).
[37] Poemen 45; GSC 10.86; *VP* 5.10.58; Budge 1.22; Bars 291 (see Appendix 2 for other parallels).
[38] Poemen 139; MD 75; Budge 1.369 (on watchfulness) (see Appendix 2 for other parallels).
[39] On silence and speech, see above, p. 192; on non-judgment, see below, pp. 202-11.
[40] Poemen 33. See also: GSC 10.82; *VP* 5.10.56; *VP* 7.36.4; MD 7; Budge 1.179 (on voluntary poverty).

responsibility for the decision. By forcing him to make up his own mind, Poemen refused to let him do this and by effectively presenting the disciple with only one legitimate option, he was forcing the monk to address the λογισμός of greed. On the other hand, presenting λογισμοί and questions to teachers for advice required disciples to be intent on spiritual advancement. As their training in διάκρισις progressed they needed to learn to exercise it themselves and Poemen may have been encouraging the monk to do this. While either interpretation is possible, the former is more likely. However, it is also probable that, as with so many apophthegms, this one was capable of various interpretations and readers were expected to meditate on it and use διάκρισις to ascertain what God was saying to them through it. In any case the disciple was forced to use his own διάκρισις to make a decision about his λογισμός.

The disciple was expected to reveal his λογισμοί to a teacher who was πνευματικός καὶ διακριτικός ('spiritual and discerning').[41] In this way he relied upon the διάκρισις and experience of his teacher and learnt διάκρισις λογισμῶν. By choosing to expose his λογισμοί to his teacher a disciple demonstrated not only humility in seeking help with his inner struggle and a desire to advance in purity, but also his growing ability to discern the presence of λογισμοί. Such exposure of λογισμοί was also understood to have a disarming effect upon them. For example, a monk struggling with blasphemy repeatedly visited Poemen for help, but was always too ashamed to admit his problem. Eventually Poemen, discerning the monk's distress, assured the monk that what he told him would remain confidential,[42] which gave the monk the confidence to confess that he was tempted to believe that God does not exist. Poemen reassured him that this had not arisen from the monk's negligence but from Satan, and told him to speak out against the suggestion each time it came to him by affirming his belief in God. The demon is then said to have left the monk because its suggestion had been exposed; the version in the Alphabetical Collection notes the immediacy of this departure after the exposure of the λογισμός.[43] The monk had discerned his need of Poemen's διάκρισις but feared the exposure this would involve. However, when the λογισμός was exposed, its power was immediately lost. Poemen also provided advice on how to deal with the λογισμός in future and the monk successfully put this into action. The point of the apophthegm is how λογισμοί were defeated by exposing

---

41 GSC 5.4. See also: *VP* 5.5.3-4; Cassian, *conf.* 2.10, 13. Exposure of λογισμοί to others is widely attested throughout the apophthegms.

42 Cf. the importance of confidentiality in modern counselling and, more significantly, in the confessional.

43 GSC 10.63. See also: Poemen 93; *VP* 3.57; *VP* 7.1.5; PE 3.30.1.1-3 p361; Budge 2.59; Dorotheos, *doctr.* 10.109.

them to a teacher.[44] This demonstrates that διάκρισις provided psychological as well as spiritual insight, since the hold many preoccupations or feelings of guilt have over an individual arises from secrecy. Once such a problem is exposed its power diminishes because the individual has admitted it more openly to himself and come to terms with the need to resolve the problem. With διάκρισις the teacher / disciple relationship became a place of cooperation and trust where, through humility and obedience, the disciple was able to learn διάκρισις and how to overcome λογισμοί so that he could advance towards purity and union with God.

Διάκρισις and Non-judgment

The relationship between teacher and disciple was only one of the many that needed to be managed and one important aspect of maintaining these was non-judgment, which is a key theme throughout the apophthegms.[45] This is a biblical precept based on an awareness of personal sin[46] and a knowledge that it is for God to judge people[47] and that to discriminate between people is to judge them.[48] Even when a disciple confessed to his teacher that he had sinned, the teacher would be reluctant to judge him. For example, on one occasion when this happened the teacher discerned (διακρίνω) in himself how to reply and said, 'Now that you have confessed it yourself, I dare not judge you before God, for perhaps God has forgiven

---

44   Cf. GSC 5.16; Nau 164; VP 5.5.13; VP 3.9; PE 1.20.8.3 p282; Budge 1.560 where a disciple suffering from the λογισμός of lust is told to return repeatedly to his teacher each time it attacks. In the PE version the disciple goes to his teacher to expose his λογισμοί without hesitation (μηδὲν διακρινόμενος). The λογισμός of lust is thus overcome by revealing it to another.

45   E.g. Ammonas discerned the veracity of an accusation that a monk was keeping a woman in his cell, but prevented those searching for her from discovering her whereabouts; he then warned the monk to be on his guard in future thereby responding to what he knew without judging the offender (Ammonas 10; cf. *vit. Pach.* G[1] 76 where Pachomius used διάκρισις to correct a penitent monk and told him to watch himself in future). Moses the Ethiopian was so aware of his own sin that he refused to judge anyone else (Moses 2). Cassian describes how Machetes learnt not to judge others hastily because on several occasions he had done so only to do the same himself and so he concluded that monks should only judge themselves (Cassian, *inst.* 5.30). Judgment of others was renounced on the understanding that God alone is the true judge (Alonius 4) and so it was presumptuous and arrogant to do so (Nau 254; Origen, *de orat.* 28.8-10).

46   Mt. 7:1-2; Rom. 2:1-3.

47   1 Cor. 4:4-5; Jas 4:11-12.

48   Jas 2:1-4.

you.'[49] Condemning others was regarded as an impurity that prevented the monk from serving God and so he needed to rid himself of any inclination to do so:

> Another brother enquired of Abba Poemen, "My λογισμοί suggest to me things which surpass me [*alph*.: Why do the demons persuade my ψυχή to be with him who is superior to me] and make me despise him who is my inferior." The old man answered him, "The apostle says, 'In a large house there are articles not only of gold and silver, but also of wood and clay. If a man cleanses himself from all these, he will be an instrument made useful and honoured to his own master ready for any good work.' [2 Timothy 2:20-21]" The brother replied, "What do these things mean?" The old man said to him, "The house represents the world and the articles men, the gold articles are those who are perfect and the silver ones those who are with them, the wood and clay ones those who are spiritually young. If then someone cleanses himself from all these, that is to say he condemns no one, he will also be a useful and honoured article to his master prepared to do any good work."[50]

The version in the Alphabetical Collection makes it clearer that this is a question concerning the temptation to discriminate between people, but it lacks the interpretation of the metaphor. The exposition of this metaphor has always been problematic. The interpretation in the Greek Systematic Collection reflects early exegeses that focussed on the need for purity and charity, expressed here in non-judgment, but avoids the identification in those exegeses of the house with wicked or unworthy persons in the Church or world. It thus avoids encouraging the enquirer's discriminatory tendencies.[51] Although διάκρισις provided the ability to distinguish

---

[49] GSC 15.130. See also: Nau 527; PE 1.3.2.2 p69. The disciple, presumably discerning the penance required of him, returned to his cell and put himself in chains and was miraculously released by God just before his death because of his endurance and humility.

[50] GSC 10.70. See also: Poemen 100; Budge 2.137.

[51] One modern interpretation understands the house as the Church and claims that an 'orthodox Christian should rigorously eschew his unworthy brethren.' (J.N.D. Kelly, *A Commentary on the Pastoral Epistles* (Black's New Testament Commentaries; London: A & C Black, 1963, repr. 1986), pp. 187-88). Early exegeses reflect the uncertainty arising from the awkwardness of the metaphor. Cyprian (*exhortatio ad pœnitentiam* 44), Augustine (*de bapt.* 3.19.26) and Gregory the Great (*ep.* 8.35) speak of false Christians in the Church, but John Chrysostom (*in epistulam ii ad Timotheum, hom.* 6) understands the house to refer to the world. Nevertheless, Augustine and Chrysostom exhort their readers to purify themselves from iniquity and prepare themselves to serve God. John of Damascus (*expositio*

between different types of people, it was not to be used for discriminating between them or making critical judgments about them, as this would be destructive of purity. Διάκρισις thus provided a critical faculty, but it was not critical of others; a distinction lost in modern English usage where criticism generally has a negative connotation. It was a sign that a monk was advancing towards his goals when he was able to use διάκρισις not to make distinctions between people but to treat everyone in the same way:

> An old man said, "He who does not receive all people equally but makes distinctions [διακρίνω], such a person cannot be perfect."[52]

With διάκρισις the monk could evaluate people and situations. However, it was διάκρισις to use the knowledge so gained not to condemn or denigrate others, but to accept them for what they were, conscious that personal shortcomings made being judgmental wrong.

The way monks treated others required that they weigh their words and actions carefully. The use of διάκρισις to ensure that words spoken to others were beneficial and not destructive is evident in the gnomic saying: 'The harsh word makes even the good evil, but the good word is useful to all.'[53] However, much the same aphorism ('The evil word makes even the good evil, but the good word makes even the evil good.') is elsewhere supported by an illustrative anecdote that contrasts the effects of good and evil speech and actions. Macarius the Egyptian's disciple so insulted a pagan priest that the priest beat him almost to death. However, Macarius subsequently greeted the priest with friendly concern about the priest's weariness[54] and, taken aback by such kindness, the priest admitted the assault and asked to become a monk. As a result many other pagans are said

---

fidei 92) says that a person must choose which type of vessel he is and so he must voluntarily purge himself of dishonour or suffer destruction.

52   GSC 21.62. See also: GSC 1.33; Budge 2.448b. Pseudo-Macarius also says that sinners and the maimed should not be despised but regarded as whole and treated with compassion (*hom. B* 15.8; *hom. H* 45.1.3).

53   GSC 10.181.

54   The narrative leaves open whether this weariness resulted from the strenuous beating he had administered or from the futile pursuit of pagan religion. The nature of pagan religion in Egypt at the time should not be understood simply as that of the Graeco-Roman world. Egypt, like any other country, was unique in its culture and religion and the endemic Egyptian religions persisted into Late Antiquity. The Christian term 'pagan' also tended to embrace anything that was neither Judaism nor Christianity. For a recent study on the continuance of native religion during the Christianisation of Egypt, see: D. Frankfurter, *Religion in Roman Egypt: Assimilation and Resistance* (Princeton: Princeton University Press, 1998).

to have become Christians.[55] Both Macarius and his disciple recognised that the priest was a pagan but they used the information differently, one to encourage the other to insult. Good words led the pagan to Christ and set him on the road to purity, whereas bad and condemnatory words only caused harm. Properly used, διάκρισις enabled the monk to use the knowledge he had discerned about someone to choose how to act upon it for the best, so that his words and actions became productive of purity and not harm.

There is one area in which erroneous discrimination could result in condemnation of others that was of particular concern to monks, that is anger. The monastic life was demanding, with contrasting periods of solitude and community life (e.g. hospitality and teaching), and so it was perhaps inevitable that there would be tensions and disagreements that resulted in anger. Syncletica acknowledges that the ideal is not to grow angry but accepts that this happens; with διάκρισις monks could be realistic about such weaknesses. She therefore says that anger needed to be resolved the same day (citing Ephesians 4:26 and Matthew 6:34) and asks:

Why do you hate the man that grieves you? It is not he who has grieved you but the devil. Hate the sickness and not the one who is sick.[56]

With διάκρισις the monk was able to distinguish between the sinner and sin, loving the one and hating the other (just as God does) because he was capable of discerning the spiritual background to what aroused his anger. Anger, then, was a condemnation of the person rather than the wrong and its evil spiritual source. This apophthegm also demonstrates the practical application of Scripture using διάκρισις, viz. that anger should be resolved quickly (Ephesians 4:26).[57] Antony linked Ephesians 4:26 with self-examination (2 Corinthians 13:5) and not condemning others,[58] which points to how διάκρισις was used for judging oneself and not others. It was understood that if a monk quarrelled it led to anger, then (spiritual) blindness and eventually deeper into sin; Evagrius also said that anger darkened the ψυχή and defiled the νοῦς.[59] To have διάκρισις meant not allowing anger and grudges to fester and grow out of control. The danger

---

[55] Macarius the Egyptian 39; GSC 10.181; *VP* 3.127; PE 2.44.1.1-2 pp549-550; Am211.2-213.2; Budge 1.186; Macarius, *apoph.* PG 34.260.

[56] GSC 10.103. See also: Syncletica 13; *VP* 5.10.71A-B; *vit. Syn.* 64.

[57] On the failure to use *discretio* to understand that anger attracts judgment (Mt. 5:22) and the implications of Eph. 4:26 to friendship see Cassian, *conf.* 16.17.

[58] *Vit. Ant.* 55.

[59] GSC 10.180; Nau 634; PE 1.42.2.2 p622; Budge 2.214. Cf. Evagrius, *prak* 23. In *vit. Pach.* the clouded conscience is incapable of διάκρισις (G¹ 8) whereas the pure νοῦς is capable of it (G¹ 12).

inherent in this is seen in an apophthegm that eulogises Christians and monks in particular as a superior race. It is said that monks are only harmed when the devil persuades them to remember wrongs and gossip about them. The Evergetinos parallel concludes that if a monk rids his καρδία of such grudges and condemnation, 'he will live the angelic life on earth.'[60] In effect, διάκρισις expressed in non-judgment not only defended the integrity of the individual but also of the monastic community as a whole. With διάκρισις the monk could discern that the devil was behind rancour and condemnation, and also the damaging effects such attitudes and behaviour had on himself and others. Διάκρισις then directed him to reject his judgmental attitude, not least because he was aware of his own faults, thus enabling him to come closer to his goals.

The power of memory could, however, be used more positively than for remembrance of wrongs; it could be used to fix the mind on God and to recall the evil of demons. The monk thus needed to use διάκρισις to distinguish between these different types of memory and to select only those that would promote union with God.

> Abba Macarius said, "If we remember the evil things spoken to us by men, we destroy the power of the remembrance of God. But if we remember that the evil things spoken to us come from demons, we will be invulnerable [Ch: we shall live spotlessly to the point that they will be unable to pierce us]." [App adds: However he sighed and said, "All the *virtutes* are begun in this cell alone, and as a result of these labours a man is established." They also asked him, "What is this *virtus*?" He answered, "That a man reproach himself."][61]

Brooding on the wrongs of others and forgetting the demonic inspiration behind them destroyed remembrance of God, which according to Evagrius is contrary to human nature.[62] The longer parallels conclude that 'inveterate anger blinds the eyes of the heart and excludes the soul from prayer,'[63] indicating that anger and forgetting God separated the monk from him. Διάκρισις kept the monk focussed on *virtus* and God, guarded and guided his thoughts, kept him from resentment and anger, and reminded him of his true spiritual enemy. The parallel in the Latin appendix of Palladius indicates that it is διάκρισις to persevere with work in the cell to acquire

---

60   GSC 10.187; PE 3.2.8.30 p48. See also: Nau 397, 615b.
61   GSC 10.48; App 15d; Ch60. See also: Macarius the Egyptian 36; *VP* 5.10.34; *VP* 7.37.4a; MD 15; PE 2.42.2.1 p540; Budge 2.206; Macarius, *apoph.* PG 34.257; Evagrius, *prak* 93; Socrates Scholasticus, *HE* 4.23.
62   Evagrius, *prak*. 93; Socrates Scholasticus, *HE* 4.23.
63   *VP* 7.37.4; MD 16. Evagrius says θυμός (anger or irritation) is wholly in accordance with human nature (*prak.* 93; Socrates Scholasticus, *HE* 4.23).

virtutes in an attitude of humility and self-deprecation rather than attempting to apportion blame. This saying also links, through a network of parallels, to Poemen S18 and Cronius 1,[64] which point to the need to be vigilant and avoid all distraction if the monk was to receive the Spirit of God and be spiritually productive. Διάκρισις was thus self-accusing and self-critical, not condemnatory, rancorous or irascible. It kept the mind on God and the search for union with him.

The value of using διάκρισις to understand that faults in others originated with demons and not the individual was that it made the monk better able to forgive.[65] The monk was expected to be forgiving by nature and forgiveness was expressive of διάκρισις, since it was to be like God. For instance, when Poemen was asked whether a monk who had sinned and reformed should be forgiven, he reminded his enquirer of Matthew 18:22 and the need to forgive repeatedly. However, Poemen used this to make the point that if this is what God requires of people, then God himself will forgive yet more so.[66] To have διάκρισις meant learning to forgive others repeatedly in order to become more like God. The suggestion here is that the monk with διάκρισις is also confident of God's willingness to forgive and restore him when he is repentant. This impression is confirmed by another saying in which Mius reassured a soldier that just as the soldier would repair a torn cloak rather than throw it away, so also God carefully mends those of his creatures in need of forgiveness and salvation.[67] Διάκρισις thus represented an attitude towards God and forgiveness that had a full hope and expectation of Divine compassion and help. It encouraged the monk to imitate God in his attitude to others by being compassionate and forgiving, and therefore not judgmental.

If this attitude of forgiveness was to be developed the monk needed to be aware of his own sin and unwilling to listen to reports about the sins of others as this might lead him to be condemnatory. For example, a monk explained to Poemen that he wished to leave the area because he had heard reports about a *confrère* that he found unhelpful. Although Poemen said the reports were untrue and that the monk's 'faithful' informant could not be faithful otherwise he would never have said such things, the monk remained insistent. When Poemen said that even God insisted on seeing with his own eyes what was happening in Sodom (Genesis 18:20-21), the monk claimed to have witnessed the faults personally. Finally, Poemen acted out the mote and beam analogy on non-judgment (Matthew 7:1-5),

---

[64]   See Appendix 2 for details.
[65]   Cf. Cassian, *conf.* 7.28: no one should be 'detested or despised' for the trials they endure because these are either permitted or brought upon a person by God to produce humility.
[66]   Poemen 86; GSC 10.62; PE 1.1.4.3 p30; Bars 371.
[67]   Mius 3; GSC 10.176; *VP* 5.21.30; PE 1.1.4.1 p30; Budge 1.599.

saying that the *confrère*'s sins were like a twig and his enquirer's like a roof
beam. In all but one version the saying ends with praise for Poemen's wise
words, but Evergetinos replaces this with: 'Therefore if you give heed to
your own sins, you will not take into account those of another.'[68] There is a
progression here in how διάκρισις is used in handling information about
the faults of others – monks should not: a) let themselves be disturbed by it;
b) speak of it; c) listen to hearsay but rely only on what they know to be
true; d) allow what they know to be true to cause them to judge others. The
monk was not to use διάκρισις to make critical judgments about others, but
to scrutinise his own spiritual condition and faults. Only by using διάκρισις
as a critical faculty to gain self-knowledge could the monk progress
towards his goals, but that same διάκρισις could also be misused to
condemn others, which resulted in a loss of purity. Poemen elsewhere takes
this combination of self-knowledge and non-judgment to a deeper and more
inward level:

> (Poemen) said, "He who knows himself is a man." He also said, "There is
> a man who seems to be silent in speech, but his heart condemns others;
> consequently he is talking constantly. Another man both talks from
> morning to evening and keeps silent; for when he talks, he never speaks
> without benefiting his hearers."[69]

This paradox demonstrates that silence was not regarded as indicative of
inward purity. The purity represented by non-judgment needed to be
expressed in both outward actions (spiritually profitable and
non-condemnatory speech) and inward attitudes. Thus διάκρισις enabled
the monk not only to guard his speech, but also to make a critical
examination of his inward state. Διάκρισις was, then, to be devoid of
judgmental thoughts as well as condemnatory words. By using διάκρισις in
this way, the monk not only preserved his own purity but encouraged it in
others too.

The interior quality of some faults and the visibility of others led to a
distinction being made between different kinds of judgmental statements;
the former was slander and the latter condemnation.

> A brother asked an old man [App: Antony], "What is slander and what is
> condemnation?" The old man replied, "Slander is talking about unseen
> and hidden things, but condemnation is talking about visible sins;
> therefore every word which one cannot say in front of his brother is

---

[68]   GSC 10.51; Nau 391 (uses Thomas in Jn 20:25 to make the same point);
        VP 5.10.37; PE 3.2.2.4 p24; Ch63.
[69]   *VP* 5.10.51. See also: Poemen 27; GSC 10.75; PE 2.47.2.1 p574; Budge 1.27 (on
        contemplation), 1.298 (on watchfulness). Cf. GSC 10.184.

slander. If someone says, 'A certain brother is virtuous and good, but also slovenly and he does not have διάκρισις,' this is slander. But if someone says, 'That brother is a trader and avaricious,' this is condemnation, for he condemns his actions and his whole life, and this is worse than slander."[70]

Using διάκρισις to weigh another's actions and judge him was a grievous fault because it condemned all the accused was visibly doing to seek God. Since the accusations could be verified, they might also have a more damaging effect on the accused and his community. Slander here, however, is understood as a value judgment (using διάκρισις) about something the accuser could not see. Making either judgment was to usurp God's rightful role as judge, but slander effectively claimed the ability to judge what only God was capable of seeing: the motivations underlying the actions. Both forms of judgment were a misuse of διάκρισις. However, it is significant that accusing a monk of lacking διάκρισις is singled out as a slanderous accusation. This suggests that not only was διάκρισις a quality essential to being a 'good monk' it was also an interior quality that only God could fully assess.

It is also helpful to consider the reaction of those who were subjected to condemnation by others. When monks were falsely accused of sin they displayed humility. Having no concern for their own reputation, they accepted the accusation and did penance.[71] For example, Nicon was falsely accused of sinning with someone's daughter. When the father confronted Nicon with a sword, his sword hand withered. Notwithstanding the miracle, when the father reported the alleged offence to the priests, they attacked Nicon and tried to drive him away. Despite his innocence, Nicon begged to do penance. He was ostracised for three years, but each Sunday begged others to pray for him. Eventually the false accuser was driven to confess and the congregation sought Nicon's forgiveness. Although Nicon forgave them, he refused to continue living among them because, he said, 'I did not find one person who had διάκρισις enough to sympathise with me.' The Evergetinos version adds a further comment reinforcing this statement and noting that Nicon also fled the area because they were about to lavish 'praise and glory' on him.[72] The priests' lack of διάκρισις resulted in their failure to weigh the case, discern the meaning of the miracle and their judgmental attitude. Nicon's διάκρισις led him to be humble and forgiving

---

[70] PE 2.49.2.2 p592. See also: Nau 417; App 13. Cf. Nau 503.

[71] E.g. Cassian (*conf.* 18.15-16) describes how a monk sought to discredit Paphnutius by hiding one of his books in Paphnutius' cell and falsely accusing him of stealing it. Paphnutius then did penance, even though he was innocent, and through his humility and trust in God's judgment the devil was forced to expose the true villain.

[72] Nicon 1; GSC 16.30; PE 2.46.4.4 p567.

but also to leave the area because of their lack of διάκρισις, which appears to be judgmental. The Evergetinos version attempts to overcome this problem by saying that Nicon left because the affair had brought him renown, which could damage his spiritual state by destroying his humility. However, this parallel also suggests that Nicon sought to correct them and his departure may have been intended to help achieve this and to teach them διάκρισις. The saying effectively contrasts the priests' lack of διάκρισις with Nicon's skill in it. Διάκρισις prompted Nicon to act with humility and to take steps to preserve his humility. It enabled him to evaluate the people and the situation and to use the understanding he gained to encourage their purity without compromising his own.

Nicon's humility in the face of false accusation draws attention to how διάκρισις prompted monks to be non-retaliatory, but there was also to be a more active response; they were to meet ill treatment with good. This reflected the command found in the Gospels to love one's enemies (Matthew 5:44; Luke 6:27). It was διάκρισις to overcome evil with good (Romans 12:21).

> (Poemen) also said, "Wickedness in no way destroys wickedness; but if someone maltreats you, do good to him, so that you destroy his wickedness through your goodness." [cf. Rom. 12:21][73]

Monks with διάκρισις were not encouraged always to be passive when mistreated. Διάκρισις prompted them to act constructively for the benefit of the offender and so διάκρισις could be used to reverse the effect of malice and encourage others towards purity.

There were, then, occasions when διάκρισις prompted monks to make judgments and make an active response, for example when they discerned that a wrong decision had been made. This is to counter wrong judgment with right judgment. Thus when Agathon boldly told some monks in Scetis that their decision on a matter was wrong, they questioned his authority to challenge it. Agathon claimed Scriptural authority because he was, 'A son of man. For it is written, "If truly you speak righteousness, judge rightly, sons of men." [Psalm 57:2 (LXX)]'[74] Not only was Agathon using διάκρισις to put his understanding of Scripture into practice,[75] he also regarded sound judgment, and therefore διάκρισις, as an expression of righteousness. Διάκρισις could thus be used assertively to uphold the truth.

Διάκρισις in relation to judgment thus provides insight into the truth of a matter and into how to act for the best. Refusing to judge others is not an

---

[73] GSC 10.77. See also: Poemen 177; *VP* 5.10.53; *VP* 3.79; *VP* 7.7.3; PE 2.40.5.2 p524; Dorotheos, *doctr.* 10.109. Cf. GSC 10.181.
[74] Agathon 14; GSC 10.15; *VP* 5.10.12.
[75] See above, pp. 180-84.

ignorance of their faults and therefore a failure to use διάκρισις. Rather it provides an awareness of their sins and the ability to determine how best to help the sinner towards purity without judging them.

> Abba Poemen said, "If a man has sinned and he does not deny it, saying, 'I have sinned,' do not reprimand him, since you will cut off his zeal. But if you say to him, 'do not lose heart, brother, and do not despair of yourself but be on guard in future,' you stir up his ψυχή to repentance."[76]

The textual evidence for the beginning of this saying is confused. The majority of manuscripts for *Vitae Patrum* agree with the versions found in the Alphabetical, Evergetinos and Syriac Collections reading: 'If a man has sinned and he denies it saying, "I have not sinned."' In some ways the version in the Greek Systematic Collection provides the most natural reading, in that if a monk confessed his sin, reproaching him would not be useful. However, the end of the saying suggests that the better attested reading is the correct one, in that a monk in denial needed to be stirred to repentance, but without judging him. If he had already confessed, why would he need to repent? In either case, διάκρισις provided the ability to stir to repentance through encouragement rather than judgment. Were a response to be condemnatory, it would not edify the sinner. Διάκρισις promoted gentleness and a concern to encourage spiritual growth, rather than the investigation of error or passing judgment. Διάκρισις is thus sound judgment, not being judgmental.

Relationships with Others

Διάκρισις had an important role in the wider aspects of how the monk related to others, for example to his natural family. When the monk renounced secular life he was expected to forsake all family ties. This can be seen as a biblical concept based on Matthew 19:29 where family and possessions are forsaken for Christ and eternal life. This abandonment could be so total that the only father a monk would recognise was God. For example, when Evagrius heard of his natural father's death he declared, 'Stop blaspheming, for my Father is immortal.'[77] This suggests that with διάκρισις doctrinal truth could be so deeply assimilated that it overrode all else, including family bonds. It was believed that such bonds could threaten to distract the monk from his vocation and so he needed διάκρισις to

---

[76]   GSC 10.68. See also: Poemen 23; *VP* 5.10.48; PE 4.48.1.5 p654; Budge 1.608 (on repentance). Further on the MS evidence for *VP*, see O. Chadwick, *Western Asceticism*, p. 352.

[77]   GSC 10.194. See also: GSC 1.5; *VP* 5.1.5; Evagrius, *prak.* 95; *HL* 38.13; Socrates Scholasticus, *HE* 4.23. Cf. Cassian 8.

recognise when this was happening. Hence when a disciple asked his teacher whether he should give alms to his poor sister like any other beggar, he was warned that he was being drawn to his charitable act by the blood bond between them.[78] Another danger of family ties laid in the way others might use them to manipulate monks, such as when a magistrate unjustly imprisoned Poemen's nephew to force Poemen into giving him an audience. However, Poemen had so cut off family ties he refused to get involved and told the magistrate to do as he wished.[79] Only the Syriac version regards this as a διάκρισις saying, but Poemen clearly discerned the threat to his purity since to accede would have been a rejection of his renunciation and possibly leave him open to pride or vainglory as a result of renown. Poemen's curt dismissal of the magistrate, 'do as you wish,' is rendered using either βούλομαι or *volo* in all but *Vitae Patrum* 3, which uses *discerno*, which suggests that he had used *discretio* and may have been advising the magistrate to do the same. In any case it makes an interesting contrast between the way *discretio* was used for spiritual discernment among monks and for exercising a personal preference or legal judgment among seculars. With διάκρισις monks chose to renounce family ties and refused to renew them because they were distractions from the more important spiritual bond with God.

The renunciation of family relationships and the retreat into the solitude of the desert did not mean, however, that all relationships were abandoned; there is also extensive comment in the apophthegms on how monks should relate to each other.[80] For all that the monastic vocation could be described in Plotinus' words as φυγὴ μόνου πρὸς μόνον,[81] the monastic search for union with God contrasts with Neo-Platonism in the value placed on others for achieving that goal.

(Poemen) said that Abba Theonas used to say, "If a man acquires an ἀρετή, God does not grant its grace to him alone [PE adds: as the ἀρετή remains in him]." For he knew that man is not faithful in his own labour, but that if he went to his companion, then he would remain with him.[82]

---

[78] GSC 10.156; Nau 233; *VP* 5.10.101.
[79] Poemen 5; GSC 8.16; *VP* 5.8.13; *VP* 3.20; PE 1.24.7.2 pp347-348; Budge 1.265 (on watchfulness).
[80] The significance of personal relationships in the apophthegms and how this is balanced with solitude is explored at length in G. Gould, *The Desert Fathers on Monastic Community*. NB also the biblical statement of new family bonds based on obedience to God's will (Mt. 12:50).
[81] *Enneads* 6.9.11.
[82] GSC 10.85; PE 1.20.3.7 p268. See also: Poemen 151.

It was διάκρισις to recognise the value of mutual support and encouragement for establishing and developing ἀρεταί, which would include διάκρισις; this was particularly evident in the teacher / disciple relationship. Only once a monk had learnt to live among others was he considered capable of living in solitude. For example, Longinus consulted Lucius about three λογισμοί concerned with living in solitude. He was told that he could not live in exile until he learned to control his tongue while living among others. Secondly, when Longinus said he wanted to fast, Lucius alluded to Isaiah 58 on the nature of the true fast and said he needed first to learn to control his 'evil λογισμοί.' Finally, when Longinus said he wanted to flee from men, Lucius replied, 'If you have not first lived rightly among men, you will not be able to live rightly alone.'[83] The use of κατορθόω here for living rightly also carries the sense (supported by the *Vitae Patrum* parallel) of correction. Life in community with others (whether in a cœnobium or in the desert) was a training ground that prepared the monk for solitude. Thus it was διάκρισις to recognise the need of others for learning to control the inner and outer life before attempting to live alone.

For these relationships with others to be of spiritual benefit, their quality needed to be maintained with διάκρισις. For example, one διάκρισις apophthegm reveals that it was διάκρισις to recognise the futility of arguing over whether someone had said something offensive or not; even if the offender admitted saying it he was only likely to snap back, 'Yes I said it, so what?'[84] Saying 474 in the Greek Anonymous Collection and the Evergetinos version point out that such exchanges result in violent dispute. In the latter the offended monk is told to 'let the word be and profound peace will come,' in other words, to forget all about it. The former parallel presents the same idea by using a short narrative in which a priest brokers peace between the pair by having them agree, in effect, to forget the incident, although the offender also repents. Thus the monk with διάκρισις was to meet provocation with ἀπάθεια, and if a squabble did occur he was to nip it in the bud before it spiralled out of control and destroyed the inner peace of both parties. Furthermore, the implication is that it is διάκρισις not to get into a dispute in the first place and to reunite divided parties.

The monk's admission of his fault in the previous example demonstrates that an outward action does not necessarily indicate inward purity or a

---

83 GSC 10.45. See also: Longinus 1; *VP* 5.10.33; PE 1.13.1.2 p188, 3.31.1.6 p372 (section on διάκρισις); Ch59; Budge 2.265. Cf. Basil the Great (*reg. fus.* 7): 'You who live alone, whose feet will you wash? For whom will you care? Who will you be less than?' Antony spoke of the value of Scripture for instruction but added that is was good to encourage each other in the faith (*vit. Ant.* 16; Am43.2).

84 Nau 232. See also: GSC 10.155; Nau 474a; *VP* 5.10.100; PE 2.37.1.9 p462. Further on quarrelling, see above, p. 205.

penitent attitude. It was διάκρισις for a monk to have a vigilant inward awareness of personal guilt and to guard against harming others if he was to be saved; exterior works of πρακτική were not sufficient per se. Thus a teacher told his disciple that fasting, solitude and loving others would not save him, rather he was 'to bear his own blame and not distress his brother in anything at all.'[85] This reflects the Gospel principles of treating others well and being merciful, forgiving and not condemnatory,[86] and it is with these principles that one senior monk was said to challenge enquirers, speaking to them as would God himself:

> Concerning a great old man, some of the fathers explained that if any one came to ask him for a word, he would habitually say, "Look, I am taking on God's role and sitting on his judgment throne. What do you want me to do for you, then? If you say, 'Have mercy on me,' God says to you, 'If you want me to have mercy on you, you too must have mercy on your brother! If you want me to forgive you, you too must forgive your neighbour.' There's no injustice in God, is there? Certainly not! But it is up to us if we wish to be saved."[87]

The monk had διάκρισις if he applied the biblical injunctions to be merciful and forgiving; then he was also able to receive God's mercy and forgiveness. This saying also indicates that the way a monk treated others was a matter of personal choice; they chose how to behave with διάκρισις.

Such a decision, made using use διάκρισις, could be arrived at by following the golden rule.[88] One monk defined this as, 'If you hate something, do not do it to someone else.' He explained that this included slander, calumny, contempt, insult and theft, and concluded that by avoiding these a monk could be saved.[89] With διάκρισις monks were able to treat others in a manner consistent with how they hoped to be treated themselves. Thus it was διάκρισις to be considerate of others. It went beyond a search for personal purity and integrity to recognising that behaviour towards others had an impact on the purity and integrity of the wider monastic community as well.

Although using διάκρισις to determine how to live in harmony with others had an outward aspect in behaviour, it grew out of an interior focus. The monk exercised διάκρισις when he was attentive to himself and did not meddle in the lives of others. One monk, concerned that he was 'neither able to bear evil nor to work and give alms,' was told to 'guard (his)

---

85   GSC 10.133.
86   Mt. 7:1-2, 12; Lk. 6:31, 36-37.
87   Nau 226. See also: GSC 10.148; *VP* 5.10.95; PE 2.37.1.2 p461; Budge 2.158.
88   Mt. 7:12; Lk. 6:31.
89   Nau 253. See also: GSC 1.31; *VP* 5.1.21; *VP* 3.153; *VP* 7.16.2; Budge 2.53.

conscience with regard to (his) neighbour and keep (himself) from all evil.' The Evergetinos version expands this to include not counting evil against his neighbour and not treating him with contempt.[90] Thus even when the monk's capacity for πρακτική was limited, he at least needed to use διάκρισις to keep his thoughts and actions pure in his relations with those around him. However, living in an isolated community would have had its problems. Under such conditions there would be the temptation to take an inappropriate interest in the lives of others, for example by prying and gossiping.

> An elder said, "It is not profitable for a monk to inquire into the condition of this or that person, for through questioning you are detached from prayer and you fall into silly chatter and back-biting and so it is better to keep silent."[91]

Curiosity and gossip were thus a misuse of διάκρισις. The attention was shifted away from interior watchfulness of personal faults to considering those of others. In doing so, the monk was distracted from prayer and therefore separated from God. Furthermore, it was also destructive of community life. A monk with διάκρισις was, then, to prefer silence and curb his inquisitiveness because being preoccupied with the lives of others meant he was not using διάκρισις to pay attention to his own. This injunction not to use διάκρισις to meddle in the affairs of others but, by implication, use it to watch his own way of life, is succinctly expressed elsewhere, where it is said that to have ἀνάπαυσις 'a foreign monk living in another country should not interfere in anything.'[92] However, it was not the interest in the lives of others that was being condemned, but the attitude and purpose behind it. Such interest exercised with διάκρισις became a charitable concern for others. For instance, it was διάκρισις to distinguish between those who were in need and those who were not, and to support the poor one, since this would give him ἀνάπαυσις.[93] In relation to others the monk's life was, then, to be exemplary and edifying:

> An elder said, "Just as the order of monks is more honourable than that of seculars, so also the foreign monk ought to be a mirror to local monks in every way."[94]

---

[90] GSC 10.40. See also: Joseph of Panephysis 4; *VP* 5.10.31; PE 3.2.2.2 pp23-24; Budge 1.373 (on watchfulness).

[91] GSC 10.128. See also: *VP* 7.30.1; App 11.

[92] GSC 10.8. See also: Arsenius 12; *VP* 5.10.6; *VP* 7.32.6; PE 4.42.1.6 p623; Budge 2.47.

[93] GSC 10.144; MD 98; PE 1.25.1.3 p351; Budge 1.167 (on voluntary poverty).

[94] GSC 10.117; Nau 250. See also: *VP* 5.10.82; Budge 2.141.

The point of this apophthegm could be that a monk coming to a new region should reflect the lifestyle of those around him. However, this does not take into account the initial comparison, which suggests that the visiting monk should live more honourably and therefore be an example to others. The mirror image in this saying is not so much the enigmatic reflection (like the obscure image in a polished metal mirror) of future knowledge found in 1 Corinthians 13:12, as 'beholding as in a mirror' (κατοπτριζόμενος) the glory of God in 2 Corinthians 3:18. Mirrors were regarded as instruments of revelation, particularly of knowledge of God, and so the monk with διάκρισις was to reflect the image of God in his life, which would be an edifying example to others. It was thus διάκρισις for a monk to live among others in such a way that his attitudes, words and behaviour encouraged and supported the monastic goals and did not detract from them.

The way in which διάκρισις could be used to discern how best to help and encourage others can be demonstrated from the story of Maria the Harlot.[95] She had been brought up by her uncle, the hermit Abraham, and became an anchorite until she was seduced by 'a monk by profession only.'[96] She failed to discern that God could forgive her and told neither Abraham nor his disciple Ephraim (the author of the life) what had happened. Instead, she fled the desert and turned to prostitution. After receiving Divine revelations and praying for two years Abraham discovered her whereabouts, disguised himself as a Roman soldier and visited her as if he were a client, even breaking his discipline to eat a sumptuous meal. Maria was first moved to tears by the reminiscent smell of asceticism on Abraham, who eventually disclosed his identity. He did not condemn her or discuss her motives, but won her back to the anchoritic life through mercy and love. At the centre of this account, Abraham's exceptional *discretio* is praised at length.[97] It is said that through such wisdom, understanding, *discretio* and a willingness to appear foolish and lacking in *discretio* he was able to save his niece. This story reflects less a commitment to family loyalty (although this must have been a factor) than a desire to win a fellow anchorite back to the monastic path. It also reveals how *discretio* was non-judgmental, willing to forgo πρακτική for charitable purposes and unconcerned about personal reputation when it was used to determine how to restore another to faith, which was considered far more important.

Διάκρισις was not only used to find the best way to encourage others, it was also used to avoid discouraging them. This required the monk to use διάκρισις to gain insight into the other person's spiritual condition. For example, Achilles said he had no time to make fishing nets for two of three monks that visited him, but agreed to make one for the third who was said

---

Ephraim the Deacon, *vit. Mar. mere.*
Ibid. 3.
Ibid. 7-8.

to have a 'bad reputation.' He later explained to the other two that they 'were not grieved' by his answer but, if he had refused the third monk, he would have assumed it was because Achilles had heard about his sin. By agreeing, Achilles said, 'I have stirred up his ψυχή so that he will not be consumed by grief. [cf. 2 Corinthians 2:7b]'[98] The allusion to 2 Corinthians 2:7b is helpful because the first half of that verse exhorts believers to forgive and comfort sinners. Διάκρισις enabled Achilles to discern both the likely reaction of the sinful monk and how best to treat him. By showing kindness and (effectively) forgiving him rather than acting in a way that would be perceived as judgmental, he not only kept the monk from despair but also encouraged him to be penitent.

The same concern to promote joyous zeal, rather than despairing resignation, is found elsewhere. Poemen praised a monk for working a field and charitably giving away his produce, with the result that the monk became more zealous in his charitable efforts. However, Anoub reprimanded Poemen for acting in this way. Two days later, in Anoub's presence, Poemen told the monk he had thought he was talking about a secular brother and said that what the monk was doing was not monastic work. Knowing he could do no other work, the monk became distressed. Afterwards Anoub sought Poemen's forgiveness and Poemen explained that he had known from the start that it was not monastic work. However, he had spoken 'to his λογισμός and so gave him zeal for advancing in charity, but now he had gone away distressed only to do the same.'[99] This apophthegm contrasts the effect of treating another with and without διάκρισις. Poemen had initially used διάκρισις to discern the monk's ability and how best to encourage him in what he was capable of doing. He thereby not only kept the monk from despair, he also encouraged him to greater charity. By taking Anoub's approach and dealing with the issue without διάκρισις, the result was destructive and condemnatory. The practical result was the same, but the spiritual and emotional effect was different. Διάκρισις provided the ability to understand people and to discern the outcome of any advice given. It therefore made the monk capable of inspiring others and kept him from harming them.

Anoub's assertiveness in the last example suggests a legalistic over confidence about what it was right and wrong for monks to do, as such it indicates a lack of the humility that was regarded as necessary for living harmoniously with others. Over confident and impudent speech (παρρησία)

---

[98] GSC 10.18. See also: *Achilles* 1; *VP* 5.10.14; PE 4.47.1.1-5 p649; Budge 1.415 (on love, charity and hospitality).

[99] GSC 10. 66. See also: *Poemen* 22; *VP* 5.10.46; PE 4.44.1.1-5 p636; Budge 2.74. If this saying reflects an actual incident, one cannot help but feel for the disciple who was used as an object lesson; whether Poemen rectified the problem later is left unanswered.

was considered destructive of spiritual 'fruit' and 'the mother of all the πάθη' and so the monk was expected to refrain from it and work hard in his cell. In the parallels to the saying where this is expressed, such a monk is called a warrior (Alphabetical Collection and *Vitae Patrum* 7) who guards against such speech (*Vitae Patrum* 7) and lives humbly (*Vitae Patrum* 3).[100] The monk was thus expected to use διάκρισις to exercise self-control over his speech and life generally. By doing so he guarded against pride and against damaging the community in which he lived.

Such self-restraint was helped by using διάκρισις to develop an awareness of personal sin and of the approach of death and judgment. Thus one monk was told: 'Cut off from yourself all love of contention in everything [*alph.* adds: and weep and mourn because the time draws near].'[101] The monk was expected to use διάκρισις to examine himself and not others, because in this way he could concentrate on purifying himself and reject any controversy that would distract him from this, damaging his own purity and that of others. This shift of focus onto the self meant that διάκρισις was used for self-blame and not for blaming others. For example, a monk who felt overburdened was reminded of how sailors, when the wind was unfavourable, tied ropes round the centre of their ship and towed it until God sent a favourable wind, then they would anchor it with a stake to keep it from drifting; 'the stake' he is told 'is to rebuke oneself.'[102] Self-blame was thus understood to keep the monk from drifting away from God when life was difficult and to persevere in the expectation that matters would improve. The suggestion here is that the monk had brought the oppressive burden on himself, and it may be that he needed to accept the blame for it. Διάκρισις was a humble awareness of personal fault and consciousness of culpability before God that could act as a form of self-restraint which would both hold the monk to God and keep him from turning his attention to the faults of others.

---

[100]   GSC 10.11. See also: Agathon 1; *VP* 5.10.8; *VP* 3.198; *VP* 7.42.1; PE 2.34.1.1 p434; Budge 1.280 (on watchfulness), 2.524; Bars 261, 340, 342, 347, 458; Dorotheos, *doctr.* 4.52. Cf. GSC 3.55-56.

[101]   GSC 10.179; Matoes 12. See also: Budge 1.142 (on weeping and mourning). There is a significant link between consciousness of death and humility. For example, in GSC 15.129 a monk, conscious of his death, asked his *confrère* to throw his body into the desert and not a tomb when he died. The *confrère* hesitated (διακρίνω) to do so, but agreed. After the monk's death the *confrère* had a dream in which the dead monk told him God had rewarded his humility by ordaining that he rest with Antony.

[102]   GSC 10.64. See also: Poemen 145; Budge 1.528 (on humility). Tying ropes round a vessel is also found in Acts 27:17, although there they appear to be used to frap the vessel to keep it from breaking up rather than for towing it. If frapping is also in mind in this apophthegm, then διάκρισις can be said to hold the monk together when he feels oppressed.

The awareness of his coming death and judgment, combined with renunciation of secular life, led the monk to regard himself as dead; this had an impact on his relationships with others in that he would refuse to engage in their affairs.[103] For example, Poemen would not allow Anoub to invite priests visiting the monasteries to see them, explaining:

It is not my business, for I died and a corpse does not speak. Therefore they should not consider me to be here among them.[104]

While this may have been a humble refusal to engage in matters that did not concern him, it is more likely that Poemen discerned that it would lead to futile conversation that would damage his purity and theirs. Just how thoroughly dead towards others monks regarded themselves is evident in the comment that a monk should consider himself 'already three years [*alph.*: days] in the tomb.'[105] Since a dead person can have no legal rights, this indicates that the monk's sense of being dead was an expression of humility towards others. This humble of rejection of rights is also evident in Sisoes' explanation of his comment that 'the monk ought to be in λογισμός beneath the idols.' He cited Psalm 113:13-14 (LXX), '(idols) have a mouth but do not speak, they have eyes but do not see, they have ears but do not hear,' and said:

The monk ought to be the same. Because the idols are an object of loathing, he too should suppose himself an object of loathing.[106]

Since διάκρισις meant, then, that a monk regarded himself as dead and without rights in relation to others; he considered himself to be without the right to react negatively to provocation:

(Poemen) said, "A monk is not faultfinding [MD: does not disparage another]; a monk does not return evil for evil; a monk is not irascible. [MD adds: a monk is not lustful, proud, avaricious, or self-exulting, or verbose; but the true monk is humble and *quies*, full of charity, having the

---

[103] Cf. above, p. 138.

[104] GSC 10.53. See also: Poemen 3; *VP* 5.10.38.

[105] GSC 10.92. See also: Moses 12; *VP* 5.10.63; *VP* 7.26.1; PE 3.2.2.5 p24; Budge 1.368 (on watchfulness). In Jewish, Eastern and early Christian belief the soul was understood to linger near the dead body for three days and then depart as corruption set in; three years therefore stresses how utterly dead monks were to regard themselves.

[106] GSC 10.97. See also: Nau 384; PE 1.45.1.52 p654; Budge 1.488 (on humility). The Nau section is entitled Περὶ Διορατικῶν, which refers to discernment, prophetic insight and the ability to read hearts and interpret Scripture, which indicates how διάκρισις was understood.

fear of God always in his heart. PE ends: That is to say those who have these are not monks, even if they appear to be.]"[107]

By extending the range of λογισμοί, *Ægyptiorum Patrum Sententiæ* lays greater stress on the importance of purity and the Evergetinos addition indicates the need for external practice to match inner purity. The former of these also highlights this integration by stressing humility, ἀπάθεια (*quies*), charity and the fear of God. Διάκρισις was thus expressed in an impassive and humble state of mind which sought a good relationship with God and other people. Being dead towards others did not mean that monks refused to engage with them, but sought to ensure the purity of those relationships as well as of their own inner being.

The interaction between monks is frequently seen in their meeting as hosts and guests, although their reactions when receiving or offering hospitality were sometimes unexpected and enigmatic.[108] For example:

> Once some fathers came to Alexandria, when they had been summoned by Theophilus the archbishop, to pray and to destroy the pagan temples. As they were eating with him, veal was set before them and they ate without hesitating [διακρίνω]. The bishop, taking a piece of meat, offered it to the old man nearest him, saying, "Look, this is a good piece of meat, eat, Abba." But they replied, "We were eating vegetables until just now; but if it is meat, we do not eat it." And not one of them agreed to eat it any more.[109]

The adjacent sayings are the same in both Systematic Collections and throw light on how this apophthegm was understood. In the preceding saying a monk stepped aside when he saw some nuns approaching and was rebuked for doing so: 'If you had been a perfect monk, you would not have looked so closely as to see we were women.' (The preceding saying in the Greek Anonymous Collection records a monk who, more positively, did not succumb to the temptation to look at others when he visited Theophilus in Alexandria.) In the second saying a monk took bread to his elders who practised an austere regime and, when they stopped eating, encouraged them to eat more. This apophthegm concludes: 'See how these true and

---

[107] GSC 10.78; MD 82; PE 2.35.1.2 p439. See also: Poemen 91; *VP* 5.10.54; App 5d; Budge 1.456 (section on humility). *Quies* is equivalent to *apathia* (ἀπάθεια) (Souter, p. 339).

[108] Sometimes διάκρισις prompted monks to do something bizarre and outside normal behaviour in order to achieve some discipline or avoid doing something wrong, e.g. feigning madness in order to avoid judging someone (Ammonas 9).

[109] Theophilus 3. See also: GSC 4.76; Nau 162; *VP* 5.4.63; PE 2.24.6.1 p286; Budge 2.529.

self-disciplined monks ate much more than they needed, for God's sake;' that is they were conscious of the duties of hospitality. Theophilus' visitors ate what was set before them without question (cf. Luke 10:8; 1 Corinthians 10:27). With διάκρισις they chose not to pay attention to the food, partly because being concerned about food was a preoccupation, but mainly because they were there to meet Theophilus and pray with him. In a sense, they used διάκρισις to choose not to use διάκρισις with regard to the food. However, their refusal to eat when their attention was drawn to what the food was,[110] suggests that they either failed the demands of hospitality or possibly exhibited commendable self-control by not eating something contrary to their normal πρακτική. The emphasis here is on self-control, the subject heading in the Anonymous and Systematic Collections. The visitors demonstrated self-control in their ability both to pay no attention to the food and to stop eating when their discipline was compromised. The visitors chose not to use διάκρισις at first, but then chose to use it to maintain their purity. However, Theophilus also had an ambiguous relationship with the monks after his opposition to Origenism and the expulsion of Origenist monks from Nitria and Kellia,[111] thus this apophthegm may also suggest provocation (by Theophilus) and resistance (by the monks). When meeting with others, monks used διάκρισις to control how they behaved and to defend their spiritual purity.

Using διάκρισις to choose how to behave when receiving hospitality, then, could result in actions contrary to expectations. For example, two natural brothers became monks, the younger first, but when one of the fathers visited them and the younger monk tried to wash his feet, the father stopped him and made his older brother do it. When other monks present questioned this (*Vitae Patrum* explains that 'they had been accustomed to the first in the monastery doing this'), the father replied 'I take away the first place from the younger and give it to the elder.'[112] This saying was understood to relate to humility (the Syriac Collection's section heading) as well as διάκρισις. While there is humble obedience to an elder here, there is also the humility to disregard the accepted norm and not expect to stand on presupposed rights. It was thus διάκρισις to forgo personal rights and not regard oneself too highly. On another occasion, Poemen (noted for his διάκρισις twice in the saying) explained that he refused to eat meat at a meal with others because the many brothers who visited him would 'suffer harm' if they discovered he had eaten meat and would ask why they should

---

110 This is reminiscent of 1 Cor. 8; 10:25-30 where knowledge that food had been sacrificed to idols (as was commonly the case with food sold at the time) was not a matter of concern to strong believers but destructive of those with a weak conscience.

111 I.e. the Anthropomorphite controversy (see above, pp. 35-36).

112 Nau 246. See also: GSC 10.175; *VP* 5.10.113; Budge 1.535.

not eat it too.[113] The monk's diet generally excluded meat, although it might be served as an expression of hospitality. The expectation of Poemen's hosts was that, as a man of διάκρισις, he would eat what was set before him and keep his own ascetic discipline secret.[114] Poemen, however, discerned the wider implications of his behaviour and so it was διάκρισις for the monk to be conscious at all times of the example he was setting, particularly if he was a teacher. Another aspect of receiving hospitality with διάκρισις can be seen in how monks discerned the needs of their host. For example, John Kolobos accepted water from an eminent elder when the rest of the company had refused it; as the youngest present he particularly was expected to decline. He explained that, since he was delighted and rewarded when others accepted water from him, he did not want to deprive the elder of a similar reward or cause him grief by refusing to accept a drink; the rest were 'amazed and profited greatly from his διάκρισις.'[115] John had used διάκρισις to determine how best to act and decided to overturn accepted practice in order to encourage rather than hurt his host. Monks with διάκρισις were therefore not bound by rules, rights or customs but freed from them. They used διάκρισις to evaluate situations and personal behaviour. It kept them alert to the wider implications of their actions and informed them of how to benefit others and not harm them.

Not every guest, however, possessed διάκρισις; some lacked it. On these occasions it was the actions of the host and not the guest that were misinterpreted. Monks were expected to keep their ascetic regime secret and to relax their normal discipline when they entertained, but this could lead a visitor to assume that his host was negligent in his ἄσκησις. For example, when some cœnobites visited an anchorite, they were received joyfully and generously. They were allowed to rest while their host kept vigil in secret. He then overheard them saying, 'the anchorites in the desert take more rest than we do in the cœnobium' and so when they left to visit a neighbouring anchorite, he asked them to greet him with the message, 'Do not water the vegetables.' When the second anchorite heard the message he made them work all day without eating, prolonged the synaxis, provided them with an austere meal and then made them say the synaxis until dawn, each time saying that he had either limited the synaxis or been more generous with the food for their sakes. When they tried to leave he implored them to stay three days longer 'according to the custom of the desert.' The cœnobites 'fled secretly.'[116] The cœnobites' lack of διάκρισις

---

[113]   Poemen 170; PE 4.47.1.6-8 p649.
[114]   Cf. Nau 256, 257.
[115]   GSC 10.37. See also: John Kolobos 7; *VP* 5.10.28; Budge 2.131.
[116]   Nau 229. See also: GSC 10.150; *VP* 5.10.97; *VP* 3.5; PE 3.3.1.1 p66; Budge 2.14.
        Cf. the encounter between Eulogius visited Joseph of Panephysis where Joseph's

is contrasted with the διάκρισις of both anchorites. The first knew how to act properly towards guests while keeping his ἄσκησις secret and recognised the cœnobites' lack of understanding. The second discerned the meaning of the message and how best to address that lack of understanding. It was διάκρισις not to make hasty judgments about a host's way of life based on the hospitality he showed. Διάκρισις was also needed for determining the intentions of visitors and how to treat them.[117]

When the actions of a host were misinterpreted, διάκρισις of his own actions made him confident that he was behaving correctly. For instance, when a secular beggar came seeking alms from a monk already entertaining other monks, he was invited to join them. The beggar declined and so the host sent out more food to the beggar than the others were eating and two cups of wine instead of the one each they had. One of the monks joked that he should go outside too so that he could have two cups of wine. The host replied that had the beggar come in he would have been pleased to have the same as them, whereas now the beggar would assume they had an easier life than him. The host concluded: 'So it is profitable that our conscience does not condemn us.'[118] The host discerned that his actions would be misinterpreted, since the beggar did not know how generous he had been in showing charity. However, the monks knew they had done nothing wrong. Although it can be said from this apophthegm that it was διάκρισις to be generous in almsgiving, the point is more that it was διάκρισις to be unconcerned about being misjudged when the conscience was clear. This is not to say that διάκρισις encourages complacency. Διάκρισις was used to weigh thoughts and actions and, when the monk found that he had behaved uprightly, he was confident in that self-knowledge. Διάκρισις was to be concerned about purity and integrity, not reputations.

Using διάκρισις to maintain integrity and purity meant, however, that monks also needed it to determine how best to respond when an encounter with another person had the potential to harm their purity. Such was the case when a prostitute propositioned Ephraim. No one had ever seen him angry or fighting and she hoped to make him angry. So he took her to a public place and told her to do as she wished. When she said she was too ashamed to do it in front of so many people, he asked how much more she should be ashamed before God who sees all that is hidden in darkness

---

relaxation of his discipline in order to show Eulogius hospitality was misinterpreted (Eulogius 1 and parallels; see above p. 169).

[117] Monks received many visitors, some genuinely seeking instruction and others little more than tourists. To tackle this problem Antony established a code with Macarius who was to say the visitors were from Egypt if they were 'idle' and from Jerusalem if they were 'pious and erudite;' the former would be fed, prayed for and sent on their way, but Antony would discuss salvation with the latter all night (HL 21.8-9).

[118] GSC 10.189; Budge 1.258 (on watchfulness).

(1 Corinthians 4:5); she left him in shame.[119] Ephraim used διάκρισις to determine how best to overcome the λογισμός of fornication (i.e. by exposing it to others[120]) and lead the prostitute to compunction.

However, monks did not only use διάκρισις to protect their purity in unavoidable brief encounters with others, they also needed it to guard against living in contact with people that might tempt them to sin. Thus it was διάκρισις for a monk to avoid over familiarity with his teacher, seculars, women, young boys and children, since such relationships were understood to be fraught with difficulty and the potential for some form of unacceptable intimacy.[121] Hence:

An elder said, "Do not have any dealings with a secular [Nau: Do not be friendly with a superior], do not have an acquaintance with a woman and do not be familiar with a young child for a long time [Nau: kind to a young lad]."[122]

---

[119] Ephraim 3; GSC 10.26; *VP* 5.10.21.

[120] See above, pp. 201-202.

[121] There are numerous examples of monks being or avoiding being sexually tempted by children and youths (Eudemon 1, John Kolobos 4, John the Persian 1, Poemen 176, Nau 456-8 [= PE 2.29.12.14-16 pp379-380], Nau 545 [= PE 2.29.12.3 p378]) or by each other (Achilles 6, Nau 181). Thus Basil the Great told young monks not to live together but to 'run away from them as from fire' (*exhortatio de renunciatione mundi* 5).

The attitude to adultery and fornication appears to have become more lenient following an edict by Callistus I (Pope from c.217; d. c.223). Before this they were regarded as irremissible (e.g. Origen, *de orat.* 28.8-10) and, while Cyprian (200-258) approved the shift in attitude (*ep.* 51.20-21), Hippolytus (c.170-c.236) and Tertullian (c.160-c.220) were more critical of it (*refutatio omnium haeresium* 9.12.23-26 and *de pud.* 1 respectively). By the Council of Ancyra (314AD) adulterers could be forgiven after due, if extensive, penance (Canon 20) and in his Canonical Epistle Gregory of Nyssa (c.330-c.395; canon 4) allowed the same, including 'unlawful lusts' and the need to use discretion. Basil the Great (c.330-379), in his third Canonical Epistle (also *ep.* 217), broadened the range of forgivable sexual sins to include adultery (canon 58), fornication (canon 59), homosexual acts (canon 62), bestiality (canon 63), incest (canon 67), sex within the prohibited degrees (canon 68) and premarital sex (canon 69). However, when Cassian discussed fornication he focused on the need for purity of heart (*inst.* 6.2 and *passim*) and the value of the practical disciplines and penance (*conf.* 5.4.3). The concern in monastic circles concentrated more often on prevention and inward purity than on penance for sins committed.

[122] GSC 10.124; Nau 125 (amending μειλακίου to μειρακίου). See also: *VP* 5.10.87; Budge 1.277a (on watchfulness).

Abba Isaac the Theban said to the brethren, "Do not bring young children here [PE: Do not allow monks to live with children], for four churches in Scetis were deserted because of young children."[123]

With διάκρισις the monk was alert to how those around him might tempt him into relationships that would compromise his purity and integrity. This was not a judgment on others, considering them to be sinful, but a self-recognition of weakness and the avoidance of the potential for temptation, hence one monk said: 'By nature I do not fear children, but what is the use of a pointless battle?'[124] With διάκρισις monks were able to anticipate struggles and guard against placing themselves in potentially damaging relationships with others.

There was also the matter of discerning when a relationship had become spiritually harmful and what to do about it, for example when a teacher became sinful with the result that his disciple suffered. One disciple realised his ψυχή was being destroyed by living with his teacher and so went to ask Poemen about it. Poemen was surprised the disciple felt the need to ask about leaving his teacher, but left the decision to the disciple. By the disciple's third visit to Poemen, he had decided to leave. Poemen said:

> When a man sees he is losing his ψυχή, he has no need to consult another. Concerning secret λογισμοί one should ask and it is up to the old men to test them, but with visible sins there is no need to consult but to cut them off immediately.[125]

Poemen refused to allow the disciple to abdicate responsibility for deciding to leave; he made him use his own διάκρισις to make the decision. More significant, however, is Poemen's concluding instruction, which suggests that inexperienced monks discussed their λογισμοί with a teacher because they had yet to learn whether or not they were wrong. By contrast, sinful acts were self-evident and so it was διάκρισις to separate oneself from them without delay. The teacher was providing a destructively bad example and so the disciple needed to break the relationship (cf. 1 Corinthians 5:11); with watchful διάκρισις a disciple was able to detect when this was necessary. Sometimes, however, a disciple would discern that he was acting for the best by remaining with his sinful teacher. For example, one teacher

---

123 GSC 10.44. See also: Isaac, Priest of the Cells 5; *VP* 5.10.32; PE 2.29.7.1 p370; Ch58. Children did not only represent a sexual temptation, their noisiness was also a source of distraction (e.g. Poemen 155 and Nau 338).

124 Nau 456; PE 2.29.12.14 p379; Budge 1.569 (on fornication).

125 GSC 10.90. See also: Poemen S2; *VP* 5.10.61; App 4a-b; Budge 1.388-389 (on watchfulness). Cf. GSC 5.9; *VP* 5.5.9.

sold the mats he and his disciple made and spent the proceeds on drink, bringing home so little food that the disciple eventually died. This brought the teacher to his senses and he went on to become an exemplary monk.[126] The contrast between these two responses rests in the nature of the harm being done, the one spiritual and the other physical. If the disciple had been suffering spiritual harm, he would have needed to break the relationship. However, physical harm was regarded as a lesser concern because it did not threaten to separate the disciple from God. A monk needed διάκρισις to distinguish between different types of threat and harm, and to then choose how best to act.

Discerning how to respond to harmful relationships did not, then, necessarily involve immediate separation from the person who was the source of the trouble. The spiritual wellbeing of the offender was the first concern and only if it proved impossible to encourage him to reform and strive for purity did separation occur. Thus Arsenius attempted to reform a monk who had been stealing from his brothers and disturbing their peace by giving him all he wanted and telling him to stop stealing, but when he continued to steal he was driven away. This apophthegm concludes:

> If there is a brother who has a weakness for some sin, it is necessary to support him [cf. Romans 15:1]; but if he steals and does not stop despite being warned, drive him away, for it damages his ψυχή and troubles everyone in the neighbourhood.[127]

It was διάκρισις to support and restore a fellow monk without condemning him. Driving the offender away could suggest that he was being removed from temptation, although it is more likely that if any further compulsion to reform was in mind it was along the lines of 1 Corinthians 5:5. It was also διάκρισις to recognise when attempts to reform had failed and to weigh the respective needs of the individiual against the wider community and the harm they were suffering.[128]

Deciding whether to support a monk in his struggle with temptation and sin depended on the nature of the fault. Διάκρισις was needed to determine what kind of struggle the monk was engaged in and then to choose how to respond. The contrasting concerns of immediate separation or support and of spiritual or other threat are brought out in another apophthegm. Theodore

---

[126] Nau 340; GSC 16.27; *VP* 5.16.18; PE 1.37.1.2 p528.
[127] GSC 10.23. See also: Daniel 6; *VP* 5.10.18; PE 4.50.1.1-3 p667; Ch 56. Cf. Dorotheos, *doctr.* 11.121.
[128] The breadth of the offender's destructive influence is brought out by PE: ... δεῖ ἐκδιώκειν αὐτόν, ἵνα μὴ σὺν αὐτῷ καὶ ἄλλοι ἀπόλωνται. ('... it is necessary to banish him, lest others perish with him.').

of Pherme said that a monk should help a brother who had fallen into the temptation of fornication to reform, however:

> If he falls into heresy and he is not persuaded by you to turn away from it, quickly cut yourself off from him [cf. Titus 3:10], in case, by delaying, you are dragged down with him into the abyss.[129]

The brother's struggle with fornication would not necessarily be a spiritual threat to the one helping him, since it was the offender's λογισμός not the helper's. However, heresy was another matter because if the offender was not quickly won back to orthodoxy, the helper was in danger of succumbing to his heretical ideas and thereby being separated from God. Thus in relating to others, it was necessary to weigh with διάκρισις the relative dangers of their sins and decide whether and how long to help the offender. While διάκρισις was expressed in a compassionate concern for others and their purity, it was also the instrument by which the monk advanced his own purity and sought union with God. When these were threatened, the monk needed to use διάκρισις to decide when to separate himself from the offender.

Balance and Integrity

The monk's way of life had, then, a significant impact on others and if he was to be an influence for good among them he needed to maintain the purity of his inner and outer life and keep them in harmony with each other. While such integrity and balanced life was particularly important for teachers,[130] it was the ideal for all monks. In a saying reminiscent of the biblical analogy of good trees bearing good fruit (e.g. Matthew 7:16-20), monks were told to ensure that their speech and πρακτική were in keeping with each other:

> An old man said, "If the ψυχή has the word but not the work, it is like a tree with leaves but no fruit. For just as a tree full of fruit also has luxuriant foliage, so also is a word prepared in a ψυχή which does good daily labour."[131]

Διάκρισις was to have an inner and outer life that were fully expressive of each other and so monks were expected to put what they said into practice. Furthermore, it was understood that only by living out the monastic

---

[129] GSC 10.32. See also: Theodore of Pherme 4; *VP* 5.10.23; Budge 1.315 (on watchfulness).

[130] See above, pp. 196-99.

[131] Nau 252. See also: GSC 10.120-121; *VP* 5.10.84; PE 4.38.3.5 p568.

discipline was the monk capable of saying anything profitable. The basis of the monk's life needed to be the truth of God, not the false premises of his old life with its misguided desires. This is expressed in a pair of διάκρισις sayings that are linked in three collections:

> An elder said, "Falsehood, this is the old man [PE adds: who is being corrupted by his deceitful desires (Ephesians 4:22)] but truth, this is the new man [PE adds: created to be like God (Ephesians 4:24)]."[132]

> He also said, "The root of good works is truth, but falsehood is death."[133]

The succinct description of the moral impact of Christ's redemptive act in the first saying is developed in the second saying. Living 'in accordance with the truth that is in Jesus' (Ephesians 4:21) is understood in terms of good works. This may derive from the understanding that as a new creature the monk was created to do the work of God (Ephesians 2:10). A monk's inner life purified from λογισμοί was to exhibit itself outwardly in his works of πρακτική and so it was διάκρισις to keep the two in harmony so that the monk could progress towards union with God. Deceit and deceitful behaviour had no part in this new life, since if the inner and outer life were not in harmony, even if his works were good they would belie his inner state. A further pair of διάκρισις sayings reinforces this need to harmonise conduct and speech with the interior life:

> (Abba Isaiah) said, "Whoever lives with his brother deceitfully will not escape sadness of καρδία."[134]

> He also said, "Whoever says one thing and has another evil one in his καρδία, his worship is worthless. [cf. James 1:26] Therefore do not attach yourself to such a man so that you are not soiled by his defiling venom."[135]

When the monk's interior life and exterior behaviour were at odds with each other it had a destructive psychological (sadness of heart) and spiritual (futile worship) impact on him as well as a damaging effect on those around him. To live without integrity and balance was to build a life on an unstable foundation of untruth and contradictions instead of on the truth of God. If the monk was to advance spiritually and be edifying to others, he needed to strive for a purity that reached through every aspect of his life and

---

[132]   GSC 10.157; PE 2.45.1.2 p552. See also: Budge 2.442a.
[133]   GSC 10.158. See also: GSC 21.61; PE 2.45.1.3 p552; Budge 2.442b.
[134]   GSC 10.29.
[135]   GSC 10.30.

behaviour, a purity that was rooted in God's truth and reached out to know him more fully. With διάκρισις he was able to make that integrity a reality.

It is apparent then, that just as διάκρισις was central to the conduct of the monk's inner life and search for union with God, so was it essential in the conduct of his life towards others. The teacher / disciple relationship, the place where διάκρισις was learnt, was built on διάκρισις, without it the relationship could not function or enable monks to pursue their goals. The way monks treated others was also governed by διάκρισις. It provided them with sound judgment in their dealings with others but kept them from being judgmental. When monks needed to evaluate how to respond to others, διάκρισις gave them the ability to encourage and edify. When confronted by people and situations that threatened their search for purity and union with God, it provided them with the means to determine how to act to defend these. Διάκρισις also enabled them to consider the wider implications of situations and of their behaviour so that the purity of the monastic community was preserved. Their whole lives, within and without, could be brought into harmony so that they became, as it were, 'salt and light' (Matthew 5:13-14) to those around them as they sought to be united with God.

CONCLUSION

In examining διάκρισις in this material, I have come to appreciate the opinions of Dingjan and Lienhard, but in view of this study it seems more likely that the monastic understanding of διάκρισις was developed from a broader understanding of biblical διάκρισις than they suggest. For example, although Dingjan notes that διάκρισις πνευμάτων is only one specific expression of διάκρισις in Scripture, he suggests a progressive development in the monastic understanding of διάκρισις, which may be summarised as beginning with the biblical charism of διάκρισις πνευμάτων, which evolved into διάκρισις λογισμῶν and finally into διάκρισις πρακτικῶν.[1] In his book, *Discretio*, Dingjan develops these ideas considering Cassian and later monastic writers, arguing that *discretio* / διάκρισις became a means of interior examination and debate developed from the charism of διάκρισις πνευμάτων into general gift of discernment required by all.[2] He also concludes that for Cassian the discernment of one's thoughts and of spirits is the same thing.[3] Lienhard[4] has also noted the fact that in the *Apophthegmata Patrum* there is no reference to διάκρισις πνευμάτων. He has suggested that there is no reason to doubt that the concept of διάκρισις / *discretio* did not derive from the older διάκρισις πνευμάτων. However, it seems more likely that the concept of διάκρισις among the Egyptian monks was a development of the biblical charism of διάκρισις πνευμάτων *and* the wider concept of διάκρισις found in Scripture generally. Διάκρισις remained for them a spiritual gift, but one that was more broadly applied than the extraordinary or occasional gift of

---

[1] F. Dingjan, 'La discrétion dans les apophtegmes des Pères', *Angelicum* 39 (1962), pp. 403-15 (esp. pp. 407-408); discernment of spirits, thoughts and practical matters respectively.

[2] F. Dingjan, *Discretio: Les origines patristiques et monastiques de la doctrine sur la prudence chez saint Thomas d'Aquin* (Assen: Van Gorcum, 1967).

[3] *Ibid.* pp. 26-29.

[4] Lienhard, '"Discernment of Spirits" in the Early Church', p. 521.

διάκρισις πνευμάτων; it was a gift that was used to govern every aspect of the monk's life, behaviour and thought. The use of διάκρισις for self-examination,[5] determining how to behave towards others,[6] weighing words[7] and distinguishing between good and evil ideas[8] is entirely biblical, as is acquiring a realistic opinion of oneself[9] and the transformation and renewal of the νοῦς.[10] The monastic understanding of διάκρισις / *discretio* and its use was very fluid and it was left to Cassian to develop and systematise the teaching on it.[11] However, among the Egyptian monks there was a radical internalisation of the concept of demonic attack so that the influence of demons took on a more interior psychological dimension than an exterior attack, as suggested by διάκρισις πνευμάτων, but they did not entirely lose this latter sense in the process.[12] Thus, while there is a demonstrable shift away from a spiritual gift of διάκρισις πνευμάτων to an independent and unqualified gift of διάκρισις, this was not so much a departure from the biblical concept of διάκρισις as an attempt to apply it practically. The monastic understanding of διάκρισις, therefore, did not develop specifically from the biblical διάκρισις πνευμάτων, but from a general understanding of biblical διάκρισις of which διάκρισις πνευμάτων was a part.

The biblical use of the διάκρισις word-group builds on the Classical usage in two ways. Firstly, the New Testament introduces the sense of wavering or doubting, that is hesitating between two contrasting ideas or opinions with the implied need to choose what is right.[13] Secondly, διάκρισις comes to express a spiritual critical faculty by which it is possible to develop the spiritual life.[14] Although the spiritual gift of διάκρισις πνευμάτων[15] is an important aspect of διάκρισις in Scripture, it would be too limiting to say that it is the only way in which διάκρισις is understood in Scripture.

The secular philosophical background to this development can be found in Plotinus. However, his use of the διάκρισις word-group reflects his concern to describe the nature of the universe and union with the One rather

---

[5] 1 Cor. 11:28-31.

[6] Jas 2:4 (cf. Jas 3:17).

[7] 1 Cor. 14:29.

[8] Heb. 5:14.

[9] Rom. 12:3.

[10] Rom. 12:2.

[11] Dingjan ('La discrétion' p. 405, n.10) also notes this and that Cassian's doctrine was hardly surpassed until the 12th century.

[12] See p. 159.

[13] See p. 9.

[14] See p. 11.

[15] 1 Cor. 12:10.

than any 'religious' or moral sense.[16] His influence, then, on the monastic understanding of διάκρισις and the development of Christian theology in Late Antiquity is indirect, through the impact of his philosophical thought and particularly his teaching on the union of the νοῦς with the One.

Although Origen drew on Plotinus' philosophical ideas (among others) to inform his own thinking and theological speculation, he remained a Christian, if Platonic, philosopher and theologian.[17] For Origen, secular philosophy was a means of discovering spiritual truth[18] and so he may be said to have used philosophy and developed his speculative theology using διάκρισις. In Origen's theology, the process by which the individual strives for union with God relies heavily on διάκρισις. For him, the acquisition of διάκρισις through practice and experience was essential for distinguishing good and evil, for nourishing the ψυχή and for discerning the mysteries of God, Scripture, the spiritual realm and the self.[19] Origen's understanding of διάκρισις shifts its usage further, towards a mystical theology technical term and places it at the centre of the mystical search for union with God.

Evagrius, renowned for his own διάκρισις,[20] took this concept further and, even though he rarely uses the word-group, διάκρισις can be said to be at the centre of his understanding of monastic spirituality.[21] That understanding is systematic and philosophical; he is more concerned (although far from exclusively concerned) about the inner life and the νοῦς gaining its ultimate goal, γνῶσις of God, than he is with practical and physical considerations. Given his stress on the work of the νοῦς in achieving γνῶσις of and union with God, and his understanding that such γνῶσις is the purpose of human existence, it is significant that he makes the νοῦς the *locus operandi* of διάκρισις.[22] This places διάκρισις at the centre of human existence, in the highest spiritual and intellectual level of being which reflects God's image. Thus διάκρισις emerges as the sense by which the νοῦς can know God, that is, the highest spiritual and intellectual human faculty that intuitively knows God and what is right without the need to analyse or reason. Furthermore, for Evagrius, διάκρισις is more fully endowed in union with God[23] and so the closer the monk comes to that union, the more intimate his knowledge of God and his will, and therefore the more instinctively he makes choices in accordance with God's will and

---

[16] See pp. 22-23.
[17] See pp. 26-28.
[18] See pp. 23-28.
[19] See pp. 31-33, 36-38.
[20] See pp. 39-40.
[21] See pp. 43, 48, 74.
[22] See pp. 43-44, 48-50, 54, 73-74.
[23] See pp. 45-47.

nature. Thus διάκρισις becomes increasingly intuitive as it is learnt and developed.

Cassian bridges the gap between these theological and philosophical considerations and the practical application of διάκρισις found in the *Apophthegmata Patrum*. However, his intellectual approach presents *discretio* as a reasoning faculty; more an intellectual exercise than the intuitive one found in Evagrius. Nevertheless, he suggests that, as the monk becomes more advanced in his use of *discretio*, it develops from being used as a reasoning faculty to an intuitive one.[24] *Discretio* comes to embrace both properties, the intuitive element developing from the reasoning element without loss of the latter, but with progressively less dependence on reason as the monk grows more experienced in *discretio* and closer to God. In both Cassian and the apophthegms, *discretio* / διάκρισις is presented both as a *virtus* and a practical discipline, so that it becomes a bridge between the inner and outer life of the monk, directing both and facilitating their integration.[25] Thus while *discretio* / διάκρισις is an intuitive knowing operating within the purified νοῦς it also has a practical application in the life of the monk at every level. Διάκρισις in its most advanced state is, then, a perceptiveness, beyond sense-perception, assumption or the need to analyse information, by which the monk is able to know increasingly by intuition how best to act or react in a given situation. The nature of διάκρισις thus becomes a technical term for perception beyond intellection and an essential property of the spiritual life. The monk fully endowed with διάκρισις so knows God that he intuitively knows what is of God and right under God.

Origen, Evagrius and Cassian, then, provide the theological background to how διάκρισις was understood, but the primary concern in the *Apophthegmata Patrum* is to demonstrate the practical application of διάκρισις. The apophthegms portray διάκρισις as a balance of analysis and reason with a view to practice. Every aspect of the inner and outer life is subjected to the critical examination of διάκρισις, and decisions and choices are made in the light of the knowledge and information gained through using διάκρισις. As such διάκρισις very often comes across, as in Cassian, as a function of the reasoning mind. At times it appears highly introspective and intense and in some respects a philosophical approach to faith, as in Evagrius.

This apparently introspective and philosophical approach is mitigated in a number of ways by the practical bias of the apophthegms. Διάκρισις was used experimentally by the first generation of monks to evaluate different attempts to seek God and find the best and most effective;[26] a natural

---

24   See pp. 91, 96, 106, 121.
25   See pp. 84-85, 87, 110-11, 140-41.
26   See pp. 143-44.

practical step in the development of monastic spirituality from biblical and received theology. The suggested introspective nature of διάκρισις is balanced by its use to discern how best to help and encourage others,[27] not being judgmental towards them,[28] following the golden rule[29] and being aware, not only of the validity of different monastic ways of life,[30] but also of the different capabilities of individual monks.[31] The monk with διάκρισις was, then, not so entirely self-absorbed that he was unaware or unconcerned about the wider implications of his actions or the community around him.[32] Διάκρισις can therefore be seen as a reasoning faculty that discerns what practical steps should be taken to advance towards the spiritual goals of the individual and wider community.

Διάκρισις is sometimes described in the same terms as the work of the Holy Spirit in the believer's life, so that the two can become almost indistinguishable.[33] Like the Holy Spirit, διάκρισις guides the monk and enables him to interpret Scripture,[34] so that he is free from impurity and ignorance and so capable of achieving his goals. Διάκρισις is a means of gaining knowledge, ultimately of God himself, and in union with God the monk fully knows both himself and God. He also uses it to discern the spiritual origin and background to his experiences and to interpret spiritual revelations correctly.[35] This association of διάκρισις with Scripture and the Holy Spirit suggests an inherent danger of relying on the gift of διάκρισις rather than on God and his Holy Spirit. But for the repeated emphasis on dependence upon God, this would result in dependence upon reason rather than developing the more intuitive spiritual ability gained by knowing God more fully. This danger is avoided by the understanding that διάκρισις properly derives from a renunciation of the will and humble obedience to God.[36] Διάκρισις needs to be understood, then, as a Divine gift and the means by which the Holy Spirit achieves these various ends,[37] not as a replacement of the Holy Spirit. Διάκρισις is a God given intuitive spiritual critical faculty as well as an intellectual reasoning one.

For all that διάκρισις is a spiritual gift and not a purely human faculty, it remains an ability that needs to be discovered, acquired,[38] learnt[39] and

---

27   See pp. 214-18.
28   See pp. 202-11.
29   See p. 214.
30   See pp. 145-46.
31   See pp. 144, 164-65.
32   See pp. 221-22, 226.
33   See pp. 131-32.
34   See pp. 179-84.
35   See pp. 184-87.
36   See e.g. pp. 179-80, 190-91.
37   See p. 184.
38   See pp. 139, 178.

developed through experience,[40] as in Scripture.[41] The development of skill in διάκρισις can be compared to a skilled artisan who is able to exercise his craft apparently without effort or conscious thought because of his years of experience.[42] The apophthegms themselves can be seen as part of this process of learning διάκρισις, since they were meant to be read with διάκρισις.[43] However, this had a practical bias as anything learnt needed to be put into practice; as with Scripture[44] and divine revelations,[45] all information was used with διάκρισις to achieve the transformation of the individual. The mere possession of διάκρισις was regarded as insufficient; monks were expected to learn how to use it and to choose to use it.[46] However, this choosing to learn and use διάκρισις is in itself an act of διάκρισις and so at every level διάκρισις directed the monk on how to behave and how to be.[47]

With διάκρισις the monk was able to gain self-knowledge. This was a realistic self-assessment of his inner condition and capabilities that enabled him to direct his inner and outer life and practice in such a way that he was able to achieve union with God.[48] An important aspect of this was learning how not to sin, then overcoming temptation and finally overcoming and eradicating his underlying motivations to sin, understood as λογισμοί.[49] The immediate impression is that a monk saved himself by his own effort as he determinedly overcame sin, temptation and λογισμοί, and engaged in austere ascetic acts to bring his body under the control of his ψυχή. This would make the monastic view of salvation and union with God a human based activity with salvation by works and not by grace. However, self-will and dependence upon personal effort to attain the monastic goals was condemned[50] and, again, there are the frequent references to dependence upon God and the assurance of his forgiveness. Διάκρισις was thus used with God to gain God, not instead of God and the saving work of Christ.

Although διάκρισις directed the monk in how to live, this was not seen in legalistic terms; it was not simply a means of interpreting and making judgments based upon a perceived set of established rules. Διάκρισις was liberating as the monk gained confidence in the way of life he had

---

[39] See pp. 153, 189-202.

[40] See pp. 139, 143-44, 163-64.

[41] Heb. 5:14 (see p. 7).

[42] See pp. 113, 134-35, 153.

[43] See pp. 189, 194.

[44] See pp. 180-84.

[45] See pp. 186-87.

[46] See p. 153.

[47] See e.g. pp. 213-14.

[48] See pp. 175-78.

[49] See pp. 55-62, 93-99, 150-66, esp. p. 150.

[50] See e.g. p. 134.

discerned was best for him.[51] It enabled him to be flexible and adapt to changing circumstances,[52] showed him when to relax his disciplines,[53] how to avoid exhausting himself with excessive asceticism[54] or by struggling with too many λογισμοί at once,[55] how to remain calm when attacked by a λογισμός that would only grow worse if he dwelt on it[56] and how not to get so caught up in the detail of πρακτική that its purpose was lost.[57] Διάκρισις is not negative, then, rather it can be seen as a spiritual tool that could be used like a surgeon's knife, which is used both for examination and for cutting away anything unhealthy. This analogy is supported by Evagrius' use of medical language and theory, and the Classical use of διάκρισις to express the diagnosis of an illness and its crisis point.[58] Διάκρισις is used to diagnose spiritual 'sickness' (sin / λογισμοί) and to establish spiritual 'health' (purity); it marks the turning point between the two. Διάκρισις was used to purify, support and vivify the monk in his search for union with God, not restrict it.

The extensive comment on διάκρισις in the apophthegms indicates its perceived value in every aspect of the spiritual life of monks. It is said to summarise the work of the monk and govern all he does.[59] The foregoing analysis of apophthegms understood to relate to διάκρισις supports this sweeping generalisation. It was regarded as the heart of the entire framework of monastic life, thought, practice, vocation and objectives. It was essential to monks as they weighed λογισμοί, πρακτική, ἀρετή, Scripture and doctrine and their implications for their lives. They needed it to avoid deceit and error. It was central to the attainment of their goals (purity of heart / ἀπάθεια and union with / γνῶσις of God), enabled them to develop all the ἀρεταί and expressed their wholehearted commitment to attaining these. It helped them to focus on their present spiritual condition and strive for their goals without attempting to achieve those aims by their own will and efforts alone. Διάκρισις enabled monks to maintain the ἀρεταί and πρακτικαί necessary for their spiritual advancement, to guard against any loss of progress they had made[60] and was bound up with the key elements of these: obedience, work and humility. In any given situation διάκρισις was used to determine how to act for the best, usually for the

---

[51] See e.g. p. 223.
[52] See p. 145.
[53] See e.g. p. 149.
[54] See pp. 141-44.
[55] See pp. 155-56.
[56] See p. 162.
[57] See p. 144.
[58] See p. 58; cf. cutting off λογισμοί (*passim*) and διάκρισις as an axe (p. 153).
[59] See pp. 128-29.
[60] See pp. 136-37.

spiritual benefit of the individual concerned, but frequently for the benefit of others too.

Διάκρισις, then, lies at the centre of the monk's spirituality, guiding every aspect of his inner and outer life, keeping them in balance, harmony and integrity and focussed on seeking purity and union with God. Although διάκρισις is described as the supreme ἀρετή / *virtus* and, at times, as a work of πρακτική, it is presented as something beyond both. Cassian describes *discretio* as the supreme and controlling *virtus* from which all others derive[61] and almost as a practical discipline as well;[62] the same is said of διάκρισις in the apophthegms.[63] But there is a sense in which διάκρισις is neither and both because it stands on the border between the two and functions as a bridge or link between the inner and outer life, governing and directing both, and facilitating their integration.[64] Διάκρισις is beyond being an ἀρετή in that it is greater than all the ἀρεταί, which it governs and examines along with every other aspect of the monk's life. Whereas ἀνάπαυσις can be had too early and ἡσυχία can be had too much, nowhere is a monk described as having too much διάκρισις or too soon. Διάκρισις is thus more than a quality, it is an essential spiritual sense or faculty. Gregory the Great expresses this when he calls *discretio* a nose that can smell the difference between *virtutes* and sins.[65] It was a positive critical faculty not critical, sound judgment not judgmental. The modern concept of judgment and criticism tends towards the negative, but in the monastic understanding it was a positive faculty that enhanced the spiritual life and was never destructive when used properly. Διάκρισις represented a tool or ability used in every aspect of the monk's life that made the monastic life and search for purity and union with God possible and in that union διάκρισις was understood to be most fully endowed. Διάκρισις was thus intrinsic both to the process towards and the attainment of union with God.

Διάκρισις was therefore woven into every aspect of the monk's life and spirituality. It both expressed and facilitated his earnest desire to seek and know God in all his saving power. With constant practice it developed beyond a critical faculty of reason into an intuition derived from experience in the monastic life and above all from personal experience and closeness to God. It did not replace the work of the Holy Spirit or grace, but was used to make them a reality in the life of the monk. In the sayings of the Desert Fathers and their interpreters, Evagrius and Cassian, διάκρισις was

---

[61] See p. 84-85.
[62] See pp. 86, 109.
[63] See pp. 128-29, 140-41.
[64] See pp. 227-29.
[65] *Reg. past.* 1.11; 3.32. Gregory's *reg. past.* was highly influential in the Middle Ages as a practical handbook on discernment.

understood to be a charism essential to the conduct of the Christian life and also became a technical term in the mystical search for God as monks sought purity, knowledge of God and union with him.

APPENDIX 1

Scripture Verses Using Διάκρισις / *Discretio*

The following table of cross references contains all occurrences in Scripture and the Old Testament apocrypha of διάκρισις, *discretio* and their cognates along with the Hebrew and Coptic (where available) parallels.

Some Coptic words in the table are marked with a superscript letter. Those with superscript 'C' (^{C}) indicate that the text is that according to Crum's dictionary[1] and those with a superscript 'T' (^{T}) indicate that the text is that according Tattam.[2]

---

[1]   W.E. Crum, *A Coptic Dictionary* (Oxford: Clarendon Press, 2000 [1939]).

[2]   H. Tattam, *Duodecim Prophetarum Minorum Libros in Lingua Ægyptiaca vulgo Coptica seu Memphitica ex Manuscripto Parisensi Descriptos et cum Manuscripto Johannes Lee, J.C.D. Collatos* (Oxford: E typographeo Academico, 1836).

Text (Eng)	BHS	Definition	LXX/UBS	Definition	Vg	Definition	Coptic B	Definition	Coptic S	Definition
Ex 18.16	שׁפט	judge	διακρίνω	discern	iudico	judge	ⲛⲟⲩⲧϥ	settle	[different]ᶜ	—
Lv 10.10	בדל	separate	διαστέλλω	distinguish	discerno	discern	ⲟⲩⲱⲧ ⲉⲃⲟⲗ	separate out	ⲡⲱⲣϫ ⲛ̄–ᶜ	divide between
Lv 24.12	פרשׁ	make distinct	διακρίνω	discern	iubeo	decree	ϯϩⲁⲡ	give judgment	—	—
Dt 33.7	רב	strive / contend	διακρίνω	discern	pugno	dispute	ⲇⲓⲁⲕⲣⲓⲛⲓⲛ	—	ϫⲓ ϩⲁⲡᶜ	go to law
2Sam 19.35	ידע (v36)	know	γινώσκω (v36)	know	discerno	discern	—	—	ⲉⲓⲙⲉ	know
1Kgs 3.9	שׁפט	judge	διακρίνω	discern	discerno	discern	—	—	—	—
1Kgs 3.11	שׁמע משׁפט	hear judgment	εἰσακούω	perceive	discerno	discern	—	—	—	—
1Chr 26.29	שׁפט	judge	διακρίνω	discern	iudico	judge	—	—	—	—
Est 8.12 E v9	—	—	διακρίνω	discern	—	—	—	—	—	—
Job 9.14	ריב	choose	διακρίνω	discern	loquor	speak	ⲇⲓⲁⲕⲣⲓⲛⲓⲛ	examine	—	—
Job 12.11	בחר	examine	διακρίνω	discern	diiudico	decide	ⲫⲟⲧϩⲉⲧ	examine	ⲙⲟⲩⲟⲩⲧᶜ	examine
Job 15.5	ריב	choose	διακρίνω	discern	imitor	imitate	ⲇⲓⲁⲕⲣⲓⲛⲓⲛ	—	ϭⲱⲃⲉᶜ	change to
Job 21.22	שׁפט	judge	διακρίνω	discern	iudico	judge	ϯϩⲁⲡ	give judgment	—	—
Job 23.10	בחן	examine	διακρίνω	discern	probo	test	ⲇⲓⲁⲕⲣⲓⲛⲓⲛ	—	—	—
Job 37.16	מפלשׂ	(uncertain)	διάκρισις	discernment	semita	path	ⲟⲩⲱⲧϥ ⲉⲃⲟⲗ	separate out	ⲙⲓⲛⲉᶜ	quality
Ps 43.1	ריב	contend	δικάζω (42.1)	decide	discerno (42.1)	discern	ϭⲓ ⲙ̄ⲡϣⲓϣ	take vengeance	ⲣ ϩⲁⲡ	go to law
Ps 50.4	דין	judge	διακρίνω (49.4)	discern	discerno (49.4)	discern	ϯϩⲁⲡ	give judgment	ⲇⲓⲁⲕⲣⲓⲛⲉ	—
Ps 68.14	פרשׂ (68.15)	spread out	διαστέλλω (67.15)	distinguish	discerno (67.15)	discern	ⲉϣⲱϣ ⲉϫⲛ	appointed over	ⲡⲱⲣϫ ⲉϩⲣⲁⲓ ⲉϫⲛ	divide
Ps 82.1	שׁפט	judge	διακρίνω (81.1)	discern	diiudico (81.1)	decide	ϯϩⲁⲡ	give judgment	ⲭⲛⲟⲩ (81.1)	question
Prov 25.1	—	—	ἀδιάκριτος	unwavering	—	—	—	—	ⲁϫⲛⲙⲉⲉⲩⲉ	lit. without thought
Prov 31.9	דין	judge	διακρίνω	discern	iudico	judge	—	—	—	—
Eccles 3.18	ברר	test	διακρίνω	discern	probo	test	—	—	—	—
Jer 15.10	דין	judge	διακρίνω	discern	discordia	disagreement	ⲫⲟⲧϩⲉⲧ	examine	ⲇⲓⲁⲕⲣⲓⲛⲉᶜ	examine
Ezek 20.35	שׁפט	judge	διακρίνω	discern	iudico	judge	ϭⲓ ϩⲁⲡ	go to law	—	—

Text (Eng)	BHS	Definition	LXX/UBS	Definition	Vg	Definition	Coptic B	Definition	Coptic S	Definition
Ezek 20.36	שׁפט	judge	διακρίνω	discern	iudicium	discretion	ϭⲓ ϩⲁⲡ	go to law	ϫⲓ ϩⲁⲡᶜ	go to law
Ezek 34.17	שׁפט	judge	διακρίνω	discern	iudico	judge	ϯϩⲁⲡ	give judgment	---	---
Ezek 34.20	שׁפט	judge	διακρίνω	discern	iudico	judge	ϯϩⲁⲡ	give judgment	---	---
Ezek 44.24	שׁפט	judge	διακρίνω	discern	iudico	judge	ϯϩⲁⲡ	give judgment	---	---
Joel 3.2	שׁפט (4.2)	judge	διακρίνω (4.2)	discern	discepto	dispute	ϭⲓ ϩⲁⲡ	go to law	---	---
Joel 3.12	שׁפט (4.12)	judge	διακρίνω (4.12)	discern	iudico	judge	ϯϩⲁⲡ	give judgment	---	---
Zech 3.7	דין	judge	διακρίνω	discern	iudico	judge	ϯϩⲁⲡ or ⲇⲓⲁⲕⲣⲓⲛⲓⲛᶜ	give judgment	ϭⲱ ϩⲓϫⲛ-ᶜ	wait upon?
4Macc 1.14	---	---	διακρίνω	discern	---	---	---	---	---	---
Wis 9.12	---	---	διακρίνω	discern	dispono	arrange	---	---	ⲕⲣⲓⲛⲉ	---
Ps Sol 17.43	---	---	διακρίνω	discern	---	---	---	---	---	---
Ep Jer 1.53	---	---	διακρίνω	discern	discerno Bar 6.53	discern	ϩⲁⲡ Bar 6.54	judgment	ⲇⲓⲁⲕⲣⲓⲛⲉ	judgment
Mt 16.3	---	---	διακρίνω	discern	diiudico (16.4)	decide	ⲥⲟⲙⲥ	consider	[omitted]	consider
Mt 21.21	---	---	διακρίνω	discern	haesito	hesitate	ϩⲏⲧ ⲃ	double minded	ϩⲏⲧ ⲥⲛⲁⲩ	be of two minds
Mk 11.23	---	---	διακρίνω	discern	haesito	hesitate	ϭⲓⲥⲁⲛⲓⲥ	doubt	ϩⲏⲧ ⲥⲛⲁⲩ	be of two minds
Lk 11.38 (Codex Bezae)	---	---	διακρίνω	discern	cogito (Bezae)	consider	---	---	---	---
Acts 4.32 (Codex Bezae)	---	---	διάκρισις	discernment	accusatio (Bezae)	accusation	---	---	---	---
Acts 10.20	---	---	διακρίνω	discern	dubito	doubt	ϩⲏⲧ ⲃ	double minded	ⲇⲓⲁⲕⲣⲓⲛⲉ	double minded
Acts 11.2	---	---	διακρίνω	discern	discepto	dispute	ϭⲓ ϩⲁⲡ	go to law	ϫⲓ ϩⲁⲡ	go to law
Acts 11.12	---	---	διακρίνω	discern	haesito	hesitate	ϩⲏⲧ ⲃ	double minded	ⲇⲓⲁⲕⲣⲓⲛⲉ	double minded
Acts 15.9	---	---	διακρίνω	discern	discerno	discern	ϭⲩⲃϯ	change	ⲡⲱⲣϫ	divide
Rom 4.20	---	---	διακρίνω	discern	haesito	hesitate	ϩⲏⲧ ⲃ	double minded	ϩⲏⲧ ⲥⲛⲁⲩ	be of two minds
Rom 14.1	---	---	διάκρισις	discernment	disceptatio	debate	ϩⲟⲓ	discussion	ϩⲟⲧϩⲧ	question

Text (Eng)	BHS	Definition	LXX/UBS	Definition	Vg	Definition	Coptic B	Definition	Coptic S	Definition
Rom 14.23	—		διακρίνω	discern	dicserno	discern	ⲍⲏⲧ ⲃ	double minded	ⲍⲏⲧ ⲥⲛⲁⲩ	be of two minds
1Cor 4.7	—		διακρίνω	discern	discerno	discern	ⲗⲁⲕⲣⲓⲛⲓⲛ		ⲗⲁⲕⲣⲓⲛⲉ	
1Cor 6.5	—		διακρίνω	discern	iudico	judge	ⲗⲁⲕⲣⲓⲛⲓⲛ		ⲗⲁⲕⲣⲓⲛⲉ	
1Cor 11.29	—		διακρίνω	discern	diiudico	decide	ⲗⲁⲕⲣⲓⲛⲓⲛ		ⲗⲁⲕⲣⲓⲛⲉ	
1Cor 11.31	—		διακρίνω	discern	diiudico	decide	ⲗⲁⲕⲣⲓⲛⲓⲛ		ⲙⲟⲩϣⲧ	examine
1Cor 12.10	—		διάκρισις	discernment	discretio	discernment	ⲃⲱⲗ	interpretation	ⲗⲁⲕⲣⲓⲥⲓⲥ	
1Cor 14.29	—		διακρίνω	discern	diiudico	decide	ⲗⲁⲕⲣⲓⲛⲓⲛ		ⲗⲁⲕⲣⲓⲛⲉ	
Heb 4.12	—		κριτικός	able to discern	discretor	discerner	ⲗⲁⲕⲣⲓⲛⲓⲛ	inquirer	ⲣⲉϥⲕⲣⲓⲛⲉ	
Heb 5.14	—		διάκρισις	discernment	discretio	discernment	ϣⲟⲧϫⲉⲧ	change	ⲗⲁⲕⲣⲓⲛⲉ	
Jas 1.6	—		διακρίνω (bis)	discern	haesito (bis)	hesitate	ⲍⲏⲧ ⲃ (bis)	double minded	ⲗⲁⲕⲣⲓⲛⲉ (bis)	
Jas 2.4	—		διακρίνω	discern	iudico	judge	ϣⲟⲃϯ	change	ϣⲟⲃϯ (ϣⲓⲃⲉ)	change
Jas 3.17	—		ἀδιάκριτος	unwavering	non iudico	not judge	ⲁⲧϯϩⲁⲡ	not judging	ⲗⲁⲕⲣⲓⲛⲉ	not judging
Jude 1.9	—		διακρίνω	discern	disputo	dispute	ϫⲱ ⲟⲩⲃⲉ	speak against	ϫⲓ ϩⲁⲡ	go to law
Jude 1.22	—		διακρίνω	discern	iudico	judge	ⲗⲁⲕⲣⲓⲛⲓⲛ		ϫⲓ ϩⲁⲡ (1.23)	go to law

Reference List of Διάκρισις / *Discretio* Apophthegms

The following table of cross references lists all the apophthegms in the Greek and Latin Systematic, Greek Alphabetical, Greek Anonymous, Bohairic and Sahidic Coptic Collections and Latin Apendices which either contain διάκρισις, *discretio*, ⲆⲒⲀⲔⲢⲒⲤⲒⲤ and their cognates or are found under a διάκρισις or *discretio* section heading along with their parallels in the anthology of Paul Evergetinos and Syriac Collection translated by Budge; some other parallels are noted in the final column.

Apophthegms marked with an asterisk (*) do not have a parallel in any of the collections considered in this study. The preparation of this table was greatly assisted by the work of Bousset and Regnault.[1] The number given to each apophthegm by Regnault is included to make it easier to compare this table with his.

---

[1]   W. Bousset, *Apophthegmata*, pp. 93-185; L. Regnault, *Les sentences des Pères du désert: Troisième recueil et tables*, pp. 201-308.

Apophthegm	Reg-nault no.	Section heading	Keyword(s)	Parallel references: Alph	GSC	Nau	VP 5	VP 3	VP 7	SP MD App	PE	Ch Am	Budge	Other
Antony 8	8		διάκρισις	cf. Poemen 106	10.1		5.10.1				3.31.1.1 p372		1.296	Antony ep. 6.106
Antony 12	12				10.2		5.10.2a				4.19.3.1-3 p341	Am16.1	2.56	Bars 413
Antony 13	13				10.3		5.10.2b				2.18.3.3 pp232-233	Am16.2		
Antony 16	16				10.4		5.10.3						2.114	
Antony 23	23				10.5		5.10.4				1.30.1.1 p434	Am17.1	2.246	
Arsenius 5	43				10.7		5.10.5						2.233	
Arsenius 12	50				10.8		5.10.6		7.32.6		4.42.1.6 p623		2.47	Bars 126
Arsenius 22	60				10.9		5.10.7				4.1.15.2 p28		2.397	
Arsenius 39	77				10.10		5.10.9	3.163a			4.37.4.1 p557		1.502	
Agathon 1	83				10.11; cf. 3.55-56		5.10.8	3.198	7.42.1		2.34.1.1 p434		1.280 2.524	Bars 261; 340; 342; 347; 458; Dorotheos doctr. 4.52
Agathon 5	87		διάκρισις (bis)		10.12		5.10.10	3.21			2.2.6.1 p56		1.183	
Agathon 8	90				10.13		5.10.11a							
Agathon 10	92				10.14		5.10.11b							
Agathon 14	96				10.15		5.10.12							
Agathon 19	101				10.16		5.10.13				2.35.1.1 p439		1.484	
Ammonas 4	116				10.20		5.10.16				1.44.3.1 p643	Ch53	1.447	Ammonas apoph. 4
Ammonas 11	123				10.116	249	5.10.81				1.42.2.3 p622		2.209	Ammonas apoph. 11
Achilles 1	124				10.18		5.10.14				4.47.1.1-5 p649		1.415	
Abraham 1	140				10.19		5.10.15	3.117			4.22.1.1.4 p369	Ch52	2.115	
Daniel 1	183				10.21						3.28.3.1 p532	Ch55	2.108	

Apophthegm	Regnault no.	Section heading	Keyword(s)	Parallel references:										
				Alph	GSC	Nau	VP 5	VP 3	VP 7	SP MD App	PE	Ch Am	Budge	Other
Daniel 4	186				10.22 cf. 10.140		5.10.17				2.15.17.3 p210	Cb54	1.99	
Daniel 6	188				10.23		5.10.18				4.50.1.1-3 p667	Cb56		cf. Dorotheos doctr. 11.121
Ephraim 3	215				10.26		5.10.21				3.26.8.2-8 pp309-310		1.322	
Eulogius 1	217		διάκρισις		8.4		5.8.4							
Euprepius 7	224			cf. Poemen 45; 139	10.24; cf. 4.94; 10.86	cf. 468	5.10.19; cf. 5.10.58			cf. MD 75	2.47.2.3 p574	Cb57	1.58 cf. 1.22 1.313 1.369	Bars 291; cf. Bars 698
Evagrius 6	232				1.4; 10.193; 17.35		5.1.4							Evagrius prak. 91; Socrates HE 4.23
Zeno 4	238				10.27		5.10.22				4.17.1.1-2 p312		1.315	
Theodore of Pherme 4	271				10.32		5.10.23				1.25.1.1 p351		2.96; 2.501	
Theodore of Pherme 8	275				10.34		5.10.25				3.36.4.1 p470		2.148 cf. 2.469	
Theodore of Pherme 10	277				10.33		5.10.24						2.149	
Theodore of Pherme 11	278				10.177				7.17.2		3.36.4.2-3 pp470-471			
Theodore of Pherme 16	283				10.35		5.10.26				1.41.1.3 p600		2.87	
Theodore of Eleutheropolis 1	301				10.153								2.19	
Theophilus 3	306		διακρίνω		4.76	162	5.4.63	3.56			2.24.6.1 p286		2.529	
John Kolobos 2	317				10.36		5.10.27				2.3.5.7 p89		2.70	
John Kolobos 7	322		διάκρισις		10.37		5.10.28						2.131	

Apophthegm	Regnault no.	Section heading	Keyword(s)	Parallel references:										
				Alph	GSC	Nau	VP 5	VP 3	VP 7	SP MD App	PE	Ch Am	Budge	Other
John Kolobos 12	327				11.40		5.11.14A	208			4.6.1.13 p137	Ch85; Am338.3	2.211	
John Kolobos 18	333		διακρίνω		11.41		5.11.15				4.41.3.1-6 pp618-619	Cb86	2.154	
John Kolobos 34	349		διάκρισις	cf. Poemen 46	1.13		5.1.8				cf. 3.11.2.1 p126	Am138.2; cf. Am333.1; Am407.2	2.128 cf. 2.118;	cf. Dorotheos doctr. 14.150; Evagrius gnos. 6
Isaac, Priest of the Cells 5	376				10.44		5.10.32				2.29.7.1 p370	Ch58		
Joseph of Panephysis 3	386				10.38		5.10.29				4.6.1.18-21 p138		2.210	Bars 432
Joseph of Panephysis 4	387				10.40		5.10.31				3.2.2.2 pp23-24		1.373	
Joseph of Panephysis 5	388				10.39		5.10.30							
James 4	398				10.111		5.10.77							
Isidore the Priest 4	412				10.41						3.29.3.1 p346		2.52	
Isidore the Priest 5	413				10.42						1.34.4.1 p507			
Isidore the Priest 6	414				10.43									
Cronius 1	435			1b= Poemen S18b	18.34	363	5.18.27 (i.e. VP 6.1.7)		7.37.4c	MD 16b	1.24.7.1 p347; 4.5.2.34 p100; 1b= 4.24.1.3b p419	Ch200	2.515	
Longinus 1	449				10.45		5.10.33				3.31.1.6 p372; 1a= 1.13.1.2 p188	Ch59	2.265	

Apophthegm	Reg-nault no.	Section heading	Keyword(s)	Parallel references:										
				Alph	GSC	Nau	VP 5	VP 3	VP 7	SP MD App	PE	Ch Am	Budge	Other
Macarius the Egyptian 20	473				20b= 10.139				7.38.2	MD 23	4.22.1.6 p369	20a= Am166.1	20= 1.232	Macarius *apoph.* *PG* 34.249 20b= *HL* 47.6; Bars 549
Macarius the Egyptian 23	476			cf. Anoub 1	23b= 10.47						3.25.1.1-3 p289	Am126.1; 214.2	1.446	Macarius *apoph.* *PG* 34.249-252; *HL* 9 (*PL* 74.357B-C)
Macarius the Egyptian 36	489				10.48		5.10.34		7.37.4a	MD 15; App 15d	2.42.2.1 p540	Ch60	2.206	Macarius *apoph.* *PG* 34.257; Evagrius *prak.* 93; Socrates, *HE* 4.23
Macarius the Egyptian 39	492 ·				39b= 10.181			3.127			2.44.1.1-2 pp549-550	Am211.2-213.2	1.186	Macarius *apoph.* *PG* 34.260
Moses 12	506				10.92		5.10.63		7.26.1		3.2.2.5 p24		1.368	
Matoes 1	513				7.16		5.7.11				3.31.1.16 p373		2.147	
Matoes 4	516				10.49		5.10.35				4.21.1 p363	Ch61	2.248	cf. Evagrius *prak.* 44
Matoes 12	524				10.179								1.142	
Megethius 4	538				10.165	238	5.10.105					Ch64	2.259	
Mius 2	540		διακριτικός		15.47		5.15.31	3.17			4.40.5.9-11 p611		2.169	
Mius 3	541				10.176		5.21.30 (i.e. VP 6.4.30)				1.1.4.1 p30		1.599	
Macarius the citizen 2	544				10.46-						4.49.1.1-2 p664			
Nicon 1	563		διάκρισις		16.30						2.46.4.4 p567			
Netras 1	564				10.50		5.10.36			App 18	2.18.3.8 p233	Ch62	2.410	

Apophthegm	Regnault no.	Section heading	Keyword(s)	Parallel references: Alph	GSC	Nau	VP 5	VP 3	VP 7	SP MD App	PE	Ch Am	Budge	Other
Poemen 3	577				10.53		5.10.38							
Poemen 5	579				8.16		5.8.13	3.20			1.24.7.2 pp347-348		1.265	
Poemen 8	582				10.54		5.10.39	3.184			4.17.1.3-8 pp312-314		2.159	
Poemen 12	586				10.57		5.10.40				1.1.4.2 p30			
Poemen 15	589				10.58		5.10.41				2.28.7.2 p345		1.255 1.538 cf. 1.603	
Poemen 18	592				10.65		5.10.45				1.23.1.4 p332		1.294	
Poemen 20	594				10.59		5.10.42				4.6.1.1 p136		2.162 2.474	
Poemen 21	595				10.60		5.10.43				4.6.1.2 p136		2.163	
Poemen 22	596				10.66		5.10.46				4.44.1.1-5 p636		2.74	
Poemen 23	597				10.68		5.10.48				4.48.1.5 p654		1.608	
Poemen 24	598				10.71		5.10.49							
Poemen 25	599				10.72		5.10.50	3.183a						
Poemen 27	601				10.75; cf. 10.184		5.10.51				4.38.3.2 p568		2.145	
Poemen 28	602				10.81		5.10.55				2.47.2.1 p574		1.27 1.298	
Poemen 29	603				10.76		5.10.52		7.36.1		3.18.7.2 p230		2.66 2.237	
Poemen 31	605				10.61		5.10.44	3.45			2.18.3.1 p232		1.102	
Poemen 32	606		διακρίνω		11.58		5.11.22			MD 32	4.32.2.5 p515		1.273	
Poemen 33	607				10.82		5.10.56		7.36.4	MD 7			1.179	
Poemen 35	609		διάκρισις		1.20		5.1.12						1.367	
Poemen 40	614				10.83		5.10.57			MD 70			2.231	

Apophthegm	Reg-nault no.	Section heading	Keyword(s)	Parallel references: Alph	GSC	Nau	VP 5	VP 3	VP 7	SP MD App	PE	Ch Am	Budge	Other
Poemen 45	619			cf. Euprepius 7; Poemen 139	10.86; cf. 4.94; 10.24	cf. 468	5.10.58; cf. 5.10.19			cf. MD 75	cf. 2.47.2.3 p574	cf. Ch57	1.22 cf. 1.58 1.313 1.369	Bars 291; cf. Bars 698
Poemen 46	620			cf. John Kolobos 34	cf. 1.13		cf. 5.1.8				3.11.2.1 p126	cf. Am138.2; Am407.2	2.118 cf. 2.128	Dorotheos *doctr.* 14.150; Evagrius *gnos.* 6
Poemen 52	626		διάκρισις		10.88		5.10.59				3.31.1.2 p372		2.134	Ammonas *apoph.* 14
Poemen 54	628			cf. Ammoes 4	10.89		5.10.60			MD 80	1.42.2.1 p622		2.77 cf. 1.531	Dorotheos *doctr.* 5.63
Poemen 56	630				8.19		5.8.14b						2.139 2.193	
Poemen 60	634		διάκρισις		1.23		5.1.14			MD 8			cf. 2.341	
Poemen 63	637			Poemen S1; 164	8.18		5.8.14a	3.183b					1.297 2.144	
Poemen 67	641				10.91		5.10.62		7.25.3		1.30.1.2 p434		2.308	
Poemen 86	660				10.62						1.1.4.3 p30			Bars 371
Poemen 91	665				10.78		5.10.54			MD 82; App.5d	2.35.1.2 p439		1.456	
Poemen 93	667				10.63			3.57	7.1.5		3.30.1.1-3 p361		2.59	Dorotheos *doctr.* 10.109
Poemen 100	674				10.70								2.137	
Poemen 103	677				10.74									
Poemen 106	680		[Migne: *discretio*; Bousset: 'Diakrisis und Tapferkeit']	cf. Antony 8	cf. 10.1		cf. 5.10.1				cf. 3.31.1.1 p372		cf. 1.296	cf. Antony *ep.* 6.106
Poemen 118	692				10.67		5.10.47				2.38.5.1 p494		1.233	
Poemen 127	701				127b= 10.55					127b= MD 79	4.38.3.1 p568		127b= 2.287	
Poemen 128	702				10.56				7.27.2	MD 102			2.288	

Apophthegm	Regnault no.	Section heading	Keyword(s)	Parallel references:										
				Alph	GSC	Nau	VP 5	VP 3	VP 7	SP MD App	PE	Ch Am	Budge	Other
Poemen 134	708								7.22.2	MD 59; App 15e	1.45.1.37 p652		2.296	Dorotheos *doctr.* 7.86
Poemen 139	713			cf. Euprepius 7; Poemen 45	cf. 4.94; 10.24; 10.86	cf. 468	cf. 5.10.19; 5.10.58			MD 75	cf. 2.47.2.3 p574	cf. Ch57	1.369; cf 1.22; 1.58; 1.313	cf. Bars 291; 698
Poemen 145	719				10.64									
Poemen 149	723				10.87						3.13.7.10 p171		1.528	cf. Bars 500; 613
Poemen 151	725				10.85						1.20.3.7 p268			
Poemen 152	726				10.69						2.6.2.1 p111		1.629c	
Poemen 154	728		διακρίνω		5.8					MD 3	2.28.7.3 p345		2.253	
Poemen 164	738			Poemen S1; 63	8.18		5.8.14a	3.183b					1.297	
Poemen 168	742		διάκρισις (bis)		10.93		5.10.64						2.144	
Poemen 170	744									MD 21		Am37.2	1.546	
Poemen 177	751				10.77		5.10.53	3.79	7.7.3		4.47.1.6-8 p649			Dorotheos *doctr.* 10.109
Poemen 184	758				8.18		5.8.14a			App 4d	2.40.5.2 p524		2.166	
Poemen S1	967			Poemen 63; 164	8.18			3.183b			2.18.3.4 p233		1.297	
Poemen S2	968				10.90; cf. 5.9		5.10.61; cf. 5.5.9			App 4a-b			2.144; 1.388-389	
Poemen S18	982			S18b= Cronius 1b	S18b= 18.34b	S18a= 124; S18b= 363b	5.18.27b (i.e. VP 6.1.7b)				4.24.1.3 p419; S18b= 1.24.7.1b p347; 4.5.2.34b p100	S18b= Ch200b	S18a= 2.89; S18b= 2.515b	
Poemen S19	983				4.38		5.4.31E			App 4c	1.42.7.2 p632			
Pambo 2	763				10.94		5.10.65				3.2.2.6 p24		1.376	cf. HL 14

Apophthegm	Regnault no.	Section heading	Keyword(s)	Parallel references: Alph	GSC	Nau	VP 5	VP 3	VP 7	SP MD App	PE	Ch Am	Budge	Other
An Abba of Rome 1	799		διακριτικός	cf. Arsenius 36	10.110		5.10.76				4.46.1.1-16 pp643-644 cf. 4.46.1.17-21 p644		cf. 1.450	cf. Bars 191
Rufus 1	801				2.35						4.5.2.12 p97			
Sisoes 6	809				10.98		5.10.68			MD 27	4.6.1.5 p136		2.241 2.528	Dorotheos doctr. 13.141
Silvanus 5	860				10.99		5.10.69	3.55			2.3.5.2 p88		2.15	
Sarmatas 1	871				10.52						1.44.3.5 p644		1.610	
Sarah 4	887				10.107		5.10.73						2.525	
Sarah 5	888				10.108		5.10.74				3.25.1.4 p289		2.75	Bars 237
Syncletica 10	901				10.101		5.10.70: 5.21.24 (i.e. VP 6.4.24)							Vit. Syn. 37
Syncletica 12	903				10.104		5.10.71C							Vit. Syn. 79
Syncletica 13	904				10.103		5.10.71A-B							Vit. Syn. 64
Syncletica 14	905				10.106						1.30.1.5 p435			Vit. Syn. 26
Syncletica 15	906		διακρίνω		10.105		5.10.72							Vit. Syn. 100
Syncletica 17	908		διάκρισις		14.18		5.14.10							Vit. Syn. 101
Syncletica S10	1001				10.102		5.10.71							Vit. Syn. 40
Or 12	945				15.79	305; 659	5.15.61	3.78b	7.7.2b	App 15b		Ch135	1.506 2.90	
GSC prol. 11			διάκρισις		10.193; 17.35									
GSC 1.4		perfection		Evagrius 6			5.1.4							Evagrius prak. 91; Socrates HE 4.23
GSC 1.5		perfection		cf. Cassian 8	10.194		5.1.5							Evagrius prak. 95; HL 38.13; Socrates HE 4.23

Apophthegm	Regnault no.	Section heading	Keyword(s)	Parallel references:										
				Alph	GSC	Nau	VP 5	VP 3	VP 7	SP MD APP	PE	Ch Am	Budge	Other
GSC 1.13		perfection	διάκρισις	John Kolobos 34; cf. Poemen 46			5.1.8				cf. 3.11.2.1 p126	Am138.2; cf. Am333.1; Am407.2	2.128 cf. 2.118	cf. Dorotheos doctr. 14.150; Evagrius gnos. 6
GSC 1.20		perfection	διάκρισις	Poemen 35			5.1.12						1.367	
GSC 1.23		perfection	διάκρισις (bis)	Poemen 60			5.1.14			MD 8			2.193 cf.	
GSC 1.31		perfection	διάκρισις			253	5.1.21	3.153					2.341	
GSC 1.32		perfection	διάκρισις			225	5.1.22		7.16.2				2.53	
GSC 1.33		perfection	διακρίνω										1.596b	
GSC 2.35		ἡσυχία	διάκρισις	Rufus 1	21.62						4.5.2.12 p97		2.436 2.448b	
GSC 4.38		self-control	διακρίνω	Poemen S19			5.4.31E			App 4c	1.42.7.2 p632			
GSC 4.76		self-control	διακρίνω	Theophilus 3		162	5.4.63				2.24.6.1 p286		2.529	
GSC 4.94		self-control		cf. Euprepius 7; Poemen 45; 139	cf. 10.24; 10.86	468	cf. 5.10.19; 5.10.58			cf. MD 75	cf. 2.47.2.3 p574	cf. Ch57	1.313 cf. 1.22 1.58 1.369	cf. Bars 291; 698
GSC 5.4		fornication	διακριτικός				5.5.3-4							Cassian conf. 2.10 & 13
GSC 5.8		fornication		Poemen 154						MD 3	2.28.7.3 p345		2.253	
GSC 5.38		fornication	διάκρισις			185	5.5.33							
GSC 5.47		fornication	διάκρισις			50								
GSC 7.16		endurance		Matoes 1			5.7.11			App 16	3.31.1.16 p373		2.147	
GSC 8.4		ostentation	διάκρισις	Eulogius 1			5.8.4				3.26.8.2-8 pp309-310		1.322	
GSC 8.16		ostentation		Poemen 5			5.8.13	3.20			1.24.7.2 pp347-348		1.265	
GSC 8.18		ostentation		Poemen S1: 63; 164			5.8.14a	3.183b					1.297 2.144	

Parallel references: (columns Alph, GSC, Nau)

Apophthegm	Regnault no.	Section heading	Keyword(s)	Alph	GSC	Nau	VP 5	VP 3	VP 7	SP MD App	PE	Ch Am	Budge	Other
GSC 8.19		ostentation		Poemen 56			5.8.14b						2.139	
GSC 8.32		ostentation	διακρίνω			408								
GSC 9.11		non-judgment					5.9.8	3.100	7.39.2	MD 39	3.13.7.7 p170			
GSC 9.16		non-judgment	διακρίνω	cf. Mark the Egyptian 1		254	5.9.11; cf. 9.6				4.28.3.5-7 p489; cf. 4.28.3.1-4 pp488-489			
GSC 10.1		διάκρισις		Antony 8 cf. Poemen 106			5.10.1				3.3.11.1 p372		1.296	Antony *ep.* 6.106
GSC 10.2		διάκρισις		Antony 12			5.10.2a				4.19.3.1-3 p341	Am16.1	2.56	Bars 413
GSC 10.3		διάκρισις		Antony 13			5.10.2b				2.18.3.3 pp232-233	Am16.2		
GSC 10.4		διάκρισις		Antony 16			5.10.3				1.30.1.1 p434		2.114	
GSC 10.5		διάκρισις		Antony 23			5.10.4				3.19.3.1 p240	Am17.1	2.246	
GSC 10.6		διάκρισις				568								
GSC 10.7		διάκρισις		Arsenius 5			5.10.5		7.32.6		4.42.1.6 p623		2.233	Bars 126
GSC 10.8		διάκρισις		Arsenius 12			5.10.6				4.1.15.2 p28		2.47	
GSC 10.9		διάκρισις		Arsenius 22			5.10.7						2.397	
GSC 10.10		διάκρισις		Arsenius 39			5.10.9	3.163a			4.37.4.1 p557		1.502	
GSC 10.11		διάκρισις		Agathon 1	cf. 3.55-56		5.10.8	3.198	7.42.1		2.34.1.1 p434		1.280; 2.524	Bars 261; 340; 342; 347; 458; Dorotheos *doctr.* 4.52
GSC 10.12		διάκρισις	διάκρισις (*bis*)	Agathon 5			5.10.10	3.21			2.2.6.1 p56		1.183	
GSC 10.13		διάκρισις		Agathon 8			5.10.11a							
GSC 10.14		διάκρισις		Agathon 10			5.10.11b							
GSC 10.15		διάκρισις		Agathon 14			5.10.12							

Apophthegm	Reg-nault no.	Section heading	Keyword(s)	Parallel references: Alph	GSC	Nau	VP 5	VP 3	VP 7	SP MD App	PE	Ch Am	Budge	Other
GSC 10.16		διάκρισις		Agathon 19			5.10.13				2.35.1.1 p439		1.484	
GSC 10.17		διάκρισις												
GSC 10.18		διάκρισις		Achilles 1		1	5.10.14				4.47.1.1-5 p649		1.415	
GSC 10.19		διάκρισις		Abraham 1			5.10.15	3.117			4.22.1.1-4 p369	Ch52	2.115	
GSC 10.20		διάκρισις		Ammonas 4			5.10.16				1.44.3.1 p643	Ch53	1.447	Ammonas apoph. 4
GSC 10.21		διάκρισις		Daniel 1							3.28.3.1 p332	Ch55	2.108	
GSC 10.22		διάκρισις		Daniel 4	cf. 10.140		5.10.17				2.15.17.3 p210	Ch54	1.99	
GSC 10.23		διάκρισις		Daniel 6			5.10.18				4.50.1.1-3 p667	Ch56		cf. Dorotheos docr. 11.121
GSC 10.24		διάκρισις		Euprepius 7; cf. Poemen 45; 139	cf. 4.94; 10.86	cf. 468	5.10.19; cf. 5.10.58			cf. MD 75	2.47.2.3 p574	Ch57	1.58 cf. 1.22 1.313 1.369	Bars 291; cf. Bars 698
GSC 10.25		διάκρισις					5.10.20				3.31.1.5 p372			Evagrius prak. 15
GSC 10.26		διάκρισις		Ephraim 3			5.10.21							
GSC 10.27		διάκρισις		Zeno 4			5.10.22				4.17.1.1-2 p312			
GSC 10.28*		διάκρισις		cf. Poemen 36										
GSC 10.29*		διάκρισις												
GSC 10.30*		διάκρισις												
GSC 10.31*		διάκρισις												
GSC 10.32		διάκρισις		Theodore of Pherme 4			5.10.23						1.315	
GSC 10.33		διάκρισις		Theodore of Pherme 10			5.10.24				3.36.4.1 p470		2.148 cf.	
GSC 10.34		διάκρισις		Theodore of Pherme 8			5.10.25				1.25.1.1 p351		2.469 2.96 2.501	
GSC 10.35		διάκρισις		Theodore of Pherme 16			5.10.26				1.41.1.3 p600		2.87	

Apophthegm	Regnault no.	Section heading	Keyword(s)	Parallel references: Alph	GSC	Nau	VP 5	VP 3	VP 7	SP MD App	PE	Ch Am	Budge	Other
GSC 10.36		διάκρισις		John Kolobos 2			5.10.27	3.56			2.3.5.7 p89		2.70	
GSC 10.37		διάκρισις	διάκρισις	John Kolobos 7			5.10.28						2.131	
GSC 10.38		διάκρισις		Joseph of Panephysis 3			5.10.29				4.6.1.18-21 p138		2.210	Bars 432
GSC 10.39		διάκρισις		Joseph of Panephysis 5			5.10.30							
GSC 10.40		διάκρισις		Joseph of Panephysis 4			5.10.31				3.2.2.2 pp23-24		1.373	
GSC 10.41		διάκρισις		Isidore the Priest 4							3.29.3.1 p346			
GSC 10.42		διάκρισις		Isidore the Priest 5							1.34.4.1 p507			
GSC 10.43		διάκρισις		Isidore the Priest 6								Ch58		
GSC 10.44		διάκρισις		Isaac, Priest of the Cells 5			5.10.32				2.29.7.1 p370			
GSC 10.45		διάκρισις		Longinus 1			5.10.33				3.31.1.6 p372; 45a= 1.13.1.2 p188; 4.49.1.1-2 p664	Ch59	2.265	
GSC 10.46		διάκρισις		Macarius the citizen 2							3.25.1.3b p289	Am126.1; 214.2	1.446b	
GSC 10.47		διάκρισις		Macarius the Egyptian 23b; cf. Anoub 1										Macarius apoph. PG 34.252; HL 9 (PL 74.357B-C)
GSC 10.48		διάκρισις		Macarius the Egyptian 36			5.10.34		7.37.4a	MD 15; App 15d	2.42.2.1 p540	Ch60	2.206	Macarius apoph. PG 34.257; Evagrius prak. 93; Socrates HE 4.23
GSC 10.49		διάκρισις		Matoes 4			5.10.35				4.21.1 p363	Ch61	2.248	cf. Evagrius prak. 44
GSC 10.50		διάκρισις		Netras 1			5.10.36			App 18	2.18.3.8 p233	Ch62	2.410	

Apophthegm	Reg-nault no.	Section heading	Keyword(s)	Parallel references: Alph	GSC	Nau	VP 5	VP 3	VP 7	SP MD App	PE	Ch Am	Budge	Other
GSC 10.51		διάκρισις				391	5.10.37				3.2.2.4 p24	Ch63		
GSC 10.52		διάκρισις		Sarmatas 1							1.44.3.5 p644		1.610	
GSC 10.53		διάκρισις		Poemen 3			5.10.38							
GSC 10.54		διάκρισις		Poemen 8			5.10.39	3.184			4.17.1.3-8 pp312-314		2.159	
GSC 10.55		διάκρισις		Poemen 127b						MD 79	4.38.3.1b p568			
GSC 10.56		διάκρισις		Poemen 128									2.287	
GSC 10.57		διάκρισις		Poemen 12			5.10.40		7.27.2	MD 102	1.1.4.2 p30		2.288	
GSC 10.58		διάκρισις		Poemen 15			5.10.41				2.28.7.2 p345		1.255 1.538 cf. 1.603	
GSC 10.59		διάκρισις		Poemen 20			5.10.42				4.6.1.1 p136		2.162	
GSC 10.60		διάκρισις		Poemen 21			5.10.43				4.6.1.2 p136		2.474	
GSC 10.61		διάκρισις		Poemen 31			5.10.44	3.45			2.18.3.1 p232		2.163	
GSC 10.62		διάκρισις		Poemen 86							1.1.4.3 p30		1.102	Bars 371
GSC 10.63		διάκρισις		Poemen 93				3.57	7.1.5		3.30.1.1-3 p361		2.59	Dorotheos *doctr.* 10.109
GSC 10.64		διάκρισις		Poemen 145									1.528	
GSC 10.65		διάκρισις		Poemen 18			5.10.45				1.23.1.4 p332		1.294	
GSC 10.66		διάκρισις		Poemen 22			5.10.46				4.44.1.1-5 p636		2.74	
GSC 10.67		διάκρισις		Poemen 118			5.10.47				2.38.5.1 p494		1.233	
GSC 10.68		διάκρισις		Poemen 23			5.10.48				4.48.1.5 p654		1.608	
GSC 10.69		διάκρισις		Poemen 152							2.6.2.1 p111		1.629c	

Apophthegm	Reg-nault no.	Section heading	Keyword(s)	Parallel references: Alph	GSC	Nau	VP 5	VP 3	VP 7	SP MD App	PE	Ch Am	Budge	Other
GSC 10.70		διάκρισις		Poemen 100									2.137	
GSC 10.71		διάκρισις		Poemen 24			5.10.49						2.145	
GSC 10.72		διάκρισις		Poemen 25			5.10.50	3.183a			4.38.3.2 p568			
GSC 10.73		διάκρισις									4.38.3.3 p568			
GSC 10.74		διάκρισις		Poemen 103	cf. 10.184								1.27	
GSC 10.75		διάκρισις		Poemen 27			5.10.51				2.47.2.1 p574		1.298	
GSC 10.76		διάκρισις		Poemen 29			5.10.52		7.36.1		3.18.7.2 p230		2.237	
GSC 10.77		διάκρισις		Poemen 177			5.10.53	3.79	7.7.3		2.40.5.2 p524		1.456	Dorotheos *doctr.* 10.109
GSC 10.78		διάκρισις		Poemen 91			5.10.54			MD 82; App 5d	2.35.1.2 p439			
GSC 10.79		διάκρισις										cf. Am30.2		cf. Ammonas *ep.* 12
GSC 10.80*		διάκρισις		Poemen 28			5.10.55						2.66	
GSC 10.81		διάκρισις		Poemen 33			5.10.56			MD 7			1.179	
GSC 10.82		διάκρισις		Poemen 40			5.10.57		7.36.4	MD 70			2.231	
GSC 10.83		διάκρισις												
GSC 10.84		διάκρισις				661					2.28.7.11 p347		1.577	
GSC 10.85		διάκρισις		Poemen 151							1.20.3.7 p268			
GSC 10.86		διάκρισις		Poemen 45; cf. Euprepius 7; Poemen 139	cf. 4.94; 10.24	cf. 468	5.10.58; cf. 5.10.19			cf. MD 75	cf. 2.47.2.3 p574	cf. Ch57	1.22 cf. 1.58 1.313 1.369	Bars 291; cf. Bars 698
GSC 10.87		διάκρισις		Poemen 149							3.13.7.10 p171			cf. Bars 500; 613
GSC 10.88		διάκρισις	διάκρισις	Poemen 52			5.10.59				3.31.1.2 p372		2.134	Ammonas *apoph.* 14
GSC 10.89		διάκρισις		Poemen 54			5.10.60			MD 80	1.42.2.1 p622		2.77 cf. 1.531	Dorotheos *doctr.* 5.63
GSC 10.90		διάκρισις		Poemen S2	cf. 5.9		5.10.61 cf. 5.5.9			App 4a-b			1.388-389	

Apophthegm	Reg-nault no.	Section heading	Keyword(s)	Parallel references: Alph	GSC	Nau	VP 5	VP 3	VP 7	SP MD App	PE	Ch Am	Budge	Other
GSC 10.91		διάκρισις		Poemen 67			5.10.62		7.25.3		1.30.1.2 p434		2.308	
GSC 10.92		διάκρισις		Moses 12			5.10.63		7.26.1		3.2.2.5 p24		1.368	
GSC 10.93		διάκρισις		Poemen 168			5.10.64			MD 21		Am37.2	1.546	
GSC 10.94		διάκρισις		Pambo 2			5.10.65				3.2.2.6 p24		1.376	cf. *HL* 14
GSC 10.95		διάκρισις				383	5.10.66				1.30.1.3 p434			
GSC 10.96		διάκρισις				662	5.10.67				1.18.1.1 p231			*Hl. Ep. Laus.* 3
GSC 10.97		διάκρισις				384					1.45.1.52 p654		1.488	
GSC 10.98		διάκρισις		Sisoes 6			5.10.68			MD 27	4.6.1.5 p136		2.241 2.528	Dorotheos *doctr.* 13.141
GSC 10.99		διάκρισις		Silvanus 5			5.10.69	3.55			2.3.5.2 p88		2.15	
GSC 10.100		διάκρισις	διάκρισις, διακριτικός, ἀδιάκριτος			217	5.10.85				1.21.1.2 p285			cf. Cassian *conf.* 2.13.4-12
GSC 10.101		διάκρισις		Syncletica 10			5.10.70; 5.21.24 (i.e. VP 6.4.24)							*Vit. Syn.* 37
GSC 10.102		διάκρισις		Syncletica S10			5.10.71							
GSC 10.103		διάκρισις		Syncletica 13			5.10.71A-B							*Vit. Syn.* 40
GSC 10.104		διάκρισις		Syncletica 12			5.10.71C							*Vit. Syn.* 64
GSC 10.105		διάκρισις	διακρίνω	Syncletica 15			5.10.72							*Vit. Syn.* 79
GSC 10.106		διάκρισις		Syncletica 14										*Vit. Syn.* 100
GSC 10.107		διάκρισις		Sarah 4			5.10.73				1.30.1.5 p435		2.525	*Vit. Syn.* 26
GSC 10.108		διάκρισις		Sarah 5			5.10.74						2.75	Bars 237
GSC 10.109		διάκρισις					5.10.75				3.25.1.4 p289 4.38.3.4 p568			
GSC 10.110		διάκρισις	διακριτικός	An Abba of Rome 1 cf. Arsenius 36			5.10.76				4.46.1.1-16 pp643-644 cf. 4.46.1.17-21 p644		cf. 1.450	cf. Bars 191

Apophthegm	Reg-nault no.	Section heading	Keyword(s)	Parallel references: Alph	GSC	Nau	VP 5	VP 3	VP 7	SP MD App	PE	Ch Am	Budge	Other
GSC 10.111		διάκρισις					5.10.77						2.52	
GSC 10.112		διάκρισις		James 4		216	5.10.78				4.47.1.9-11 pp649-650		2.502-503	
GSC 10.113		διάκρισις				247	5.10.79							
GSC 10.114		διάκρισις				86					2.3.4.3 p88			
GSC 10.115		διάκρισις				248	5.10.80							
GSC 10.116		διάκρισις		Ammonas 11		249	5.10.81				1.42.2.3 p622		2.209	Ammonas *apoph.* 11
GSC 10.117		διάκρισις				250	5.10.82				1.40.4.1 p576		2.141	
GSC 10.118		διάκρισις				446								
GSC 10.119		διάκρισις				251	5.10.83							
GSC 10.120		διάκρισις				252a	5.10.84a				4.38.3.5a p568			
GSC 10.121		διάκρισις				252b	5.10.84b				4.38.3.5b p568			
GSC 10.122				This apophthegm does not exist. Guy (*Recherches*, pp. 150-51; *Les Apophtegmes des Pères*, SC 474, p. 97, n. 1) made a mistake in his numeration and chose not to correct it to avoid confusion.										
GSC 10.123		διάκρισις				218	5.10.86				4.6.1.11 p137		1.277a	
GSC 10.124		διάκρισις				125	5.10.87						1.302	
GSC 10.125		διάκρισις				219	5.10.88				4.6.1.10 p137			
GSC 10.126		διάκρισις				83:220	5.10.89						1.126a 2.453a	
GSC 10.127		διάκρισις				221	5.10.90		7.19.6				1.125d 2.451	
GSC 10.128		διάκρισις							7.30.1	App 11				
GSC 10.129*		διάκρισις												
GSC 10.130		διάκρισις						3.180	7.28.1					
GSC 10.131		διάκρισις							7.25.4					
GSC 10.132*		διάκρισις												
GSC 10.133*		διάκρισις												

Apophthegm	Regnault no.	Section heading	Keyword(s)	Parallel references:										
				Alph	GSC	Nau	VP 5	VP 3	VP 7	SP MD App	PE	Ch Am	Budge	Other
GSC 10.134		διάκρισις				24							134a= 1.126b 2.453b 134b= 1.338 1.500c	
GSC 10.135		διάκρισις	ἀδιακρισία		134b= 11.82	134b= 650								
GSC 10.136		διάκρισις	διακρίνω			222	5.10.91	3.178			1.18.1.2 p231		2.31a	
GSC 10.137		διάκρισις				223	5.10.92				1.15.4.3 p210		2.41	
GSC 10.138		διάκρισις				404					4.19.3.4-6 pp341-342		1.300	
GSC 10.139		διάκρισις		Macarius the Egyptian 20b		224	5.10.93		7.38.2b	MD 23b	4.22.1.6b p369	cf. Am166.1	cf. 1.232	Macarius apoph. PG 34.249 HL 47.6; Bars 549
GSC 10.140*		διάκρισις		cf. Daniel 4	cf. 10.22		cf. 5.10.17							
GSC 10.141*		διάκρισις									cf. 2.15.17.3 p210	cf. Ch54	cf. 1.99	cf. Evagrius *prak.* 56
GSC 10.142*		διάκρισις												
GSC 10.143		διάκρισις												
GSC 10.144		διάκρισις								MD 98	1.28.2.4 p404		1.167	
GSC 10.145		διάκρισις				J674					1.25.1.3 p351			
GSC 10.146		διάκρισις				J675								
GSC 10.147		διάκρισις				385	5.10.94		7.41.2		3.29.3.3 p346		2.98	cf. Evagrius *schol.* 14 in Ps. 88:26.
GSC 10.148		διάκρισις				226	5.10.95				2.37.1.2 p461		2.250	
GSC 10.149		διάκρισις				227	5.10.96				4.8.6.2.4 p224		2.158 1.249	

Apophthegm	Reg-nault no.	Section heading	Keyword(s)	Parallel references:										
				Alph	GSC	Nau	VP 5	VP 3	VP 7	SP MD App	PE	Ch Am	Budge	Other
GSC 10.150		διάκρισις				229	5.10.97	3.5			3.3.1.1 p66		2.14	
GSC 10.151		διάκρισις				645					4.15.1.3 p298			
GSC 10.152		διάκρισις				230	5.10.98						2.19	
GSC 10.153		διάκρισις		Theodore of Eleutheropolis 1										
GSC 10.154		διάκρισις				231	5.10.99	3.48	7.1.3		2.18.3.6 p233			
GSC 10.155		διάκρισις				232; 474a	5.10.100				2.37.1.9 p462			
GSC 10.156		διάκρισις				233	5.10.101						2.442a	
GSC 10.157		διάκρισις									2.45.1.2 p552		2.442b	
GSC 10.158		διάκρισις			158a= 21.61						2.45.1.3 p552		1.33b	
GSC 10.159		διάκρισις				386	5.10.102							
GSC 10.160		διάκρισις			21.64	234	5.10.103							
GSC 10.161		διάκρισις				235	5.10.103A		7.28.3		1.24.2.1 p340; 4.5.2.31 p99			
GSC 10.162		διάκρισις				236	5.10.103B		7.19.5b		1.13.1.3 p188			
GSC 10.163		διάκρισις				237	5.10.103C				1.38.4.2 pp541-542		1.340	
GSC 10.164		διάκρισις				646	5.10.104				4.17.1.9 p314		2.79	
GSC 10.165		διάκρισις		Megethius 4		238	5.10.105					Ch64	2.259	
GSC 10.166		διάκρισις			166a= 11.103	239; 166a= 272	5.10.106; 166a=166 5.11.45					Ch65	2.486	
GSC 10.167		διάκρισις				240	5.10.107					Ch66		
GSC 10.168		διάκρισις				241	5.10.108	3.179	7.26.3		4.7.3.2 p200	Ch67		
GSC 10.169		διάκρισις				387					3.31.1.15 p373	Ch68	1.390a	

Apophthegm	Regnault no.	Section heading	Keyword(s)	Parallel references:										
				Alph	GSC	Nau	VP 5	VP 3	VP 7	SP MD APP	PE	Ch Am	Budge	Other
GSC 10.170		διάκρισις				242	5.10.109				3.3.1.2 pp66-67	Ch69		
GSC 10.171		διάκρισις				394					4.6.10.7-8 p191		2.62	
GSC 10.172		διάκρισις				243	5.10.110				1.41.1.1 p600	Ch70	2.422	
GSC 10.173		διάκρισις				111; 244	5.10.111				3.29.3.2 p346	Ch71	2.504	Bars 693
GSC 10.174		διάκρισις				245	5.10.112					Ch72	2.17	
GSC 10.175		διάκρισις				246	5.10.113						1.535	
GSC 10.176		διάκρισις		Mius 3			5.21.30 (i.e. VP 6.4.30)				1.1.4.1 p30		1.599	
GSC 10.177		διάκρισις		Theodore of Pherme 11					7.17.2		3.36.4.2-3 pp470-471		2.149	
GSC 10.178		διάκρισις	διακρίνω			70					4.5.2.23 p99			
GSC 10.179		διάκρισις											1.142	
GSC 10.180		διάκρισις		Matoes 12		634					1.42.2.2 p622		2.214	cf. Evagrius prak. 23
GSC 10.181		διάκρισις		Macarius the Egyptian 39b				3.127b			2.44.1.2 pp549-550	Am213.2	1.186b	Macarius apoph. PG 34.260
GSC 10.182		διάκρισις				J665					1.44.3.9 p645			
GSC 10.183		διάκρισις				26					1.15.4.1 p210			
GSC 10.184*		διάκρισις		cf. Poemen 27	cf. 10.75		cf. 5.10.51				cf. 2.47.2.1 p574		cf. 1.27 1.298	
GSC 10.185		διάκρισις				396					3.33.7.4 p427			
GSC 10.186		διάκρισις				395				cf. MD 41				
GSC 10.187		διάκρισις				397; 615b					3.2.8.30 p48		cf. 1.497	
GSC 10.188*		διάκρισις												
GSC 10.189		διάκρισις											1.258	

Apophthegm	Reg-nault no.	Section heading	Keyword(s)	Parallel references:										
				Alph	GSC	Nau	VP 5	VP 3	VP 7	SP MD App	PE	Ch Am	Budge	Other
GSC 10.190		διάκρισις				59								
GSC 10.191		διάκρισις				228	5.10.114				4.15.1.1 p298		1.250	
GSC 10.192		διάκρισις				55	5.10.115						2.483a	cf. Evagrius *prak.* prol. 2, 4 & 5; Cassian *inst.* 1.3, 4 & 11; Dorotheos *doctr.* 1.19
GSC 10.193		διάκρισις		Evagrius 6	1.4; 17.35		5.1.4							Evagrius *prak.* 91; Socrates *HE* 4.23
GSC 10.194		διάκρισις		cf. Cassian 8	1.5		5.1.5							Evagrius *prak.* 95; *HL* 38.13; Socrates *HE* 4.23
GSC 11.40		vigilance		John Kolobos 12			5.11.14A	208			4.6.1.13 p137	Ch85 Am338.3	2.211	
GSC 11.41		vigilance	διακρίνω	John Kolobos 18			5.11.15				4.41.3.1-6 pp618-619	Ch86	2.154	
GSC 11.58		vigilance	διακρίνω	Poemen 32			5.11.22			MD 32	4.32.2.5 p515		1.273	
GSC 11.63		vigilance		Poemen S18a		124	5.11.25				4.24.1.3a p419		2.89	
GSC 11.82		vigilance			10.134b	24b; 650							1.338; 1.500c	
GSC 11.103		vigilance			10.166a	239a; 272	5.10.106a; 5.11.45					Ch65a	2.486a	
GSC 12.14		prayer				635								
GSC 14.18		obedience	διάκρισις	Syncletica 17			5.14.10	3.17			4.40.5.9-11 p611		2.169	*Vit. Sym.* 101
GSC 15.47		humility		Mius 2			5.15.31							
GSC 15.78		humility				304; 658	5.15.60		7.13.12	App 15a	1.45.1.65 p655; 3.38.1.42 p500	Ch134	2.463	
GSC 15.79		humility		Or 12		305; 659	5.15.61	3.78b	7.7.2b	App 15b		Ch135	1.506; 2.90	

Apophthegm	Reg- nault no.	Section heading	Keyword(s)	Parallel references: Alph	GSC	Nau	VP 5	VP 3	VP 7	SP MD App	PE	Ch Am	Budge	Other
GSC 15.129		humility	διακρίνω			129a= 519; 129b= 520					129a= 1.5.6.5 p88; 129b= 4.37.4.9-18 pp558-559			
GSC 15.130		humility	διακρίνω			527					1.3.2.2 p69			
GSC 16.30		endurance	διάκρισις	Nicon 1							2.46.4.4 p567			
GSC 17.35		ἀγάπη		Evagrius 6	1.4; 10.193		5.1.4							Evagrius *prak.* 91; Socrates *HE* 4.23
GSC 18.34		visions		Cronius 1; 34b= Poemen S18b		363	5.18.27 (i.e. VP 6.1.7)		7.37.4c	MD 16b	1.24.7.1 p347; 4.5.2.34 p100; 34b= 4.24.1.3b p419	Ch200	2.515	
GSC 20.15		virtuous living				132A	5.20.11 (i.e. VP 6.3.11)					Ch268		
GSC 20.22		virtuous living				67; 490		3.130	7.15.2		1.45.1.83 pp658-659		2.2	
GSC 21.9		apophthegms in brief	διάκρισις			93	5.23.6 (i.e. SP 6)			SP 6 (i.e. VP 5.23.6)	3.31.1.3 p372		2.313	
GSC 21.25		apophthegms in brief	διάκρισις			106	5.23.20 (i.e. SP 20)			SP 20 (i.e. VP 5.23.20)	3.31.1.4 p372		2.201 2.281	
GSC 21.61		apophthegms in brief			10.158a						2.45.1.3a p552		2.442b	
GSC 21.62		apophthegms in brief	διακρίνω		1.33								2.448b	
GSC 21.64		apophthegms in brief			10.159	386	5.10.102							
Nau 1	1002				10.17									

Apophthegm	Regnault no.	Section heading	Keyword(s)	Parallel references: Alph	GSC	Nau	VP 5	VP 3	VP 7	SP MD App	PE	Ch Am	Budge	Other
Nau 24	1024				10.134 24b= 11.82	24b= 650							24= 1.126b 2.453b 24b= 1.338 1.500c	
Nau 26	1026				10.183							1.15.4.1 p210			
Nau 50	1050	magistrates	διάκρισις		5.47					App 16				
Nau 53	1053	magistrates	ἀδιακρίτως											
Nau 55	1055	monastic habit			10.192		5.10.115				1.33.4.6 p488		2.483a	cf. Evagrius *prak.* prol. 2, 4 & 5; Cassian *inst.* 1.3, 4 & 11; Dorotheos *doctr.* 1.19
Nau 59	1059	monastic habit			10.190									
Nau 67	1067	monastic habit			20.22	490		3.130	7.15.2		1.45.1.83 pp658-659		2.2	
Nau 70	1070	monastic habit	διακρίνω		10.178						4.5.2.23 p99			
Nau 83	1083	monastic habit			10.126	220	5.10.89				2.3.4.3 p88		1.126a 2.453a	
Nau 86	1086	monastic habit			10.114									
Nau 93	1093	monastic habit	διάκρισις		21.9		5.23.6 (i.e. SP 6)			SP 6 (i.e. VP 5.23.6)	3.31.1.3 p372		2.313	
Nau 106	1106	monastic habit	διάκρισις		21.25		5.23.20 (i.e. SP 20)			SP 20 (i.e. VP 5.23.20)	3.31.1.4 p372		2.201 2.281	
Nau 111	1111	monastic habit			10.173	244	5.10.111				3.29.3.2 p346	Ch71	2.504	
Nau 124	1124	monastic habit		Poemen S18a	11.63		5.11.25				4.24.1.3a p419		2.89	Bars 693
Nau 125	1125	monastic habit			10.124		5.10.87						1.277a	

Apophthegm	Reg-nault no.	Section heading	Keyword(s)	Parallel references: Alph	GSC	Nau	VP 5	VP 3	VP 7	SP MD App	PE	Ch Am	Budge	Other
Nau 132A	1132A	anchorites	διακρίνω		20.15		5.20.11 (i.e. VP 6.3.11)					Ch268		
Nau 162	1162	self-control	διακρίνω	Theophilus 3	4.76		5.4.63				2.24.6.1 p286		2.529	
Nau 185	1185	fornication	διάκρισις		5.38		5.5.33							
Nau 216	1216	διάκρισις			10.112		5.10.78				4.47.1.9-11 pp649-650		2.502-503	
Nau 217	1217	διάκρισις	διάκρισις ἀδιάκριτος		10.100		5.10.85				1.21.1.2 p285			cf. Cassian conf 2.13.4-12
Nau 218	1218	διάκρισις			10.123		5.10.86				4.6.1.11 p137			
Nau 219	1219	διάκρισις			10.125		5.10.88				4.6.1.10 p137		1.302	
Nau 220	1220	διάκρισις			10.126	83	5.10.89						1.126a 2.453a	
Nau 221	1221	διάκρισις			10.127		5.10.90		7.19.6				1.125d 2.451 2.31a	
Nau 222	1222	διάκρισις	διάκρισις ἀδιακρισία		10.135		5.10.91							
Nau 223	1223	διάκρισις			10.136		5.10.92	3.178			1.18.1.2 p231		2.41	
Nau 224	1224	διάκρισις			10.138		5.10.93				4.19.3.4-6 pp341-342		1.300	
Nau 225	1225	διάκρισις	διάκρισις		1.32		5.1.22						1.596b 2.436 2.158	
Nau 226	1226	διάκρισις			10.148		5.10.95				2.37.1.2 p461			
Nau 227	1227	διάκρισις			10.149		5.10.96				4.8.6.2-4 p224		1.249	
Nau 228	1228	διάκρισις			10.191		5.10.114				4.15.1.1 p298		1.250	
Nau 229	1229	διάκρισις			10.150		5.10.97	3.5			3.3.1.1 p66		2.14	
Nau 230	1230	διάκρισις			10.152		5.10.98							
Nau 231	1231	διάκρισις			10.154		5.10.99	3.48	7.1.3		2.18.3.6 p233			

Apophthegm	Reg-nault no.	Section heading	Keyword(s)	Parallel references: Alph	GSC	Nau	VP 5	VP 3	VP 7	SP MD App	PE	Ch Am	Budge	Other
Nau 232	1232	διάκρισις			10.155	474a	5.10.100				2.37.1.9 p462			
Nau 233	1233	διάκρισις			10.156		5.10.101							
Nau 234	1234	διάκρισις			10.160		5.10.103						1.33b	
Nau 235	1235	διάκρισις			10.161		5.10.103A		7.28.3		1.24.2.1 p340; 4.5.2.31 p99			
Nau 236	1236	διάκρισις			10.162		5.10.103B		7.19.5b		1.13.1.3 p188			
Nau 237	1237	διάκρισις			10.163		5.10.103C				1.38.4.2 pp541-542		1.340	
Nau 238	1238	διάκρισις		Megethius 4	10.165		5.10.105					Ch64	2.259	
Nau 239	1239	διάκρισις			10.166; 239a= 11.103	239a= 272	5.10.106; 239a= 5.11.45					Ch65	2.486	
Nau 240	1240	διάκρισις			10.167		5.10.107					Ch66		
Nau 241	1241	διάκρισις			10.168		5.10.108	3.179	7.26.3		4.7.3.2 p200	Ch67		
Nau 242	1242	διάκρισις			10.170		5.10.109				3.3.1.2 pp66-67	Ch69		
Nau 243	1243	διάκρισις			10.172		5.10.110				1.41.1.1 p600	Ch70	2.422	
Nau 244	1244	διάκρισις			10.173	111	5.10.111				3.29.3.2 p346	Ch71	2.504	Bars 693
Nau 245	1245	διάκρισις			10.174		5.10.112					Ch72	2.17	
Nau 246	1246	διάκρισις			10.175		5.10.113						1.535	
Nau 247	1247	διάκρισις			10.113		5.10.79							
Nau 248	1248	διάκρισις			10.115		5.10.80							
Nau 249	1249	διάκρισις		Ammonas 11	10.116		5.10.81				1.42.2.3 p622		2.209	Ammonas apoph. 11
Nau 250	1250	διάκρισις			10.117		5.10.82						2.141	
Nau 251	1251	διάκρισις			10.119		5.10.83							
Nau 252	1252	διάκρισις			10.120-121		5.10.84				4.38.3.5 p568			
Nau 253	1253	διάκρισις			1.31		5.1.21	3.153	7.16.2				2.53	

Apophthegm	Regnault no.	Section heading	Keyword(s)	Parallel references: Alph	GSC	Nau	VP 5	VP 3	VP 7	SP MD App	PE	Ch Am	Budge	Other
Nau 254	1254	non-judgment	διακρίνω	cf. Mark the Egyptian 1	9.16; cf. 9.6		5.9.11				4.28.3.5-7 p489; cf. 4.28.3.14 pp488-489			
Nau 272	1272	vigilance			10.166a; 11.103	239a	5.10.106a; 5.11.45					Ch65a	2.486a	
Nau 304	1304	humility			15.78	658	5.15.60		7.13.12	App 15a	1.45.1.65 p655; 3.38.1.42 p500	Ch134	2.463	
Nau 305	1305	humility		Or 12	15.79	659	5.15.61	3.78b	7.7.2b	App 15b		Ch135	1.506 2.90	
Nau 363	1363	visions		Cronius 1 363b= Poemen S18b	18.34		5.18.27 (i.e. VP 6.1.7)		7.37.4c	MD 16b	1.24.7.1 p347; 4.5.2.34 p100; 363b= 4.24.1.3b p419	Ch200	2.515	
Nau 383	1383	visions			10.95		5.10.66				1.30.1.3 p434			
Nau 384	1384	visions			10.97						1.45.1.52 p654		1.488	
Nau 385	1385	visions			10.147		5.10.94		7.41.2		3.29.3.3 p346		2.250	
Nau 386	1386	visions			10.159; 21.64		5.10.102							
Nau 387	1387	visions			10.169						3.31.1.15 p373	Ch68	1.390a	
Nau 391	1391	visions			10.51		5.10.37				3.2.2.4 p24	Ch63		
Nau 394	1394	visions			10.171						4.6.10.7-8 p191		2.62	
Nau 395	1395	visions			10.186					cf. MD 41			cf. 1.497	
Nau 396	1396	visions			10.185						3.33.7.4 p427			

Apophthegm	Reg-nault no.	Section heading	Keyword(s)	Parallel references:										
				Alph	GSC	Nau	VP 5	VP 3	VP 7	SP MD App	PE	Ch Am	Budge	Other
Nau 397	1397	visions			10.187	615b					3.2.8.30 p48			
Nau 404	1404	visions			10.137						1.15.4.3 p210			
Nau 408	1408	visions			8.32									
Nau 417	1417	visions	διάκρισις? sc. as PE			cf. 503				App 13	2.49.2.2 p592			
Nau 446	1446	visions			10.118						1.40.4.1 p576			
Nau 451	1451	visions	διακριτικός					3.26			1.37.1.1 pp527-528			
Nau 468	1468	fornication		cf. Euprepius 7; Poemen 45; 139	4.94; cf. 10.24; 10.86		cf. 5.10.19; 5.10.58			cf. MD 75	cf. 2.47.2.3 p574	cf. Ch57	1.313 cf. 1.22 1.58 1.369	cf. Bars 291; 698
Nau 474	1474	fornication			474a= 10.155	474a= 232	474a= 5.10.100				474a= 2.37.1.9 p462			
Nau 490	1490		ἀδιάκριτος? sc. as PE		20.22	67		3.130	7.15.2		1.45.1.83 pp658-659		2.2	
Nau 519	1519	compunction			15.129a						1.5.6.5 p88			
Nau 520	1520	compunction	διακρίνω? sc. as GSC		15.129b						4.37.4.9-18 pp558-559			
Nau 527	1527	compunction	διακρίνω? sc. as GSC		15.130						1.3.2.2 p69			
Nau 568	1568	compunction			10.6						3.19.3.1 p240			
Nau 615	1615				615b= 10.187	615b= 397					615b= 3.2.8.30 p48			
Nau 634	1634				10.180						1.42.2.2 p622		2.214	cf. Evagrius prak. 23

Apophthegm	Regnault no.	Section heading	Keyword(s)	Parallel references:										
				Alph	GSC	Nau	VP 5	VP 3	VP 7	SP MD App	PE	Ch Am	Budge	Other
Nau 635	1635		διάκρισις? (GSC = διορατικός)		12.14									
Nau 641	1641		διάκρισις? (PE= ἀδιαφορέω)											
Nau 645	1676										3.29.3.5-20 pp346-348			
Nau 646	1677				10.151						4.15.1.3 p298			
					10.164		5.10.104				4.17.1.9 p314		2.79	
Nau 650	1681				10.134b; 11.82	24b							1.338 1.500c	
Nau 658	1690				15.78	304	5.15.60		7.13.12	App 15a	1.45.1.65 p655; 3.38.1.42 p500	Ch134	2.463	
Nau 659	1691			Or 12	15.79	305	5.15.61	3.78b	7.7.2b	App 15b		Ch135	1.506	
Nau 661	1693				10.84						2.28.7.11 p347		2.90	
Nau 662	1694				10.96		5.10.67				1.18.1.1 p231		1.577	
J665	1665				10.182						1.44.3.9 p645			HL Ep. Laus. 3
J674	1674				10.145									
J675	1675				10.146								2.98	cf. Evagrius schol. 14 in Ps. 88:26.
VP 5.1.4		perfection		Evagrius 6	1.4; 10.193; 17.35									Evagrius prak. 91; Socrates HE 4.23
VP 5.1.5		perfection		cf. Cassian 8	1.5; 10.194									Evagrius prak. 95; HL 38.13; Socrates HE 4.23
VP 5.1.8		perfection	discretio	John Kolobos 34; cf. Poemen 46	1.13						cf. 3.11.2.1 p126	Am138.2; cf. Am333.1; Am407.2	2.128 cf. 2.118	cf. Dorotheos doctr. 14.150; Evagrius gnos. 6

Apophthegm	Reg-nault no.	Section heading	Keyword(s)	Parallel references: Alph	GSC	Nau	VP 5	VP 3	VP 7	SP MD App	PE	Ch Am	Budge	Other
VP 5.1.12		perfection	*discretio*	Poemen 35	1.20								1.367	
VP 5.1.14		perfection	*discretio; discerno*	Poemen 60	1.23					MD 8			2.193 cf. 2.341	
VP 5.1.21		perfection			1.31	253		3.153	7.16.2				2.53	
VP 5.1.22		perfection	*discretio*		1.32	225							1.596b 2.436	
VP 5.4.31E		self-control		Poemen S19	4.38					App 4c	1.42.7.2 p632			
VP 5.4.63		self-control	*discerno*	Theophilus 3	4.76	162					2.24.6.1 p286		2.529	
VP 5.5.3		fornication	*discretio*		5.4a									Cassian *conf.* 2.10
VP 5.5.4		fornication			5.4b									Cassian *conf.* 2.13
VP 5.5.33		fornication	*discretio*		5.38	185								
VP 5.7.11		patience		Matoes 1	7.16						3.31.1.16 p373		2.147	
VP 5.8.4		ostentation	*discretio*	Eulogius 1	8.4						3.26.8.2-8 pp309-310		1.322	
VP 5.8.13		ostentation		Poemen 5	8.16			3.20			1.24.7.2 pp347-348		1.265	
VP 5.8.14		ostentation		14a= Poemen S1; 63; 164 14b= Poemen 56	14a= 8.18 14b= 8.19			14a= 3.183b					14a= 1.297 2.144 14b= 2.139	
VP 5.9.8		non-judgment			9.11			3.100	7.39.2	MD 39	3.13.7.7 p170			
VP 5.9.11		non-judgment		cf. Mark the Egyptian 1	9.16; cf. 9.6	254					4.28.3.5-7 p489; cf. 4.28.3.14 pp488-489			
VP 5.10.1		*discretio*	*discretio*	Antony 8 cf. Poemen 106	10.1						3.31.1.1 p372		1.296	Antony *ep.* 6.106

Apophthegm	Reg-nault no.	Section heading	Keyword(s)	Parallel references: Alph	GSC	Nau	VP 5	VP 3	VP 7	SP MD App	PE	Ch Am	Budge	Other
VP 5.10.2		*discretio*		Antony 12-13	10.2-3						2a= 4.19.3.1-3 p341; 2b= 2.18.3.3 pp232-233	Am16.1-2	2a= 2.56	2a= Bars 413
VP 5.10.3		*discretio*		Antony 16	10.4								2.114	
VP 5.10.4		*discretio*		Antony 23	10.5						1.30.1.1 p434	Am17.1	2.246	
VP 5.10.5		*discretio*		Arsenius 5	10.7								2.233	Bars 126
VP 5.10.6		*discretio*		Arsenius 12	10.8				7.32.6		4.42.1.6 p623		2.47	
VP 5.10.7		*discretio*		Arsenius 22	10.9						4.1.15.2 p28		2.397	
VP 5.10.8		*discretio*		Agathon 1	10.11; cf. 3.55-56			3.198	7.42.1		2.34.1.1 p434		1.280 2.524	Bars 261; 340; 342; 347; 458; Dorotheos doctr. 4.52
VP 5.10.9		*discretio*		Arsenius 39	10.10			3.163a			4.37.4.1 p557		1.502	
VP 5.10.10		*discretio*	*discretio (bis)*	Agathon 5	10.12			3.21			2.2.6.1 p56		1.183	
VP 5.10.11		*discretio*		Agathon 8 and 10	10.13-14									
VP 5.10.12		*discretio*		Agathon 14	10.15									
VP 5.10.13		*discretio*		Agathon 19	10.16		5.10.13				2.35.1.1 p439		1.484	
VP 5.10.14		*discretio*		Achilles 1	10.18						4.47.1.1-5 p649		1.415	
VP 5.10.15		*discretio*		Abraham 1	10.19			3.117			4.22.1.1-4 p369	Ch52	2.115	
VP 5.10.16		*discretio*		Ammonas 4	10.20						1.44.3.1 p643	Ch53	1.447	Ammonas *apoph.* 4
VP 5.10.17		*discretio*		Daniel 4	10.22 cf. 10.140						2.15.17.3 p210	Ch54	1.99	
VP 5.10.18		*discretio*		Daniel 6	10.23						4.50.1.1-3 p667	Ch56		cf. Dorotheos doctr. 11.121

Apophthegm	Reg-nault no.	Section heading	Keyword(s)	Parallel references:										
				Alph	GSC	Nau	VP 5	VP 3	VP 7	SP MD App	PE	Ch Am	Budge	Other
VP 5.10.19		*discretio*		Euprepius 7; cf. Poemen 45; 139	10.24; cf. 4.94; 10.86	cf. 468	cf. 5.10.58			cf. MD 75	2.47.2.3 p574	Ch57	1.58 cf. 1.22 1.313 1.369	Bars 291; cf. Bars 698
VP 5.10.20		*discretio*			10.25						3.31.1.5 p372			Evagrius *prak.* 15
VP 5.10.21		*discretio*		Ephraim 3	10.26									
VP 5.10.22		*discretio*		Zeno 4	10.27						4.17.1.1-2 p312			
VP 5.10.23		*discretio*		Theodore of Pherme 4	10.32								1.315	
VP 5.10.24		*discretio*		Theodore of Pherme 10	10.33						3.36.4.1 p470		2.148 cf. 2.469	
VP 5.10.25		*discretio*		Theodore of Pherme 8	10.34						1.25.1.1 p351		2.96 2.501	
VP 5.10.26		*discretio*		Theodore of Pherme 16	10.35						1.41.1.3 p600		2.87	
VP 5.10.27		*discretio*		John Kolobos 2	10.36		5.10.27	3.56			2.3.5.7 p89		2.70	
VP 5.10.28		*discretio*	*discretio*	John Kolobos 7	10.37								2.131	
VP 5.10.29		*discretio*		Joseph of Panephysis 3	10.38						4.6.1.18-21 p138		2.210	Bars 432
VP 5.10.30		*discretio*		Joseph of Panephysis 5	10.39									
VP 5.10.31		*discretio*		Joseph of Panephysis 4	10.40			.			3.2.2.2 pp23-24		1.373	
VP 5.10.32		*discretio*		Isaac, Priest of the Cells 5	10.44						2.29.7.1 p370	Ch58		
VP 5.10.33		*discretio*		Longinus 1	10.45						3.31.1.6 p372; 33a= 1.13.1.2 p188	Ch59	2.265	

Apophthegm	Regnault no.	Section heading	Keyword(s)	Parallel references: Alph	GSC	Nau	VP 5	VP 3	VP 7	SP MD App	PE	Ch Am	Budge	Other
VP 5.10.34		*discretio*		Macarius the Egyptian 36	10.48				7.37.4a	MD 15; App 15d	2.42.2.1 p540	Ch60	2.206	Macarius *apoph.* PG 34.257; Evagrius *prak.* 93; Socrates *HE* 4.23
VP 5.10.35		*discretio*		Matoes 4	10.49						4.21.1 p363	Ch61	2.248	cf. Evagrius *prak.* 44
VP 5.10.36		*discretio*		Netras 1	10.50					App 18	2.18.3.8 p233	Ch62	2.410	
VP 5.10.37		*discretio*			10.51	391					3.2.2.4 p24	Ch63		
VP 5.10.38		*discretio*		Poemen 3	10.53									
VP 5.10.39		*discretio*		Poemen 8	10.54			3.184			4.17.1.3-8 pp312-314		2.159	
VP 5.10.40		*discretio*		Poemen 12	10.57						1.14.2 p30			
VP 5.10.41		*discretio*		Poemen 15	10.58						2.28.7.2 p345		1.255 1.538 cf. 1.603	
VP 5.10.42		*discretio*		Poemen 20	10.59						4.6.1.1 p136		2.162	
VP 5.10.43		*discretio*		Poemen 21	10.60						4.6.1.2 p136		2.163	
VP 5.10.44		*discretio*		Poemen 31	10.61			3.45			2.18.3.1 p232		1.102	
VP 5.10.45		*discretio*		Poemen 18	10.65						1.23.1.4 p332		1.294	
VP 5.10.46		*discretio*		Poemen 22	10.66						4.44.1.1-5 p636		2.74	
VP 5.10.47		*discretio*		Poemen 118	10.67						2.38.5.1 p494		1.233	
VP 5.10.48		*discretio*		Poemen 23	10.68						4.48.1.5 p654		1.608	
VP 5.10.49		*discretio*		Poemen 24	10.71									
VP 5.10.50		*discretio*		Poemen 25	10.72			3.183a			4.38.3.2 p568		2.145	

Apophthegm	Regnault no.	Section heading	Keyword(s)	Parallel references:										
				Alph	GSC	Nau	VP 5	VP 3	VP 7	SP MD App	PE	Ch Am	Budge	Other
VP 5.10.51		discretio		Poemen 27	10.75 cf. 10.184						2.47.2.1 p574		1.27 1.298	
VP 5.10.52		discretio		Poemen 29	10.76				7.36.1		3.18.7.2 p230		2.237	
VP 5.10.53		discretio		Poemen 177	10.77			3.79	7.7.3		2.40.5.2 p524			Dorotheos doctr. 10.109
VP 5.10.54		discretio		Poemen 91	10.78					MD 82; App 5d	2.35.1.2 p439		1.456	
VP 5.10.55		discretio		Poemen 28	10.81								2.66	
VP 5.10.56		discretio		Poemen 33	10.82				7.36.4	MD 7			1.179	
VP 5.10.57		discretio		Poemen 40	10.83					MD 70			2.231	
VP 5.10.58		discretio		Poemen 45; cf. Euprepius 7; Poemen 139	10.86; cf. 4.94; 10.24	cf. 468	cf. 5.10.19			cf. MD 75	cf. 2.47.2.3 p574	cf. Ch57	1.22 cf. 1.58 1.313 1.369	Bars 291; cf. Bars 698
VP 5.10.59		discretio	discretio	Poemen 52	10.88						3.31.1.2 p372		2.134	Ammonas apoph. 14
VP 5.10.60		discretio	discretio	Poemen 54	10.89					MD 80	1.42.2.1 p622		2.77 cf. 1.531	Dorotheos doctr. 5.63
VP 5.10.61		discretio		Poemen S2	10.90 cf. 5.9		cf. 5.5.9			App 4a-b			1.388-389	
VP 5.10.62		discretio		Poemen 67	10.91				7.25.3		1.30.1.2 p434		2.308	
VP 5.10.63		discretio		Moses 12	10.92				7.26.1		3.2.2.5 p24		1.368	
VP 5.10.64		discretio	discretio	Poemen 168	10.93					MD 21	3.2.2.6 p24	Am37.2	1.546	
VP 5.10.65		discretio	discretio	Pambo 2	10.94						1.30.1.3 p434		1.376	cf. Hl. 14
VP 5.10.66		discretio			10.95	383					1.18.1.1 p231			HL Ep. Laus. 3
VP 5.10.67		discretio			10.96	662								
VP 5.10.68		discretio		Sisoes 6	10.98					MD 27	4.6.1.5 p136		2.241 2.528	Dorotheos doctr. 13.141
VP 5.10.69		discretio		Silvanus 5	10.99			3.55			2.3.5.2 p88		2.15	

Apophthegm	Reg-nault no.	Section heading	Keyword(s)	Parallel references:										
				Alph	GSC	Nau	VP 5	VP 3	VP 7	SP MD App	PE	Ch Am	Budge	Other
VP 5.10.70		discretio		Syncletica 10	10.101		5.21.24 (i.e. VP 6.4.24)							Vit. Syn. 37
VP 5.10.71		discretio			10.102									Vit. Syn. 40
VP 5.10.71A		discretio		Syncletica S10	10.103a									Vit. Syn. 64
VP 5.10.71B		discretio		Syncletica 13a	10.103b									Vit. Syn. 64
VP 5.10.71C		discretio		Syncletica 13b	10.104									
VP 5.10.72		discretio	discerno	Syncletica 12	10.105									Vit. Syn. 79
VP 5.10.73		discretio		Syncletica 15	10.107								2.525	Vit. Syn. 100
VP 5.10.74		discretio		Sarah 4	10.108						3.25.1.4 p289		2.75	Bars 237
VP 5.10.75		discretio		Sarah 5	10.109						4.38.3.4 p568			
VP 5.10.76		discretio	discerno	An Abba of Rome 1 cf. Arsenius 36	10.110						4.46.1.1-16 pp643-644 cf. 4.46.1.17-21 p644		cf. 1.450	cf. Bars 191
VP 5.10.77		discretio		James 4	10.111	216							2.52	
VP 5.10.78		discretio			10.112						4.47.1.9-11 pp649-650		2.502-503	
VP 5.10.79		discretio			10.113	247								
VP 5.10.80		discretio			10.115	248								
VP 5.10.81		discretio		Ammonas 11	10.116	249					1.42.2.3 p622		2.209	Ammonas apoph. 11
VP 5.10.82		discretio			10.117	250								
VP 5.10.83		discretio			10.119	251							2.141	
VP 5.10.84		discretio			10.120-121	252					4.38.3.5 p568			
VP 5.10.85		discretio	discretio (bis); discretor		10.100	217					1.21.1.2 p285			cf. Cassian conf. 2.13.4-12
VP 5.10.86		discretio			10.123	218					4.6.1.11 p137			
VP 5.10.87		discretio			10.124	125							1.277a	
VP 5.10.88		discretio			10.125	219					4.6.1.10 p137		1.302	
VP 5.10.89		discretio			10.126	83; 220							1.126a 2.453a	

Apophthegm	Reg-nault no.	Section heading	Keyword(s)	Parallel references:										
				Alph	GSC	Nau	VP 5	VP 3	VP 7	SP MD App	PE	Ch Am	Budge	Other
VP 5.10.90		*discretio*			10.127	221			7.19.6				1.125d 2.451	
VP 5.10.91		*discretio*	*discretio (bis)*		10.135	222							2.31a	
VP 5.10.92		*discretio*			10.136	223		3.178			1.18.1.2 p231		2.41	
VP 5.10.93		*discretio*			10.138	224					4.19.3.4-6 pp341-342		1.300	
VP 5.10.94		*discretio*			10.147	385			7.41.2		3.29.3.3 p346		2.250	
VP 5.10.95		*discretio*			10.148	226					2.37.1.2 p461		2.158	
VP 5.10.96		*discretio*			10.149	227					4.8.6.2-4 p224		1.249	
VP 5.10.97		*discretio*			10.150	229		3.5			3.3.1.1 p66		2.14	
VP 5.10.98		*discretio*			10.152	230								
VP 5.10.99		*discretio*			10.154	231		3.48	7.1.3		2.18.3.6 p233			
VP 5.10.100		*discretio*			10.155	232; 474a					2.37.1.9 p462			
VP 5.10.101		*discretio*			10.156	233								
VP 5.10.102		*discretio*			10.159; 21.64	386								
VP 5.10.103		*discretio*			10.160	234							1.33b	
VP 5.10.103A		*discretio*			10.161	235			7.28.3		1.24.2.1 p340; 4.5.2.31 p99			
VP 5.10.103B		*discretio*			10.162	236			7.19.5b		1.13.1.3 p188			
VP 5.10.103C		*discretio*			10.163	237					1.38.4.2 pp541-542		1.340	
VP 5.10.104		*discretio*			10.164	646					4.17.1.9 p314		2.79	
VP 5.10.105		*discretio*		Megethius 4	10.165	238						Ch64	2.259	

Apophthegm	Regnault no.	Section heading	Keyword(s)	Parallel references:										
				Alph	GSC	Nau	VP 5	VP 3	VP 7	SP MD App	PE	Ch Am	Budge	Other
VP 5.10.106		discretio			10.166; 106a= 11.103	239; 106a= 272	106a= 5.11.45					Ch65	2.486	
VP 5.10.107		discretio			10.167	240						Ch66		
VP 5.10.108		discretio			10.168	241		3.179	7.26.3		4.7.3.2 p200	Ch67		
VP 5.10.109		discretio			10.170	242					3.3.1.2 pp66-67	Ch69		
VP 5.10.110		discretio			10.172	243					1.41.1.1 p600	Ch70	2.422	
VP 5.10.111		discretio			10.173	111; 244					3.29.3.2 p346	Ch71	2.504	Bars 693
VP 5.10.112		discretio			10.174	245						Ch72	2.17	
VP 5.10.113		discretio			10.175	246							1.535	
VP 5.10.114		discretio			10.191	228					4.15.1.1 p298		1.250	
VP 5.10.115		discretio			10.192	55							2.483a	cf. Evagrius *prak. prol.* 2, 4 & 5; Cassian *inst.* 1.3, 4 & 11; Dorotheos *doctr.* 1.19
VP 5.11.14A		sober living		John Kolobos 12	11.40			208			4.6.1.13 p137	Ch85; Am338.3	2.211	
VP 5.11.15		sober living		John Kolobos 18	11.41						4.41.3.1-6 pp618-619	Ch86	2.154	
VP 5.11.22		sober living	discerno	Poemen 32	11.58						4.32.2.5 p515		1.273	
VP 5.11.25		sober living		Poemen S18a	11.63	124				MD 32	4.24.1.3a p419		2.89	
VP 5.11.45		sober living			10.160a; 11.103	239a; 272	5.10.106a					Ch65a	2.486a	
VP 5.14.10		obedience	discretio	Syncletica 17	14.18									
VP 5.15.31		humility		Mius 2	15.47			3.17			4.40.5.9-11 p611		2.169	Vit. Sym. 101

Apophthegm	Reg-nault no.	Section heading	Keyword(s)	Parallel references: Alph	GSC	Nau	VP 5	VP 3	VP 7	SP MD App	PE	Ch Am	Budge	Other
VP 5.15.60		humility			15.78	304; 658			7.13.12	App 15a	1.45.1.65 p655; 3.38.1.42 p500	Ch134	2.463	
VP 5.15.61		humility		Or 12	15.79	305; 659		3.78b	7.7.2b	App 15b		Ch135	1.506 2.90	
VP 5.18.27 (i.e. VP 6.1.7)		visions		Cronius 1; 27b= Poemen S18b	18.34	363			7.37.4c	MD 16b	1.24.7.1b p347; 4.5.2.34b p100; 27b= 4.24.1.3b p419	Ch200	2.515	
VP 5.20.11 (i.e. VP 6.3.11)		holy men			20.15	132A						Ch268		Vit. Syn. 37
VP 5.21.24 (i.e. VP 6.4.24)		7 chapters of Moses etc.		Syncletica 10	10.101		5.10.70							
VP 5.21.30 (i.e. VP 6.4.30)		7 chapters of Moses etc.		Mius 3	10.176						1.1.4.1 p30		1.599	
VP 5.23.6 (i.e. SP 6)		sententiae	discretio		21.9	93				SP 6 (i.e. VP 5.23.6)	3.31.1.3 p372		2.313	
VP 5.23.20 (i.e. SP 20)		sententiae	discretio		21.25	106				SP 20 (i.e. VP 5.23.20)	3.31.1.4 p372		2.201 2.281	
VP 3.5					10.150	229	5.10.97				3.3.1.1 p66		2.14	
VP 3.17				Mius 2	15.47		5.15.31				4.40.5.9-11 p611		2.169	
VP 3.20			discerno	Poemen 5	8.16		5.8.13				1.24.7.2 pp347-348		1.265	
VP 3.21				Agathon 5	10.12		5.10.10				2.2.6.1 p56		1.183	
VP 3.26						451					1.37.1.1 pp527-528			
VP 3.45				Poemen 31	10.61		5.10.44				2.18.3.1 p232		1.102	

Apophthegm	Reg-nault no.	Section heading	Keyword(s)	Parallel references: Alph	GSC	Nau	VP 5	VP 3	VP 7	SP MD App	PE	Ch Am	Budge	Other
VP 3.48					10.154	231	5.10.99		7.1.3		2.18.3.6 p233			
VP 3.55				Silvanus 5	10.99		5.10.69				2.3.5.2 p88		2.15	
VP 3.56				John Kolobos 2	10.36		5.10.27				2.3.5.7 p89		2.70	
VP 3.57				Poemen 93	10.63				7.1.5		3.30.1.1-3 p361		2.59	Dorotheos doctr. 10.109
VP 3.75			discretio											
VP 3.78				78b= Or 12	78b= 15.79	78b= 305; 659	78b= 5.15.61		78b= 7.7.2b	78b= App 15b		78b= Ch135	78b= 1.506 2.90	
VP 3.79				Poemen 177	10.77		5.10.53		7.7.3		2.40.5.2 p524			Dorotheos doctr. 10.109
VP 3.100					9.11		5.9.8		7.39.2	MD 39	3.13.7.7 p170			
VP 3.117				Abraham 1	10.19		5.10.15				4.22.1.1-4 p369	Ch52	2.115	
VP 3.127				Macarius the Egyptian 39	127b= 10.181						2.44.1.1-2 pp549-550	Am211.2-213.2	1.186	
VP 3.130			discretio		20.22	67; 490			7.15.2		1.45.1.83 pp658-659		2.2	Macarius apoph. PG 34.260
VP 3.153					1.31	253	5.1.21							
VP 3.163				163a= Arsenius 39	163a= 10.10		163a= 5.10.9		7.16.2		163a= 4.37.4.1 p557		2.53 163a= 1.502	
VP 3.178					10.136	223	5.10.92				1.18.1.2 p231		2.41	
VP 3.179					10.168	241	5.10.108		7.26.3		4.7.3.2 p200	Ch67		
VP 3.180					10.130				7.28.1					

Apophthegm	Reg-nault no.	Section heading	Keyword(s)	Parallel references: Alph	GSC	Nau	VP 5	VP 3	VP 7	SP MD App	PE	Ch Am	Budge	Other
VP 3.183				183a= Poemen 25 183b= Poemen S1; 63; 164	183a= 10.72 183b= 8.18		183a= 5.10.50 183b= 5.8.14a				183a= 4.38.3.2 p568		183a= 2.145 183b= 1.297 2.144	
VP 3.184				Poemen 8	10.54		5.10.39				4.17.1.3-8 pp312-314		2.159	
VP 3.198				Agathon 1	10.11 cf. 3.55-56		5.10.8		7.42.1		2.34.1.1 p434		1.280 2.524	Bars 261; 340; 342; 347; 458; Dorotheos doctr. 4.52
VP 3.206									7.43.2	MD 108		cf. Am139.2		
VP 3.208				John Kolobos 12	11.40	231	5.11.14A	3.48			4.6.1.13 p137	Ch85; Am338.3	2.211	
VP 7.1.3		gluttony			10.154		5.10.99				2.18.3.6 p233			
VP 7.1.5		gluttony		Poemen 93	10.63			3.57			3.30.1.1-3 p361		2.59	Dorotheos doctr. 10.109
'VP 7.4' (PL 73.1064D-1066A)		worthless clothing	discretio					3.75						
VP 7.7.2		returning good for evil		2b= Or 12	2b= 15.79	2b= 305; 659	2b= 5.15.61	2b= 3.78b		2b= App 15b		2b= Ch135	2b= 1.506 2.90	
VP 7.7.3		returning good for evil		Poemen 177	10.77		5.10.53	3.79			2.40.5.2 p524			Dorotheos doctr. 10.109
VP 7.13.12		pride			15.78	304; 658	5.15.60			App 15a	1.45.1.65 p655; 3.38.1.42 p500	Ch134	2.463	
VP 7.15.2		unclean thoughts	discretio		20.22	67; 490		3.130			1.45.1.83 pp658-659		2.2	
VP 7.16.2		distraction		Theodore of Pherme 11	1.31	253	5.1.21	3.153			3.36.4.2.3 pp470-471		2.53	
VP 7.17.2		acquiring neighbours' good-will			10.177								2.149	

Apophthegm	Reg-nault no.	Section heading	Keyword(s)	Parallel references:										
				Alph	GSC	Nau	VP 5	VP 3	VP 7	SP MD App	PE	Ch Am	Budge	Other
VP 7.19.5		obeying weakness			5b= 10.162	5b= 236	5b= 5.10.103B				5b= 1.13.1.3 p188			
VP 7.19.6		obeying weakness			10.127	221	5.10.90						1.125d 2.451	
VP 7.22.2		penitence		Poemen 134						MD 59; App.15e	1.45.1.37 p652		2.296	Dorotheos doctr. 7.86
VP 7.25.3		fighting demons		Poemen 67	10.91		5.10.62				1.30.1.2 p434		2.308	
VP 7.25.4		fighting demons			10.131									
VP 7.26.1		destroying vices		Moses 12	10.92		5.10.63				3.2.2.5 p24		1.368	
VP 7.26.3		destroying vices			10.168	241	5.10.108	3.179			4.7.3.2 p200	Ch67		
VP 7.27.2		steadfastness		Poemen 128	10.56					MD 102			2.288	
VP 7.28.1		labour of the saints			10.130				3.180					
VP 7.28.3		labour of the saints			10.161	235	5.10.103A				1.24.2.1 p340; 4.5.2.31 p99			
VP 7.30.1		avoiding curiosity			10.128					App 11				
VP 7.32.6		silence		Arsenius 12	10.8		5.10.6				4.42.1.6 p623		2.47	
VP 7.36.1		equal merits		Poemen 29	10.76		5.10.52				3.18.7.2 p230		2.237	
VP 7.36.4		equal merits		Poemen 33	10.82		5.10.56			MD 7			1.179	
VP 7.37.4		charity		4a= Macarius the Egyptian 36; 4c= Cronius 1	4a= 10.48; 4c= 18.34	4c= 363	4a= 5.10.34; 4c= 5.18.27 (i.e. VP 6.1.7)			4a= MD 15; App 15d; 4b-c= MD 16	4a= 2.42.2.1 p540; 4c= 1.24.7.1 p347; 4.5.2.34 p100	4a= Ch60; 4c=Ch200	4a= 2.206; 4c= 2.515	4a= Macarius apoph. PG 34.257 Evagrius prak. 93; Socrates HE 4.23

Apophthegm	Regnault no.	Section heading	Keyword(s)	Parallel references: Alph	GSC	Nau	VP 5	VP 3	VP 7	SP MD App	PE	Ch Am	Budge	Other
VP 7.38.2		devotion to weeping and poverty		Macarius the Egyptian 20	2b= 10.139					MD 23	4.22.1.6 p369	2a= Am166.1	2a= 1.232	Macarius *apoph.* PG 34.249 2b= HL 47.6; Bars 549
VP 7.39.2		rest			9.11		5.9.8	3.100		MD 39	3.13.7.7 p170			
VP 7.41.2		virtues			10.147	385	5.10.94				3.29.3.3 p346		2.250	
VP 7.42.1		living in the coenobium		Agathon 1	10.11 cf. 3.55-56		5.10.8	3.198			2.34.1.1 p434		1.280 2.524	Bars 261: 340; 342; 347; 458; Dorotheos *doctr.* 4.52
VP 7.43.2		spiritual discipline						3.206		MD 108		cf. Am139.2		
SP 6 (i.e. VP 5.23.6)			*discretio*		21.9	93	5.23.6 (i.e. SP 6)				3.31.1.3 p372		2.313	
SP 20 (i.e. VP 5.23.20)			*discretio*		21.25	106	5.23.20 (i.e. SP 20)				3.31.1.4 p372		2.201 2.281	
MD 3				Poemen 154	5.8						2.28.7.3 p345		2.253	
MD 7				Poemen 33	10.82		5.10.56		7.36.4				1.179	
MD 8			*discretio (bis)*	Poemen 60	1.23		5.1.14						2.193 cf. 2.341	
MD 15				Macarius the Egyptian 36	10.48		5.10.34		7.37.4a	App 15d	2.42.2.1 p540	Ch60	2.206	Macarius *apoph.* PG 34.257; Evagrius *prak.* 93; Socrates *HE* 4.23
MD 16				16b= Cronius 1	16b= 18.34	16b= 363	16b= 5.18.27 (i.e. VP 6.1.7)		7.37.4b -c		16b= 1.24.7.1 p347; 4.5.2.34 p100	Ch200	16b= 2.515	

Apophthegm	Regnault no.	Section heading	Keyword(s)	Parallel references:										
				Alph	GSC	Nau	VP 5	VP 3	VP 7	SP MD App	PE	Ch Am	Budge	Other
MD 21				Poemen 168	10.93		5.10.64					Am37.2	1.546	
MD 23				Macarius the Egyptian 20	23= 10.139				7.38.2		4.22.1.6 p369	23a= Am166.1	23a= 1.232	Macarius *apoph.* PG 34.249 23b= *HL* 47.6; Bars 549
MD 27				Sisoes 6	10.98		5.10.68				4.6.1.5 p136		2.241 2.528	Dorotheos *doctr.* 13.141
MD 32			discerno	Poemen 32	11.58		5.11.22				4.32.2.5 p515		1.273	
MD 39			discretio		9.11		5.9.8	3.100	7.39.2		3.13.7.7 p170			
MD 59				Poemen 134	10.83				7.22.2	App 15e	1.45.1.37 p652		2.296	Dorotheos *doctr.* 7.86
MD 70				Poemen 40			5.10.57						2.231	
MD 75				Poemen 139; cf. Euprepius 7; Poemen 45	cf. 4.94; 10.24; 10.86	cf. 468	cf. 5.10.19; 5.10.58				cf. 2.47.2.3 p574	cf. Ch57	1.369 cf. 1.22 1.58 1.313	cf. Bars 291; 698
MD 79				Poemen 127b	10.55						4.38.3.1b p568		2.287	
MD 80				Poemen 54	10.89		5.10.60				1.42.2.1 p622		2.77 cf. 1.531	Dorotheos *doctr.* 5.63
MD 82				Poemen 91	10.78		5.10.54			App 5d	2.35.1.2 p439		1.456	
MD 98					10.144					MD 98	1.25.1.3 p351		1.167	
MD 102				Poemen 128	10.56				7.27.2				2.288	
MD 108			discretio; discerno					3.206	7.43.2			cf. Am139.2		

Apophthegm	Reg-nault no.	Section heading	Keyword(s)	Parallel references: Alph	GSC	Nau	VP 5	VP 3	VP 7	SP MD App	PE	Ch Am	Budge	Other
App 4			4d: *discretio*	4a-b= Poemen S2 4c= Poemen S19 4d= Poemen 184	4a-b= 10.90 cf. 5.9 4c= 4.38		4a-b= 5.10.61 cf. 5.5.9 4c= 5.4.31E				4c= 1.42.7.2 p632 4d= 2.18.3.4 p233		4a-b= 1.388-389 4d= 2.166	
App 5				5d= Poemen 91	5d= 10.78		5d= 5.10.54				5d= 2.35.1.2 p439		5d= 1.456	
App 11					10.128	417 cf. 503								
App 13									7.30.1		2.49.2.2 p592			
App 15				15b= Or 12 15d= Macarius the Egyptian 36 15e= Poemen 134	15a= 15.78 15b= 15.79 15d= 10.48	15a= 304; 658 15b= 305; 659	15a= 5.15.60 15b= 5.15.61 15d= 5.10.34	15b= 3.78b	15a= 7.13.12 15b= 7.7.2b 15d= 7.37.4a 15e= 7.22.2	15d= MD 15 15e= MD 59	15a= 1.45.1.65 p655; 3.38.1.42 p500 15d= 2.42.2.1 p540 15e= 1.45.1.37 p652	15a= Ch134 15b= Ch135 15d= Ch60	15a= 2.463 15b= 1.506 2.90 15d= 2.206 15e= 2.296	15d= Evagrius *prak.* 93; Socrates *HE* 4.23 Macarius *apoph.* PG 34.257 15e= Dorotheos *doctr.* 7.86
App 16			*discretio*		5.47	50								

Apophthegm	Reg-nault no.	Section heading	Keyword(s)	Parallel references: Alph	GSC	Nau	VP 5	VP 3	VP 7	SP MD App	PE	Ch Am	Budge	Other
App 18				Netras 1	10.50		5.10.36				2.18.3.8 p233	Ch62	2.410	
QRT 5			διάκρισις sc. as PE								1.29.5.6 pp427-428 1.30.1.7 p435			See above, p. 163, n. 178.
Chaîne 52				Abraham 1	10.19		5.10.15	3.117			4.22.1.1-4 p369		2.115	
Chaîne 53				Ammonas 4	10.20		5.10.16				1.44.3.1 p643		1.447	Ammonas *apoph.* 4
Chaîne 54				Daniel 4	10.22 cf. 10.140		5.10.17				2.15.17.3 p210		1.99	
Chaîne 55				Daniel 1	10.21						3.28.3.1 p332		2.108	
Chaîne 56				Daniel 6	10.23		5.10.18				4.50.1.1-3 p667			cf. Dorotheos *doctr.* 11.121
Chaîne 57				Euprepius 7 cf. Poemen 45; 139	10.24; cf. 4.94; 10.86	cf. 468	5.10.19; cf. 5.10.58			cf. MD 75	2.47.2.3 p574		1.58 cf. 1.22 1.313 1.369	Bars 291; cf. Bars 698
Chaîne 58				Isaac, Priest of the Cells 5	10.44		5.10.32				2.29.7.1 p370			
Chaîne 59				Longinus 1	10.45		5.10.33				3.31.1.6 p372; 1a= 1.13.1.2 p188		2.265	
Chaîne 60				Macarius the Egyptian 36	10.48		5.10.34		7.37.4a	MD 15; App 15d	2.42.2.1 p540		2.206	Macarius *apoph.* PG 34.257; Evagrius *prak.* 93; Socrates *HE* 4.23
Chaîne 61				Matoes 4	10.49		5.10.35				4.21.1 p363		2.248	cf. Evagrius *prak.* 44

Apophthegm	Regnault no.	Section heading	Keyword(s)	Parallel references:										
				Alph	GSC	Nau	VP 5	VP 3	VP 7	SP MD App	PE	Ch Am	Budge	Other
Chaîne 62				Netras 1	10.50		5.10.36			App 18	2.18.3.8 p233; 3.2.2.4 p24		2.410	
Chaîne 63					10.51	391	5.10.37							
Chaîne 64				Megethius 4	10.165	238	5.10.105						2.259	
Chaîne 65					10.166; 65a= 11.103	239; 65a= 272	5.10.106; 65a= 5.11.45						2.486	
Chaîne 66					10.167	240	5.10.107							
Chaîne 67				10.168	241	5.10.108	3.179	7.26.3			4.7.3.2 p200			
Chaîne 68					10.169	387	5.10.109				3.31.1.15 p373		1.390a	
Chaîne 69					10.170	242	5.10.110				3.3.1.2 pp66-67; 1.41.1.1 p600			
Chaîne 70					10.172	243	5.10.111						2.422	
Chaîne 71					10.173	111; 244					3.29.3.2 p346		2.504	Bars 693
Chaîne 72					10.174	245	5.10.112						2.17	
Chaîne 85				John Kolobos 12	11.40		5.11.14A	208			4.6.1.13 p137	Am338.3	2.211	
Chaîne 86				John Kolobos 18	11.41		5.11.15	·			4.41.3.1-6 pp618-619		2.154	
Chaîne 134					15.78	304; 658	5.15.60		7.13.12	App 15a	1.45.1.65 p655; 3.38.1.42 p500		2.463	
Chaîne 135				Or 12	15.79	305; 659	5.15.61	3.78b	7.2b	App 15b			1.506; 2.90	
Chaîne 200				Cronius 1; 363b= Poemen S18b	18.34	363	5.18.27 (i.e. VP 6.1.7)		7.37.4c	MD 16b	1.24.7.1 p347; 4.5.2.34 p100; 363b= 4.24.1.3b p419		2.515	

Apophthegm	Reg-nault no.	Section heading	Keyword(s)	Alph	GSC	Nau	VP 5	VP 3	VP 7	SP MD App	PE	Ch Am	Budge	Other
				Parallel references:										
Chaîne 268					20.15	132A	5.20.11 (i.e. VP 6.3.11)							
Amélineau 16.1				Antony 12	10.2		5.10.2a				4.19.3.1-3 p341		2.56	Bars 413
Amélineau 16.2				Antony 13	10.3		5.10.2b				2.18.3.3 pp232-233			
Amélineau 17.1				Antony 23	10.5		5.10.4				1.30.1.1 p434		2.246	
Amélineau 22.3*			ДІАКРІСІС											
Amélineau 30.2					cf. 10.79									cf. Ammonas ep. 12
Amélineau 37.2				Poemen 168	10.93		5.10.64			MD 21			1.546	
Amélineau 96.2*			ДІАКРІСІС											
Amélineau 126.1				Macarius the Egyptian 23 cf. Anoub 1	23b= 10.47						3.25.1.1-3 p289	Am214.2	1.446	Macarius apoph. PG 34.249-252; HL 9 (PL 74.357B-C)
Amélineau 138.2				John Kolobos 34; cf. Poemen 46	1.13		5.1.8				cf. 3.11.2.1 p126	cf. Am333.1; Am407.2	2.128 cf. 2.118	cf. Dorotheos doctr. 14.150; Evagrius gnos. 6
Amélineau 139.2								cf. 3.206	cf. 7.43.2 7.38.2a	cf. MD 108				
Amélineau 166.1				Macarius the Egyptian 20a	cf. 10.139					MD 23a	4.22.1.6a p369		1.232	Macarius apoph. PG 34.249; HL 47.6; Bars 549
Amélineau 211.2-213.2				Macarius the Egyptian 39	213.2= 10.181			3.127			2.44.1.1-2 pp549-550		1.186	Macarius apoph. PG 34.260

Apophthegm	Regnault no.	Section heading	Keyword(s)	Parallel references:										
				Alph	GSC	Nau	VP 5	VP 3	VP 7	SP MD App	PE	Ch Am	Budge	Other
Amélineau 214.2				Macarius the Egyptian 23 cf. Anoub 1	23b= 10.47						3.25.1.1-3 p289	Am126.1	1.446	Macarius apoph. PG 34.249-252; HL 9 (PL 74.357B-C)
Amélineau 326.1*			ΔΙΑΚΡΙCΙC											
Amélineau 333.1	.		ΔΙΑΚΡΙCΙC (bis)	cf. John Kolobos 34	cf. 1.13		cf. 5.1.8				cf. 3.11.2.1 p126	cf. Am138.2; Am407.2	cf. 2.128 2.118	cf. Dorotheos doctr. 14.150; Evagrius gnos. 6
Amélineau 338.3			ΔΙΑΚΡΙΤΙΚΩC	John Kolobos 12	11.40		5.11.14A	3.208			4.6.1.13 p137	Ch85	2.211	
Amélineau 370.2*			ΔΙΑΚΡΙCΙC											

SELECT BIBLIOGRAPHY

Scripture

Bohairic Coptic

Bsciai, A. (ed.), *Liber Baruch Prophetae* (Rome: Typis S. Congregationis de Propaganda Fide, 1870).

Burmester, O.H.E. and E. Dévaud (eds), *Psalterii versio memphitica e recognitione Pauli de Legarde. Réédition avec le texte copte en caractères coptes* (Louvain: J.B. Istas, 1925 [1875]).

De Lagarde, P. (ed.), *Der Pentateuch Koptisch* (Leipzig: Teubner, 1867).

Horner, G. (ed.), *The Coptic Version of the New Testament in the Northern Dialect Otherwise Called Memphitic and Bohairic* (4 vols; Oxford: Clarendon Press, 1898-1905).

Porcher, E. (ed.), 'Le Livre de Job: version copte bohaïrique', *PO* 18.2 (1924).

Tattam, H. (ed.), *The Ancient Coptic Version of the Book of Job the Just* (London: William Straker, 1846).

— *Prophetae Majores, in dialecto linguae Aegyptiacae Memphitica seu Coptica* (2 vols; Oxford: E typographeo Academico, 1852).

— *Duodecim Prophetarum Minorum Libros in Lingua Ægyptiaca vulgo Coptica seu Memphitica ex Manuscripto Parisensi Descriptos et cum Manuscripto Johannes Lee, J.C.D. Collatos* (Oxford: E typographeo Academico, 1836).

Greek

Aland, K., M. Black, C.M. Martini, B.M. Metzger and A. Wikgren (eds), *The Greek New Testament* (London: United Bible Societies, 3rd edn, 1983).

Codex Bezae: *Codex Bezae Cantabrigiensis quattuor Evangelica et Actus Apostolorum complectens Graece et Latine sumptibus Academiae phototypice repraesentatus* (2 vols; Cambridge: C.J. Clay et filios in emporio Preli Academici Catabrigiensis, 1899).

Rahlfs, A. (ed.), *Septuaginta: Id est Vetus Testamentum graece iuxta LXX interpretes* (Stuttgart: Deutsche Bibelgesellschaft, 1979).

Hebrew

Ellinger, K. and W. Rudolph (eds), *Biblica Hebraica Stuttgartensia* (Stuttgart: Deutsche Bibelgesellschaft, 1984).

Latin

Weber R., B. Fischer, H.I. Frede, H.F.D. Sparks and W. Thiele (eds), *Biblia Sacra iuxta Vulgatam Versionem* (Stuttgart: Deutsche Bibelgesellschaft, 1994).

Sahidic Coptic

Budge, E.A. Wallis, *The Earliest Known Coptic Psalter: The Text, in the Dialect of Upper Egypt, edited from the unique Papyrus Codex Oriental 5000 in the British Museum* (London: Kegan Paul, Trench, Trübner, 1898).

Drescher, J. (ed.), *The Coptic (Sahidic) Version of Kingdoms I, II (Samuel I, II)* (*CSCO* 313-14, Scriptores Coptici 35-36; Louvain: Secrétariat du *CSCO*, 1970).

Horner, G. (ed.), *The Coptic Version of the New Testament in the Southern Dialect Otherwise Called Sahidic and Thebaic* (7 vols; Oxford: Clarendon Press, 1911-1924).

Kasser, R. (ed.), *Papyrus Bodmer VI Livres des Proverbes* (*CSCO* 194-95, Scriptores Coptici 27-28; Louvain: Secrétariat du *CSCO*, 1960).

– *Papyrus Bodmer XXII et Mississippi Coptic Codex II: Jérémie, XL,3-LII,34 Lamentations Epître de Jérémie Baruch I,1-V,5 en Sahidique*, (Colgony-Genève: Bibliotheca Bodmeriana, 1964).

Thompson, H. (ed.), *The Coptic (Sahidic) Version of Certain Books of the Old Testament from a Papyrus in the British Museum* (London: Oxford University Press, 1908).

Worrell, W.H. (ed.), *The Coptic Manuscripts in the Freer Collection* (New York: Macmillan, 1923).

– *The Proverbs of Solomon in Sahidic Coptic According to the Chicago Manuscript* (The University of Chicago Oriental Institute Publications 12; Chicago: University of Chicago Press, 1931).

Primary Sources

Acta Ioannis: R.A. Lipsius and M. Bonnet (eds), *Acta apostolorum apocrypha post Constantinum Tischendorf denuo*, (2 vols; Hildesheim: Olms, 1972 [1891-1903]), II.1, pp. 151-215. [TLG 0317 001 and 0317 002]

Aesop, *Proverbia*: B.E. Perry (ed.), *Aesopica Volume 1: Greek and Latin texts* (Urbana: University of Illinois Press, 1952), pp. 265-91. [TLG 0096 017]

Alexander Aphrodisiensis, *Problemata* 3-4 (sp.): H. Usener (ed.), *Alexandri Aphrodisiensis quae feruntur problematorum liber III et IIII* (Berlin: Druckerei der Königl. Akademie der Wissenschaften, 1859), pp. 1-37. [TLG 0732 017]

Ambrose, *De officiis ministrorum*: *PL* 16.23-184.

– *De officiis ministrorum* (Eng. trans.): H. de Romestin, E. de Romestin and H.T.F. Duckworth, NPNF Series 2, X, pp. 35-211.

– *De Spiritu Sanctu*: *PL* 16.703-816.

– *De Spiritu Sanctu* (Eng. trans.): H. de Romestin, E. de Romestin and H.T.F. Duckworth, NPNF Series 2, X, pp. 214-345.

Ammonas, *Apophthegmata* (*apoph.*; references are to Greek numeration): F. Nau, 'Ammonas, successeur de Saint Antoine: texts grecs et syriaques', *PO* 11.4 (1915), pp. 403-409.

– *Epistolae* (*ep*.; references are to Syriac numeration):
– *Epp*. 1-7 (Greek): ed. F. Nau, 'Ammonas, successeur de Saint Antoine: texts grecs et syriaques' (*PO* 11.4; Paris: Firmin-Didot, 1915), pp. 432-54.
– *Ep*. 8 (Greek) published as *hom*. 7 of Pseudo-Macarius: G.L. Marriott, *Macarii Anecdota: Seven Unpublished Homilies of Macarius* (Harvard Theological Studies 5; Cambridge, Mass.: Harvard University Press, 1918; repr. New York: Kraus, 1969), pp. 19-48. [TLG 2109 004]
– *Epp*. (Latin trans. of Arabic attrib. Antony the Great): *PG* 40.1019-1066.
– *Epp*. (Eng. trans. of Syriac): D.J. Chitty, *The Letters of Ammonas: Successor to Antony the Great*, (Oxford: SLG Press, 1979).
Antony the Great, *Apophthegmata* (Bohairic Coptic): É. Amélineau, *Monuments pour servir à l'histoire de l'Égypte chrétienne: Histoire des monastères de la Basse-Égypte. Vies des saints Paul, Antoine, Macaire, Maxime et Domèce, Jean le Nain, et autres* (Annales du Musée Guimet 25; Paris: E. Leroux, 1894), pp. 15-45.
– *Epistolae* (*ep*.; numeration follows Rubenson):
– *Epp*. (Greek): *PG* 40.977-1000.
– *Epp*. (Eng. trans.): S. Rubenson, *The Letters of St Antony: Monasticism and the Making of a Saint* (Studies in Antiquity and Christianity; Minneapolis: Fortress Press, 1995).
– *Epp*. (Eng. trans.): D.J. Chitty, *The Letters of Saint Antony the Great* (Oxford: SLG Press, 1975).
Apophthegmata, Greek Alphabetical Collection (*alph*.): *PG* 65.71-440. [TLG 2742 001]
– *Alph*. supplement: J.-C. Guy, *Recherches sur la Tradition Grecque des Apophthegmata Patrum* (Subsidia Hagiographica 36; Brussels: Société des Bollandistes, 1962), pp. 13-58.
– *Alph*. (Eng. trans.): B. Ward, *The Sayings of the Desert Fathers: The Alphabetical Collection* (Oxford: Cistercian Publications), 1975.
Apophthegmata, Greek Anonymous Collection (Nau):
– Nau 1-392, 421, 430-436, 438: F. Nau, 'Histoire des Solitaires Égyptiens', *ROC* 12 (1907), pp. 43-69, 171-89, 393-413; *ROC* 13 (1908), pp. 47-66, 266-97; *ROC* 14 (1909), pp. 357-79; *ROC* 17 (1912), pp. 204-11, 294-301; *ROC* 18 (1913), pp. 137-46. [TLG 2742 002]
– Nau 132A-D: F. Nau, 'Le Chapitre Περὶ Ἀναχωρητῶν Ἁγίων et les Sources de la Vie de Saint Paul de Thèbes', *ROC* 10 (1905), pp. 387-417. [TLG 2742 003]
– Nau 487: J.-C. Guy, 'La collation des douze anachorètes', *Analecta Bollandiana* 76 (1958), pp. 419-27. [TLG 2742 006]
– Nau 506-508, 623-624, 627, 636, J765 included in Διάλεξις γερόντων πρὸς ἀλλήλοις περὶ λογισμῶν: J.-C. Guy, 'Un dialogue monastique inédit', *RAM* 33 (1957), pp. 171-88. [TLG 2742 007]
– Nau 599: M. Jugie, 'Un apophthegme des pères inédit sur le purgatoire', in *Mémorial Louis Petit. Mélanges d'histoire et d'archéologie Byzantines* (Archives de l'Orient chrétien 1; Bucharest: Institut français d'études byzantines, 1948), pp. 245-53. [TLG 2742 004]
– J714 (*On How to Live in the Cell and on Contemplation: Questions and Answers*): J.-C. Guy (ed.), 'Un entretien monastique sur la contemplation', *Recherches de science religieuse* 50 (1962), pp. 230-41. [TLG 2742 008]

– Nau supplement: J.-C. Guy, *Recherches sur la Tradition Grecque des Apophthegmata Patrum* (Subsidia Hagiographica 36; Brussels: Société des Bollandistes, 1962), pp. 59-115.

– Nau 1-132 (Eng. trans.): C. Stewart, *The World of the Desert Fathers: Stories and sayings from the Anonymous Series of the Apophthegmata Patrum* (Oxford: SLG Press, 1986).

– Nau 133-369 (Eng. trans.): B. Ward, *The Wisdom of the Desert Fathers: Systematic Sayings from the Anonymous Series of the Apophthegmata Patrum* (Oxford: SLG Press, rev. edn, 1986).

– French trans. of whole Greek Anonymous Collection: L. Regnault, *Les Sentences des Pères du Désert: Série des anonymes* (Spiritualité Orientale 43, Solesmes-Bellefontaine: Abbayes, 1985).

Apophthegmata, Greek Anthology of Paul Evergetinos (PE): M. Langis (ed.), Εὐεργετινός ἤτοι συναγωγή τῶν θεοφθόγγων ῥημάτων καί διδασκαλιῶν τῶν θεοφόρων καὶ ἁγίων πατέρων (4 vols; Athens: Monastery of the Transfiguration, 6ᵗʰ edn, 1997-2000).

Apophthegmata, Greek Systematic Collection (GSC): J.-C. Guy, *Les Apophthegmes des Pères: Collection Systématique* (SC 387, 474, 498; Paris: Cerf, 1993-2005). [GSC 1-9: TLG 2742 005]

– GSC supplement: J.-C. Guy, *Recherches sur la Tradition Grecque des Apophthegmata Patrum* (Subsidia Hagiographica 36; Brussels: Société des Bollandistes, 1962), pp. 117-200.

– GSC (French trans.): L. Regnault, *Les Chemins de Dieu au Désert: La Collection Systématique des Apophtegmes des Pères* (Solesmes: Éditions de Solesmes, 1992).

Apophthegmata, Latin Systematic Collection:

– Pelagius (*VP* 5) and John (*VP* 6): *PL* 73.851-1024.

– Supplement (*Sententiae partum* [*SP*]): A. Wilmart (ed.), 'Le Recueil Latin des Apophtegmes', *RB* 34 (1922), pp. 185-98.

– *VP* 5 (Eng. trans. of with additional Latin texts and textual apparatus): O. Chadwick, *Western Asceticism*, (The Library of Christian Classics 12; London: SCM Press, 1958), pp. 37-189, 338-60.

– *VP* 5 (Eng. trans.): B. Ward, *The Desert Fathers: Sayings of the Early Christian Monks* (London: Penguin Books, 2003).

Apophthegmata, Latin Collection Appendices (*Appendix as Vitas Patrum*):

– Martin of Dumio, *Ægyptiorum Patrum Sententiæ* (MD): *PL* 74.381-394.

– Palladius, *Palladii Lausiaca XX* (App): *PL* 74.377-382.

Apophthegmata, Latin Collection of Paschasius of Dumio (*VP* 7): *PL* 73.851-1064.

– J.G. Freire (ed.), *A versão latina por Pascásio de Dume dos Apophthegmata Patrum* (2 vols; Coïmbra: Instituto de Estudos Classicos, 1971).

Apophthegmata, Latin Collection attrib. Rufinus (*VP* 3): *PL* 73.739-814.

Apophthegmata, Bohairic Coptic Collection (Am): É. Amélineau (ed.), *Monuments pour servir à l'histoire de l'Égypte chrétienne: Histoire des monastères de la Basse-Égypte. Vies des saints Paul, Antoine, Macaire, Maxime et Domèce, Jean le Nain, et autres* (Annales du Musée Guimet 25; Paris: E. Leroux, 1894).

Apophthegmata, Sahidic Coptic Collection (Ch): M. Chaîne (ed.), *Le Manuscrit de la Version Copte en Dialecte Sahidique des 'Apophthegmata Patrum'*, (Bibliothèque d'études coptes 6; Cairo: L'institut français d'archéologie orientale, 1960).

Apophthegmata, Syriac Collection (Eng. trans.): E.A. Wallis Budge, *The Paradise or Garden of the Holy Fathers being Histories of the Anchorites Recluses Monks Coenobites and Ascetic Fathers of the Deserts of Egypt between A.D. CCL and A.D. CCCC circiter Compiled by Athanasius Archbishop of Alexandria, Palladius Bishop of Helenopolis, Saint Jerome and Others* (2 vols; London: Chatto & Windus, 1907), II.

Apostolic Fathers: F.X. Funk (ed.), *Patres Apostolici* (2 vols; Tubingen: H. Laupp, 2nd edn, 1901).

– (Eng. trans.): M. Staniforth, *Early Christian Writings: The Apostolic Fathers* (Harmondsworth: Penguin Books, 1968).

Aquinas, Thomas, *Summa Theologiae*: T. Gilby (ed.), *Summa Theologiae: Latin text and English translation* (61 vols; London: Eyre & Spottiswoode, 1964-1981).

Aristotle, *Ethica Nicomachea*, (*eth. Nic.*): I. Bywater (ed.), *Aristotelis ethica Nicomachea* (Oxford: Clarendon Press, repr. 1962 (1894]), pp. 1-224. [TLG 0086 010]

– *Eth. Nic.* (Eng. trans.): J.A.K. Thompson, *The Ethics of Aristotle: The Nichomachean Ethics* (ed. H. Tredennick; Harmondsworth: Penguin Books, rev. edn, 1976).

Arnobius, *Adversus Gentes* (Eng. trans.): H. Bryce and H. Campbell, ANF, VI, pp. 779-1002.

Athanasius, *Contra gentes*: R.W. Thomson (ed.), *Athanasius: Contra gentes and de incarnatione* (Oxford: Clarendon Press, 1971), pp. 2-132. [TLG 2035 001]

– *Expositiones in Psalmos*: *PG* 27.60-589. [TLG 2035 061]

– *Vita Antonii* (*vit. Ant.*; references follow Greek numeration):

– *Vit. Ant.* (Greek): *PG* 26.835-976. [TLG 2035 047]

– *Vit. Ant.* (Latin): *PL* 73.127-168.

– *Vit. Ant.* (Sahidic Coptic): G. Garitte (ed.), *S. Antonii vitae versio Sahidica* (*CSCO* 117-118, Scriptores Coptici 4.1; Paris: E Typographeo Republicae, 1949).

– *Vit. Ant.* (Eng. trans. of Greek): R.C. Gregg, *Athanasius: The Life of Antony and the Letter to Marcellinus* (New York: Paulist Press, 1980).

– *Vit. Ant.* (Eng. trans. of Latin): C. White, *Early Christian Lives* (London: Penguin Books, 1998), pp. 7-70.

– *Vit. Ant.* (Eng. trans. of Coptic and Greek): T. Vivian and A.N. Athanassakis, *Athanasius of Alexandria: The Life of Antony: The Coptic Life and the Greek Life* (Cistercian Studies Series 202; Kalamazoo: Cistercian Publications, 2003).

– *Vit. Ant.* (Eng. trans. of Syriac): E.A. Wallis Budge, *The Paradise or Garden of the Holy Fathers being Histories of the Anchorites Recluses Monks Coenobites and Ascetic Fathers of the Deserts of Egypt between A.D. CCL and A.D. CCCC circiter Compiled by Athanasius Archbishop of Alexandria, Palladius Bishop of Helenopolis, Saint Jerome and Others* (2 vols; London: Chatto & Windus, 1907), I, pp. 3-76.

Athanasius, (Pseudo-), *Vita sanctae Syncleticae* (*vit. Syn.*; sp.): *PG* 28.1487-1558. [TLG 2035 104]

– *Vit. Syn.* (Eng. trans.): E.A. Castelli, 'Pseudo-Athanasius: The Life and Activity of the Holy and Blessed Teacher Syncletica', in V.L. Wimbush (ed.), *Ascetic Behavior in Greco-Roman Antiquity: A Sourcebook* (Studies in Antiquity & Christianity; Minneapolis: Fortress Press, 1990), pp. 265-311.

– *Vitae monasticae institutio* (*vit. mon. inst.*; sp.): *PG.* 28.845-849. [TLG 2035 084]

Augustine, *Confessiones* (*confess.*): L. Verheijen (ed.), *Sancti Augustini: Confesssionum Libri XIII* (*CCL* 27; Turnholt: Brepols, 1981).

– *Confess.* (Latin and Eng. trans.): W. Watts (ed.), *St. Augustine's Conffessions* (LCL 26-27; London: William Heinemann Ltd, 1912).

– *De baptismo contra donatistas* (*de bapt.*): *PL* 43.107-244.

– *De bapt.* (Eng. trans.): J.R. King, NPNF Series 1, IV, pp. 755-961.

– *De civitate Dei* (*de civ. Dei*; Latin and Eng. trans.): G.E. McCracken, W.M. Green, etc. (eds), *Saint Augustine: The City of God Against the Pagans* (LCL 411-417; London: William Heinemann Ltd, 1957-1972).

– *De civ. Dei* (Eng. trans.): H. Bettenson and J. O'Meara, *Augustine: Concerning the City of God Against the Pagans* (Penguin Books: Harmondsworth, 1984).

– *De utilitate credendi*: *PL* 42.65-92.

– *De utilitate credendi* (Eng. trans.): C.L. Cornish, NPNF Series 1, III, pp. 653-88.

– *Epistolae* (*ep.*): A. Goldbacher (ed.), *S. Aureli Augustini Hipponensis Episcopi Epistulae* (*CSEL* 34, 44, 57, 58; Vienna: Tempsky, 1895-1923).

– *Epp.* (Eng. trans.): J.G. Cunningham, NPNF Series 1, I, pp. 395-1194.

– *Enarrationes in Psalmos* (*Enarr. in Ps.*): D.E. Dekkers and J. Fraipont (eds), *Sancti Aurelii Augustini: Enarrationes in Psalmos* (*CCL* 38-40; Turnhout: Brepols, 1956).

– *Enarr. in Ps.*: C. Weidmann (ed.), *Sancti Augustini Opera: Enarrationes in Psalmos 1-50 Pars 1A: Enarrationes in Psalmos 1-32 (Expos.)* (*CSEL* 93.1A; Wien: Verlag der Österreichischen Akademie der Wissenschaften, 2003).

– *Enarr. in Ps.*: F. Gori (ed.), *Sancti Augustini Opera: Enarrationes in Psalmos 101-150 Pars 3: Enarrationes in Psalmos 119-133* (*CSEL* 95.3; Wien: Verlag der Österreichischen Akademie der Wissenschaften, 2001).

– *Enarr. in Ps.*: F. Gori and A.F. Recananti (eds), *Sancti Augustini Opera: Enarrationes in Psalmos 101-150 Pars 4: Enarrationes in Psalmos 134-1140* (*CSEL* 95.4; Wien: Verlag der Österreichischen Akademie der Wissenschaften, 2002).

– *Enarr. in Ps.* (Eng. trans.): A.C. Coxe, NPNF Series 1, VIII, pp. 13-1482.

Barsanuph and John of Gaza, *Epistolae* (French trans.): L. Regnault, P. Lemaire and B. Outtier (eds), *Barsanuphe et Jean de Gaza: Correspondance*, (Solesmes: Éditions des Solesmes, 2nd edn, 1993).

Basil the Great, *De spiritu sancto*: B. Pruche (ed.), *Basile de Césarée: Sur le Saint-Esprit* (SC 17; Paris: Cerf, 2nd edn, 1968). [TLG 2040 003]

– *De spiritu sancto* (Eng. trans.): B. Jackson, NPNF Series 2, VIII, pp. 119-210.

– *Epistolae*: Y. Courtonne (ed.), *Saint Basile: Lettres* (3 vols; Paris: Les Belles Lettres, 1957-1966). [TLG 2040 004]

– *Epistolae* (Eng. trans.): B. Jackson, NPNF Series 2, VIII, pp. 314-726.

– *Epistolae*; canonical epistles (Eng. trans.): H.R. Percival, NPNF Series 2, XIV, pp. 1133-54.

– *Exhortatio de renuntiatione mundi*: *PG* 31.625-648. [TLG 2040 041]

– *Homiliae in hexaemeron* (*hom. in hex.*): S. Giet (ed.), *Basile de Césarée: Homélies sur l'hexaéméron* (SC 26; Paris: Cerf, 2nd edn 1968). [TLG 2040 001]

– *Hom. in hex.* (Eng. trans.): B. Jackson, NPNF Series 2, VIII, pp. 214-312.

– *Homiliae super Psalmos* (*hom. in Ps.*): *PG* 29.209-494. [TLG 2040 018]

– *Regulae brevius tractatae* (*reg. brev.*): *PG* 31.1052-1305. [TLG 2040 050]

– *Regulae fusius tractatae* (*reg. fus.*): *PG* 31.901-1052. [TLG 2040 048]

– *Reg. fus.* (Eng. trans.): W.K.L. Clarke, *The Ascetic Works of Saint Basil* (Translations of Christian Literature, Series 1 Greek Texts: London: SPCK, 1925).

Benedict of Nursia, *Regula Benedicti* (*reg. Ben.*): A. de Vogüé and J. Neufville (eds), *Le Règle de Saint Benoît* (SC 181-186a; Paris: Cerf, 1971-1977).
– *Reg. Ben.* (Eng. trans.): O. Chadwick, *Western Asceticism* (The Library of Christian Classics 12; London: SCM Press, 1958), pp. 291-337.
Bernard of Clairvaux, *Sermones super Cantica canticorum* (*serm. in Cant.*): J. Leclercq, C.H. Talbot and H.M. Rochais (eds), *Sermones super Cantica canticorum* (*Sancti Bernardi Opera* 1-2; Rome: Editiones Cistercienses, 1957-1958).
Cassian, John, *Collationes XXIIII* (*conf.*): E. Pichery (ed.), *Conférences* (SC 42, 54, 64; Paris: Cerf, 1955-1959).
– *Conf.* (Eng. trans.): B. Ramsey, *John Cassian: The Conferences* (Ancient Christian Writers 57; New York: Paulist Press, 1997).
– *De Incarnatione domini libri VII* (*de. inc.*): M. Pestchenig (ed.), *Iohannis Cassieni: De Incarnatione Domini contra Nestorium Libri VII* (*CSEL* 17; Vienna: Tempsky, 1888).
– *De inc.* (Eng. trans.): E.C.S. Gibson, NPNF Series 2, XI, pp. 1105-1248.
– *De institutis cœnobiorum et de octo principalium vitiorum remediis libri XII* (*inst.*): J-C. Guy (ed.), *Institutions Cénobitiques* (SC 109; Paris: Cerf, 1965).
– *Inst.* (Eng. trans.): J. Bertram, *The Monastic Institutes* (London: Saint Austin Press, 1999).
Clement of Alexandria, *Quis dives salvatur*: O. Stählin, L. Früchtel and U. Treu (eds), *Clemens Alexandrinus III: Stromata Buch VII und VIII, Excerpta ex Theodoto, Eclogae proheticae, Quis dives salvetur, Fragmente* (*GCS* 17; Berlin: Akademie-Verlag, 2nd edn, 1970), pp. 159-91. [TLG 0555 006]
– *Quis dives salvatur* (Eng. trans.): W. Wilson, ANF, II, pp. 1197-1224.
– *Stromata* (*strom.*):
– *Strom.* 1-6: O. Stählin, L. Früchtel and U. Treu (eds), *Clemens Alexandrinus II: Stromata Buch I-VI* (*GCS* 52(15); Berlin: Akademie-Verlag, 3rd edn, 1960).
– *Strom.* 7-8: O. Stählin, L. Früchtel and U. Treu (eds), *Clemens Alexandrinus III: Stromata Buch VII und VIII, Excerpta ex Theodoto, Eclogae proheticae, Quis dives salvetur, Fragmente* (*GCS* 17; Berlin: Akademie-Verlag, 2nd edn. 1970), pp. 3-102. [TLG 0555 004]
– *Strom.* (Eng. trans.): J. Donaldson and A. Roberts, ANF, II, pp. 588-1157.
Clement of Rome, *Epistula I ad Corinthios* (*1 Clem.*): A. Jaubert (ed.), *Clément de Rome: Épître aux Corinthiens* (SC 167; Paris: Cerf, 1971). [TLG 1271 001]
Concilia Oecumenica: N.P. Tanner (ed.), *Decrees of the Ecumenical Councils* (2 vols; London: Sheend & Ward, 1990).
Constitutiones apostolorum: M. Metzger (ed.), *Les constitutions apostoliques* (SC 320, 329, 336; Paris: Cerf, 1985-1987). [TLG 2894 001]
– Eng. trans.: J. Donaldson, ANF, VII, pp. 774-1008.
Council of Gangra (Eng. trans.): O.L. Yarbrough, 'Canons from the Council of Gangra', in V.L. Wimbush (ed.), *Ascetic Behavior in Greco-Roman Antiquity: A Sourcebook* (Studies in Antiquity & Christianity; Minneapolis: Fortress Press, 1990), pp. 448-55.
Cyprian, *Epistolae* (*ep.*): *PL* 3.721-864; *PL* 4.193-452.
– *Epp.* (Eng. trans.): E. Wallace, ANF, V, pp. 565-843.
– *Exhortatio ad pœnitentiam*: *PL* 4.859-902.
– *Exhortatio ad pœnitentiam*: (partial Eng. trans.): E. Wallace, ANF, V, pp. 1204-10.
Demosthenes, *Philippi epistula* (*Phil. ep.*): S.H. Butcher (ed.), *Demosthenis orationes* (3 vols; Oxford: Clarendon Press, 1966 [1903-1931]), I, pp. 158-65. [TLG 0014 012]

– *Phil. ep.* (Greek and Eng. trans.): J.H. Vince (ed.), *Demosthenes I: Olynthiacs, Philippics, Minor Public Speeches, Speech Against Leptines I-XVII, XX* (LCL 238; London: William Heinemann Ltd, 1930), pp. 334-49.

Didache: J.P. Audet (ed.), *La Didachè: Instructions des Apôtres* (Paris: Lecoffre, 1958), pp. 226-42. [TLG 1311 001]

Dorotheos of Gaza, *Doctrinae* (*doctr.*): L. Regnault and J. de Préville (eds), *Dorothée de Gaza: Œuvres Spirituelles* (SC 92; Paris: Cerf, 1963).

– *Doctr.* (Eng. trans.): E.P. Wheeler, *Dorotheos of Gaza: Discourses and Sayings* (Cistercian Studies Series 33; Kalamazoo: Cistercian Publications, 1977).

Ephraim the Deacon, *Vita Sanctae Mariae meretricis* (*vit. Mar. mere.*):
– *Vit. Mar. mere.* (Latin): *PL* 73.651-660.
– *Vit. Mar. mere.* (Greek): K.G. Phrantzoles (ed.), Ὁσίου Ἐφραίμ τοῦ Σύρου ἔργα (7 vols; Thessalonica: Το περιβόλι της Παναγίας, 1998), VII, pp. 356-94. [TLG 4138 155]
– *Vit. Mar. mere.* (Eng. trans. of Latin): B. Ward, *Harlots of the Desert: A study of repentance in early monastic sources* (Cistercian Studies Series 106; Kalamazoo: Cistercian Publications, 1987), pp. 92-101.

Epiphanius Constantiensis, *Adversus haereses* (=*Panarion*): K. Holl (ed.), *Epiphanius: Ancoratus und Panarion* (*GCS* 25, 31, 37; Leipzig: Hinrichs, 1915-1933). [TLG 2021 002]

Eunapius, *Vitae sophistarum* (*vit. soph.*): J. Giangrande (ed.), *Eunapii vitae sophistarum* (Rome: Polygraphica, 1956), pp. 1-101. [TLG 2050 001]

Eusebius of Caesarea, *De martyribus Palaestinae*: G. Bardy (ed.), *Eusèbe de Césarée: Histoire ecclésiastique* (SC 55; Paris: Cerf, 1958), pp. 121-74. [TLG 2018 003 and TLG 2018 004]

– *Historia ecclesiastica* (*HE*): G. Bardy (ed.), *Eusèbe de Césarée: Histoire ecclésiastique* (SC 31, 41, 55; Paris: Cerf, 1952-1958). [TLG 2018 002]

– *Praeparatio Evangelica* (*praep. Ev.*): K. Mras (ed.), *Eusebius Werke VIII: Die Praeparatio evangelica* (*GCS* 43.1, 43.2: Berlin: Akademie-Verlag, 1954-1956). [TLG 2018 001]

– *Vita Constantini* (*vit. Const.*): F. Winkelmann (ed.), *Eusebius Werke I: Über das Leben des Kaisers Konstantin* (*GCS* 68 (7), Berlin: Akademie-Verlag, 1975), pp. 3-151. [TLG 2018 020]

Evagrius Ponticus, *Ad monachos* (*ad mon.*): J. Driscoll (ed.), *The 'Ad Monachos' of Evagrius Ponticus: Its Structure and a Select Commentary* (Studia Anselmiana 104; Rome: Abbazia S. Paolo, 1991).

– *Ad mon.*: H. Gressmann (ed.), 'Nonnenspiegel und Mönchsspiegel des Euagrios Pontikos', *TU* 39.4 (1913), pp. 153-65. [TLG 4110 007]

– *Ad mon.* (Eng. trans.): R.E. Sinkewicz, *Evagrius of Pontus: The Greek Ascetic Corpus* (Oxford: Oxford University Press, 2003), pp. 122-31.

– *Ad virgines* (*ad virg.*): H. Gressmann (ed.), 'Nonnenspiegel und Mönchsspiegel des Euagrios Pontikos', *TU* 39.4 (1913), pp. 146-51. [TLG 4110 008]

– *Ad virg.* (Latin): *PG* 40.1283-1286.

– *Ad virg.* (Latin): D.A. Wilmart (ed.), 'Les versions Latines des sentences d'Évagre pour les vierges', *RB* 28 (1911), pp. 148-50.

– *Ad virg.* (Eng. trans.): A.M. Casiday, *Evagrius Ponticus* (The Early Church Fathers; Routledge: Abingdon, 2006), pp. 165-71.

– *Ad virg.* (Eng. trans.): R.E. Sinkewicz, *Evagrius of Pontus: The Greek Ascetic Corpus* (Oxford: Oxford University Press, 2003), pp. 131-35.

– *Aliae sententiae*: *PG* 40.1269-1270.

– *Aliae sententiae*: A. Elter (ed.), *Gnomica* (2 vols; Leipzig: Teubner, 1892), I, pp. liii-liv. [TLG 4110 018]

– *Aliae sententiae* (Eng. trans.): A.M. Casiday, *Evagrius Ponticus* (The Early Church Fathers; Routledge: Abingdon, 2006), pp. 181-82

– *Aliae sententiae* (Eng. trans.): R.E. Sinkewicz, *Evagrius of Pontus: The Greek Ascetic Corpus* (Oxford: Oxford University Press, 2003), pp. 231-32.

– *Antirrhetikos* (*Antirr.*: partial Eng. trans.): M. O'Laughlin, 'Evagrius Ponticus: Antirrheticus (Selections)', in V.L. Wimbush (ed.), *Ascetic Behavior in Greco-Roman Antiquity: A Sourcebook* (Studies in Antiquity & Christianity; Minneapolis: Fortress Press, 1990), pp. 243-62.

– *Capita paraenetica*: *PG* 79.1249-1252.

– *Capita paraenetica*: A. Elter (ed.), *Gnomica* (2 vols; Leipzig: Teubner, 1892), I, p. lii. [TLG 4110 016]

– *Capita paraenetica* (Eng. trans.): R.E. Sinkewicz, *Evagrius of Pontus: The Greek Ascetic Corpus* (Oxford: Oxford University Press, 2003), pp. 229-30.

– *Capitula XXXIII: Definitiones passionum animae rationalis*: *PG* 40.1263-1268. [TLG 4110 015]

– *Capitula XXXIII* 17-33: P. Géhin (ed.), *Évagre le Pontique: Scholies aux Proverbes* (SC 340; Paris: Cerf, 1987), pp. 487-89.

– *Capitula XXXIII* (Eng. trans.): R.E. Sinkewicz, *Evagrius of Pontus: The Greek Ascetic Corpus* (Oxford: Oxford University Press, 2003), pp. 224-27.

– *De magistris et discipulis*: P. van den Ven (ed.), 'Un opuscule inédit attribué à S. Nil', in *Mélanges Godefroid Kurth: Recueil de mémoires relatifs à l'histoire, à la philologie et à l'archéologie* (2 vols; Liège: Faculté de Philosophie et Lettres de l'Université de Liège, 1908), II, pp. 73-81. [TLG 4110 043]

– *De octo spiritibus malitiae* (*de octo*): *PG* 79.1145-1164. [TLG 4110 023]

– *De octo* (Greek text with Italian trans.): F. Moscatelli, *Evagrio Pontico: Gli Otto Spiriti della Malvagità* (Milan: Edizioni San Paolo, 1996).

– *De octo* (Eng. trans.): R.E. Sinkewicz, *Evagrius of Pontus: The Greek Ascetic Corpus* (Oxford: Oxford University Press, 2003), pp. 73-90.

– *De oratione* (*de orat.*; numeration follows Migne): *PG* 79.1165-1200. [TLG 4110 024]

– *De orat.* (Eng. trans.): J.E. Bamberger, *Evagrius Ponticus: The Praktikos & Chapters on Prayer* (Cistercian Studies Series, 4; Kalamazoo: Cistercian Publications, 1972).

– *De orat.* (Eng. trans.): A.M. Casiday, *Evagrius Ponticus* (The Early Church Fathers; Routledge: Abingdon, 2006), pp. 185-201.

– *De orat.* (Eng. trans.): G.E.H. Palmer, P. Sherrard and K. Ware (eds), *The Philokalia: The Complete Text compiled by St Nikodemos of the Holy Mountain and St Makarios of Corinth* (4 vols; London: Faber and Faber, 1979-1995), I, pp. 55-71.

– *De orat.* (Eng. trans.): R.E. Sinkewicz, *Evagrius of Pontus: The Greek Ascetic Corpus* (Oxford: Oxford University Press, 2003), pp. 193-209.

– *De orat.* (Eng. trans.): S. Tugwell, *Evagrius Ponticus: Praktikos and on Prayer; Dionysius the Areopagite: Mystical Theology* (Oxford: Faculty of Theology, 1987).

– *De orat.* (French trans.): I. Hausherr, 'Le traité de l'oraison d'Évagre le Pontique (Pseudo Nil)', *RAM* 15 (1934), pp. 34-93, 113-70.

- *De vitiis quae opposita sunt virtutibus*: *PG* 79.1139-1144. [TLG 4110 021]
- *De vitiis quae opposita sunt virtutibus* (Eng. trans.): R.E. Sinkewicz, *Evagrius of Pontus: The Greek Ascetic Corpus* (Oxford: Oxford University Press, 2003), pp. 61-65.
- Εἰς τὸ πιπι (sp.): P. de Lagarde (ed.), *Onomastica sacra* (Hildesheim: Olms, 1966 [1887]), pp. 229-30. [TLG 4110 040]
- *Epistulae*:
- *Epp.* (Syriac with Greek retroversion): W. Frankenberg, *Euagrius Ponticus*, (Abhandlungen der königlichen Gesellschaft der Wissenschaften zu Göttingen, Philologisch-Historische Klasse, Neue Folge, 13.2; Berlin: Weidmannsche Buchhandlung, 1912), pp. 564-619.
- *Epp.* (Greek fragments in *codex Sinaiticus 462*): C. Guillaumont, 'Fragments grecs inédits d'Evagre le Pontique', in Jürgen Dummer (ed.), *Texte und Textkritik: Eine Aufsatzsammlung* (*TU* 133; Berlin: Akademie-Verlag, 1987), pp. 218-21.
- *Epistula fidei* (= Basil, *ep.* 8): Y. Courtonne (ed.), *Saint Basile: Lettres*, (3 vols; Paris: Les Belles Lettres, 1957-1966), I, pp. 22-37. [TLG 2040 004]
- *Epistula ad Melaniam* 33-68 (Syriac and French trans.; numeration follows Casiday): G. Vitestam, *Seconde partie du traité qui passe sous le nom de 'La grande lettre d'Évagre le Pontique à Mélanie l'Ancienne': Publiée et traduite d'après le manuscrit du British Museum Add. 17192* (Scripta Minora Regiae Societatis Humaniorum Litterarum Lundensis 1963-1964.3; Lund: Gleerup, 1964).
- *Epp.* (German trans. and commentary): G. Bunge, *Evagrios Pontikos: Briefe aus der Wüste* (Sophia Quellen Östlicher Theologie 24; Trier: Paulinus-Verlag, 1986).
- *Epp.* 7, 8, 19, 20, *ep. fidei* and *ep. ad Melaniam* (Eng. trans.): A.M. Casiday, *Evagrius Ponticus* (The Early Church Fathers; Routledge: Abingdon, 2006), pp. 45-77.
- *Excerpta*: J. Muyldermans (ed.), *À travers la tradition manuscrite d'Évagre le Pontique: Essai sur les manuscrits grecs conservés à la Bibliothèque Nationale de Paris* (Bibliothèque du Muséon 3; Louvain: Bureaux du Muséon, 1932), pp. 79-94.
- *Excerpta* (Eng. trans.): A.M. Casiday, *Evagrius Ponticus* (The Early Church Fathers; Routledge: Abingdon, 2006), pp. 172-80.
- *Expositio in Proverbia Salomonis* (= Codex *Patmiacus 270*): C. Tischendorf, *Notitia editionis codicis bibliorum Sinaitici* (Leipzig: F.A. Brockhaus, 1860), pp. 76-122. [TLG 4110 028]
- *Expositio in Proverbia Salomonis* (extracts and discussion): P. Géhin (ed.), *Évagre le Pontique: Scholies aux Proverbes* (SC 340; Paris: Cerf, 1987), pp. 55-62.
- *Gnostikos* (*gnos.*): A. Guillaumont and Claire Guillaumont (eds), *Évagre le Pontique: Le gnostique ou à celui qui est devenu digne de la science* (SC 356; Paris: Cerf, 1989). [TLG 4110 002].
- *Institutio ad monachos* (*inst. ad mon.*): *PG* 79.1235-1240. [TLG 4110 025]
- *Inst. ad mon.* longer recension (*inst. suppl.*) J. Muyldermans (ed.), 'Evagriana: Le Vatic. Barb. Graecus 515', *Le Muséon* 51 (1938), pp. 191-226.
- *Inst. ad mon.* (Eng. trans.): R.E. Sinkewicz, *Evagrius of Pontus: The Greek Ascetic Corpus* (Oxford: Oxford University Press, 2003), pp. 218-23.
- *Kephalaia Gnostica* (*KG*):
- *KG* (Syriac and French trans. of *KG* S¹ and *KG* S²): A. Guillaumont (ed.), *Les six Centuries des 'Kephalaia Gnostica' d'Évagre le Pontique: Édition critique de la*

version Syriaque commune et édition d'une nouvelle version Syriaque, intégrale, avec une double traduction française (*PO* 28.1; Paris: Firmin-Didot, 1958).

– *KG* (Greek fragments): I. Hausherr (ed.), 'Nouveau fragments grecs d'Évagre le Pontique', *OCP* 5 (1939), pp. 229-33.

– *KG* (S²) (Eng. trans.): D. Bundy, 'Evagrius Ponticus: The Kephalaia Gnostica', in V.L. Wimbush (ed.), *Ascetic Behavior in Greco-Roman Antiquity: A Sourcebook* (Studies in Antiquity & Christianity; Minneapolis: Fortress Press, 1990), pp. 175-86.

– *Περὶ λογισμῶν* (Περὶ Λογ. Formerly: *de diversis malignis cogitationibus*): P Géhin, C. Guillaumont and A. Guillaumont (eds), *Évagre le Pontique: Sur les pensées* (SC 438; Paris: Cerf, 1998).

– Περὶ Λογ. (Short recension: *capita XXVII de diversis malignis cogitationibus*): *PG* 79.1199-1234 and *PG* 40.1236-1244. [TLG 4110 022]

– Περὶ Λογ. (Eng. trans.): A.M. Casiday, *Evagrius Ponticus* (The Early Church Fathers; Routledge: Abingdon, 2006), pp. 89-116.

– Περὶ Λογ. (Eng. trans.): R.E. Sinkewicz, *Evagrius of Pontus: The Greek Ascetic Corpus* (Oxford: Oxford University Press, 2003), pp. 153-82.

– Περὶ Λογ. (Eng. trans. of a shorter version): G.E.H. Palmer, P. Sherrard and K. Ware (eds), *The Philokalia: The Complete Text compiled by St Nikodemos of the Holy Mountain and St Makarios of Corinth* (4 vols; London: Faber and Faber, 1979-1995), I, pp. 38-52.

– *Praktikos* (*prak.*): A. Guillaumont and C. Guillaumont (eds), *Évagre le Pontique: Le Traité practique ou le moine* (SC 170, 171; Paris: Cerf, 1971). [TLG 4110 001]

– *Prak.*: *PG* 40.1219-1252 (*capita practica ad Anatolium*) and *PG* 40.1271-1276 (*de octo vitiosis cogitationibus ad Anatolium*).

– *Prak.*: (Eng. trans.): J.E. Bamberger, *Evagrius Ponticus: The Praktikos & Chapters on Prayer* (Cistercian Studies Series, 4; Kalamazoo: Cistercian Publications, 1972).

– *Prak.* (Eng. trans.): R.E. Sinkewicz, *Evagrius of Pontus: The Greek Ascetic Corpus* (Oxford: Oxford University Press, 2003), pp. 95-114.

– *Prak.* (Eng. trans.): S. Tugwell, *Evagrius Ponticus: Praktikos and on Prayer; Dionysius the Areopagite: Mystical Theology* (Oxford: Faculty of Theology, 1987).

– *Rerum monachalium rationes* (*rer. mon. rat.*): *PG* 40.1251-1264. [TLG 4110 010]

– *Rer. mon. rat.* (Eng trans.): A.M. Casiday, *Evagrius Ponticus* (The Early Church Fathers; Routledge: Abingdon, 2006), pp. 81-88.

– *Rer. mon. rat.* (Eng. trans.): G.E.H. Palmer, P. Sherrard and K. Ware (eds), *The Philokalia: The Complete Text compiled by St Nikodemos of the Holy Mountain and St Makarios of Corinth* (4 vols; London: Faber and Faber, 1979-1995), I, pp. 31-37.

– *Rer. mon. rat.* (Eng. trans.): R.E. Sinkewicz, *Evagrius of Pontus: The Greek Ascetic Corpus* (Oxford: Oxford University Press, 2003), pp. 4-11.

– *Scholia in Ecclesiasten* (*schol. in Eccl.*): P. Géhin (ed.), *Évagre le Pontique: Scholies à l'Ecclésiaste* (SC 397; Paris: Cerf, 1993). [TLG 4110 031]

– *Schol. in Eccl.* (Eng trans.): A.M. Casiday, *Evagrius Ponticus* (The Early Church Fathers; Routledge: Abingdon, 2006), pp. 130-49.

– *Scholia in Iob* (*schol. in Job*; Eng. trans.): A.M. Casiday, *Evagrius Ponticus* (The Early Church Fathers; Routledge: Abingdon, 2006), pp. 123-29.

– *Scholia in Proverbia* (*schol. in Prov.*): P. Géhin (ed.), *Évagre le Pontique: Scholies aux Proverbes* (SC 340; Paris: Cerf, 1987). [TLG 4110 030]

– *Scholia in Psalmos* (*schol. in Ps.*; Greek and Eng. trans.): L. Dysinger, http://www.ldysinger.com/Evagrius/08_Psalms/00a_start.htm (accessed 23 August

2006); a key to published sources can be found in M.-J. Rondeau, 'Le commentaire sur les Psaumes d'Évagre le Pontique', *OCP* 26 (1960), pp. 307-48.

- *Skemmata (skem. = capita cogniscitiva)*: J. Muyldermans (ed.), 'Evagriana', *Le Muséon* 44 (1931), pp. 37-68, 369-83.
- *Skem.* (Eng. trans.): W. Harmless, 'The Sapphire Light of the Mind: The Skemmata of Evagrius Ponticus', *Theological Studies* 62 (2001), pp. 498-529.
- *Skem.* (Eng. trans.): R.E. Sinkewicz, *Evagrius of Pontus: The Greek Ascetic Corpus* (Oxford: Oxford University Press, 2003), pp. 211-16.
- *Spiritales sententiae per alphabeticum dispositae (sp. sent.)*: *PG* 40.1267-1270.
- *Sp. Sent.*: A. Elter (ed.), *Gnomica* (2 vols; Leipzig: Teubner, 1892), I, p. liii. [TLG 4110 017]
- *Sp. Sent.* (Eng. trans.): R.E. Sinkewicz, *Evagrius of Pontus: The Greek Ascetic Corpus* (Oxford: Oxford University Press, 2003), pp. 230-31.
- *Tractatus ad Eulogium (tract. ad Eulog.*; numeration follows Migne): *PG* 79.1093-1140. [TLG 4110 020]
- *Tract. ad Eulog.* (Eng. trans. and Greek text of Lavra *Γ* 93): R.E. Sinkewicz (ed.), *Evagrius of Pontus: The Greek Ascetic Corpus* (Oxford: Oxford University Press, 2003), pp.29-59, 310-33.

Gellius, Aulus, *Noctes Atticae*: J.C. Rolfe (ed.), *The Attic Nights of Aulus Gellius* (LCL 195, 200, 212; London: William Heinemann Ltd, 1927-1928).

Gennadius, *De viris inlustribus (de vir. inl.)*: C.A. Bernoulli (ed.), *Hieronymus und Gennadius: De viris inlustribus* (Sammlung augeswählter kirchen und dogmengeschichtlicher Quellenschriften 11; Freiburg und Leipzig: Mohr, 1895).
- *De vir. inl.* (Eng. trans.): E.C. Richardson, NPNF Series 2, III, pp. 781-818.

Gregory of Nazianzus, *Orationes (orat.)*:
- *Orat.* 28 *(de theologia)*: J. Barbel (ed.), *Gregor von Nazianz: Die fünf theologischen Reden* (Düsseldorf: Patmos-Verlag, 1963), pp. 62-126. [TLG 2022 008]
- *Orat.* 42 *(supremum vale)*: *PG* 36.457-492. [TLG 2022 050]

Gregory of Nyssa, *De vita Mosis (de vit. Mos.)*: J. Daniélou (ed.), *Grégoire de Nysse: La vie de Moïse* (SC 1; Paris: Cerf, 3rd edn, 1968). [TLG 2017 042]
- *De vit. Mos.* (Eng. trans.): A.J. Malherbe and E. Ferguson, *Gregory of Nyssa: The Life of Moses* (The Classics of Western Spirituality; New York: Paulist Press, 1978).
- *Epistula canonica ad Letoium*: *PG* 45.221-236 [TLG 2017 076]
- *Epistula canonica ad Letoium* (Eng. trans.): H.R. Percival, NPNF Series 2, XIV, pp. 1154-56.

Gregory Thaumaturgus, *In Origenem oratio panegyrica (Orig. orat. pan.)*: H. Crouzel (ed.), *Grégoire le Thaumaturge: Remerciement à Origène suivi de la lettre d'Origène à Grégoire* (SC 148: Paris: Cerf, 1969). [TLG 2063 001]
- *Orig. orat. pan.* (Eng. trans.): S.D.F. Salmond, ANF, VI, pp. 10-79.

Gregory the Great, *Dialogues (dial.)*: A. de Vogüé and P. Antin (eds), *Grégoire le Grand: Dialogues* (SC 251, 260, 265; Paris: Cerf, 1978-1980).
- *Dial.* (Eng. trans.): M.L. Uhlfelder, *The Dialogues of Gregory the Great, Book Two, Saint Benedict* (The Library of the Liberal Arts; New York: The Bobb-Merrill Company, 1967).
- *Dial.* (Eng. trans.): C. White, *Early Christian Lives*, (London: Penguin Books, 1998), pp. 165-204.
- *Epistolae (ep.)*: *PL* 77.441-1368.
- *Epp.* (Eng. trans.): J. Barmby, NPNF Series 2, XII, pp. 632-976.

– *Liber Regula Pastoralis (reg. past.)*: *PL* 77.13-128.
– *Reg. past.* (Eng. trans.): H. Davis, *St. Gregory the Great: Pastoral Care – Regula Pastoralis* (Ancient Christian Writers 11; London: Longmans, Green and Co., 1950).
– *Moralia in Iob (mor. in Iob)*: *PL* 75.509-1162; *PL* 76.9-782.
– *Mor. in Iob*: M. Adriaen (ed.), *S. Gregorii Magni: Moralia in Iob (CCL* 143, 143A, 143B; Turnhout: Brepols, 1979-85).
– *Mor. in Iob*: R. Gillet, A. de Gaudemaris and A. Bocognano, *Grégoire le Grand: Morales sur Job* (SC 32 *bis*, 212, 221; Paris: Cerf, 1952-1989).
– *Mor. in Iob* (Eng. trans.): J. Bliss, *Morals on the Book of Job by S. Gregory the Great* (Library of the Fathers of the Catholic Church, 18, 21, 23, 31; Oxford: John Henry Parker, 1844-1850).
Hermas, *Pastor*: M. Whittaker (ed.), *Die apostolischen Väter I: Der Hirt des Hermas (GCS* 48; Berlin: Akademie-Verlag, 2nd edn, 1967), pp. 1-98. [TLG 1419 001]
– *Pastor*: K. Lake (ed.), *Facsimiles of the Athos Fragments of the Shepherd of Hermas* (Oxford: Claredon Press, 1907).
Herodotus, *Historiae (hist.)*: Ph.-E. Legrand (ed.), *Hérodote: Histoires* (9 vols; Paris: Les Belles Lettres, rev. edn, 1963-1970). [TLG 0016 001]
– *Hist.* (Eng. trans.): Aubrey de Sélincourt, *Herodotus: The Histories* (Harmondsworth: Penguin Books, rev edn, 1972).
Hippocrates, *Coa praesagia*: É. Littré (ed.), *Oeuvres complètes d'Hippocrate* (10 vols; Amsterdam: Hakkert, 1962 [1839-1861]), V, pp. 588-732. [TLG 0627 017]
– *De diaeta*: É. Littré (ed.), *Oeuvres complètes d'Hippocrate*, (10 vols; Amsterdam: Hakkert, 1962 [1839-1861]), VI, pp. 466-662. [TLG 0627 031]
– *De semine, de natura pueri, de morbis iv (de semine)*: É. Littré (ed.), *Oeuvres complètes d'Hippocrate* (10 vols; Amsterdam: Hakkert, 1962 [1839-1861]), VII, pp. 470-614. [TLG 0627 024]
Hippolytus, *Refutatio omnium haeresium*: M. Marcovich (ed.), *Hippolytus: Refutatio omnium haeresium (PTS* 25; Berlin: De Gruyter, 1986), pp. 53-417. [TLG 2115 060]
– *Refutatio omnium haeresium* (Eng. trans.): J.H. MacMahon, ANF, V, pp. 16-316.
Historia monachorum in Aegypto (HM): A.-J. Festugière (ed.), *Historia Monachorum in Aegypto: Édition critique du texte grec et traduction annotée* (Subsidia Hagiographica 53; Brussels: Société des Bollandistes, 1971). [TLG 2744 001]
– Latin version of Rufinus: *PL* 21.387-462.
– Latin version of Rufinus: E. Schultz-Flügel (ed.), *Tyrannius Rufinus: Historia Monachorum sive de vita sanctorum partum (PTS* 34; Berlin; Hew York: De Gruyter, 1990).
– Eng. trans.: N. Russell and B. Ward, *The Lives of the Desert Fathers: The historia monachorum in Aegypto* (Cistercian Studies Series 34; London: Mowbray, 1981).
Homer, *Iliad*: T.W. Allen (ed.), *Homeri Ilias* (3 vols; Oxford: Clarendon Press, 1931). [TLG 0012 001]
– *Iliad* (Eng. trans.): E.V. Rieu, *Homer: The Iliad* (Harmondsworth: Penguin Books, 1950).
– *Odyssey*: P. vón der Mühll (ed.), *Homeri Odyssea* (Basel: Helbing & Lichtenhahn, 1962). [TLG 0012 002]
– *Odyssey* (Eng. trans.): E.V. Rieu, *Homer: The Odyssey* (Harmondsworth: Penguin Books, 1946).
Horace, *Epistolae (ep.)*: H.R. Fairclough, *Horace: Satires, Epistles and Art of Poetry* (LCL 194; London: William Heinemann Ltd, 1926).

Ignatius Antiochenus, *Epistulae*: P.T. Camelot (ed.), *Ignace d'Antioche. Polycarpe de Smyrne. Lettres. Martyre de Polycarpe* (SC 10; Paris: Cerf, 4th edn, 1969). [TLG 1443 001]

Irenaeus, *Adversus haereses*: A. Rousseau, L. Doutreleau, B. Hemmerdinger and C. Mercier, *Irénée de Lyon: Contre les hérésies* (SC 100 *bis*, 152-153, 263-264, 293-294, 210-211; Paris: Cerf, 1965-1982).

– *Adversus haereses* (Eng. trans.): A. Cleveland Coxe, ANF, I, pp. 623-1138.

James the Deacon, *Vita Sanctae Pelagiae meretricis*:

– *Vita Sanctae Pelagiae meretricis* (Latin trans. of Greek of Eustochius): *PL* 73.663-672.

– *Vita Sanctae Pelagiae meretricis* (Eng. trans.): B. Ward, *Harlots of the Desert: A study of repentance in early monastic sources* (Cistercian Studies Series 106; Kalamazoo: Cistercian Publications, 1987), pp. 66-75.

Jerome, *Apologia contra Rufinum* (*apol. cont. Ruf.*): *PL* 23. 397-492.

– *Apol. Cont. Ruf.*: P. Lardet (ed.), *S. Hieronymi Presbyteri Opera pars III Opera Polemica I Contra Rufinum* (*CCL* 79; Turnhout: Brepols, 1982).

– *Apol. Cont. Ruf.* (Eng. trans.): W.H. Fremantle, NPNF Series 2, III, pp. 974-1091.

– *De viris inlustribus* (*de vir. inl.*): C.A. Bernoulli (ed.), *Hieronymus und Gennadius: De Viris Inlustribus* (Sammlung augeswählter kirchen und dogmengeschichtlicher Quellenschriften 11; Freiburg und Leipzig: Mohr, 1895).

– *De vir. Inl.* (Eng. trans.): E.C. Richardson, NPNF Series 2, III, pp. 727-78.

– *Dialogus adversus Pelagianos* (*dial. adv. Pel.*): C. Moreschini (ed.), *S. Hieronymi Presbyteri Opera pars III opera polemica 3* (*CCL* 80; Turnhout: Brepols, 1990).

– *Dial. adv. Pel.* (Eng. trans.): W.H. Fremantle, G. Lewis and W. G. Martley, NPNF Series 2, VI, pp. 939-1009.

– *Epistolae* (*ep.*): *PL* 22.325-1224.

– *Epp.*: I. Hilberg (ed.), *Sancti Eusebii Hieronymi Epistulae* (*CSEL* 54-56; Vienna: Tempsky, 1910-18).

– *Epp.* (partial Eng. trans.): W.H. Fremantle, G. Lewis and W. G. Martley, NPNF Series 2 VI, pp. 68-651.

– *Ep. to Pammachius against John of Jerusalem* (Eng. trans.): W.H. Fremantle, G. Lewis and W.G. Martley, NPNF Series 2, VI, pp. 892-936.

– *Commentarium in Hieremiam* (*comm. in Hierem.*): S. Reiter (ed.), *S. Hieronymi Presbyteri Opera pars I opera exegetica 3* (*CCL* 74; Turnhout: Brepols, 1960).

– *Vita Pauli Primi Eremitae* (*vit. Pauli*): *PL* 23.17-28.

– *Vit. Pauli* (Eng. trans.): P.B. Harvey, 'Jerome: Life of Paul, the First Hermit', in V.L. Wimbush (ed.), *Ascetic Behavior in Greco-Roman Antiquity: A Sourcebook* (Studies in Antiquity & Christianity; Minneapolis: Fortress Press, 1990), pp. 357-69.

– *Vit. Pauli* (Eng. trans.): C. White, *Early Christian Lives* (London: Penguin Books, 1998), pp. 75-84.

John Chrysostom, *Ad populum Antiochenum, homiliae 1-21* (*ad pop. Antioch.*): *PG* 49.15-222. [TLG 2062 024]

– *ad pop. Antioch.* (Eng. trans.): W.R.W. Stevens, NPNF Series 1, IX, pp. 539-834.

– *In epistulam ad Romanos, homiliae 1-32* (*hom. in Rom.*): *PG* 60.391-682 [TLG 2062 155]

– *Hom. in Rom.* (Eng. trans.): J.R. Morris, W.H. Simcox and G.B. Stevens, NPNF Series 1, XI, pp. 575-1016.

– *In epistulam ii ad Timotheum, homiliae 1-10*: *PG* 62.599-662. [TLG 2062 165]

– *In epistulam ii ad Timotheum, homiliae 1-10* (Eng. trans.): P. Schaff, NPNF Series 1, XIII, pp. 974-1067.

John Climacus, *Scala paradisi* (*scala parad.*): *PG* 88.631-1164.

– *Scala parad.* (Eng. trans.): C. Luibheid and N. Russell, *John Climacus: The Ladder of Divine Ascent* (The Classics of Western Spirituality; Mahwah: Paulist Press, 1982).

John of Damascus, *Expositio fidei*: B. Kotter (ed.), *Die Schriften des Johannes von Damaskos* (*PTS* 12; Berlin: De Gruyter, 1973), pp. 3-239. [TLG 2934 004]

– *Expositio fidei* (Eng. trans.): S.D.F. Salmond, NPNF Series 2, IX, pp. 639-833.

John Moschus, *Pratum spirituale*: *PG* 87.2851-3116.

– *Pratum spirituale*: *PL* 74.119-240.

Josephus, Flavius, *Contra Apionem* (*cont. Ap.*): B. Niese (ed.), *Flavii Iosephi opera* (7 vols; Berlin: Weidmann, 1889, repr. 1955), V, pp. 3-99. [TLG 0526 003]

– *Cont. Ap.* (Eng. trans.): W. Whiston, *Josephus: Complete Works* (London: Pickering & Inglis, rev. edn, 1981), pp. 607-36.

Justin Martyr, *Apologia* (*apol.*): E.J. Goodspeed (ed.), *Die ältesten Apologeten* (Göttingen: Vandenhoeck & Ruprecht, 1915), pp. 26-77. [TLG 0645 001]

– *Apol.* (Eng. trans.): A.C. Coxe, ANF, I, pp. 292-344.

Lactantius, *De mortibus persecutorum*: J. Moreau (ed.), *Lactance: De la mort des persécuteurs* (SC 39; Paris: Cerf, 1954).

Macarius (Pseudo-), *Apophthegmata* (*apoph.*):

– *Apoph.* (Greek): *PG* 34.229-262. [TLG 2109 011]

– *Apoph.* (Latin): D.A.B. Caillau and D.M.N.S. Guillon (eds), *Collectio Selecta SS. Ecclesiæ Patrum complectens exquisitissima opera, tum dogmatica et moralia tum apologetica et oratoria* (133 vols; Paris: Parent-Desbarres, 1836), XLVIII, pp. 419-38.

– *Apoph.* (Bohairic Coptic with French trans.): É. Amélineau, *Monuments pour servir à l'histoire de l'Égypte chrétienne: Histoire des monastères de la Basse-Égypte. Vies des saints Paul, Antoine, Macaire, Maxime et Domèce, Jean le Nain, et autres* (Annales du Musée Guimet 25; Paris: E. Leroux, 1894), pp. 203-34.

– *De elevatione mentis*: *PG* 34.889-908.

– *De patientia et discretione*: *PG* 34.865-889.

– *Homiliae*:

– *Homiliae* Collectio H (*hom. H*): H. Dörries, E. Klostermann and M. Krüger (eds), *Die 50 geistlichen Homilien des Makarios* (*PTS* 4; Berlin: De Gruyter, 1964), pp. 1-322. [TLG 2109 002]

– *Homiliae* Collectio B (*hom. B*): H. Berthold (ed.), *Makarios/Symeon: Reden und Briefe. Die Sammlung I des Vaticanus Graecus 694* (2 vols; GCS; Berlin: Akademie-Verlag, 1973). [TLG 2109 001]

– *hom. H* (Eng. trans.): G.A. Maloney, *Pseudo-Macarius: The Fifty Spiritual Homilies and the Great Letter* (The Classics of Western Spirituality; New York: Paulist Press,1992).

Musonius Rufus, *Dissertationum a Lucio digestarum reliquiae* (*dissert.*): C.E. Lutz (ed.), *Musonius Rufus 'The Roman Socrates'* (New Haven: Yale University Press, 1947), pp. 32-128. [TLG 0628 001]

Origen, *Commentarii in Canticum* (*com. in Cant.*):

– *Com. in Cant.* (Greek): W.A. Baehrens (ed.), *Origenes Werke 8* (GCS 33; Leipzig: Teubner, 1925). [TLG 2042 026]

- *Com. in Cant.* (Latin): L. Brésard and H. Crouzel (eds), *Origène: Commentaire sur le Cantique des Cantiques* (SC 375, 376; Paris: Cerf, 1991-2).
- *Com. in Cant.* (Eng. trans.): R.P. Lawson, *Origen: The Song of Songs – Commentary and Homilies* (Ancient Christian Writers 26; New York: Newman Press, 1957).
- *Com. in Cant.* prologue (Eng. trans.): R.A. Greer, *Origen: An Exhortation to Martyrdom, Prayer, First Principles Book IV, Prologue to the Commentary on the Song of Songs, Homily XXVII on Numbers* (The Classics of Western Spirituality; London: SPCK, 1979), pp. 217-44.
- *Commentarii in evangelium Joannis* (*comm. in Joh.*):
- *Comm. in Joh.* 1, 2, 4, 5, 6, 10, 13: C. Blanc (ed.), *Origène: Commentaire sur saint Jean* (SC 120, 157, 222; Paris: Cerf, 1966-1975). [TLG 2042 005]
- *Comm. in Joh.* 19, 20, 28, 32: E. Preuschen (ed.), *Origenes Werke 4* (GCS 10; Leipzig: Hinrichs, 1903), pp. 298-480. [TLG 2042 079]
- *Comm. in Joh.* 1, 2, 4, 5, 6, 10 (Eng. trans.): A. Menzies, ANF, X, pp. 451-676.
- *Contra Celsum* (*cont. Cels.*): M. Borret (ed.), *Origène: Contre Celse* (SC 132, 136, 147, 150, 227: Paris: Cerf, 1967-1976). [SC 132, 136, 147, 150: TLG 2042 001]
- *Cont. Cels.* (Eng. trans.): F. Crombie, ANF, IV, pp. 755-1336.
- *De oratione* (*de orat.*): P. Koetschau (ed.), *Origenes Werke 2* (GCS 3; Leipzig: Hinrichs, 1899), pp. 297-403. [TLG 2042 008]
- *De orat.* (Eng. trans.): R.A. Greer, *Origen: An Exhortation to Martyrdom, Prayer, First Principles Book IV, Prologue to the Commentary on the Song of Songs, Homily XXVII on Numbers* (The Classics of Western Spirituality; London: SPCK, 1979), pp. 81-170.
- *De principiis* (*de prin.*):
- *De prin.* (Greek): H. Görgemanns and H. Karpp (eds), *Origenes vier Bücher von den Prinzipien* (Darmstadt: Wissenschaftliche Buchgesellschaft, 1976). [TLG 2042 002 and 2042 003]
- *De prin.* (Latin): H. Crouzel and M. Simonetti (eds), *Origène: Traité Des Principes* (SC 252, 253, 268, 269, 312; Paris: Cerf, 1978-1984).
- *De prin.* (Eng. trans.): G.W. Butterworth, *Origen: On First Principles* (London: SPCK, 1936).
- *De prin.* (Eng. trans.): F. Crombie, ANF, IV, pp. 456-730.
- *De prin.* 4 (Eng. trans. of Greek): R.A. Greer, *Origen: An Exhortation to Martyrdom, Prayer, First Principles Book IV, Prologue to the Commentary on the Song of Songs, Homily XXVII on Numbers* (The Classics of Western Spirituality; London: SPCK, 1979), pp. 171-216.
- *Dialogus cum Heraclide* (*dial. Herac.*): J. Scherer (ed.), *Origène: Entretien avec Héraclide* (SC 67; Paris: Cerf, 1960). [TLG 2042 018]
- *Exhortatio ad martyrium* (*exhort. ad mart.*): P. Koetschau (ed.), *Origenes Werke 1*, (GCS 2; Leipzig: Hinrichs, 1899), pp. 3-47. [TLG 2042 007]
- *Exhort. ad mart.* (Eng. trans.): R.A. Greer, *Origen: An Exhortation to Martyrdom, Prayer, First Principles Book IV, Prologue to the Commentary on the Song of Songs, Homily XXVII on Numbers* (The Classics of Western Spirituality; London: SPCK, 1979), pp. 41-79.
- *Fragmenta ex commentariis in epistulam I ad Thessalonicenses* (*frag. in I Thess.*): PG 14.1297-1304.
- *Fragmenta in Jeremiam* (*frag. in Jer.*): E. Klostermann (ed.), *Origenes Werke 3* (GCS 6; Leipzig: Hinrichs, 1901), pp. 199-232. [TLG 2042 010]

- *Fragmenta in Psalmos 1-150* (Pitra): J.B. Pitra (ed.), *Analecta sacra spicilegio Solesmensi parata* (8 vols; Farnborough: Gregg Press, 1966-1967 [1876-1891]), II, pp. 444-83; III, pp. 1-364. [TLG 2042 044]
- *Homiliae in Canticum* (*hom. in Cant.*): O. Rousseau (ed.), *Origène: Homélies sur le Cantique des Cantiques* (SC 37; Paris: Cerf, 2nd edn, 1966).
- *Hom. in Cant.* (Eng. trans.): R.P. Lawson, *Origen: The Song of Songs – Commentary and Homilies* (Ancient Christian Writers 26; New York: Newman Press, 1957).
- *Homiliae in Genesim* (*hom. in Gen.*): *PG* 12.145-262.
- *Hom. in Gen.* (Greek): W.A. Baehrens (ed.), *Origenes Werke 6* (*GCS* 29; Leipzig: Teubner, 1920), pp. 23-30. [TLG 2042 022]
- *Hom. in Gen.* (Latin): L. Doutreleau (ed.), *Origène: Homélies sur la Genèse* (SC7 *bis*; Paris: Cerf, 1976).
- *Homiliae in Jeremiam* (*hom. in Jer.*):
- *Hom. in Jer.* 1-11: P. Nautin (ed.), *Origène: Homélies sur Jérémie I* (SC 232; Paris: Cerf, 1976). [TLG 2042 009]
- *Hom. in Jer.* 12-20: E. Klostermann (ed.), *Origenes Werke 3* (*GCS* 6; Leipzig: Hinrichs, 1901), pp. 85-194. [TLG 2042 021]
- *Homiliae in Josue* (*hom. in Jos.*): A. Jaubert (ed.), *Origène: Homélies sur Josué* (SC 71; Paris: Cerf, 1960).
- *Homiliae in Lucam* (*hom. in Luc.*):
- *Hom. in Luc.* (Greek): M. Rauer (ed.), *Origenes Werke 9* (*GCS* 49 (35); Berlin: Akademie-Verlag, 2nd edn, 1959). [TLG 2042 016]
- *Hom. in Luc.* (Latin with Greek fragments): H. Crouzel, F. Fournier, P. Périchon (eds), *Origène: Homélies sur S. Luc – Latin et Fragments Grecs* (SC 87; Paris: Cerf, 1962).
- *Homiliae in Numeros* (*hom. in Num.*): W.A. Baehrens, *Origenes Werke 7.2* (*GCS* 30; Leipzig: Hinrichs, 1921).
- *Hom. in Num.* 27 (Eng. trans.): R.A. Greer, *Origen: An Exhortation to Martyrdom, Prayer, First Principles Book IV, Prologue to the Commentary on the Song of Songs, Homily XXVII on Numbers* (The Classics of Western Spirituality; London: SPCK, 1979), pp. 245-69.
- *Philocalia 1-27*: J.A. Robinson (ed.), *The philocalia of Origen* (Cambridge: Cambridge University Press, 1893). [TLG 2042 019]
- *Selecta in Psalmos*: *PG* 12.1053-1320, 1368-1369, 1388-1389, 1409-1685. [TLG 2042 058]

Pachomius, *Vita Pachomii graeca prima* (*vit. Pach.* G[1]) and *secunda* (*vit. Pach.* G[2]): F. Halkin, *Sancti Pachomii: Vitae Graecae* (Subsidia Hagiographica 19; Brussels: Société des Bollandistes, 1932).
- *Vita Pachomii* (Latin trans. of Dionysius Exiguus): *PL* 73.227-272.
- *Vita Pachomii* (Eng. trans.): A. Veilleux, *Pachomian Koinonia* (Cistercian Studies Series 45-47; Kalamazoo: Cistercian Publications), 1980-1982.

Palladius, *Dialogus de vita Joannis Chrysostomi* (*dial.*): P.R. Coleman-Norton (ed.), *Palladii dialogus de vita S. Joanni Chrysostomi* (Cambridge: Cambridge University Press, 1928), pp. 3-147. [TLG 2111 004]
- *Epistula ad Lausum* (*ep. Laus.*): C. Butler (ed.), *The Lausiac History of Palladius: A Critical Discussion Together with Notes on Early Egyptian Monachism* (2 vols; Hildesheim: Olms, 1967 [1898-1904]), II, pp. 6-7. [TLG 2111 003]
- *Historia Lausiaca* (*HL*):

- *HL* (Greek): G.J.M. Bartelink (ed.), *Palladio: La storia Lausiaca* (Verona: Fondazione Lorenzo Valla, 1974). [TLG 2111 001]
- *HL* (Latin): *PL* 73.1085-1218; *PL* 74.343-382.
- *HL* (Eng. trans. of Greek): R.T. Meyer, *Palladius: The Lausiac History* (Ancient Christian Writers 34; New York: Paulist Press, 1965).
- *HL* 9-10 (Eng. trans. of Coptic): T. Vivian, 'Coptic Palladiana I: The Life of Pambo (Lausiac History 9-10)', *Coptic Church Review* 20.3 (1999), pp. 66-95.
- *HL* 38 (Eng. trans. of Coptic): T. Vivian, 'Coptic Palladiana II: The Life of Evagrius (Lausiac History 38)', *Coptic Church Review* 21.1 (2000), pp. 8-23.
- *HL* 17 (Eng. trans. of Coptic): T. Vivian, 'Coptic Palladiana III: The Life of Macarius of Egypt (Lausiac History 17)', *Coptic Church Review* 21.3 (2000), pp. 82-109.
- *HL* 18 (Eng. trans. of Coptic): T. Vivian, 'Coptic Palladiana IV: The life of Macarius of Alexandria (Lausiac History 18)', *Coptic Church Review* 22.1 (2001), pp. 2-22.
- *HL* (Eng. trans. of Syriac): E.A. Wallis Budge, *The Paradise or Garden of the Holy Fathers being Histories of the Anchorites Recluses Monks Coenobites and Ascetic Fathers of the Deserts of Egypt between A.D. CCL and A.D. CCCC circiter Compiled by Athanasius Archbishop of Alexandria, Palladius Bishop of Helenopolis, Saint Jerome and Others* (2 vols; London: Chatto & Windus, 1907), I, pp. 77-281.
- *Prooemium ad historiam Lausiacam* (sp.): C. Butler (ed.), *The Lausiac History of Palladius: A Critical Discussion Together with Notes on Early Egyptian Monachism* (2 vols; Hildesheim: Olms, 1967 [1898-1904]), II, pp. 3-5. [TLG 2111 002]
Philo Judaeus, *Collected works* (Greek and Eng. trans.): F.H. Coulson, G.H. Whitaker, J.W. Earp and R. Marcus (eds), *Philo* (LCL 226, 227, 247, 261, 275, 289, 320, 341, 363, 379, 380, 401; London: William Heinemann Ltd, 1929-1971).
- *De congressu eruditionis gratia*: L. Cohn and P. Wendland (eds), *Philonis Alexandrini: opera quae supersunt*, (7 vols; Berlin: De Gruyter, 1962 [1896-1930]), III, pp. 72-109. [TLG 0018 016]
- *De migratione Abrahami*: L. Cohn and P. Wendland (eds), *Philonis Alexandrini: opera quae supersunt* (7 vols; Berlin: De Gruyter, 1962 [1896-1930]), II, pp. 268-314. [TLG 0018 014]
- *De vita contemplativa*: L. Cohn and P. Wendland (eds), *Philonis Alexandrini: opera quae supersunt* (7 vols; Berlin: De Gruyter, 1962 [1896-1930]), VI, pp. 46-71. [TLG 0018 028]
- *De vita contemplativa*: (Eng. trans.): G.P. Corrington, 'Philo. On the Contemplative Life: Or, On the Suppliants (The Fourth Book on the Virtues)', in V.L. Wimbush (ed.), *Ascetic Behavior in Greco-Roman Antiquity: A Sourcebook* (Studies in Antiquity & Christianity; Minneapolis: Fortress Press, 1990), pp. 134-55.
Photius, *Bibliotheca*: R. Henry (ed.), *Photius: Bibliothèque* (8 vols; Paris: Les Belles Lettres, 1959-1977). [TLG 4040 001]
Pindar, *Olympia*: H. Maehler (ed.), *Pindari carmina cum fragmentis* (Leipzig: Teubner, 5th edn, 1971), I, pp. 2-58. [TLG 0033 001]
Plato, *Epistulae* (*ep.*): J. Burnet (ed.), *Platonis opera* (5 vols; Oxford: Clarendon Press, 1967-1968 [1900-1907]), V. [TLG 0059 036]
- *Epp.*: R.G. Bury, *Plato IX: Timaeus, Critias, Cleitophon, Menexenus, Epistles* (LCL 234; London: William Heinemann Ltd, 1929).
- *Leges* (*leg.*): J. Burnet (ed.), *Platonis opera* (5 vols; Oxford: Clarendon Press, 1967-1968 [1900-1907]), V. [TLG 0059 034]

- *Phaedo*: J. Burnet (ed.), *Platonis opera* (5 vols; Oxford: Clarendon Press, 1967-1968 [1900-1907]), I. [TLG 0059 004]
- *Phaedo*: H.N. Fowler (ed.), *Plato I: Euthyphro, Apology, Crito, Phaedo, Phaedrus* (LCL 36; London: William Heinemann Ltd, 1938).
- *Respublica (rep.)*: J. Burnet (ed.), *Platonis opera* (5 vols; Oxford: Clarendon Press, 1967-1968 [1900-1907]), IV. [TLG 0059 030]
- *Rep.*: P. Shorey, *Plato: The Republic* (LCL 237, 276; London: William Heinemann Ltd, 1930-1935).
- *Rep.* (Eng. trans.): H.D.P. Lee, *Plato: The Republic* (Harmondsworth: Penguin Books, rev. edn, 1987).
- *Sophista*: J. Burnet (ed.), *Platonis opera* (5 vols; Oxford: Clarendon Press, 1967-1968 [1900-1907]), I. [TLG 0059 007]

Plotinus, *Enneads*: P. Henry and H.-R. Schwyzer (eds), *Plotini opera* (3 vols; Leiden: Brill, 1951-1973). [TLG 2000 001]
- *Enneads*: A.H. Armstrong (ed.), *Plotinus* (LCL 440-445, 468; London: William Heinemann Ltd, 1966-1988).
- *Enneads* (Eng. trans.): S. MacKenna, *Plotinus: The Enneads* (ed. B.S. Page; London: Faber and Faber, rev. edn, 1961), pp. 21-625.

Polybius, *Historiae (hist.)*: T. Büttner-Wobst (ed.), *Polybii historiae* (5 vols; Stuttgart: Teubner 1962-1967 [1889-1905]). [TLG 0543 001]

Porphyry, *Vita Plotini (vit. Plot.)*: P. Henry and H.-R. Schwyzer (eds), *Plotini opera* (3 vols; Leiden: Brill, 1951-1973), I, 1951, pp. 1-41. [TLG 2034 001]
- *Vit. Plot.*: A. H. Armstrong (ed.), *Plotinus I: Porphyry's Life of Plotinus, Ennead I* (LCL 440; London: William Heinemann Ltd, 1966).
- *Vit. Plot.* (Eng. trans.): S. MacKenna, *Plotinus: The Enneads* (ed. B.S. Page; London: Faber and Faber, rev. edn, 1961), pp. 1-20.

Prosper of Aquitaine, *Contra collatorem*: *PL* 51.214-276.
- *Contra collatorem* (Eng. trans.): P. de Letter, *Prosper of Aquitaine: Defense of St. Augustine* (Ancient Christian Writers 32; Westminster, Md.: Newman Press, 1963), pp. 70-137.

Rufinus, *Apology of Rufinus addressed to Anastasius* (*apol. Anas.*; Eng. trans.): W.H. Fremantle, NPNF Series 2, III, pp. 864-68.
- *Apology against Jerome* (*apol. Jer.*; Eng. trans.): W.H. Fremantle, NPNF Series 2, III, pp. 874-971.
- *Historia monachorum in Aegypto* (see separate entry above)
- *Preface to Origen's De Principiis* (*de prin. praef. Ruf.*; Eng. trans.): F. Crombie, ANF, IV, pp. 453-55.

Seneca, *Epistulae morales ad Lucilium*: L.D. Reynolds (ed.), *L. Annaei Senecae: Ad Lucilium Epistulae Morales* (2 vols; Oxford: Oxford University Press, 1965).

Socrates Scholasticus, *Historia ecclesiastica* (*HE*): W. Bright (ed.), *Socrates' Ecclesiastical History* (Oxford: Clarendon Press, 2nd edn, 1893). [TLG 2057 001]
- *HE* (Eng. trans.): A.C. Zenos, NPNF Series 2, II, pp. 39-396.

Soranus, *Gynaeciorum libri iv*: J. Ilberg (ed.), *Sorani Gynaeciorum libri iv, de signis fracturarum, de fasciis, vita Hippocratis secundum Soranum* (Corpus medicorum Graecorum 4; Leipzig: Teubner, 1927), pp. 3-152. [TLG 0565 001]

Sozomen, *Historia ecclesiastica* (*HE*): J. Bidez and G.C. Hansen (eds), *Sozomenus: Kirchengeschichte* (GCS 50; Berlin: Akademie-Verlag, 1960). [TLG 2048 001]
- *HE* (Eng. trans.): C.D. Hartranft, NPNF Series 2, II, pp. 507-924.

Sulpicius Severus, *Dialogi* (*dial.*): *PL* 20.183-222.
- *Dial.* (Eng. trans.): A. Roberts, NPNF Series 2, XI, pp. 52-117.
- *Historia Sacra* (*HS*): *PL* 20.95-160.
- *HS* (Eng. trans.): A. Roberts, NPNF Series 2, XI, pp. 150-255.
Synesius of Cyrene, *Epistulae* (*ep.*): R. Hercher (ed.), *Epistolographi Graeci* (Amsterdam: Hakkert, 1965 [1873]), pp. 638-739. [TLG 2006 001]
- *Epp.*(Eng. trans.): A. Fitzgerald, *The Letters of Synesius of Cyrene* (London: Oxford University Press, 1926).
Tertullian, *De pallio* (*de pall.*): A. Gerlo (ed.), *Tertullianus II, Opera monastica* (*CCL* 2; Turnhout: Brepols, 1954), pp. 731-50.
- *De pall.* (Eng. trans.): S. Thelwall, ANF, IV, pp. 7-22.
- *De pudicitia* (*de pud.*): C. Micaelli and C. Munier (eds), *Tertullien: La Pudicité* (SC 394-395; Paris: Cerf, 1993).
- *De pud.* (Eng. trans.): S. Thelwall, ANF, IV, pp. 150-205.
Testamenta xii patriarcharum: M. de Jonge (ed.), *Testamenta xii patriarcharum* (Pseudepigrapha veteris testamenti Graece 1; Leiden: Brill, 2nd edn, 1970), pp. 1-86. [TLG 1700 001]
- *Testamenta xii patriarcharum* (Eng. trans.): A.C. Coxe, ANF, VIII, pp. 7-65.
Theodoret, *Historia ecclesiastica* (*HE*; references are to *GCS* edition): L. Parmentier and F. Scheidweiler (eds), *Theodoret: Kirchengeschichte* (*GCS* 44; Berlin: Akademie-Verlag, 2nd edn, 1954), pp. 1-349. [TLG 4089 003]
- *HE* (Eng. trans.): B. Jackson, NPNF Series 2, III, pp. 72-307.
Thucydides, *Historiae* (*hist.*): H.S. Jones and J.E. Powell (eds), *Thucydidis historiae* (2 vols; Oxford: Clarendon Press, rev. edn. 1967-1970). [TLG 0003 001]
- *Hist.* (Eng. trans.): R. Warner, *Thucydides: History of the Peloponnesian War* (Harmondsworth: Penguin Books, rev. edn, 1972).
Xenophon, *Hellenica*: E.C. Marchant (ed.), *Xenophontis opera omnia* (5 vols; Oxford: Clarendon Press, rev. edn, 1967-1970), I. [TLG 0032 001]

Secondary Sources

Alexe, S., 'Le discernement selon Saint Jean Cassien', in E.A. Livingstone (ed.), *Biblica et Apocrypha, Ascetica, Liturgica* (*Studia Patristica* 30; Leuven: Peeters, 1997), pp. 129-35.
Bagnall, R.S., *Egypt in Late Antiquity* (Princeton: Princeton University Press, 1993).
- *Currency and Inflation in Fourth Century Egypt* (Bulletin of the American Society of Papyrologists, Supplements 5; Chico, CA: Scholars Press, 1985).
Baker, D. 'St Antony & the Biblical Precedents for the Monastic Tradition', *Ampleforth Journal* 76 (1971), pp. 6-11.
Bauer, W. (ed.), *A Greek-English Lexicon of the New Testament and other Early Christian Literature*, (trans. W.F. Arndt, and F.W. Gingrich; Chicago: University of Chicago Press, rev. edn, 1979).
Bertrand, D., 'Le discernement bernadin entre les Pères du Désert et Ignace de Loyola', *Collectanea Cisterciensia* 64 (2002), pp. 6-16.
Bloomfield, M.W., 'The Origin of the Concept of the Seven Cardinal Sins', *Harvard Theological Review* 34 (1941), pp. 121-28.

Bousset, W., *Apophthegmata: Studien zur Geschichte des ältesten Mönchtums* (Tübingen: Mohr, 1923).

Bouyer, L., *The Spirituality of the New Testament and the Fathers* (A History of Christian Spirituality 1; London: Burns & Oates, 1963).

Brougher, R.F. and Goehring, J.E., 'Egyptian Monasticism (Selected Papyri)', in V.L. Wimbush (ed.), *Ascetic Behavior in Greco-Roman Antiquity: A Sourcebook* (Studies in Antiquity & Christianity; Minneapolis: Fortress Press, 1990), pp. 456-63.

Brown, C. (ed.), *The New International Dictionary of New Testament Theology* (4 vols; Grand Rapids: Zondervan, 1986).

Brown, F., S.R. Driver and C.A. Briggs (eds.), *A Hebrew and English Lexicon of the Old Testament* (Oxford: Clarendon Press, 1951).

Bruce, F.F., *The Epistle to the Hebrews: The English text with introduction, exposition and notes* (The New International Commentary on the New Testament; Grand Rapids: Eerdmans, 1964).

Budge, E.A. Wallis (ed.), *An Egyptian Hieroglyphic Dictionary* (London: John Murray, 1920).

Bunge, G., *Evagrios Pontikos: Briefe aus der Wüste* (Sophia Quellen Östlicher Theologie 24; Trier: Paulinus-Verlag, 1986).

Burton-Christie, D., *The Word in the Desert: Scripture and the Quest for Holiness in Early Christian Monasticism* (New York: Oxford University Press, 1993).

Cabrol, F. and H. Leclercq (eds.), *Dictionnaire d'archéologie chrétienne et de liturgie*, (15 vols in 30; Paris: Letouzey et Ané, 1907-1953).

Casiday, A.M., *Evagrius Ponticus* (The Early Church Fathers; Routledge: Abingdon, 2006)

– 'Gabriel Bunge and the Study of Evagrius Ponticus: Review Article', *St Vladimir's Theological Quarterly* 48.2 (2004), pp. 249-89

Chadwick, H., 'The Ascetic Ideal in the History of the Church', in W.J. Shiels (ed.), *Monks, Hermits and the Ascetic Tradition* (Studies in Church History 22; Oxford: Blackwell, 1985), pp. 1-23.

Chadwick, O., *John Cassian* (Cambridge: Cambridge University Press, 2nd edn, 1968).

Chitty, D.J. *The Desert a City: An Introduction to the Study of Egyptian and Palestinian Monasticism under the Christian Empire* (Crestward, NY: St Vladimir's Seminary Press, 1995 [1966]).

Chollet, A., 'Discernement des esprits', in J.M.A Vacant (ed.), *Dictionnaire de théologie catholique* (15vols; Paris: Letouzey et Ané, 1899-1950), IV, pp. 1375-1415.

Corrigan, K., '"Solitary" Mysticism in Plotinus, Proclus, Gregory of Nyssa, and Pseudo-Dionysius', *Journal of Religion* 76.1 (January, 1996), pp28-42.

Craigie, P.C., *The Book of Deuteronomy* (The New International Commentary on the Old Testament; Grand Rapids: Eerdmans, 1976).

Crum, W.E. (ed.), *A Coptic Dictionary*, (Oxford: Clarendon Press, 2000 [1939]).

Daniélou, J., *From Glory To Glory: Texts from Gregory of Nyssa's Mystical Writings* (trans. H. Musurillo; London: Murray, 1962).

Davids, P.H., *The Epistle of James: A Commentary on the Greek Text* (The New International Greek Testament Commentary; Exeter: Paternoster Press, 1982).

De Lubac, H., *Medieval Exegesis: The Four Senses of Scripture* (trans. M. Sebanc; 2 vols; Grand Rapids: Ressourcement, 1998).

Dingjan, F. *Discretio: Les origines patristiques et monastiques de la doctrine sur la prudence chez saint Thomas d'Aquin* (Assen: Van Gorcum, 1967).

– 'La discrétion dans les apophtegmes des Pères', *Angelicum* 39 (1962), pp. 403-15.

Draguet, R., *Index Copte et Grec-Copte de la Concordance du Nouveau Testament Sahidique* (*CSCO* 196 Subsidia 16, Louvain: Secrétariat du *CSCO*, 1960).

Driot, M., *Fathers of the Desert: Life and Spirituality* (trans. F. Audette; Slough: St Paul Publications, 1992).

Dunn, M., *The Emergence of Monasticism: From the Desert Fathers to the Early Middle Ages* (Oxford: Blackwell, 2003).

Dysinger, L., 'The Relationship between Psalmody and Prayer in the Writings of Evagrius Ponticus' (DPhil thesis, St Benet's Hall, Oxford, 1999)

– 'The Significance of Psalmody in the Mystical Theology of Evagrius of Pontus', in E.A. Livingstone (ed.), *Biblica et Apocrypha, Ascetica, Liturgica* (*Studia Patristica* 30; Leuven: Peeters, 1997), pp. 176-82.

Ellingworth, P., *The Epistle to the Hebrews: A Commentary on the Greek Text* (Carlisle: Paternoster, 1993).

Elm, S., 'Evagrius Ponticus' *Sententiae ad Virginem*', *Dumbarton Oaks Papers* 45 (1991), pp. 97-120.

– *Virgins Of God: The Making of Ascetism in Late Antiquity* (Oxford Classical Monographs; Oxford: Claredon Press, 1996).

Epp, E.J., 'Coptic Manuscript G67 and the Rôle of Codex Bezae as a Western Witness in Acts', *Journal of Biblical Literature*, 85.2 (June 1966), pp. 197-212.

Fitzgerald, P.J., 'A Model for Dialogue: Cyprian of Carthage on Ecclesial Discernment', *Theological Studies* 59.2 (June, 1998), pp. 236-253.

Frankfurter, D., *Religion in Roman Egypt: Assimilation and Resistance* (Princeton: Princeton University Press, 1998).

Gerson, L.P. 'Plotinus's Metaphysics: Emanation or Creation?', *The Review of Metaphysics* 46 (1993), pp. 559-74.

Gordis, R., *The Book of Job: Commentary and translation and special studies* (Moreshet Series 2; New York: Jewish Theological Seminary of America, 1978).

Gould, G., 'A Note on the *Apophthegmata Patrum*', *JTS* 37 (1986), pp. 133-38.

– *The Desert Fathers on Monastic Community* (Oxford Early Christian Studies; Oxford: Clarendon Press, 1993).

– 'The Life of Antony and the Origins of Christian Monasticism in Fourth Century Egypt', *Medieval History* 1.2 (1991), pp. 3-11.

Gressmann, H., 'Nonnenspiegel und Mönchsspiegel des Euagrios Pontikos', *TU* 39.4 (1913), pp. 143-65.

Guillaumont, C., 'Fragments grecs inédits d'Évagre le Pontique', in J. Dummer (ed.), *Texte und Textkritik: Eine Aufsatzsammlung* (*TU* 133; Berlin: Akademie-Verlag, 1987), pp. 209-21.

Guy, J.-C., 'Note sur l'évolution du genre apophtegmatique', *RAM* 32 (1956) pp. 63-68.

– *Recherches sur la Tradition Grecque des Apophthegmata Patrum* (Subsidia Hagiographica 36; Brussels: Société des Bollandistes, 1962).

– 'Remarques sur la texte des *Apophthegmata Patrum*', *Recherches de Science Religieuse* 43 (1955), pp. 252-58.

Habel, N.C., *The Book of Job: A Commentary* (Old Testament Library; London: SCM Press, 1985).

Hagedorn U. and D. Hagedorn (eds), *Die älteren griechischen Katenen zum buch Hiob* (*PTS* 40, 48, 53, 59; Berlin: De Gruyter, 1994-2004).

Harlow, M. and W. Smith, 'Between fasting and feasting: The literary and archaeobotanical evidence for monastic diet in Late Antique Egypt', *Antiquity* 75.290 (2001), pp. 758-68.

Harmless, W., *Desert Christians: An Introduction to the Literature of Early Monasticism* (Oxford: Oxford University Press, 2004),

– 'Remembering Poemen Remembering: The Desert Fathers and the Spirituality of Memory', *Church History* 69 (2000), pp. 483-518.

– 'The Sapphire Light of the Mind: The Skemmata of Evagrius Ponticus', *Theological Studies* 62 (2001), pp. 498-529.

Harper, J., 'John Cassian and Sulpicius Severus', *Church History* 34.4 (1965), pp. 371-80.

Hartley, J.E., *The Book of Job* (The New International Commentary on the Old Testament; Grand Rapids: Eerdmans, 1988).

Hausherr, I., 'Le "De Oratione" d'Évagre le Pontique en Syriaque et en Arabe', *OCP* 5 (1939), pp. 7-71.

– 'Le traité de l'oraison d'Évagre le Pontique (Pseudo Nil)', *RAM* 15 (1934), pp. 34-93, 113-70.

– 'Les grands courants de la spiritualité orientale', *OCP* 1 (1935), pp. 114-38.

– *Les leçons d'un contemplatif: Le traité de l'Oraison d'Évagre le Pontique* (Paris: Beauchesne, 1960).

– 'Les versions Syriaque et Arménienne d'Évagre le Pontique', *OC* 22.2 (1931), pp. 69-118.

– 'L'hésychasme: Étude de spiritualité', *OCP* 22 (1956), pp. 5-40, 247-85 repr. as 'Hésychasme et prière', *OCA* 176 (1966), pp. 164-237.

– 'L'origine de la théorie orientale des huits péchés capitaux', *OC* 30.3 (1933), pp. 164-75 repr. as 'Études de Spiritualité Orientale', *OCA* 183 (1969), pp. 11-22.

– 'Nouveaux fragments grecs d'Évagre le Pontique', *OCP* 5 (1939), pp. 229-33.

Heaton, H., *A Septuagint Translation Technique in the Book of Job* (The Catholic Biblical Quarterly Monograph Series 2; Washington: Catholic Biblical Association of America, 1982).

Hopfner, T., *Über die koptisch-sa'idischen Apophthegmata Patrum Aegyptiorum und verwandte griechische, lateinische, koptisch-bohairische und syrische Sammlungen* (Kaiserliche Akademie der Wissenschaften in Wien, Philosophisch-historische Klasse, Denkschriften 61.2; Abhandlungen, Wien: A. Hölder, 1918).

Horden, P., 'The Death of Ascetics: Sickness and Monasticism in the Early Byzantine Middle East', in W.J. Shiels (ed.), *Monks, Hermits and the Ascetic Tradition* (Studies in Church History 22; Oxford: Blackwell, 1985), pp. 41-52.

Horsley, G.H.R., *New Documents Illustrating Early Christianity: A review of the Greek inscriptions and papyri published in 1976* (North Ryde, N.S.W: Ancient History Documentary Research Centre, Macquarie University, 1981).

Hughes, P.E., *A Commentary on the Epistle to the Hebrews* (Grand Rapids: Eerdmans, 1977).

Inowlocki, S., 'Eusebius of Caesarea's *Interpretatio Christiana* of Philo's *De vita contemplativa*', *Harvard Theological Review* 97.3 (2004), pp. 305-28.

Irvine, I., 'Acedia, Tristitia and Sloth: Early Christian Forerunners to Chronic Ennui', *Humanitas* 12.1 (1999), pp. 89-103.

Jacob, K.A., *Coins and Christianity* (London: B.A. Seaby Ltd, 1959).

Jeremias, J., *Unknown Sayings of Jesus* (London: SPCK, 1957).

Kelly, J.N.D., *A Commentary on the Epistles of Peter and of Jude* (Black's New Testament Commentaries; London: Adam & Charles Black, 1969).

– *A Commentary on the Pastoral Epistles* (Black's New Testament Commentaries; London: A & C Black, 1963).

King, C., 'Roman Copies', in C.E. King and D.G. Wigg (eds), *Coin Finds and Coin Use in the Roman World*, (Studien zu Fundmünzen der Antike 10; Berlin: Gebr. Mann, 1996), pp. 237-63.

Lampe, G.W.H. (ed.), *A Patristic Greek Lexicon* (Oxford: Clarendon Press, 1995 [1961]).

Lane, W.L., *Hebrews 1-8* (Word Bible Commentary 47A; Dallas: Word Books, 1991).

Larchet, J.-C., *Thérapeutique des maladies spirituelles: Une introduction à la tradition ascétique de l'Église orthodoxe* (Paris: Cerf, 1997).

Lefort, L.-Th. and M. Wilmet (eds), *Concordance du Nouveau Testament Sahidique* (*CSCO* 124, 173, 183, 185 Subsidia 1, 11, 13, 15; Louvain: Secrétariat du *CSCO*, 1950-1959.

Leloir, L., 'La discrétion des Pères du désert, d'après les "Paterica" Arméniens', *Collectanea Cisterciensia* 37.1 (1975), pp. 15-32.

Levko, J., 'The Relationship of Prayer to Discretion and Spiritual Direction for John Cassian', *St Vladimir's Theological Quarterly* 40.2 (1996), pp. 155-71.

Lewis, C.T. and C. Short (eds), *A Latin Dictionary* (Oxford: Clarendon Press, 1996 [1879]).

Liddell, H.G. and R. Scott (eds), *A Greek-English Lexicon* (Oxford: Clarendon Press, 9th rev. edn with supplement, 1996).

Lienhard, J.T., '"Discernment of Spirits" in the Early Church', *Studia Patristica* 17.2 (1982), pp. 519-22.

– 'On "Discernement of Spirits" in the Early Church', *Theological Studies* 41.3 (1980), pp. 505-29.

Louth, A., 'Envy as the Chief Sin in Athanasius and Gregory of Nyssa' (*Studia Patristica* 15, *TU* 128; Berlin: Akademie Verlag, 1984), pp. 458-60.

– 'St Athanasius and the Greek *Life of Antony*', *JTS* 39 (1988), pp. 504-509.

– 'The Literature of the Monastic Movement', in F. Young, L. Ayres, A. Louth and A. Casiday (eds), *The Cambridge History of Early Christian Literature* (Cambridge: Cambridge University Press, 2004).

– *The Origins of the Christian Mystical Tradition from Plato to Denys* (Oxford: Clarendon Press, 1983).

Macleod, C.W., 'Allegory and Mysticism in Origen and Gregory of Nyssa', *JTS* 22.2 (October, 1971), pp. 362-79.

Marty, F., 'Le discernement des esprits dans le *Peri Archôn* d'Origène', *RAM* 34 (1958) pp. 147-64, 253-74.

McGuckin, J.A., 'Christian Asceticism and the Early School of Alexandria', in W.J. Shiels (ed.), *Monks, Hermits and the Ascetic Tradition* (Studies in Church History 22; Oxford: Blackwell, 1985), pp. 25-39.

Merton, T., *The Wisdom of the Desert: Sayings from the Desert Fathers of the Fourth Century* (London: Darley Anderson, 1988 [1961]).

Molland, E., *The Conception of the Gospel in the Alexandrian Theology* (Skrifter utgitt av det Norske Videnskaps-Akademi i Oslo II. Hist.-Filos. Klasse 2; Oslo: I kommisjon hos J. Dybwad, 1938).

Montefiore, H.W., *A Commentary on the Epistle to the Hebrews* (Black's New Testament Commentaries; London: A & C Black, 1964).

Morris, L., *The Epistle to the Romans* (Leicester: IVP, 1988).

Munz, P., 'John Cassian', *JEH* 11.2 (1960), pp. 1-22.

Murray, J. *The Epistle to the Romans* (The New London Commentary on the New Testament; London: Marshall, Morgan & Scott, 1967).

Muyldermans, J., *À travers la tradition manuscrite d'Évagre le Pontique: Essai sur les manuscrits grecs conservés à la Bibliothèque Nationale de Paris* (Bibliothèque du Muséon 3; Louvain: Bureaux du Muséon, 1932).

— 'Evagriana', *Le Muséon* 44 (1931), pp. 37-68.

— 'Evagriana: Le Vatic. Barb. Graecus 515', *Le Muséon* 51 (1938), pp. 191-226.

— *Evagriana Syriaca: Textes inédits du British Museum et de la Vaticane* (Bibliothèque du Muséon 31; Louvain: Publications Universitaires, 1952).

— 'Note Additionnelle A: Evagriana', *Le Muséon* 44 (1931), pp. 369-83.

Nygren, A., *Commentary on Romans* (Phildelphia: Fortress Press, 1972 [1949]).

O'Laughlin, M., 'Evagrius Ponticus in Spiritual Perspective', in E.A. Livingstone (ed.), *Biblica et Apocrypha, Ascetica, Liturgica* (*Studia Patristica* 30; Leuven: Peeters, 1997), pp. 224-30.

Orlandi, T., 'A Catechesis against Apocryphal Texts By Shenute and the Gnostic Texts of Nag Hamadi', *Harvard Theological Review* 75.1 (1982), pp. 85-95.

Palmer, G.E.H., P. Sherrard and K.Ware (eds), *The Philokalia: The Complete Text compiled by St Nikodemos of the Holy Mountain and St Makarios of Corinth* (4 vols; London: Faber and Faber, 1979-1995).

Pearson, B.A. and J.E. Goehring (eds), *The Roots of Egyptian Christianity* (Studies in Antiquity and Christianity; Philadelphia: Fortress Press, 1986).

Penkett, R., 'Discerning the Divine and the Demonic in the *Life of Antony*', *Reading Medieval Studies* 24 (1998), pp. 79-94.

Peterson, R.M., '"The Gift of Discerning Spirits" in the *Vita Antonii* 16-44', *Studia Patristica* 17.2 (1982), pp. 523-27.

Quasten, J., *Patrology* (3 vols; Antwerp: Spectrum, 1943-1946).

Ramfos, S., *Like a Pelican in the Wilderness: Reflections on the sayings of the Desert Fathers* (trans. N. Russell; Brookline, Mass.: Holy Cross Orthodox Press, 2000).

Regnault, L., *Les sentences des Pères du désert nouveau recueil: Apophtegmes inédits ou peu connus* (Solesmes: Abbaye Saint-Pierre de Solesmes, 2nd edn, 1977).

— *Les sentences des Pères du désert: Troisième recueil et tables* (Solesmes: Abbaye Saint-Pierre de Solesmes, 1976).

— 'The Beatitudes in the *Apophthegmata Patrum*', *Eastern Churches Review* 6 (1974), pp. 22-43.

Roberts, C.H., *Manuscript, Society and Belief in Early Christian Egypt* (The Schweich Lectures 1977; Oxford: Oxford University Press, 1979).

Rondeau, M.-J., 'Le commentaire sur les Psaumes d'Évagre le Pontique', *OCP* 26 (1960), pp. 307-48.

Rousseau, P., *Ascetics, Authority, and the Church in the Age of Jerome and Cassian* (Oxford: Oxford University Press, 1978).

– 'Cassian, Contemplation and the Coenobitic Life', *JEH* 26.2 (April, 1975), pp. 119-26.
– *Pachomius: The Making of a Community in Fourth-Century Egypt* (London: University of California, rev. edn, 1999).
– 'The Spiritual Authority of the "Monk-Bishop": Eastern Elements in Some Western Hagiography of the Fourth and Fifth Centuries', *JTS* 22.2 (1971), pp. 380-419.
Rowley, H.H., *The Book of Job* (The New Century Bible Commentary; London: Marshall, Morgan & Scott, 1980 [1976]).
Russell, K.C., 'The unanswered question in John Cassian's Second Conference', *Église et Théologie* 29.3 (1998), pp. 291-302.
Scholl, E., 'The Mother of Virtues: *Discretio*', *Cistercian Studies Quarterly* 36.3 (2001), pp. 389-401.
Shaw, I. and P.T. Nicholson, (eds), *British Museum Dictionary of Ancient Egypt* (London: British Museum Press, 1995).
Simon, M. 'Recent French Studies on Early Church History: A Bibliographical Note', *JEH* 4 (1953), pp. 85-91.
Sinkewicz, R.E. *Evagrius of Pontus: The Greek Ascetic Corpus – Translation, Introduction, and Commentary* (Oxford: Oxford University Press, 2003).
Souter, A. (ed.), *A Glossary of Later Latin to 600 AD* (Oxford: Clarendon Press, 1996 [1949]).
Špidlík, T., *The Spirituality of the Christian East: A Systematic Handbook* (trans. A.P. Gythiel; Cistercian Studies Series 79; Kalamazoo: Cistercian Publications, 1986).
Stewart, C., *Cassian the Monk* (Oxford: Oxford University Press, 1998).
– 'Radical honesty about the self: The practice of the Desert Fathers', *Sobornost* 12 (1990), pp. 25-39.
– *Working the Earth of the Heart: The Messalian Controversy in History, Texts, and Language to AD 431* (Oxford: Clarendon Press, 1991).
Viller, M., F. Cavallera, J. de Guibert, C. Baumgartner and M. Olphe-Galliard (eds), *Dictionnaire de Spiritualité Ascétique et Mystique Doctrine et Histoire* (16 vols; Paris: Beauchesne, 1932-1995).
Vivian, T., 'Words to Live by: A conversation the Elders had with one another Concerning Thoughts (ΠΕΡΙ ΛΟΓΙΣΜΩΝ)', *St Vladimir's Theological Quarterly* 39.2 (1995), pp. 127-41.
Vogüé, A. de. *De Saint Pachôme à Jean Cassien: Études littéraires et doctrinales sur le monachisme égyptien à ses débuts* (Studia Anselmiana 120; Rome: Editrice Anselmiana, 1996).
Waaijman, K., 'Discernment: Its history and meaning', *Studies in Spirituality* 7 (1997), pp. 5-41.
Waddell, H., *The Desert Fathers* (London: Constable & Co., 1987 [1936]).
Ward, B., 'Discernment: A Rare Bird', *The Way* Supplement 64 (Spring, 1989), pp. 10-18.
– *Harlots of the Desert: A study of repentance in early monastic sources* (Cistercian Studies Series 106; Kalamazoo: Cistercian Publications, 1987).
Ware, K.T., '"Pray Without Ceasing": The Ideal of Continual Prayer in Eastern Monasticism', *Eastern Churches Review* 2 (1968-9), pp. 253-61.
– 'Prayer in Evagrius of Pontus and the Macarian Homilies', in R. Waller and B. Ward (eds), *An Introduction to Christian Spirituality* (London: SPCK, 1999), pp. 14-30.

Weaver, R.H., 'Access to Scripture: Experiencing the Text', *Interpretation* 52.4 (1998), pp. 367-379.

White, C., *Early Christian Lives* (London: Penguin Books, 1998).

White, H.G.E., *The Monasteries of the Wâdi 'n Natrûn: Part II – The History of the Monasteries of Nitria and of Scetis* (New York: Metropolitan Museum of Art Egyptian Expedition, 1932).

Widnmann, I., 'Discretio (διάκρισις): Zur Bedeutungsgeschichte', *Studien und Mitteilungen zur Geschichte des Benediktiner-Ordens und seiner Zweige* 58.1 (1940), pp. 21-28.

Williams, R., *Arius: Heresy and Tradition* (London: SCM Press, 2nd edn, 2001).

– *Slience and Honey Cakes: The Wisdom of the Desert* (Oxford: Lion Publishing, 2003).

Wilmart, A., 'Le Recueil Latin des Apophtegmes', *RB* 34 (1922), pp. 185-98.

– 'Les versions Latines des sentences d'Évagre pour les vierges', *RB* 28 (1911), pp. 143-53.

Yoder, J.D. (ed.), *Concordance to the Distinctive Greek Text of Codex Bezae* (New Testament Tools and Studies 2; Leiden: E.J. Brill, 1961).

Young, R.D.. 'Evagrius the Iconographer: Monastic Pedagogy in the *Gnostikos*', *Journal of Early Christian Studies* 9.1 (2001), pp. 53-71.

Youssef, Y.N., 'Concordance des Apophthegmata Patrum', *Vigiliae Christianae* 52.3 (August 1998), pp. 319-22.

Index of Scripture References

General Index

324

General Index

Basil the Great, 213, 224
bees, 33, 117
beggar, 212, 223
Benedict of Nursia, 75
Benjamin, monk, 89
Beryllus, 28
Bethlehem, 75, 76
blasphemy, 4, 69, 201, 211
blindness, spiritual, 52, 88, 99, 108,
121, 205, 206
body: attitude to, 15, 150; control of,
143, 150
boredom, 173
Bousset, W., 141, 243
bride, 32, 34
Bridegroom, 32, 89
Brown, C., 2
Budge, E.A. Wallis, 126
Bundy, D., 40
Bunge, G., 43, 70
Burton-Christie, D., 19

Callistus I, 224
Calvin, John, 108
cardinal virtues, 68, 88
Casiday, A.M., 39, 40, 41, 43
Cassian, John, xxiv, 12, 35, 36, 41, 47,
123, 124, 129, 130, 143, 149, 150,
171, 194, 202, 230, 231, 233, 237;
indebtedness to Origen and
Evagrius, 77; influence, 79
Castor, 77, 79
cell, 69, 70, 71, 86, 96, 135, 146, 159,
168, 176, 180, 187, 193, 202, 206,
218
Chadwick, O., 41, 76, 126, 211
Chæremon, 83, 98, 119
Chaîne, M., 125, 126
change, 145, 148, 186
charity, 61, 128, 217, 219
chastity, 98
children, 224, 225
Christ: nature of, 28, 77
Christotocos, 77
Church: nature of, 34
Clement of Alexandria, 12, 157
Clysma, 148

Codex Bezae, 6, 10, 11
cœnobites: compared to anchorites, 56,
78, 82, 86, 92, 93, 100, 116, 140,
145, 179, 196, 213, 222
cœnobium, 81, 103, 114, 115, 190;
return to, 118
coinage, 37, 108, 112, 156
commitment, 61
community, 206, 215, 218, 226, 234
compunction, 61
condemnation, 7, 177, 203, 206, 208,
217
Conferences, 77, 78
confession, 202, 211, 213
confidentiality, 201
Constantine, 14
Constantinople, 77
contemplation, 18, 20, 31, 44, 48, 49,
50, 53, 58, 66, 81, 82, 85, 90, 99,
101, 146; undistracted, 82
contemplative knowledge, 87
Contra Celsum, 26
controversy, 200
Corrigan, K., 21
Council of Ancyra, 224
Council of Gangra, 25
Council of Nicaea, 14
counterfeit: and genuine, 96, 111;
coins, 112, 156
Cronius, 207
Crum, W.E., 239
Cyprian, 203, 224
Cyril of Alexandria, 145

Daniel of Scetis, 99, 142, 187
Daniel, prophet, 141
David, king, 93
Davids, P.H., 46
de Lubac, H., 109
De principiis, 26
dead: raising, 137; regarding self as,
92, 138, 219
death, 136, 203, 211; remembrance of,
70, 154, 218
deceit, 5, 32, 36, 42, 55, 59, 60, 65, 66,
69, 70, 72, 87, 108, 112, 113, 114,
117, 185, 228

Studies in Christian History and Thought
(All titles uniform with this volume)
Dates in bold are of projected publication

David Bebbington
Holiness in Nineteenth-Century England
David Bebbington stresses the relationship of movements of spirituality to changes in their cultural setting, especially the legacies of the Enlightenment and Romanticism. He shows that these broad shifts in ideological mood had a profound effect on the ways in which piety was conceptualized and practised. Holiness was intimately bound up with the spirit of the age.

2000 / 0-85364-981-2 / viii + 98pp

J. William Black
Reformation Pastors
Richard Baxter and the Ideal of the Reformed Pastor
This work examines Richard Baxter's *Gildas Salvianus, The Reformed Pastor* (1656) and explores each aspect of his pastoral strategy in light of his own concern for 'reformation' and in the broader context of Edwardian, Elizabethan and early Stuart pastoral ideals and practice.

2003 / 1-84227-190-3 / xxii + 308pp

James Bruce
Prophecy, Miracles, Angels, *and* Heavenly Light?
The Eschatology, Pneumatology and Missiology of Adomnán's Life of Columba
This book surveys approaches to the marvellous in hagiography, providing the first critique of Plummer's hypothesis of Irish saga origin. It then analyses the uniquely systematized phenomena in the *Life of Columba* from Adomnán's seventh-century theological perspective, identifying the coming of the eschatological Kingdom as the key to understanding.

2004 / 1-84227-227-6 / xviii + 286pp

Colin J. Bulley
The Priesthood of Some Believers
Developments from the General to the Special Priesthood in the Christian Literature of the First Three Centuries
The first in-depth treatment of early Christian texts on the priesthood of all believers shows that the developing priesthood of the ordained related closely to the division between laity and clergy and had deleterious effects on the practice of the general priesthood.

2000 / 1-84227-034-6 / xii + 336pp

Anthony R. Cross (ed.)
Ecumenism and History
Studies in Honour of John H.Y. Briggs
This collection of essays examines the inter-relationships between the two fields in which Professor Briggs has contributed so much: history—particularly Baptist and Nonconformist—and the ecumenical movement. With contributions from colleagues and former research students from Britain, Europe and North America, *Ecumenism and History* provides wide-ranging studies in important aspects of Christian history, theology and ecumenical studies.
2002 / 1-84227-135-0 / xx + 362pp

Maggi Dawn
Confessions of an Inquiring Spirit
Form as Constitutive of Meaning in S.T. Coleridge's Theological Writing
This study of Coleridge's *Confessions* focuses on its confessional, epistolary and fragmentary form, suggesting that attention to these features significantly affects its interpretation. Bringing a close study of these three literary forms, the author suggests ways in which they nuance the text with particular understandings of the Trinity, and of a kenotic christology. Some parallels are drawn between Romantic and postmodern dilemmas concerning the authority of the biblical text.
2006 / 1-84227-255-1 / approx. 224 pp

Ruth Gouldbourne
The Flesh and the Feminine
Gender and Theology in the Writings of Caspar Schwenckfeld
Caspar Schwenckfeld and his movement exemplify one of the radical communities of the sixteenth century. Challenging theological and liturgical norms, they also found themselves challenging social and particularly gender assumptions. In this book, the issues of the relationship between radical theology and the understanding of gender are considered.
2005 / 1-84227-048-6 / approx. 304pp

Crawford Gribben
Puritan Millennialism
Literature and Theology, 1550–1682
Puritan Millennialism surveys the growth, impact and eventual decline of puritan millennialism throughout England, Scotland and Ireland, arguing that it was much more diverse than has frequently been suggested. This Paternoster edition is revised and extended from the original 2000 text.
2007 / 1-84227-372-8 / approx. 320pp

Galen K. Johnson
Prisoner of Conscience
John Bunyan on Self, Community and Christian Faith
This is an interdisciplinary study of John Bunyan's understanding of conscience across his autobiographical, theological and fictional writings, investigating whether conscience always deserves fidelity, and how Bunyan's view of conscience affects his relationship both to modern Western individualism and historic Christianity.

2003 / 1-84227-223-3 / xvi + 236pp

R.T. Kendall
Calvin and English Calvinism to 1649
The author's thesis is that those who formed the Westminster Confession of Faith, which is regarded as Calvinism, in fact departed from John Calvin on two points: (1) the extent of the atonement and (2) the ground of assurance of salvation.

1997 / 0-85364-827-1 / xii + 264pp

Timothy Larsen
Friends of Religious Equality
Nonconformist Politics in Mid-Victorian England
During the middle decades of the nineteenth century the English Nonconformist community developed a coherent political philosophy of its own, of which a central tenet was the principle of religious equality (in contrast to the stereotype of Evangelical Dissenters). The Dissenting community fought for the civil rights of Roman Catholics, non-Christians and even atheists on an issue of principle which had its flowering in the enthusiastic and undivided support which Nonconformity gave to the campaign for Jewish emancipation. This reissued study examines the political efforts and ideas of English Nonconformists during the period, covering the whole range of national issues raised, from state education to the Crimean War. It offers a case study of a theologically conservative group defending religious pluralism in the civic sphere, showing that the concept of religious equality was a grand vision at the centre of the political philosophy of the Dissenters.

2007 / 1-84227-402-3 / x + 300pp

Byung-Ho Moon
Christ the Mediator of the Law
*Calvin's Christological Understanding of the Law as the Rule of Living
and Life-Giving*
This book explores the coherence between Christology and soteriology in
Calvin's theology of the law, examining its intellectual origins and his position
on the concept and extent of Christ's mediation of the law. A comparative study
between Calvin and contemporary Reformers—Luther, Bucer, Melancthon and
Bullinger—and his opponent Michael Servetus is made for the purpose of
pointing out the unique feature of Calvin's Christological understanding of the
law.

2005 / 1-84227-318-3 / approx. 370pp

John Eifion Morgan-Wynne
Holy Spirit and Religious Experience in Christian Writings, c.AD 90–200
This study examines how far Christians in the third to fifth generations (c.AD
90–200) attributed their sense of encounter with the divine presence, their sense
of illumination in the truth or guidance in decision-making, and their sense of
ethical empowerment to the activity of the Holy Spirit in their lives.

2005 / 1-84227-319-1 / approx. 350pp

James I. Packer
The Redemption and Restoration of Man in the Thought of Richard Baxter
James I. Packer provides a full and sympathetic exposition of Richard Baxter's
doctrine of humanity, created and fallen; its redemption by Christ Jesus; and its
restoration in the image of God through the obedience of faith by the power of
the Holy Spirit.

2002 / 1-84227-147-4 / 432pp

Andrew Partington,
Church and State
*The Contribution of the Church of England Bishops to the House of Lords
during the Thatcher Years*
In *Church and State*, Andrew Partington argues that the contribution of the
Church of England bishops to the House of Lords during the Thatcher years was
overwhelmingly critical of the government; failed to have a significant influence
in the public realm; was inefficient, being undertaken by a minority of those
eligible to sit on the Bench of Bishops; and was insufficiently moral and
spiritual in its content to be distinctive. On the basis of this, and the likely
reduction of the number of places available for Church of England bishops in a
fully reformed Second Chamber, the author argues for an evolution in the
Church of England's approach to the service of its bishops in the House of
Lords. He proposes the Church of England works to overcome the genuine
obstacles which hinder busy diocesan bishops from contributing to the debates
of the House of Lords and to its life more informally.
2005 / 1-84227-334-5 / approx. 324pp

Michael Pasquarello III
God's Ploughman
Hugh Latimer: A 'Preaching Life' (1490–1555)
This construction of a 'preaching life' situates Hugh Latimer within the larger
religious, political and intellectual world of late medieval England. Neither
biography, intellectual history, nor analysis of discrete sermon texts, this book is
a work of homiletic history which draws from the details of Latimer's milieu to
construct an interpretive framework for the preaching performances that formed
the core of his identity as a religious reformer. Its goal is to illumine the
practical wisdom embodied in the content, form and style of Latimer's
preaching, and to recapture a sense of its overarching purpose, movement, and
transforming force during the reform of sixteenth-century England.
2006 / 1-84227-336-1 / approx. 250pp

Alan P.F. Sell
Enlightenment, Ecumenism, Evangel
Theological Themes and Thinkers 1550–2000
This book consists of papers in which such interlocking topics as the
Enlightenment, the problem of authority, the development of doctrine,
spirituality, ecumenism, theological method and the heart of the gospel are
discussed. Issues of significance to the church at large are explored with special
reference to writers from the Reformed and Dissenting traditions.
2005 / 1-84227-330-2 / xviii + 422pp

Alan P.F. Sell
Hinterland Theology
Some Reformed and Dissenting Adjustments
Many books have been written on theology's 'giants' and significant trends, but
what of those lesser-known writers who adjusted to them? In this book some
hinterland theologians of the British Reformed and Dissenting traditions, who
followed in the wake of toleration, the Evangelical Revival, the rise of modern
biblical criticism and Karl Barth, are allowed to have their say. They include
Thomas Ridgley, Ralph Wardlaw, T.V. Tymms and N.H.G. Robinson.
2006 / 1-84227-331-0 / approx. 350pp

Alan P.F. Sell and Anthony R. Cross (eds)
Protestant Nonconformity in the Twentieth Century
In this collection of essays scholars representative of a number of
Nonconformist traditions reflect thematically on Nonconformists' life and
witness during the twentieth century. Among the subjects reviewed are biblical
studies, theology, worship, evangelism and spirituality, and ecumenism. Over
and above its immediate interest, this collection provides a marker to future
scholars and others wishing to know how some of their forebears assessed
Nonconformity's contribution to a variety of fields during the century leading up
to Christianity's third millennium.
2003 / 1-84227-221-7 / x + 398pp

Mark Smith
Religion in Industrial Society
Oldham and Saddleworth 1740–1865
This book analyses the way British churches sought to meet the challenge of
industrialization and urbanization during the period 1740–1865. Working from a
case-study of Oldham and Saddleworth, Mark Smith challenges the received
view that the Anglican Church in the eighteenth century was characterized by
complacency and inertia, and reveals Anglicanism's vigorous and creative
response to the new conditions. He reassesses the significance of the centrally
directed church reforms of the mid-nineteenth century, and emphasizes the
importance of local energy and enthusiasm. Charting the growth of
denominational pluralism in Oldham and Saddleworth, Dr Smith compares the
strengths and weaknesses of the various Anglican and Nonconformist
approaches to promoting church growth. He also demonstrates the extent to
which all the churches participated in a common culture shaped by the influence
of evangelicalism, and shows that active co-operation between the churches
rather than denominational conflict dominated. This revised and updated edition
of Dr Smith's challenging and original study makes an important contribution
both to the social history of religion and to urban studies.
2006 / 1-84227-335-3 / approx. 300pp

July 2005

Martin Sutherland
Peace, Toleration and Decay
The Ecclesiology of Later Stuart Dissent
This fresh analysis brings to light the complexity and fragility of the later Stuart Nonconformist consensus. Recent findings on wider seventeenth-century thought are incorporated into a new picture of the dynamics of Dissent and the roots of evangelicalism.
2003 / 1-84227-152-0 / xxii + 216pp

G. Michael Thomas
The Extent of the Atonement
A Dilemma for Reformed Theology from Calvin to the Consensus
A study of the way Reformed theology addressed the question, 'Did Christ die for all, or for the elect only?', commencing with John Calvin, and including debates with Lutheranism, the Synod of Dort and the teaching of Moïse Amyraut.
1997 / 0-85364-828-X / x + 278pp

David M. Thompson
Baptism, Church and Society in Britain from the Evangelical Revival to *Baptism, Eucharist and Ministry*
The theology and practice of baptism have not received the attention they deserve. How important is faith? What does baptismal regeneration mean? Is baptism a bond of unity between Christians? This book discusses the theology of baptism and popular belief and practice in England and Wales from the Evangelical Revival to the publication of the World Council of Churches' consensus statement on *Baptism, Eucharist and Ministry* (1982).
2005 */ 1-84227-393-0 / approx. 224pp*

Mark D. Thompson
A Sure Ground on Which to Stand
The Relation of Authority and Interpretive Method of Luther's Approach
to Scripture
The best interpreter of Luther is Luther himself. Unfortunately many modern studies have superimposed contemporary agendas upon this sixteenth-century Reformer's writings. This fresh study examines Luther's own words to find an explanation for his robust confidence in the Scriptures, a confidence that generated the famous 'stand' at Worms in 1521.
2004 / 1-84227-145-8 / xvi + 322pp

Carl R. Trueman and R.S. Clark (eds)
Protestant Scholasticism
Essays in Reassessment

Traditionally Protestant theology, between Luther's early reforming career and the dawn of the Enlightenment, has been seen in terms of decline and fall into the wastelands of rationalism and scholastic speculation. In this volume a number of scholars question such an interpretation. The editors argue that the development of post-Reformation Protestantism can only be understood when a proper historical model of doctrinal change is adopted. This historical concern underlies the subsequent studies of theologians such as Calvin, Beza, Olevian, Baxter, and the two Turrentini. The result is a significantly different reading of the development of Protestant Orthodoxy, one which both challenges the older scholarly interpretations and clichés about the relationship of Protestantism to, among other things, scholasticism and rationalism, and which demonstrates the fruitfulness of the new, historical approach.

1999 / 0-85364-853-0 / xx + 344pp

Shawn D. Wright
Our Sovereign Refuge
The Pastoral Theology of Theodore Beza

Our Sovereign Refuge is a study of the pastoral theology of the Protestant reformer who inherited the mantle of leadership in the Reformed church from John Calvin. Countering a common view of Beza as supremely a 'scholastic' theologian who deviated from Calvin's biblical focus, Wright uncovers a new portrait. He was not a cold and rigid academic theologian obsessed with probing the eternal decrees of God. Rather, by placing him in his pastoral context and by noting his concerns in his pastoral and biblical treatises, Wright shows that Beza was fundamentally a committed Christian who was troubled by the vicissitudes of life in the second half of the sixteenth century. He believed that the biblical truth of the supreme sovereignty of God alone could support Christians on their earthly pilgrimage to heaven. This pastoral and personal portrait forms the heart of Wright's argument.

2004 / 1-84227-252-7 / xviii + 308pp

Paternoster:
thinking faith

Paternoster
9 Holdom Avenue,
Bletchley,
Milton Keynes MK1 1QR,
United Kingdom
Web: www.authenticmedia.co.uk/paternoster

July 2005